DEFENCE
The Legal Implications

Military Law and the Laws of War

Brassey's titles of related interest

SWEETMAN
Sword & Mace: 20th Century History of
Civil-Military Relations in Britain

COKER
A Nation in Retreat? Britain's Defence Commitment

RUSI
Rusi Brassey's Defence Yearbook 1987

Defence Analysis
An International Journal

DEFENCE
The Legal Implications

Military Law and the Laws of War

by

PETER ROWE, LL.M.,
of Lincoln's Inn, Barrister
Senior Lecturer in Law, University of Liverpool

BRASSEY'S DEFENCE PUBLISHERS
(A member of the Pergamon Group)

LONDON · OXFORD · WASHINGTON · NEW YORK · BEIJING
FRANKFURT · SÃO PAULO · SYDNEY · TOKYO · TORONTO

U.K. (Editorial)	Brassey's Defence Publishers, 24 Gray's Inn Road, London WC1X 8HR
(Orders)	Brassey's Defence Publishers, Headington Hill Hall, Oxford OX3 0BW, England
U.S.A. (Editorial)	Pergamon-Brassey's International Defense Publishers, 8000 Westpark Drive, 4th Floor, McLean, Virginia 22102, U.S.A.
(Orders)	Pergamon Press, Maxwell House, Fairview Park, Elmsford, New York 10523, U.S.A.
PEOPLE'S REPUBLIC OF CHINA	Pergamon Press, Room 4037, Qianmen Hotel, Beijing, People's Republic of China
FEDERAL REPUBLIC OF GERMANY	Pergamon Press, Hammerweg 6, D-6242 Kronberg, Federal Republic of Germany
BRAZIL	Pergamon Editora, Rua Eça de Queiros, 346, CEP 04011, Paraiso, São Paulo, Brazil
AUSTRALIA	Pergamon-Brassey's Defence Publishers, P. O. Box 544, Potts Point, N.S.W. 2011, Australia
JAPAN	Pergamon Press, 8th Floor, Matsuoka Central Building, 1−7−1 Nishishinjuku, Shinjuku-ku, Tokyo 160, Japan
CANADA	Pergamon Press Canada, Suite No. 271, 253 College Street, Toronto, Ontario, Canada M5T 1R5

First edition 1987

Library of Congress Cataloging in Publication Data
Rowe, P. J. (Peter J.)
Defence: the legal implications.
Includes index.
1. Military law. 2. War (International law)
I. Title.
K4720.R69 1987   342.31   87-8031

British Library Cataloging in Publication Data
Rowe, Peter
Defence: the legal implications: military law and the laws of war.
1. Military law
I. Title
342'.31   K4720

ISBN 0-08-033596-9

Front cover illustration: Sketch for
Nuremberg Trial 1946 by Laura Knight, reproduced with
the kind permission of the Trustees of the Imperial
War Museum

Printed in Great Britain by A. Wheaton & Co. Ltd., Exeter

'If such is the law, the Army must become a deliberative body, and ought to be composed of attorneys, and the Lord Chancellor should be made Commander-in-Chief.' Sir Charles Napier, in Clode, *The Military Forces of the Crown, Their Administration, and Government* (1869).

Foreword

The compliment paid me of being invited to write the Foreword to Mr. Rowe's new book carried with it the privilege of being allowed to read it in proof before publication. I did so with growing pleasure.

In his preface Mr. Rowe identifies two sorts of reader at whom his book is primarily aimed. One is the layman, widely read on defence matters and eager to inform himself more fully about their legal aspects. The other is the lawyer, looking to use it as a text or reference book.

Reading it, I felt that I probably came into both categories. Though I lay no claim to wide reading on defence matters outside my own specialised legal field, I would be the first to concede that I have no very deep reservoir of immediate learning in many of the areas which this book explores. The ordinary run of my day to day professional work does not involve the consideration of questions of international law or the niceties of the laws of war (or 'the laws of armed conflict', as they are now more properly to be termed). I have, therefore, read the second part of the book, dealing with these aspects, through very much the same eyes as any interested layman with some acquaintance with these subjects. It has been easy and absorbingly interesting to read. My knowledge and understanding of these matters has been greatly enlarged by Mr. Rowe's book. When occasion does next require me to consider professionally any question arising in these areas, it will be to this book and its index that I shall be able to turn, in some confidence that it will at least point me in the right direction even if it does not provide of itself a comprehensive answer.

The past 32 years of my professional life have, however, been mainly spent in helping to apply, administer and develop the system of law which governs British servicemen at all times and which, when they are serving overseas, can also bring their families and other civilians working in the military community within its jurisdiction. Just how this machinery works is not, perhaps, very well understood outside the services. It is refreshing, and to me a pleasure, to read such clear and simple but comprehensive explanations of our military legal systems as appear in the first three chapters of this book, supported by a wealth of source material in their footnotes for the more serious inquirer.

Though Mr. Rowe himself may have had in mind the two specific types of reader he describes, I would have thought his book could well have a wider appeal to the intelligent general reader interested in the constitutional issues of the day. It discusses thoughtfully and with clarity the legalities of such highly topical questions as the deployment of our troops in Northern Ireland and their rights and responsibilities there; the use of servicemen in emergencies created by industrial action; the conflict between the need for state security and the 'right to know' of the media and the public they serve; the activities of the Greenham Common women; and the legalities of that ultimate question, the nuclear deterrent. It is certainly no dry-as-dust legal textbook but a lively and engaging explanation of these fields of law, clear in its explanations and often stimulating.

JAMES STUART-SMITH, C.B.
Judge Advocate General of the Armed Forces,
President of the International Society for
Military Law and the Laws of War

Preface

In writing this book I had in mind two distinct types of reader. First, there was what might be called the lay reader. He was envisaged as a person who read widely on defence matters. He will have found it difficult in the past to find out about the legal aspects of defence, which has had generally a low profile in law textbooks. Secondly, there was the lawyer who would look for more than a general introduction to the subject. He might seek an answer to a specific inquiry or he might wish to follow up a point raised in the text. It is hoped that the notes to the text of each chapter will satisfy his demands. It is also hoped that the inclusion of the four Geneva Conventions of 1949 and the First and Second Protocols of 1977 to them will prove useful to both the lay reader and the lawyer.

Limits of space inevitably force a choice of topics to discuss in the text. I have attempted to deal with those matters that I perceive both types of reader would demand of a book dealing with this subject-matter. The lay reader should bear in mind that international law bears hallmarks that make it quite distinct from national law. A State cannot be compelled to enter into a treaty and, if it does not do so, it is, of course, not bound by it. The norms set out in a treaty may, however, reflect customary international law and to the extent that they do they will bind all States, whether High Contracting Parties or not. Customary international law can be established by the practice of States and, in addition, the presence of a subjective element, the *opinio juris*, when States believe that practice to be a binding one. Virtually all States in the world are bound by the four Geneva Conventions of 1949 because they are High Contracting Parties to them, but many fewer are parties to the 1977 Protocols to the Geneva Conventions. Debate may therefore take place as to whether some of the 'rules' in the Protocol reflect customary international law and are therefore binding on all States or whether their application is limited to States who are bound by the Protocol itself.

Although only my name will appear on the spine of this book, I should like to acknowledge my gratitude to those who offered me assistance in various ways. In so doing I am mindful of the fact that the help that each gave to me is hardly matched by this short acknowledgement. It was Geoffrey Kinley of King's College, University of London, who first led me down the path of military law and the laws of war and who had sufficient confidence in me to allow me to teach his courses while he was on sabbatical leave. Christina Zachrisson, a member of the Board of Directors of the International Society for Military Law and the Laws of War, invited me to lecture in her native

Sweden and gave me an insight into some of the problems that might be faced by a neutral State during an armed conflict. Michael Meyer, the Head of Committee and Legal Services at the British Red Cross, read through the draft chapters dealing with the laws of war and made many helpful suggestions. Christopher Ryan and Brian Thompson, my colleagues at Liverpool, and Patrick Thornberry, also undertook the task of reading draft chapters in their own fields of interest and gave me freely of their knowledge. I wish to thank the *Military Law and Law of War Review* for permission to include in Chapter 4 extracts from my paper "Legal Aspects of the Use of the Army in Maintaining Order" given at the Xth International Congress held in Garmisch-Partenkirchen and published in Issue XXVI-4 (1987) of the Review. Jenny Shaw of Brassey's Defence Publishers showed immense patience with me when time was pressing and my speed of production was not matched by my earlier promises. Finally, my wife, Anne, encouraged me when it appeared that I would be chained to my word processor for ever. I have attempted to give an account of the law as it stood at the end of January 1987.

Liverpool   PETER ROWE

Contents

Table of Cases

Table of Statutes

1

The Legal Status of the Armed Forces

'The Army raised by the Crown, officered by the Crown, commanded by the Crown, puts at its disposal a force which is more than equivalent to a thousand little prerogatives.' Sir William Holdsworth, quoting Blackstone.

The Army, like many British institutions, is the product of long historical development, and this is no less true of its legal status. The beginnings of the modern army are to be found in the seventeenth century and in the struggle between Parliament and the Crown.

The Petition of Right in 1628 had declared that soldiers were to be governed by the ordinary law and not by commissions of martial law, but of much greater significance was the Bill of Rights 1688, which succeeded in wresting control over the creation of a standing Army from the Crown and placed it firmly in the hands of Parliament. Seventeen years earlier Parliament had declared in the Militia Act that the 'supreme government of the militia and of all forces by sea and land was the undoubted right of the King', but, in the light of experience during the Commenwealth, it fought shy of permitting the King to keep a standing Army. The Bill of Rights therefore declared that 'the raising or keeping of a standing Army within the Kingdom in time of peace, unless it be with consent of Parliament, is against law'.[1]

In attempting to control the power of the King, Parliament had made the country vulnerable to invasion. The solution was essentially a pragmatic one. A standing Army was established by Parliament, but its existence would be limited to a fixed period. The Mutiny Act 1689 not only recited the terms of the Bill of Rights but it also provided a basic disciplinary code for its members and it set the pattern that was to continue until 1881.[2] It was to remain in force for less than a year, to be replaced by another Act. Parliament had therefore stamped its authority over the very existence of the Army, but it had also given the right to the military authorities to try a limited number of offences, and, if need be, to exact the death penalty. Moreover, the Act made it very clear that soldiers were liable also to the ordinary law of the land.

Parliament continued to pass annual Mutiny Acts, and in so doing steadily increased the number of military offences, until 1881 when the Army Act of that year put the government of the Army on a more modern footing. But the impact of the Bill of Rights was not lost in the zeal for reform. It became the practice to pass an annual Act to continue in force the 1881 Act for a further year and in each annual Act there appeared the words from the Bill of Rights. This process continued until the Army Act of 1955, from when the present legal regime begins.

The Royal Navy was never subject to the Bill of Rights procedure, since its very existence never posed the threat that the standing Army did. Parliament was able to keep control over it through the supply of funds to keep it in existence.

The Royal Air Force was created in 1917 and given a statutory basis by the Air Force (Constitution) Act of that year. It fell in line with the Army over its continuation as a separate force and this continues to the present day.

The Current Legal Basis

The Army Act 1955, the Air Force Act 1955 and the Naval Discipline Act 1957 are now the governing Acts of the three Services, but they are dependent on an Armed Forces Act every 5 years to keep them in force. So, the Armed Forces Act 1986 provides that the 1955 and 1957 Acts are to continue in force for a further year and may be renewed by an Order in Council on an annual basis until 1991, when another Armed Forces Act will be required. Parliament could, therefore, in theory refuse to renew the Acts, when in course of time they would lapse. The armed forces would, in consequence, become illegal bodies to whom Parliament could vote no sums of money and any court-martial sentences would be void.[3] Such a consequence may seem very far-fetched, but the very argument—that the Army is an illegal body—was made in 1981. The basis of the argument was that the Bill of Rights of 1688 required 'the positive consent of Parliament through an Act and not its passive and unrecorded consent'.[4]

This had been given by Parliament in annual Acts up until 1955 when the Army Act was placed on a quinquennial basis subject to annual Orders in Council which have to be passed by affirmative resolutions of both Houses of Parliament. Did the Bill of Rights in fact require an annual Act of Parliament to be passed to legalise the very existence of the Army or could its consent be shown in other ways? There is no doubt that the practice of Parliament from 1688 to 1955 was to pass an annual Act, but that is not to suggest that that is the only way in which the consent of Parliament could be shown. It is difficult to imagine that the very existence of the Army at the present time is without the consent of Parliament. The requirement in each successive Armed Forces Act of annual renewal by an Order in Council, which must be passed by an affirmative resolution of each House, the annual Appropriation Acts and the debates on the Defence Estimates clearly show the consent of Parliament.[5]

This process of quinquennial review has been likened, by the minister responsible, to a naval refit. 'Once every five years', he said, 'we take the Army Act 1955, the Air Force Act 1955 and the Naval Discipline Act 1957 out of the legislative waters and let the experts swarm all over them, tapping here and prodding there, to consider whether any provisions need amendment, strengthening or scrapping.' The traditional place for the tapping and prodding has been an *ad hoc* select committee, but this procedure was considered inappropriate by the 1986 Select Committee who thought that the matter should be taken in future to the Defence Committee.

Command of the Armed Forces

Following the Restoration, the Militia Act of 1661 had declared that the 'sole supreme government, command and disposition of the militia and of all forces by sea and land' was the undoubted right of the King and this position has remained to the present day, although that Act has now been repealed.[6] This prerogative right, now exercised by ministers responsible to Parliament, has been confirmed in the courts and it is well illustrated by the case of *China Navigation Co. Ltd. v Attorney-General* in 1932.[7] The plaintiffs, who were an English shipping company, carried on trade in the China seas, an area in which pirates operated. The plaintiffs had agreed with the Crown to pay for armed soldiers to be placed on their ships to protect them and the passengers from pirates. Subsequently they sought to argue that, as British citizens, they were entitled to the protection of the Crown wherever they went and so the Crown was under a duty, at no cost to them, to provide the soldiers. Had the court accepted this argument, at least two consequences would have flown from it. First, the Crown would then be under a duty to 'follow and protect the missionary and send armed forces to rescue him from his self-imposed danger',[8] and secondly, the courts would be able to tell the Crown where it should place its forces. These arguments led the Court of Appeal to decide that the right of the Crown in peacetime[9] to determine the disposition and use of the armed forces was a prerogative right and that the exercise of that right could not be challenged in the courts.

This view was supported by the House of Lords in *Chandler v. Director of Public Prosecutions* in 1962 when Lord Reid spoke of the 'disposition and armament of the armed forces' being within 'the exclusive direction of the Crown' and Lord Radcliffe of 'the disposition, armament and direction' being matters 'decided upon by the Crown and within its jurisdiction as the executive power of the State'.[10] The effect of these decisions is that matters related to the way in which the Crown decides to employ the armed forces are not justiciable; they are not matters that can be decided in a court of law. Were it to be otherwise, the accused in *Chandler* could have argued that it was not in the interests of this country to allow the United States Air Force to use bases here from which to operate aircraft capable of carrying nuclear weapons. This is clearly a matter for the Crown, whose prerogative power is exercised by ministers responsible to Parliament, and not, in this particular case, to the courts.[11]

The use of prerogative powers is not without its disadvantages. There may be difficulty in determining whether a particular prerogative right exists or not. In *Attorney-General v. Nissan* the claimant was a British subject who managed a hotel in Cyprus. During the civil strife on the island in 1963 British forces then operating in Cyprus took possession of his hotel and subsequently the British government refused to pay any compensation. The House of Lords decided that he could sue the government, but in the course of the judgment some of their lordships spoke about the Crown's claim to take possession of the hotel under the prerogative. Lord Pearce thought that the taking of the hotel was an exercise of the prerogative (since the claimant was a British subject), but Lord Reid was not prepared to offer an opinion on the argument that the 'taking of the hotel was an exercise of the prerogative to regulate the activities of Her Majesty's forces wherever they may be'.[12] Although it is '350 years and a civil war too late for the Queen's courts to broaden the prerogative',[13] a matter that can arise is the relationship between a prerogative and a statutory power. Much of the law relating to the armed forces is contained in statutes and occasionally this may overlap with a prerogative power. An example of this was in *Attorney-General v. De Keyser's Royal Hotel* when the Army Council claimed to requisition, under the prerogative and without compensation, a hotel as a headquarters for the Royal Flying Corps. The Defence of the Realm Regulations made under an Act of 1914 also dealt with the same subject matter, but did allow compensation as of right to the owners. The House of Lords decided that the Crown had requisitioned the hotel under the statutory power and as a result compensation was payable to the owner. The effect of the statute was to place the claimed prerogative power (to take the land of the subject in time of war) in abeyance.[14]

Command over the armed forces is exercisable, on behalf of the Crown, by the Secretary of State for Defence acting through the Defence Council. Each of the three Services is headed by a Chief of Staff and governed by a Board responsible to the Defence Council. Each is therefore able to retain a degree of autonomy over its administration, traditions, discipline and the like.[15] Unlike civil ministries, where the responsible minister represents his department in government, the Chief of the Defence Staff and the Chiefs of Staff may be invited to attend a Cabinet committee, the Committee on Defence and Overseas Policy, under the chairmanship of the Prime Minister, and they also have the right of direct access to the Prime Minister if their advice to the Secretary of State is rejected. This right may rarely have been exercised, but it has been suggested that 'if a government came to power with the Labour Party's present defence policy, and rejected the Service chiefs' advice, they would probably seek a formal meeting with the Prime Minister, and if their advice was still rejected each would have to consider his position'.[16]

What could a Chief of Staff do if his advice to the Prime Minister was rejected? He could resign his post, but it will be shown later that he has no automatic right to resign his commission. Nor has he a right to go over the head of the Prime Minister to the sovereign, since Her Majesty's prerogative powers (the armament of the armed forces) are exercised by the Secretary of State for Defence. He may, of course, be replaced in the post of Chief of Staff,[17] but if no suitably qualified senior officer is willing to serve to carry out the government's defence policy a constitutional crises would ensue. Even more would this be the case if all the Chiefs were of like mind.[18]

The Legal Position of the Serviceman

The Lewis Committee in 1946 thought that 'In the matter of legal safeguards, citizens should be no worse off when they are in the Forces than in civil life unless considerations of discipline or other circumstances make such a disadvantage inevitable.'[19] Whether they are at a disadvantage or not is for the reader to decide, but their position is certainly anomalous.

A soldier (or other Serviceman) is not employed on a contract of service. He is instead appointed under the prerogative and he can therefore be dismissed at the will of the Crown if his services are no longer required. In 1986 a number of Gurkha soldiers were dismissed on the ground that their services were no longer required after refusing to assist in the investigation of an alleged fight in Hawaii between Gurkha soldiers and an officer seconded from another regiment. One reason that might be given for the development of such a position is that since it was necessary to renew annually the various Mutiny Acts or the Army Act 1881 the Crown could not enter into commitments for any longer period.[20]

A consequence of this position was that the courts could not intervene to compel the Crown to continue the service of a particular Serviceman, nor could they be used in complaints over pay. So, in *Leaman v. R.* a soldier claimed before the High Court that he had not been paid according to the correct pay scale and that the Crown should be compelled to pay him at the higher rate. The court decided that the matter was completely outside their control and that a Serviceman could not bring such a matter before the courts.[21]

If the Crown can require a Serviceman to leave prematurely, it can also compel him to stay in the Service, even though he may wish to resign. In *Hearson v. Churchill* an officer serving aboard HMS *Pembroke* left the ship to take up an offer of better paid employment and claimed that he was entitled to resign. The court found against him and explained, 'An officer who has accepted a commission in Her Majesty's Navy cannot, under any circumstances whatever, resign without the consent of Her Majesty the Queen.'[22] This consent would normally be given, since the Services are generally not anxious to retain someone who wishes to leave, but this may not always be the case, particularly where he has had the benefit of a particular course of training.

The Advisory Committee on Conscientious Objectors was established in 1970 to hear cases by Servicemen anxious to be discharged. The Committee released an Army captain in 1979 who successfully pleaded that he had a conscientious objection to serving in Northern Ireland but who had been refused permission to leave the Army prematurely. He had been seconded to undertake a university course and in consequence was required to serve a longer period than the terms of his original commission.[23]

From time to time complaints are made about the difficulty in leaving the Army faced by soldiers who have been recruited at a young age. Each new recruit is permitted to leave within the first 3 or 6 months, depending on whether he was under or over the age of 18 when he enlisted. Thereafter he is not permitted to leave, or buy himself out, for a period of 3 years or until his 21st birthday, whichever is the later. During the course of passage of the Armed Forces Act 1986 an amendment was tabled in the House of Lords which, if it had been passed, would have permitted a person who had been recruited under the age of 18 to leave with 1 month's notice and with 3 months' notice if he had been recruited after that age. The Army is keen to retain the present system and has argued that there are sufficient guarantees built into it to prevent a young person taking on longer service than he desired.[24]

It follows from the nature of the Serviceman's engagement that he cannot take any of the benefits of the labour legislation which has turned an employment contract into a valuable personal right to be protected by law. A Serviceman cannot claim the right to time off for trade union activities, or for unfair dismissal, nor can his female counterpart claim maternity leave or equal pay.[25]

The law imposes an obligation on a person to pay any damages to which his employee is liable if he commits a tort in the course of his employment. A bus driver, for instance, who drives his bus negligently and who causes an accident will render his employer liable to pay the damages, on the principle of vicarious liability. What then of the soldier who commits a tort while carrying out his duties? Can he make the Ministry of Defence liable to pay the damages? The answer would appear to be in the negative, since, as we have seen, a soldier is not employed on a contract of service, an essential precondition to the operation of the rules of vicarious liability. This conclusion would also seem to follow from the case of *Attorney-General for New South Wales v. Perpetual Trustee Co.* where the Lord Chancellor was of the opinion that 'there is a fundamental difference between the domestic relation of master and servant and that of the holder of a public office and the State which he is said to serve' and a rule that applied to the former should not apply to the latter 'unless there is compelling authority to do so'.[26]

This is not, however, the practice of the Ministry of Defence, who have accepted responsibility for the torts of soldiers. In 1980 a man who had been shot by a soldier in Northern Ireland sued the Ministry of Defence for the action of the soldier, claiming that it was a tort and committed without any legal justification. The court found in his favour and awarded him £15,000 damages. This sum was paid by the Ministry, who in theory could recover it from the soldier concerned, but who would be very unlikely to do so.[27] This case illustrates further that the Crown, through a government ministry, can be sued for damages where a civilian has suffered harm at the hands of a government employee, but what of the position of one Serviceman who causes injury to another? No one would doubt that at times service in the armed forces can pose a greater risk of injury or death than in civilian life. In 1947, when it became possible for the first time to sue the Crown in tort, the question arose whether one soldier who negligently injured another, for example on exercise, could make the Crown liable for that under the common law or whether it would be better to treat the injury as qualifying for a pension based, not on what the courts might award by way of damages, but by periodic payments assessed under the pension regulations. The latter approach was adopted.

Section 10 of the Crown Proceedings Act of 1947 has the effect of excluding the common law right to bring an action for damages against a person who has caused injury or death by way of a tort. This will apply where both the person who causes the injury or death and his victim are members of Her Majesty's forces and the latter was either on duty or on any land, premises, ship, aircraft or vehicle used for the purposes of the armed forces of the Crown. In addition, the section will only apply if the Secretary of State certifies that the injury or death is attributable to service for pension purposes.

A recent example of the working of this rule is the decision of the Court of Appeal in *Bell v. Secretary of State for Defence*. Trooper Bell suffered a head injury as a result of horseplay in barracks and he was taken to the Army medical centre. Some time later the Army doctor sent him to a civilian hospital but did not provide the hospital with accurate notes of the injuries suffered with the result that there was a significant delay at the hospital in treating him. Shortly afterwards Trooper Bell died of his injuries. His father brought the present action alleging that the Army doctor had been negligent in failing to supply notes to the civilian hospital to indicate the nature of his son's injuries. The sole issue before the court was whether section 10 of the 1947 Act excluded the father's common law action for damages. If it did have this effect, no present financial liability would be incurred by the Ministry of Defence, since Trooper Bell was dead and his parents were not eligible to receive any pension in consequence of his death. The court decided that the section did not apply, on the ground that when the alleged negligence of the doctor took place Trooper Bell was neither on duty nor on premises used by the armed forces; he was in the civilian hospital.[28]

Had the facts been slightly different in this case the father's action for damages would have been caught by the section. So, if the claim had been that the Army doctor had treated Trooper Bell negligently in the medical centre or that another soldier was negligent in causing him head injuries in the barracks, no right to sue for damages would have arisen. It is because of what some see as the draconian nature of the section that there has been considerable publicity directed at prompting Parliament to repeal the section.[29] The Secretary of State for Defence announced in December 1986 that section 10 will be amended when a Bill can be presented to Parliament. He did, however, issue a warning that, 'We will need to be able to reactivate the provisions of section 10 in the event of impending, or actual, hostilities, or grave national emergency.'[29a]

Unlike the civilian, the Serviceman is unable to take any form of 'industrial action' should he be dissatisfied with the terms and conditions of his employment. He cannot lawfully strike, go-slow, or ban 'overtime' and his rights to hold meetings or to express himself as he wishes may be curtailed. All these restrictions are, of course, seen to be necessary in the national interest and essential to preserve the armed forces as a disciplined body. That is not to say that individual members of the armed forces have no right to make heard any grievances they may have. Each of the Service Discipline Acts provides a right to make a complaint either directly to the Defence Council in the case of an officer, or to a commanding officer in the case of other ranks. Where the complaint has been made to a commanding officer and the soldier is not satisfied with the result, or where he claims to have been wronged by his commanding officer, he may also make a complaint to the Defence Council.[30]

Any widespread discontent in the armed forces would probably show itself in the form of an increase in the numbers deserting or absent without leave. The statistics show that the numbers concerned have been reducing since 1981 and represented only 0.19 of total strength in 1985.[31] Offences under military law that are specifically relevant to the terms and conditions of the soldier are those dealing with desertion, absence without leave, mutiny and the obligation to obey military commands. Soldiers who hold a meeting to discuss their grievances and in consequence defy military authority, anxious to retain the force as a disciplined body, run the risk of committing the serious offence of mutiny. This is what happened in 1931 during the Invergordon Mutiny where the complaints of sailors related to the sudden announcement that their rates of pay were to be cut by a quarter. A meeting was held on shore at which sailors from a number of warships were present and resisted attempts to get them to return to their ships. It lasted only a short time and resulted in the ringleaders being dismissed from the Service.[32]

Mutiny involves a combination between two or more persons subject to military law to overthrow or resist lawful authority in Her Majesty's forces or to disobey such authority so as to make the disobedience subversive of discipline or to impede the performance of any duty. It is well illustrated by the case of *R. v. Grant and others* in 1957. A number of reservists had been recalled in the summer of 1956 to serve in Cyprus. The men considered they had grievances and were prevented from making a complaint to their commanding officer and so they held a meeting on the roof of the hotel where they were billeted. The guard commander called out the guard and a warrant officer unsuccessfully ordered the men to come down from the roof. Eventually, the regimental sergeant-major was resorted to with desirable effect and the men were told that they could put their grievances to the commanding officer the following morning. When they did so they were either charged with mutiny or with failing to report a mutiny. At the court-martial the judge-advocate summed up to the court by saying that 'if the purpose of the men was to get their grievances heard at all costs no matter what authority were going to do about it' that was mutiny. The Court-Martial Appeal Court drew a distinction between collective disobedience, which was not mutiny and collective insubordination, defiance or disregard of authority, which was.[33]

Apart from mutiny, the military authorities can restrict the freedom, both of assembly and of expression, if the interests of discipline require it. In 1976 five Dutch soldiers, who had been dealt with by their military authorities for disciplinary offences, brought a case before the European Court of Human Rights and argued that their treatment was an infringement of the European Convention on Human Rights of 1950. One of their claims was that, contrary to Article 10, they had been punished for publishing and distributing a paper critical of the military authorities. The court rejected this argument and stated, 'Of course the freedom of expression guaranteed by Article 10 applies to Servicemen just as much as it does to other persons within the jurisdiction of the Contracting States. However, the proper functioning of the Army is hardly imaginable without legal rules designed to prevent servicemen from undermining military discipline, for example, by writing.'[34]

From time to time the question of whether trades unions should be recognised in the armed forces is aired. They exist in the armed forces of six NATO countries. In the Federal Republic of Germany, for instance, all members of the armed forces are permitted to join a civilian trade union and they may take part in demonstrations providing they are not in uniform and the dispute is over industrial issues. Of the other countries that permit a Serviceman to join a union there is a 'no strike' restriction and in Denmark the Minister of Defence can render void earlier agreements and terms of service in times of tension or hostilities.[35] In some countries there are Servicemen's unions, which are consulted by the military authorities but which have no right to negotiate. In the British armed forces a Serviceman may join a trade union but he may not take an active part in political issues; any direct action against the military authorities could amount to mutiny. During the passage of the Armed Forces Act 1986 through Parliament there was some debate on the role of trades unions towards Service personnel. In the House of Commons it was suggested that 'If there was a trade union in the Services many of the problems arising from the Cyprus incident (see page 17) would possibly not have arisen ... but when we come to power we shall investigate the possibility of such organisations. People should feel that there is a way in which they can somehow ventilate their grievances among themselves and through their elected representatives.'[36] On the other hand, in the House of Lords Lord Mayhew drew a distinction between the conscript armies in the European members of NATO and expressed the opinion that 'There is a much better case for a conscript citizens' army to be highly unionised than is the case for the much smaller highly professional forces that we have in this country.'[37]

There is clearly an important difference in permitting Servicemen to form their own union or association, which like its counterparts in other NATO countries might take the form of a consultative body but have no rights to negotiate terms and conditions of employment, and permitting Servicemen to form or to join a union with full bargaining rights. The latter approach would require a fundamental change in the relationship between the Crown and its armed forces since a 'bargaining right' implies that a union can exert pressure upon an employer to act in a particular way. Any endeavour by civilians (or indeed anyone) to 'seduce a member of the armed forces from his duty or allegiance to the Crown' is a criminal offence.[38] So in *R. v Arrowsmith* the accused was found guilty of this offence when she distributed literature to soldiers at Warminster suggesting that they should leave the Army or desert rather than serve in Northern Ireland.[39] It may be difficult to seduce a soldier from his allegiance to the Crown, but the same can hardly be said about seducing him from his duty. To endeavour to seduce him from his duty to guard a base in which are stored nuclear weapons or not to take part in fire-fighting duties when the firemen's union are on strike would clearly be unlawful.

Considerable criticism might be expected if the Serviceman was subjected to a regime in which the basic human rights that he possessed as a civilian were forfeited to the perceived needs of the military organisation. Any restrictions imposed on him and that find no place in the life of the civilian must therefore by justified.[40] It is axiomatic that the armed forces must be kept at a state of readiness and efficiency to be able to carry out any of the functions which the government directs it to do. To achieve this goal the armed forces must instil within its members a degree of discipline that does not stultify individual initiative and responsibility and to do this certain rights that each possessed as a civilian may have to be restricted. The aim must be to strike the right balance between the needs of discipline and the rights of the individual Serviceman. To lean too heavily in favour of discipline is likely to make the armed forces an unpopular career in these days of volunteer recruitment and to restrict individual initiative, but to permit Servicemen the same rights as a citizen is to place in jeopardy the very purposes of the armed forces. It is therefore understandable that any restrictions on the individual rights of the Serviceman are justified in terms of the need 'to maintain discipline' or 'to preserve the efficiency of the armed forces'.

Whether this balance of competing interests has been achieved can be tested against the issue of the continued retention of homosexuality as an offence in itself under the Service Discipline Acts. Homosexuality between consenting adults was abolished as a crime by the Sexual Offences Act 1967, but it was specifically retained by that Act as a military offence. A soldier can therefore be charged under section 66 of the Army Act 1955 with 'disgraceful conduct of an indecent kind' for an act of homosexuality that would not be an offence if he were a civilian.[41]

The offence can be committed on or off duty and there is no requirement that it should have interfered with good order or military discipline.[42] Statistics put before the Select Committee in 1981 showed that in 1980 thirty-one soldiers, twenty-seven sailors and twelve airmen were dealt with for homosexual conduct.[43] The view of the Ministry of Defence continues to be that 'The nature of service operations means that absolute trust and confidence within and between all ranks is essential and any activities, such as homosexual practices, which might disrupt such trust and confidence must be avoided. ... Homosexuality in the Armed Forces more than in many careers makes people liable to blackmail and hence may present a security risk.'[44]

The issue of homosexuality in the armed forces is unlikely to be forgotten and it will almost certainly arise again during the passage of the next Armed Forces Bill in 1990-1, but it may also be a matter fought out under the European Convention on Human Rights. The court has already decided that there was an infringement of individual human rights when homosexual conduct was retained as an offence in Northern Ireland[45] and it is possible that it would take the same view in relation to Servicemen where the acts take place off the base and between adult soldiers.

Notes

1.   Article 9 of the Bill of Rights 1688, which is still in force. The Bill was relied upon by Lord Denning M.R. in *Congreve v. The Home Office* (1976) 1 All E.R. 697, 710 and in *R v. Pentonville Prison et al. ex p. Herbage (No. 2) The Times*, 7 November 1986. See also Jaconelli, *Enacting a Bill of Rights, The Legal Problems*, Oxford, Clarendon Press (1980), at p. 16.

2.   See, generally, Maitland, *Constitutional History of England*, Cambridge U.P. (1931), pp. 175-288, 324-329, 447-462; Dicey, *An Introduction to the Study of the Law of the Constitution*, London, Macmillan, 10th edn (1959), chap. IX; Holdsworth, *History of England Law*, vol. X, Methuen & Co., Sweet & Maxwell, pp. 376-393. The terms of the first Mutiny Act can be seen in Walton, *History of the British Standing Army 1660-1700*, London, Harrison & Sons (1895), at p. 539. The Articles of War relating to the Low Countries and Ports Beyond the Seas of 1692 are set out at pp. 809 et seq.

3. The Petition of Right 1628 would seem to prevent the holding of courts-martial under the prerogative of the Crown.

4. State Research Bulletin (1981), pp. 149, 154.

5. See also Professor Colonel G. I. A. D. Draper, *The Times*, 17 June 1981. There was an attempt to abolish the requirements of annual continuation orders by Order in Council, but this was rejected by the Select Committee in 1976, *Special Report from the Select Committee on the Armed Forces Bill 1975-76*, H.C. 429 (1976), p.v. Even if it is assumed that the 1955 Acts deal with discipline and not the raising and keeping of a standing army, see s. 3(1) of the Army Act 1955 and the Ulster Defence Regiment Act 1969. All the reserve forces are established and governed by Statute: see the Reserve Forces Act 1980 and, briefly, the Reserve Forces Act 1981.

6. The relevant part of the Militia Act 1661 was repealed by the Statute Law (Repeals) Act 1969. It had been relied upon by the Court of Appeal in *China Navigation Co. Ltd. v. A.G.* (1932) 2 K.B. 197 to show that 'When Parliament has given its consent to the raising and keeping of the army for the year, it leaves the Crown to exercise its prerogative powers as to the manner in which the army is to be raised and kept and in respect to the disposition and use of the army and the administration of its affairs', *per* Lawrence L. J. at p. 220.

7. (1932) 2 K.B. 197 (Court of Appeal). See, generally, Wade and Bradley, *Constitutional Law*, Longmans, 10th edn (1985), chap. 13.

8. *Ibid*. per Scrutton L. J. at pp. 211-212.

9. *A fortiori* in wartime.

10. (1964) A.C. 736. The case concerned a prosecution under the Official Secrets Act 1911 for being in a prohibited place—an R.A.F. base—in order to protest about nuclear weapons.

11. The general trend of decisions is to make acts of government ministers subject to judicial review, but not where the matter is considered to be non-justiciable. Prerogative powers relating to the defence of the realm are non-justifiable, see *Council of Civil Service Unions et al. v. Minister for the Civil Service* (1984) 3 W.L.R. 117 (the G.C.H.Q. case). See also *The Zamora* (1916) 2 A.C. 77, 'those who are responsible for the national security must be the sole judges of what the national security requires', *per* Lord Parker at p. 107.

12. (1969) 1 All E.R. 629, 639. Lord Pearce's view is at p. 652; *Attorney-General v. De Keyser's Royal Hotel* (1920) A.C. 508; see also Bridge, *The Legal Status of British Troops Forming Part of the United Nations Force in Cyprus* (1971) 34 M.L.R. 121, who shows the dual status of the British forces in Cyprus when they became a part of UNICYP. He concludes as follows: 'The British occupation of the hotel for the second as well as for the first period (when they were not part of UNICYP) continued to be justified by virtue of the crown of England so that in that respect the British troops were not acting within the jurisdiction of UNFICYP.'

13. *B.B.C. v. Johns* (1965) Ch. 32, Diplock L. J. at p. 79.

14. (1920) A.C. 508 See s.11 Crown Proceedings Act 1947 which has the effect of preserving prerogative powers. The Crown's claim to a prerogative power, to take the land of the subject in time of war, was seriously denied by the House. The Crown has a prerogative right to requisition merchant ships during an emergency, see Requisitioning of Ships Order 1981 relating to the Falklands War, Order in Council, 4 April 1982.

15. See Central Organisation for Defence (1963), Cmnd 2097, and Defence (Transfer of Functions) Act 1964. The Ministry of Defence is now under the control of a Secretary of State for Defence, a minister of State and parliamentary under-secretary for defence procurement and equipment. See also David Owen, *The Politics of Defence* (1972), London Jonathan Cape, chap. 2: *The Machinery of Defence Decisions;* Edmonds (ed.), *The Defence Equation*, London, Brassey's Defence Publishers (1986), chap. 4.

16. *The Times*, 6 October 1986.

17. See s. 177 of the Army Act 1955 and the Air Force Act 1955.

18. See, generally, Finer, *The Man on Horseback, The Role of the Military in Politics*, Penguin Books, London, 2nd edn 1975; Edmonds (ed.), *The Defence Equation*, London, Brassey's Defence Publishers (1986), p. 65.

19. *Report of the Army and Air Force Court-Martial Committee* Cmnd 7608, para. 138 (1946); see also Sir James Mansfield C.J. in *Burdett v Abbott* (1812) 4 Taunt. 401, 405; 'It is highly important that the mistake should be corrected which supposes that an Englishman, by

taking upon him the additional character of a soldier, puts off any of the rights and duties of an Englishman.' Servicemen are paid an amount, the 'X factor', to compensate them for the burdens, additional to the civilian, they bear in military service; see the Review Body on Armed Forces Pay, 15th Report, Cmnd 9784 (1986).
20. See the arguments of the Attorney-General in *Leaman v. R.* (1920) 3 K.B. 663.
21. (1920) 3 K.B. 663.
22. (1892) 2 Q.B. 144. For an account of the various forms of discharge see Select Committee on the Armed Forces Bill 1985-86, H.C. 170, pp. 124-150.
23. *The Guardian*, 16 May 1979. The applicant was the eighth soldier out of thirty-two applicants to succeed before the committee.
24. See Select Committee on the Armed Forces Bill 1985-86, H.C. 170, p. 110. Compare the memorandum from AT EASE counselling service at p. 106.
25. Sect. 138(3) Employment Protection Consolidation Act 1978; S. 7 Equal Pay Act 1970.
26. (1955) A.C. 457, 488, Viscount Simonds L.C. *Quaere* whether the difference is as fundamental as Viscount Simonds thought. A soldier is certainly not an independent contractor in respect of whom no vicarious liability can arise. See further, Cowan, *Armed Forces of the Crown* (1950) 66 L.Q.R. 478 at 481; S. 2 Crown Proceedings Act 1947.
27. *Doherty v. Ministry of Defence* (unreported) discussed in Rowe, *Liability in Tort for the Use of Lethal Weapons* (1981) 44 M.L.R. 466. See also Chapter 4.
28. (1985) 3 All E.R. 661. Donaldson M. R. dissented. The fact that Trooper Bell's parents were not entitled to a pension in consequence of their son's death was not decisive; see *Adams v. War Office* (1955) 3 All E.R. 245. *Bell's* case was concerned with whether section 10 immunity applied, and it did not decide whether the doctor was or was not negligent. This can now be considered in fresh proceedings. Compare *Pearce v. Secretary of State for Defence and Another*, *The Times*, 31 December 1986, when the plaintiff, a soldier serving on Christmas Island in 1958, was seriously injured when the British government began testing nuclear weapons there. Caulfield J. in the High Court decided that the Crown could not rely on the immunity of section 10 since the negligence was that of the Atomic Energy Authority, whose members were not serving soldiers.
29. During passage of the Armed Forces Act 1986 through Parliament an amendment was proposed, but not carried, that would have repealed section 10 of the Crown Proceedings Act 1947. There is also a pressure group led by Jack Ashley M.P., the Section Ten Action Group, which has also called for its repeal.
29a. *The Times*, 9 December 1986. See Crown Proceedings (Armed Forces) Act 1987.
30. Sections 180 and 181 of the Army Act 1955. Statistics are given in Select Committee on the Armed Forces Bill (1980-81) H.C. 253 at p. 107. A Serviceman may not make a complaint to the Ombudsman, Parliamentary Commissioner Act 1967, Sched. 3. For a comparative study of complaints procedures in armed forces see *Les Droits de l'Homme Dans Les Forces Armées*, Recueils de la Société Internationale de Droit Pénal Militaire et de Droit de la Guerre (1976), vol. 1, pp. 300-311. There, mere submission of complaints by a group of Servicemen would not, in itself, amount to a military offence, but compare the position in Italy, *ibid.*, p. 303. A complaint concerning a military order would not have the effect of suspending that order. See also *Engel et al.* (European Court of Human Rights), Series A, vol. 22, Judgment of 8 June, 1976 (below).
31. Select Committee on the Armed Forces Bill (1985-86) H.C. 170, p. 211. In the eleven months of 1985, 507 members of the Army deserted or were absent without leave for more than 21 days. During that period 575 were returned (including some from previous years), *ibid.*, p. 198.
32. See Wincott, *Invergordon Mutineer*, Weidenfeld and Nicholson, London, 1974.
33. (1957) 1 W.L.R. 906. The case was based on the Army Act 1881 and not on the 1955 Act, which contains a more extensive definition of the offence. Their convictions were affirmed. See also Durant, *The Times* (letter) of 3 March 1982, concerning the Mutiny at Etaples in 1917, which he states was officially admitted only in 1978. The Salerno mutiny of 1943 is discussed in Keijzer, *Military Obedience*, Sijthoff & Noordhoff (1978), p. 58.
34. *Engel et al.*, E. Ct. H.R. Series A, vol. 22, Judgment of 8 June 1976. A claim based under Article 11 (freedom of association) was also rejected; see Articles 10(2) and 11(2). The European Convention is not directly applicable in English law, but an individual does have the right to petition the European Commission on Human Rights.

35. Select Committee on the Armed Forces Bill (1985-86) H.C. 170, p. 162.
36. H.C. Deb. vol. 87, cols. 443 and 444, 21 November 1985, Mr. McNamara. See also H.L. Deb. cols. 475, 66, 19 May 1986. For the position in the United States, see Siemer *et al.*, *Prohibition on Military Unionization: A Constitutional Appraisal* (1978) 78 Mil. L.R. 1. The Department of Defence Directive of 1977 which prohibits certain union activity is included as an Appendix.
37. H.L. Deb. vol. 475, col. 67, 19 May 1986. In relation to civil servants at G.C.H.Q., see *Council of Civil Service Unions et al. v Minister for the Civil Service* (1984) 3 W.L.R. 1174.
38. Incitement to Disaffection Act 1934. See also sections 192 (procuring or assisting desertion or absence without leave) and 193 (obstructing a member of the armed forces in the execution of his duty) of the Army Act 1955. Civilians could be prevented from entering a military base, but if they nevertheless broke in they might be charged under the Official Secrets Act 1911 with being in 'prohibited place', see *Chandler v. DPP* (1964) A.C. 763.
39. (1975) Q.B. 678.
40. The European Court of Human Rights in the *Engel* case (see note 30) emphasised that the European Convention applied to members of the armed forces as well as to civilians.
41. Homosexuality is retained as an offence under the Merchant Shipping Acts, see s. 2 Sexual Offences Act 1967.
42. The Campaign for Homosexual Equality proposed that a homosexual act should only be an offence if it is prejudicial to good order and discipline, but that any homosexual conduct that is committed off duty and outside Service premises should be disregarded, Select Committee on the Armed Forces Bill 1985-86, H.C. 170, p. 233.
43. Select Committee on the Armed Forces Bill 1980-81, H.C. 253, p. 81. One Serviceman is reported as intending to bring a claim under the European Convention on Human Rights 1950, *Sunday Times*, 12 April, 1981.
44. Select Committee on the Armed Forces Bill 1986, H.C. Paper 170, p. 161, *Supplementary Memorandum from the Ministry of Defence. The Treatment of Homosexuals in the Armed Forces*, and see pp. 183-192. See also *Report by David Calcutt, Q.C. on his Inquiry into the Investigations carried out by the Service Police in Cyprus in February and March 1984*, Cmnd 9781 (1986), para. 1.
45. *Dudgeon v. The United Kingdom*, Eur. Court H.R. Series A, vol. 45; Judgment of 22 October 1981. Compare A. 9237/81 6 EHRR 354, where a soldier dismissed from the Army under s. 66 of the Army Act 1955 had his claim dismissed by the Commission. The Commission's view was that penalties for homosexual acts were necessary in the Army for the 'prevention of disorder' (see Article 8(2) of the European Convention on Human Rights 1950). In addition, the applicant's offence under s. 66 involved a person under the age of 21 years.

2

The Courts-Martial of Servicemen

'For the punishing of military offences there is the further reason that unless discipline in Armies be preserved such forces are but a mob—dangerous to all but the enemies of their country.' Darling Committee (1919), Cmnd 428.

In 1869 the Commissioners appointed to inquire into the constitution and practice of courts-martial in the Army explained that the 'necessity for some exceptional tribunal better adapted to the exigencies of military service than the civil courts appears to have been recognised from very ancient times, in all nations, and under all forms of government'.[1] The modern system of trial by court-martial developed to deal with the increasing range of offences encompassed within each successive Mutiny Act. These were mainly of a military nature, but gradually courts-martial came to try cases of offences against the ordinary criminal law. Once they took on this role, they ceased to be merely courts of discipline; they also became courts of law.[2]

Liability to Military Law

A person is subject to military jurisdiction if he is a member of the regular forces or while he is on duty as a member of the reserve forces. So, a member of the Territorial Army will be subject to military law whilst he is attending drills, parades or is undergoing training but not when he returns home.[3] At one time a Serviceman who was discharged from the Service would cease then to be subject to military law and could not be tried by court-martial. In *R. v. Governor of Wormwood Scrubs, ex p. Boydell* an officer had been tried by court-martial and convicted of the civil offence of conversion and sentenced to imprisonment. He successfully applied to the High Court for a writ of *habeas corpus* on the ground that when he was tried by court-martial he was no longer subject to military law.[4] The so-called '*Boydell* gap' is one that it has taken some time to close. It has been tackled by the device of imposing a 6 months' time limit by which a person must be tried by court-martial after he has ceased to be subject to military law.[5]

One important effect of the continued liability to military law is that a member of the Territorial Army remains liable to be dealt with by his commanding officer within 3 months of his ceasing to be subject to military law, by returning home after a training session. Should the offence be of a more serious nature, he can be tried by court-martial within 6 months of that date.[6]

Although a person has ceased to be subject to military law, he can be dealt with during these time limits by the military authorities as though he were still a member. He can therefore be arrested, placed in custody, tried and sentenced.[7] In this way discipline can be enforced over Servicemen until the last day of their service, although any offences committed will have to be investigated quickly and disposed of within the time limits.

Military Offences

There are a wide range of military offences contained in the Service Discipline Acts and they emphasise the important differences between the nature of employment in the military and in the civilian spheres. By way of example, a few offences will be highlighted. A soldier may commit an offence if he fails to attend for duty without reasonable excuse or if he negligently performs any duty,[8] if he malingers[9] or if he damages or loses public Service property.[10] In addition, it has been shown in Chapter 1 that his obligations also encompass the offences of mutiny, desertion and absence without leave.

A military offence that is primarily concerned with the overriding need to enforce discipline is contained in section 69 of the Army Act 1955. This provides that a person will be guilty of an offence if by any act or omission or otherwise his conduct is to the prejudice of good order and military discipline. The offence is a very unusual one in not setting out clearly the type of conduct or omission it is intended to prohibit, but the *Manual of Military Law* points the way. Improper use of a military vehicle or improperly borrowing money from subordinates along with a failure to do one's duty might be considered so blameworthy as to deserve punishment.[11] The section has come to the attention of the Court-Martial Appeal Court in recent years; in *R v. Davies and Hamilton* two soldiers had broken into a civilian theatre in West Germany and had taken some paintings and etchings belonging to a civilian. At their court-martial they were acquitted of burglary, since the court accepted that they had no intention permanently to deprive the owner of the property, but they were convicted of a section 69 offence. The appellants argued that this offence could only be committed by interfering with Service and not civilian property. The court considered that there was evidence upon which the court-martial could find that the appellants' conduct was prejudicial to good order and military discipline since they were acts committed by members of the armed forces of a guest state in the host country.[12]

Section 2 of the Armed Forces Act 1986 introduces further military offences that do not have a counterpart in the civil law. These are intentionally impairing the efficiency or effectiveness of any Service property or intentionally interfering with or modifying any message or signal. The section goes on to provide for a lesser offence of being guilty of conduct that has any of the prohibited effects unless the accused can show that he acted with reasonable care. The object of this section is primarily to deal with the Serviceman who interferes with a computer, by altering its program. Since military law is reviewed every 5 years, the opportunity can be taken to introduce a new criminal offence, an alteration to the laws of evidence or a new type of sentence.[13] The legal difficulty in dealing with an alteration to a computer program is in the requirement that under the civil (or non-military) law to prove that the program has been damaged. This new section avoids any such consequence and may well presage the creation of a similar offence in the civil law. The offence might be charged were a soldier to erase an entry on a computer tape that recorded the withdrawal of his British Forces Germany driving licence and, of course, a soldier who intentionally erased part of the program of a weapons system could be dealt with under this section if it were considered that he did not merit a more serious charge.[14]

Section 70 of the Army Act 1955 enables a Serviceman to be charged with any offence that is punishable by the law of England, whether the offence is committed in England or elsewhere. A soldier could therefore be tried by court-martial for committing murder against a German taxi driver in Berlin or for stealing a cheque book from a fellow soldier in England.[15] The section brings in to the disciplinary code the whole of the criminal law (including all its defences) which the soldier, unlike the civilian, carries with him wherever he goes. There are only a limited number of offences that are triable in England if committed abroad by a British subject. Murder, bigamy and an offence under the Official Secrets Acts come within this category. It was on this basis that eight Servicemen were tried in 1985 at the Old Bailey and not by court-martial for an alleged breach of the Official Secrets Act 1911 when stationed in Cyprus.

In 1962 the Court-Martial Appeal Court considered the argument of an appellant that he could not be prosecuted under this section of the Army Act 1955 for driving without due care and attention on a West German road since the Road Traffic Act (which created the offence) presupposed that the road would be in England or Wales. The court decided, however, that the offence was 'translatable' and that it could form the basis of a charge under section 70 of the Act.[16]

One unusual feature of the offence is that it can be condoned by a soldier's commanding officer who has full knowledge of all the relevant circumstances. In the civilian sphere there is no similar provision whereby an official has power not merely to decide that no prosecution will be brought but to dispense with the law of the land. Should the offence be properly condoned, an accused can plead this as a bar to his trial by court-martial if he is later prosecuted for that offence. Lord Justice Lawton spoke for the Courts-Martial Appeal Court when he said, 'We wish to stress that the jurisdiction to condone offences is a most unusual one. In effect it is a power to dispense soldiers from the consequences of breaking the law, a power which was taken away from ministers of the Crown by the Bill of Rights 1688 save under the authority of Parliament. When Parliament gave this power to commanding officers it probably had in mind that when those subject to military law are on active service, and in particular when they are on operations, condonation of offences, whether civil or military may be necessary in order to secure military efficiency.'[17]

A soldier who commits a criminal offence in England renders himself liable to be prosecuted by the civilian and the military authorities. Take two instances. In the first a soldier steals goods from a shop in the High Street of his garrison town and in the second he steals petrol from an Army store. For both offences he could be prosecuted as if he were a civilian, but he could also have a charge brought against him under section 70 of the Army Act. The Army authorities might be keen to deal with the matter because of their desire not only to impose a military sentence upon him should he be convicted, but also to avoid any interference with their operational needs should soldiers be prosecuted in a civilian court. The civilian police may not wish to give up any of their authority over crimes committed within their police area to the military. The courts have taken a very practical approach in what might otherwise cause a conflict of jurisdiction. The Lord Chief Justice stated in a case in 1950 that 'Where an offence has been committed by a serving soldier in relation to government property or the barracks ... the proper person to deal with it is the commanding officer.'[18] A Home Office Circular[19] now sets out the guidelines and suggests that where an offence is committed by a Serviceman which affects the person or the property of a civilian it should normally be dealt with by the civilian courts. A soldier who is stopped by the police for dangerous driving would therefore come before the civilian courts as would the soldier, alluded to above, who steals goods from a shop in the High Street. The operational needs of the armed forces are not ignored in the circular, which makes it clear that it is not desirable to prevent Servicemen, who have been posted abroad, from travelling with their units. In this case jurisdiction would be given to the military authorities, unless the offence was sufficiently serious as not to be triable by court-martial at all.[20] Finally, the military authorities will normally assume jurisdiction where the offence is committed by a Serviceman while on duty or if committed on Service premises even if the person affected is a civilian.

At one time a soldier who had been tried by court-martial might be tried again for the same offence by a civilian court. Dicey was therefore able to say that the authority of the civil court prevailed in all questions of jurisdiction between a military and a civil court.[21] This is now no longer the case. A soldier who has been tried by court-martial (or by his commanding officer) cannot be tried again for that offence in a civilian court.

The Court-Martial

Courts-martial are courts that have to be specifically set up for each trial brought before them. This means that they can sit wherever and whenever the convening officer directs and so fit in the better with the operational needs of the Army.[22] The numbers of court-martial in any one year give some indication of the disciplinary health of the Army and of the efficiency in disposing of cases. In 1867 there were 23,535 courts-martial,[23] in 1909 there were 10,761, in 1937, 2158,[24] in 1976 between 1600 and 1800[25] and in 1986, 845.[26] In large measure the dramatic decline in the numbers can be explained by the fact that the strength of the Army is now much reduced from its earlier levels and it has become an all volunteer force. But of equal importance has been the transfer of jurisdiction from courts-martial to a commanding officer, who can now deal summarily with a wider range of offences and who can impose quite substantial penalties. Summary hearings render the dual advantages of a speedier disposal of cases and therefore less interruption in the life of the unit and, of course, they reduce the numbers of courts-martial.

These distinct advantages can be seen clearly in the procedures adopted by the Royal Navy, where the commanding officer's summary powers are wider than those possessed by his counterpart in the Army or in the Royal Air Force. The Select Committee in 1986 was told that at a naval court-martial the president had to be a captain from a ship other than the one on which the accused served, and that the other officers had to be from at least two ships. There then had to be taken into account attendance of lawyers and witnesses and the fact that 'H.M. ships spend much of their time deployed at sea on tight schedules, often operating as single ships, often away from their base ports for long periods.' The conclusion was drawn that 'it is rarely practicable to prepare and hold courts-martial when ships are deployed. Without the present powers, trial of many cases would entail delays in the administration of justice, with a weakening of the commanding officer's ability to maintain discipline and morale in the confines of a small ship, sometimes while the ship is at a high state of readiness.'[27] Moreover, it was estimated that if this wider level of summary jurisdiction was reduced in line with that possessed by commanding officers in the Army and in the Royal Air Force the numbers of courts-martial in the Royal Navy would increase from some forty to about two hundred each year.

Courts-martial in the Army and the Royal Air Force can be of two types, the general and the district. There is a third, the field general, but this is merely a form of the general and can be convened where it is not possible without serious detriment to the public service for the offence to be tried by one of the other types of courts-martial.[28]

A general court-martial is comprised of a president and four other serving officers who have held their commissions for at least 3 years while on a district court-martial there are, apart from the president, two officers of at least 2 years' standing.[29] A general court-martial will, and a district court-martial may, be assisted by a judge advocate from the staff of the Judge Advocate General. The judge advocate is an independent legally qualified official appointed by the Lord Chancellor and is not therefore a member of the military command structure.[30]

The convening officer appoints the prosecutor who will normally be a member of the Army Legal Corps, and so will be legally qualified. In such cases the accused is entitled to seek the services of a lawyer, either on the basis that he will foot the bill himself or that he will apply for legal aid under the scheme administered by the Ministry of Defence. In 1985 93 per cent of legal aid applications were granted to soldiers but the accused was represented under the legal aid scheme in just over 36 per cent of all courts-martial. The comparable figures for the Royal Air Force were 97 per cent and 69 per cent respectively.[31] These figures suggest that an application for legal aid is made only where it stands a very good chance of success and these must be in the more serious cases (or possibly in less serious cases where the nature of the defence involves legal argument).[32] An officer, who is not legally qualified, will represent the accused where a lawyer is not present to do so.

A court-martial is normally held in open court and it follows broadly the style of a trial in the Crown Court in England. The accused may object on any reasonable grounds to an individual member of the court; for example, that he was likely to be biased against him and he may plead that the court has no jurisdiction to try him. This may be because he is no longer a person subject to military law or he claims that the offence has been condoned by his commanding officer or he has already been tried for the offence by a civil court. When the trial commences it is governed by the same rules of evidence as in a civil trial.[33] The function of the judge-advocate is similar to, but not identical with, that of a Crown Court judge. He advises the court as to the law and procedure and he sums up at the end of the case. He may also rule on the admissibility of evidence[34] on the direction of the president and in the absence of the members of the court-martial. The importance of this role can be seen if the admissibility of a confession is challenged by the defence. The judge-advocate rules on its admissibility and if he decides that it is not admissible the court never hears of it and the prosecution must prove their case without it. In 1956 the Lord Chief Justice explained that the 'position of a judge-advocate is certainly not that of a judge. He has not the authority over a court-martial that a judge has in a court over which he is presiding. ... I cannot imagine a judge-advocate directing a court-martial to acquit.' His lordship went on to consider the nature of a court-martial itself and he concluded that he did not 'think it is analogous to a jury, and there is no true analogy between a court-martial, a jury or a bench of magistrates. It is a court *sui generis*.'[35]

The court-martial sits in closed session to deliberate on its finding and in the absence of the judge-advocate. The member of the court who is the most junior in rank offers his opinion first followed by the next senior and so on. The finding is made on a majority vote and if it is one of guilty of the charge it is subject to confirmation by the confirming officer.[36] This enables legal advice to be taken of the Judge Advocate General and is therefore an important safeguard for the accused that the trial was conducted according to law.

When the court deliberates on sentence the judge-advocate may be present to advise on the appropriate level. He will be familiar not only with the range of sentences for similar offences but where the accused has been convicted of an offence under section 70 of the Army Act (a civil offence) he will be aware of the sentencing policies of the civil courts. The sentence will also be subject to confirmation by the confirming officer.

The range of sentences available to a court-martial have been steadily increasing and reflect the greater flexibility given over the years to the civilian courts. The pattern of the Army Act 1955 is to list the possible sentences in decreasing order of severity, a format that can be traced to the very earliest Mutiny Acts. The most severe penalty that can be imposed is death, a sentence that is still available upon conviction of any one of five separate offences. Over the years the various Select Committees on the Armed Forces Bills have required the Ministry of Defence to justify the retention of the death sentence in its absence from the range of available civilian penalties. In 1986 the Select Committee was informed that seven NATO countries had abolished the death penalty but that all other NATO countries retained it as a penalty in peacetime (except Spain) or in wartime.[37] Four of the five death-penalty offences[38] require the offence to be committed with an 'intent to assist the enemy'. This term was considered by the court in *R. v. Steane* in 1947 when the accused had assisted the German authorities by broadcasting for them. The Court of Criminal Appeal decided that the accused had no intent to assist the enemy; his only purpose was to protect his family.[39] In the light of the interpretation now given to the meaning of 'intent' it might not be at all clear that someone in Steane's position would be acquitted.

Imposition of the death penalty hinges therefore on the meaning given to the word, 'enemy', which is defined in the Army Act 1955 as including 'all persons engaged in armed operations against any of Her Majesty's forces . . . and also includes all armed mutineers, armed rebels, armed rioters and pirates'. Various attempts have been made to improve on this definition but without success.[40] It would, in theory, be wide enough to catch a soldier who, in Northern Ireland, did an act with intent to assist the IRA, or in the

Falklands Islands in 1982 to assist the Argentine forces, or in the United Kingdom to assist armed rioters attacking an Army barracks, but it has been stated by the Ministry of Defence that there is no intention of imposing this sentence in peacetime. The reason commonly given for its retention in the British armed forces is that it can be the only ultimate deterrent 'given that a potential offender on the battlefield, who may be killed at any time as a result of obeying orders, is unlikely to be deterred from assisting the enemy by the possibility of no more than imprisonment'.[41] Since 1939 the death sentence has been carried out on forty-nine Servicemen, the last execution having taken place in 1953.[42]

In descending order of severity the range of sentences that can be imposed by a court-martial includes imprisonment, a custodial order, dismissal, detention, forfeiture of seniority, reduction in rank, fine reprimand, stoppages from pay and lesser punishments. These reflect the position of the court-martial as a court of law but also as a court representing the employer and the need to enforce discipline. As with the finding of a court-martial, the sentence is subject to confirmation by the convening officer. The Military Corrective Training Centre at Colchester receives Servicemen who have been sentenced to detention and trains them to improve their Service efficiency, discipline and morale. The average age of those undergoing this sentence is just over 22 years, about one-fifth are married and the average period spent at Colchester is about 6 months. The most common offences that attract this sentence are violent assault, absence and wilful disobedience with drunkenness and dishonesty offences as runners up.[43]

In the military legal system there are a number of avenues open to the soldier convicted by court-martial to challenge the validity of the finding or the nature of the sentence imposed. These are much more extensive than in the civilian courts and have been developed to counterbalance a system that relies to a great extent on the services of lay persons to administer justice. In all cases the procedures that have been adopted can only work to the advantage of the accused and at no stage, for instance, can his sentence be increased.

Once convicted by a court-martial the soldier can petition the confirming officer both against his conviction or his sentence. Since the latter will seek the advice of the Judge Advocate General the petition can be considered along with the proceedings of the court-martial itself.[44]

The powers of the confirming officer are very similar to those possessed by the Court of Appeal and enable him to withold confirmation, *inter alia*, if the finding is unsafe or unsatisfactory. In the light of the advice from the Judge Advocate General he can therefore substitute his own view that the accused should not have been convicted. In addition, the finding of guilt and the sentence are automatically reviewed after they have been confirmed. The reviewing authority is superior in command to the confirming officer and it also has extensive powers to quash a finding or to reduce the sentence imposed.[45] Whether or not the accused takes any steps to challenge his conviction or sentence the process of confirmation and review takes place.

It has been argued that the whole process of confirmation and review under the United States Uniform Code of Military Justice, which is not dissimilar to the British system, provides extra safeguards to the wrongful conviction of the accused or to an excessive sentence which do not exist in the civilian legal system.[46] In 1963 the view was expressed that 'The military experience demonstrates the essential fact that free access to appellate review is an indispensable feature of an enlightened system of criminal justice.'[47] It is always possible for a court-martial to impose deliberately an excessive sentence, especially in relation to a military offence, and to leave it to the confirming officer to reduce it to the level that he thinks is correct and so in effect to place the sentencing power in the hands of a superior officer. But the system of seeking independent advice from the Judge Advocate General and the process of review makes such a course futile.[48] In any event the same argument might be made in the civil system where the Court of Appeal has no power to increase a sentence imposed at the Crown Court.

A Serviceman convicted by court-martial may appeal to the Courts Martial Appeal Court, established in 1951 despite the recommendations of a number of governmental committees that there was no need for such a court.[49] An appeal cannot be brought as of right but only if the convicted Serviceman has presented a petition to the Defence Council, which has been rejected, and the court gives leave to appeal. In this connection they may seek the opinion of the Judge Advocate General.[50] The court has, however, no jurisdiction to consider the sentence imposed, a matter that is left entirely to the process of confirmation and review to correct. The powers of the court are in other matters similar to the Court of Appeal (Criminal Division) on an appeal from the Crown Court.[51]

The importance of the Court-Martial Appeal Court lies not only in the fact that it provides a means by which an accused can argue that his conviction was wrong, but it also enables a civilian court to oversee the military legal system. The judges of the court are those who would hear appeals from the Crown Court and they are not therefore within the military command structure. Weiner expressed the view in 1967 that with 'surprising unanimity, the common law world concluded virtually at the same moment in time that, just as war is too important to be left to the generals, so military justice is too vital to be entrusted to judge-advocates'.[52]

Summary Disposal

It has been shown that the powers of a commanding officer to deal with a case himself were increased by the Armed Forces Act of 1976 in an attempt to reduce the burden of courts-martial. He can try a wide range of military offences, indeed all but the most serious such as those which attract the death penalty, or desertion.[53] He also has power to deal with a number of offences charged under section 70 of the Army Act 1955, a civil offence. So, a soldier might be brought before his commanding officer on a charge of theft, taking a vehicle without authority, criminal damage, common assault, unlawful possession of drugs, and certain offences related to road traffic.[54]

Where a commanding officer, after hearing the case, considers that the accused is guilty and he would impose a penalty that involved a loss of liberty or pay he must give the accused the right to elect trial by court-martial.[55] With the permission of the appropriate superior authority a commanding officer can 'award' detention of up to 60 days, a fine of up to 28 days' pay and, on his own initiative, a range of military punishments such as reprimands and reductions in rank.[56] Once convicted, there is no appeal to a court-martial and the finding and sentence is not subject to confirmation, but it will be reviewed in the normal course of events.[57]

It is difficult to draw any meaningful analogy between the summary hearing of a case by a soldier's commanding officer for a charge, say, under the Theft Act 1968 and a civilian court. When a commanding officer deals with a charge under section 70 of the Army Act (a civil offence) he is in reality performing the same function as a magistrate, although with much more limited powers, and not *merely* acting to enforce discipline upon those under his command. The procedures before the commanding officer are quite different from a magistrates' court. The accused is not entitled to legal representation, although he does get advice, he does not plead to the charge, the laws of evidence do not apply and the proceedings are not open to the public. It is fair to say, however, that these procedures appear to be acceptable to those subject to them[58] and any widespread dissatisfaction would come to light in the number of complaints made under section 181 of the Army Act 1955 to the Defence Council.

The European Convention on Human Rights of 1950 has been referred to earlier, but a decision of the European Court of Human Rights in 1976 has more than minimal relevance to this discussion. In *Engel and Others* five Dutch soldiers were dealt with by their respective commanding officers for military and not civil offences. They received sentences ranging from confinement to a disciplinary unit, strict arrest in which the soldier was locked in a cell and prevented from performing his normal duties, and other forms of arrest that merely involved restrictions on the soldier's movements. The court decided that there had been no deprivation of liberty in respect of the latter punishments, since it was necessary to consider liberty in the light of the ordinary incidents of military life. Confinement in a disciplinary unit and strict arrest did involve the deprivation of liberty, which was therefore contrary to Article 5 of the Convention. This Article prohibited the deprivation of liberty except if it had been imposed by a 'competent court'. In the *Engel* case Dutch law provided that the sentence imposed by the commanding officer was to be suspended if appeal was made to the Supreme

Military Court and that if it was confirmed it was to be treated as if it had originally been imposed by that court. This solved the problem of whether confinement to a disciplinary unit had been imposed by a 'competent court', but the sentence of strict arrest had not been subject to this procedure and so the court held that it could not be justified by this part of Article 5.[59]

The European Convention is not a part of the law of England and any divergence between its requirements and English law can only be considered under the machinery established by the Convention.[60] It is not therefore open to a soldier who has been sentenced by his commanding officer to detention to argue that the sentence is invalid because it conflicts with Article 5 of the Convention, since he has been deprived of his liberty other than by a 'competent court'. Suppose he were to take a case to the Commission on Human Rights established under the Convention. Would he succeed?[61] His argument would be, essentially, that a commanding officer is not a court and that there is no court to which he can appeal following conviction. There is, in other words, no court to supervise the lawfulness of any detention imposed.[62] The opposing argument is that the accused could have elected trial by court-martial, which it will be recalled he has a statutory right to do, and his acceptance of the summary disposal cures any possible defect in the procedure. The issue is therefore essentially one of whether the accused can agree to be dealt with under a procedure that might not conform to the Convention. The jurisprudence of the court would suggest an answer in the negative. The court emphasised in the *Vagrancy Cases* that the right to liberty in a democratic society was too important to be waived and that 'detention might violate Article 5 even though the person concerned might have agreed to do it'.[63]

There is the further point that whenever a commanding officer deals with a criminal, rather than a disciplinary offence, Article 6 of the Convention requires, *inter alia*, that he be permitted 'to defend himself in person or through legal assistance of his own choosing'. One solution to both these problems might be to give the accused a right to appeal from the finding of his commanding officer to a court-martial, in circumstances similar to those where a civilian is convicted by a standing civilian court. An appeal would only be brought in very few cases; those in which the accused had elected not to be tried by court-martial and in which he disputed the case against him.

Court-Martial—A Court of Law or a Court of Discipline?

When a court-martial is hearing a charge of a civil offence it is, without doubt, acting as a court of law and not merely as a disciplinary body. In a sense it is also enforcing discipline since no army could allow its members to commit criminal offences without punishment. In modern conditions, with all volunteer armed forces, it is hardly conceivable that military commanders would wish their legal system to be other than fair to an accused soldier. All the indications suggest that in general members of the armed forces are not dissatisfied with the legal procedures to which they are subject.[64] Their rights are not identical[65] with the civilian, but then neither is their role nor the nature of their employment.

The major difference between the military and the civil legal systems is in the absence of a jury. The accused Serviceman is tried only by officers and it has been suggested from time to time that non-commissioned officers should be permitted to sit as members of the court.[66] On the one hand, it is argued that fairness requires an accused to be 'tried by his peers', but on the other, there is no call from Servicemen to change the system and that an officer's training fits him well for this role. Following the Select Committee in 1981 consultations were conducted in the three Services, but none of these showed any pressure for change.[67]

Given that courts-martial may try civil offences in what amounts to a legal system within a legal system, it might be expected that the civil courts would play an important part in supervising them to ensure that they do not act without, or exceed, their jurisdiction.[68] A clear example would be where a court-martial purported to try someone who was not subject to military law. The High Court has, however, shown itself reluctant to intervene unless the civil rights of the soldier have been affected.[69] The reason for this approach is no doubt that the High Court does not wish to become involved in the minutiae of military procedure. Where a convicted soldier alleges that an error has occurred, this is something that the Judge Advocate General can advise the confirming officer or reviewing authority upon.[70] The plain fact of the matter is that with the introduction of the Courts-Martial Appeal Court in 1951 the role of the High Court in ensuring that courts-martial do not overstep their statutory powers has become less important in practice.

Notes

1. Reports from Commissioners 1868-9, vol. XII. Court-Martial Commission, Second Report, 1869.
2. For a good account of the historical development of courts-martial see Stuart-Smith, *Military Law, Its History, Administration and Practice* (1969) 85 L.Q.R. 478. In 1869 the Court-Martial Commission (note 1 above) showed that ordinary crimes (felonies) were charged as 'disgraceful' or 'scandalous' conduct.
3. See section 205 of the Army Act 1955. It is proposed to deal with the statutory provisions contained in the Army Act 1955, but reference will be made to the Air Force Act 1955 and the Naval Discipline Act 1957 wherever any substantial differences occur. Section 208 of the Army Act 1955 permits an attached member of the Royal Navy or Royal Air Force to be tried by court-martial under the Army Act. See also *R. v Garth* (1985) 2 W.L.R. 569 where the accused claimed (unsuccessfully) that he was not subject to Air Force law when he committed an offence while on terminal leave.
4. (1948) 2 K.B. 193. The High Court also decided that an Army Order of 1945, the effect of which was to continue the accused in the Service, was invalid since it was inconsistent with the principal Act, the Army Act 1881.
5. Section 132 of the Army Act 1955. Section 6 of the Armed Forces Act 1981 imposed a time limit of 6 months if the accused was to be tried by court-martial and 3 months if he was to be proceeded against summarily.

6. Should the accused man remain liable to military law, there is no longer any special time limit by which his trial must begin after the commission of the offence, s. 7 of the Armed Forces Act 1986.
7. Section 131 of the Army Act 1955.
8. Section 29A of the Army Act 1955.
9. Section 42 of the Army Act 1955.
10. Section 44 of the Army Act 1955.
11. *Manual of Military Law*, Part I, 12th edn H.M.S.O.
12. (1980) Crim. L.R. 582 and commentary by Professor Smith. See also *R. v. Miller* (1983) Crim. L.R. 622 where the Court-Martial Appeal Court criticised the addition to the charge-sheet of an offence under s. 69 of the Army Act 1955.
13. See s. 9 of the Armed Forces Act 1981 (now repealed) dealing with evidence from computers. The law is now contained in s. 69 of the Police and Criminal Evidence Act 1984.
14. See the Select Committee on the Armed Forces Bill (1986) H.C. 170, paras. 37 et seq. The section was strongly criticised by the National Council for Civil Liberties, *ibid*, p. 248.
15. There would be concurrent jurisdiction with the West German authorities to try the soldier for the murder of the taxi driver. How this conflict is resolved is discussed in Chapter 6.
16. *Cox v. Army Council* (1962) 1 All E.R. 880 and see *Secretary of State for Defence v. Warn* (1968) 2 All E.R. 300.
17. Section 134 of the Army Act 1955 and see *R. v. Bissett* (1980) 1 W.L.R. 335 and see Lawton L. J. at p. 339. There are no occasions on which a civilian is free from prosecution for a crime. He may be prosecuted but acquitted on the facts or by way of the prosecution offering no evidence against him (perhaps in return for giving evidence for the prosecution), when the judge will direct the jury to acquit. Once he is acquitted of a charge, he cannot thereafter be charged again with that offence.
18. *R. v. Kirkup* (1950) 34 Cr. App. R. 150; *R. v. Hogan* (1955) Crim. L.R. 181.
19. See Select Committee on the Armed Forces Bill 1986, H.C. 170, p. 202, where it is reproduced. When the Serviceman is serving abroad, conflicts of jurisdiction are normally resolved by a status of forces agreement. See Chapter 6.
20. Section 70(4) of the Army Act 1955 prevents a court-martial dealing with the offences of treason, murder, manslaughter or rape if committed in the United Kingdom.
21. *An Introduction to the Study of the Law of the Constitution*, London, Macmillan (1959), 10th edn, p. 302.
22. For the sake of convenience it is proposed to consider courts-martials convened under the Army Act 1955. Courts-martial under the Air Force Act 1955 are virtually identical in form, while the naval system has a number of distinct features to which attention will be drawn. For the history of courts-martial, see Stuart-Smith, *Military Law, Its History, Administration and Practice* (1969) 85 L.Q.R. 478.
23. Reports from the Commissioners (see note 1 above), p.v.
24. Report of the Army and Air Force Court-Martial Committee (the Oliver Committee) (1938), Cmnd 6200, p. 6.
25. Select Committee on the Armed Forces Bill (1976) H.C. 429, para. 30.
26. Select Committee on the Armed Forces Bill (1986) H.C. 170, p. 210.
27. *Ibid.*, p. 228.
28. Sections 84(2) and 85(3) of the Army Act 1955. At one time there existed the regimental court-martial which tried the majority of drunkenness and absence without leave offences, see Commissioners, 1869 (see note 1 above), p.v. It was comprised of officers from the accused's regiment and could award a punishment of no greater than 42 days' imprisonment.
29. See sections 87 and 88 of the Army Act 1955.
30. For a history of the office of the Judge Advocate General see Stuart-Smith, *Military Law, Its History, Administration and Practice* (1969) 85 L.Q.R. 478, 481; and for the modern role of the judge advocate, *ibid.*, p. 487.
31. Select Committee on the Armed Forces Bill (1986) H.C. 170, p. 210.
32. This does not, however, explain the fact that in almost twice as many courts-martial in the Royal Air Force the accused is represented under legal aid. One explanation might be that in Air Forces courts-martial serious offences are a higher proportion of the total cases than

in Army courts-martial. When the court-martial is held abroad, a member of the Army Legal Corps may be instructed to defend. A soldier may, of course, obtain the services of a lawyer if he is prepared to pay him from his own funds. Legal aid in the civilian courts shows that 75 per cent and 98 per cent of indictable offences in the magistrates' courts and the Crown Courts respectively involved a defendant receiving legal aid; see *Judicial Statistics*, Annual Report (1985), Cmnd 9864, p. 115.

33. Sections 99 and 198 of the Army Act 1955; see also the Police and Criminal Evidence Act 1984. While in custody a soldier is entitled to the protection of the codes of practice issued under the 1984 Act, see s. 67(12)(a) of the 1984 Act. Before that Act came into force Service police were bound by the Judges' Rules (1964), see *R. v. Malcolm* (unrep.), 29 January 1979. Once the accused has been arrested the charge is investigated by his commanding officer. Section 75 of the Army Act 1955 requires the commanding officer to make a special report to the person who will be the convening officer if a court-martial has not been assembled within 8 days. This report must then be made every 8 days explaining the cause of the delay. Rules of Procedures (Army) 1972, rules 4 and 5. There is no power to hold a Serviceman in custody without arresting him; see Calcutt (below), chap. 3. For an account of the pre-trial procedures adopted in the Cyprus case see *Report by David Calcutt Q.C. on his Inquiry into the Investigations Carried out by the Service Police in Cyprus in February and March 1984*, Cmnd 9781 (1986), chap. 3. The code of practice relating to the questioning of Servicemen by the Service police is contained in the Inquiry Report as Appendix M.

34. See Rules of Procedure Procedure (Army) 1972, rules 80 and 81. His position cannot be compared with a clerk to the magistrates who cannot rule on admissibility; *Jones v. Nicks* (1977) R.T.R. 72. The problems caused when an accused attempts to challenge, in a magistrates' court, the admissibility of an item of evidence (e.g. a confession) are well illustrated by *F. (an infant) v. Chief Constable of Kent* (1982) Crim. L.R. 682. For the Crown Court, see Rowe, *The Voire Dire and the Jury* (1986) Crim. L.R. 226.

35. *R. v. Linzee and O'Driscoll* (1956) 3 All E.R. 980.

36. Section 107 of the Army Act 1955. Where a sentence of death is passed the court must be unanimous, see s. 96 of the 1955 Act. The finding and sentence imposed at a Royal Naval court-martial is not subject to confirmation.

37. Select Committee on the Armed Forces Bill (1986) H.C. 170, p. 84.

38. The five offences are: section 24 (misconduct in action); section 25 (assisting the enemy); section 26 (obstructing operations); section 31 (mutiny) and section 32 (failure to suppress a mutiny). In addition, treason is a civil offence triable under section 70, all of the Army Act 1955.

39. (1947) 1 K.B. 997. See also *R. v. Ahlers* (1915) 1 K.B. 616 and Smith and Hogan, *Criminal Law*, Butterworths, London, 5th edn (1983), pp. 48 and 49.

40. See Select Committee on the Armed Forces Bill (1986) H.C. 170, p. 15.

41. See Select Committee on the Armed Forces Bill (1981) H.C. 253, p. 61.

42. Select Committee on the Armed Forces Bill (1981) H.C. 253, p. 61 and Select Committee on the Armed Forces Bill (1986) H.C. 170, p. 103. There has been an enemy on at least forty or fifty occasions since the end of the Second World War, *ibid.*, para. 422. For statistics relating to the imposition of the death penalty on U.S. Servicemen between 1941 and 1961 see Select Committee (1986), p. 200.

43. Select Committee on the Armed Forces Bill (1986) H.C. 170, pp. 212 et seq.

44. See, generally, sections 107-112 of the Army Act 1955. Confirmation can only take place where an accused has been convicted by a court-martial. The confirming officer can substitute any other finding to which the court could originally have come at the trial (s. 110)).

45. See section 113 of the Army Act 1955. There did exist a power to reconsider sentences of detention or imprisonment, but this was repealed by section 6 of the Armed Forces Act 1986. In the Australian armed forces a convicted man may, ultimately, bring his case to the attention of the Service Ombudsman, see Lusink, *The Australian Report in Recueils de la Société Internationale de Droit Pénal Militaire et de Droit de la Guerre*, 1976, vol. 2, p. 494.

46. Moyer, *Procedure Rights of the Military Accused: Advantages Over a Civilian Defendant* (1971) 51 Mil. L.R. 1.

47. Report of the Attorney General's Commission on Poverty and the Administration of

Federal Criminal Justice, quoted *ibid.*, p. 32. Moyer shows that in all naval and marine corps general courts-martial during the fiscal year 1967, the sentence adjudged at trial was reduced on review in more than 87 per cent of the cases, *ibid.*, p. 31.

48. The criticism expressed by Sherman in *Military Justice is to Justice as Military Music is to Music* (1970) was that, 'it was commonplace in World War II for courts-martial panels to administer stupefying heavy sentences and then leave it up to "the old man" to cut them down to whatever dimensions and shape he envisioned justice to be'. This would seem to reflect a possible practice in wartime, but it can hardly be an accurate assessment of the modern system.

49. See the *Report of the Army and Air Force Court-Martial Committee* (the Oliver Committee), Cmnd 6200 (1938). At para. 21 the committee expressed its view that no appeal should be permitted to the civil courts and gave as a reason that, 'the essence of the great majority of military offences is that they are offences against discipline. They must be punished from the point of view of discipline; they would certainly seem to be better handled at every stage by persons who are familiar with service discipline. . . . ' See also *Report of the Commission Constituted by the Army Council to Enquire into the Law and Rules of Procedure Regulating Military Courts-Martial (Darling Committee)*, Cmnd 428 1919, 'it is undesirable to set up any formal court of appeal from the decisions of a court-martial since these courts sit and adjudicate in circumstances wholly different from those in which civil courts exercise their powers'; p. 103.

50. Section 11 of the Courts-Martial (Appeals) Act 1968. A civilian has a right of appeal if his application is based on a point of law; in other cases he will require the leave of the court, Criminal Appeal Act 1968, s. 1(2)(a).

51. The court can therefore affirm or quash the conviction and can order a retrial only in cases where fresh evidence has come to light, section 19 of the Courts-Martial (Appeals) Act 1968. The court can impose a lower sentence if a conviction has been varied to an offence that attracts a lesser punishment, see section 15. The Court Martial Appeal Court has no power to restore the status of an appellant if his conviction is quashed, *R. v. Swabey (No. 2)* (1973) 1 All E.R. 711, 715. For a good account of review and appeal see *R. v. Swabey* (1972) 2 All E.R. 1094. In this case the Home Secretary referred the case to the court under section 34 of the 1968 Act, but there is also power for the Judge Advocate General to do so.

52. Weiner, *Civilians Under Military Justice, The British Practice since 1689*, University of Chicago Press (1967), p. 232. Weiner shows that appeals from courts-martial to civil tribunals were established in the United States (1950), Canada (1952), New Zealand (1953), Australia (1955).

53. For a full list, see Select Committee on the Armed Forces Bill (1976) II.C. 429, p. 156.

54. Schedule 1 to Army Summary Jurisdiction Regulations 1972. These would involve the following criminal offences, section 1 of the Theft Act 1968; section 12 of that Act; section 1(1) of the Criminal Damage Act 1971 (where the amount of damage does not exceed £150); section 47 of the Offences against the Person Act 1861; section 5(2) of the Misuse of Drugs Act 1971; sections 3, 6, 17, 18, 29 of the Road Traffic Act 1972.

55. Section 78(5) of the Army Act 1955. In *Heddon v. Evans* (1919) 35 T.L.R. 642, the commanding officer failed to offer the accused the right to elect, but this did not appear to invalidate the summary proceedings. However, it is likely that a failure to offer an election to the accused would result in the award being quashed on review.

56. Should the commanding officer wish to award between 28 and 60 days detention there are a number of conditions that need to be fulfilled. The accused must admit the facts, legal advice must be obtained and an abstract or summary of evidence must be prepared, s. 78 of the Army Act 1955. Certain minor punishments can also be awarded in the Army and in the Royal Air Force.

57. Section 115 of the Army Act 1955; all soldiers can have an interview with the reviewing officer and there are a number of external checks to see that the proceedings and 'awards' are in order, see Select Committee on the Armed Forces Bill (1986) H.C. 170, p. 225. In 1976 the Select Committee on the Armed Forces Bill was told that in one year a reviewing authority quashed eight or ten awards made by a commanding officer, H.C. paper 429, para. 548.

58. See Select Committee on the Armed Forces Bill (1976) H.C. 429, para. 547; Select Committee on the Armed Forces Bill (1986) H.C. Paper 170, p.72.

59. European Court of Human Rights, Series A, No. 22, Judgment of 8 June 1976; see Andrews, (1975-76) Eur. Law Rev. 589; Rowe, *Military Justice Within the British Army* (1981) 94 Mil. L.R. 99, 121. The Military Court (of the Netherlands) is a 'competent court' within Article 5(3) of the Convention; Application No. 11013/84, 8 E.H.H.R. 252. The strict arrest could not be justified under Article 5(1)(b) which provided for the lawful detention of a person, 'in order to secure the fulfilment of any obligation prescribed by law'. The court could not accept that a person could be lawfully detained in order to effect his compliance with military law. Article 5(1)(b), it declared, permitted detention only in order to compel a person to fulfil a specific and concrete obligation which he has until then failed to rectify. The programme for a soldier sentenced to detention involves, certainly in the initial stages, being locked in at night, which would amount to a deprivation of liberty according to the *Engel* case.

60. *Malone v. Commissioner of Police for the Metropolis (No. 2)* (1979) 2 All E.R. 620, where the High Court held that telephone tapping was not against English law, although it may be contrary to Article 8 of the European Convention.

61. An individual may petition the European Commission under Article 27 of the Convention.

62. See Article 5(4) of the Convention and *De Wilde, Ooms and Versyp.*, European Court of Human Rights, Series A, No. 12, Judgment of 18 June 1971, paras. 72-73, and for the definition of a 'court', *ibid.*, paras. 76 and 78. See also *Ireland v. The U.K.*, European Court of Human Rights, Series A, No. 25, Judgment of 18 January 1978, p. 78. See also *De Jong, Baljet and Van Den Brink v. The Netherlands*, 8 E.H.H.R. 20 (1984), where the Dutch *auditeur militaire* was held not to be a 'judicial officer' within Article 5(3). The Court of Human Rights also held that there was a breach of Article 5(4) of the Convention.

63. *De Wilde, Ooms and Versyp* (see note 62) at p. 36. See, generally, Bing *Les Droits de l'Homme Dans Les Forces Armées*, in Recueils de la Société Internationale de Droit Pénal et de Droit de la Guerre (1976), vol. 11, pp. 971-983. See also *De Jong et al.* (note 62 *supra*) at p. 34, where the judgment speaks of the 'existence of a violation being conceivable even in the absence of detriment'. It would seem that the existence of a violation of the Convention is independent of the effect on the victim and, it might be argued, his consent.

64. It should be stated that not all share this view. The Richmond and Barnes Constituency Labour Party argued in a memorandum to the Select Committee on the Armed Forces Bill (1976) that the powers of a commanding officer should not be increased, H.C. 429, at p. 152. The memorandum from AT EASE Counselling Service also criticises many features of the military legal system; see Select Committee on the Armed Forces Bill (1986) H.C. 170, p. 240. See also Professor (now Sir Gordon) Borrie, *Courts-Martial, Civilians and Civil Liberties* (1969) 32 M.L.R. 35, 40-51.

65. There are a number of important differences between civil and military procedures. An accused soldier cannot, if held in close arrest, apply to the High Court for bail; he has no right of peremptory challenge of the members of a court-martial; he is not tried by jury; he can be convicted on a majority verdict; he may or may not be legally represented at his trial; the finding of the court and sentence is subject to confirmation; he cannot appeal as of right or against sentence. This is not to suggest, however, that the military accused is denied a fair trial or that the procedures operate harshly against him. The process of confirmation and review give him more opportunities to secure an eventual acquittal or reduction in sentence than a civilian. In two main areas he has the same rights as a civilian. Codes of practice made under the Police and Criminal Evidence Act 1984 dealing with detention and questioning by the military police have been brought into force for Servicemen and are similar to those applicable to civilians, and the laws of evidence apply in a court-martial. See Police and Criminal Evidence Act (Application to Armed Forces) Order 1985.

66. The Lewis Committee in 1946 concluded that non-commissioned officers should not sit as members of courts-martial (although compare the dissenting opinion of Mr. R. Blackburn who believed that an accused should have the right to demand that a person of his own rank should serve), Cmnd 7608. The issue was also raised in the Select Committee on the Armed Forces Bill (1981) H.C. 253 and in the Select Committee on the Armed Forces Bill (1986) H.C. 170.

67. See the Supplementary Memorandum from the Ministry of Defence on Consultations on Composition of Courts-Martial in the Select Committee on the Armed Forces Bill (1986)

H.C. 170, p. 200. See also H.L. Deb. vol. 475, cols. 53-58, 19 May 1986. An enlisted man in the United States armed forces may 'demand that at least one-third of the court membership be enlisted men', Moyer, *Procedural Rights of the Military Accused: Advantages Over a Civilian Defendant* (1971) 51 Mil. L.R. 1, 36. The problem may not be as great as it seems, since about 22 per cent of all Army officers have risen through the ranks, Select Committee (1986), p. 201.

68. Courts-martial, being inferior courts, are subject to the supervisory jurisdiction of the Queens's Bench Division of the High Court, see *Grant v. Gould* (1792) 2 Hy. B1 69. This would apply even if the court-martial had sat in B.A.O.R., *R. v. Secretary of State, ex p. Price* (1949) 1 K.B. 1.

69. *R. v. Secretary of State for War, ex p. Martyn* (1949) 1 All E.R. 242. 'Civil rights' of the soldier refers to his 'life, liberty or property', *In re Mansergh* (1861) 1 B. & S., 400, 406-407. See also Storkman, *Canadian Military Law: The Citizen as Soldier* (1965) Can. Bar. Rev. 414, 416 et seq., who discusses the supervisory powers of the civil courts and describes it as 'the fountain of ambiguity'.

70. Whether the High Court has any jurisdiction to supervise a commanding officer's disposal is a matter not clear of doubt; *Ex parte Fry* (1954) 2 All E.R. 118, 119, and compare *R. v. Hull Prison Board of Visitors, ex parte, St. Germain* (1979) 1 All E.R. 701, 717-718 (Shaw L. J.). In *R. v. Governor of Pentonville Prison and Another, ex parte Herbage (No. 2) The Times*, 7 November 1986, the court of appeal upheld a decision for judicial review of a prison governor's decision concerning the physical custody of the applicant. The basis of this majority decision was that the governor had breached a 'fundamental right' of a prisoner contained in the Bill of Rights 1688. However, a decision by the prison governor concerned only with discipline is not reviewable by the High Court, *R. v. Deputy Governor of Camphill Prison, ex parte King* (1985) Q.B. 735, where Griffiths L. J. stated, 'Judicial review goes to review the decision of an inferior court but not to review that of the commanding officer or headmaster.' The court of appeal relied upon *The King v. Army Council, ex parte Ravenscroft* (1917) 2 K.B. 504, but, with respect, this decision was concerned only with a matter of military discipline and not with the hearing of a criminal charge against a person subject to military law. A decision of the Defence Council was reviewed by the Divisional Court in *Barty-King v. Ministry of Defence* (1979) 2 All E.R. 80.

3

The Courts-Martial of Civilians

'The thought of trying civilians by court-martial, particularly dependent female civilians, was difficult to accept; public opinion had come a long way since the eighteenth century, when misbehaving soldiers' wives and women followers were flogged at the cart's tail.'
Wiener (1967).

Civilians who followed the armed forces on active service outside the United Kingdom were liable to military law and could be dealt with in much the same terms as a soldier.[1] Such jurisdiction would not, however, exist where the Army was stationed abroad in peacetime. Civilians who accompanied the Army in Egypt were immune from the local jurisdiction following a treaty between the United Kingdom and Egypt in 1936, but they could be tried by British consular courts. When these courts were abolished in 1950, there was left in existence no machinery for the trial of accompanying civilians. They were not subject to military law because the Army was not on active service in Egypt, nor were they liable to Egyptian law. They could only be dealt with administratively, such as by being sent back to the United Kingdom in the case of a serious matter. Upon repatriation they could not be tried by the civil courts unless the alleged offence was one that could be tried in England wherever it was committed, such as murder.

When it was envisaged that large numbers of civilians would accompany the Army in West Germany, thought had to be given to the question of criminal jurisdiction. The result was the NATO Status of Forces Agreement of 1951, which dealt with accompanying civilians as well as members of the armed forces and, unlike the treaty with Egypt, it did not grant total immunity from the jurisdiction of the West German courts. A system of a primary right to try criminal offences was established between the British military command and the West German authorities, and this required all accompanying civilians to be subject to military law. A change was therefore required in British law which had previously only subjected civilians to military jurisdiction when the force was on active service. This requirement was retained in the Army Act of 1955,[2] but it was supplemented by the Fifth Schedule. This schedule to the 1955 Act subjects a wide range of civilians to military law, but only outside the United Kingdom. The effect of it is that anyone with an employment connection with the armed forces, or a member of the family of a Serviceman, will be within its terms, but a British tourist in Germany would not. It would therefore include teachers, civil servants, NAAFI personnel, welfare workers and those working for the British Forces Broadcasting Service, along with their wives and families.[3] These civilians must be within the limits of the command of a British forces commanding officer and so if a NAAFI worker stole goods from a shop while on holiday in France he could not be tried under the Army Act upon his return.

There are, of course, certain military offences that could not be committed by a civilian. Mutiny and misconduct in action could not, but they may be liable for certain military offences, such as disobedience to standing orders, obstruction of provost officers or resistance to arrest.[4] In practice the most important offence-creating section to which civilians will be liable is section 70, the commission of a civil offence. This, it will be recalled, gives jurisdiction to the military authorities to try a person subject to military law for any offence against the English criminal calendar.

The question might be asked, why do we subject civilians to military law outside the United Kingdom when the force is not on active service? The answer would seem to be that in the interests of discipline a commander should have authority over all those who are connected, directly or indirectly, with the force which he commands. But perhaps the major reason is that 'Public opinion at home is naturally aroused if a soldier (let alone a civilian) is subject to harsh procedures or punishment at the hands of a foreign court.'[5] This is unlikely to be the case in the British Army of the Rhine, but in more distant parts it might be a relevant consideration.

The position of civilians accompanying the United States forces is quite different. Originally their liability to military jurisdiction was similar to the British pattern except that 'in the field' was the phrase adopted rather than on 'active service'. In 1955, however, a series of cases began to challenge the right of the military authorities to subject accompanying civilians to court-martial procedures. In 1960 the position had been reached where the United States Supreme Court decided that in time of peace civilians accompanying the armed forces, whether as employees or as dependants, could not be tried by court-martial.[6] In 1969 the Supreme Court went so far as to deny the right of the military authorities to try by court-martial a Serviceman for a crime that was not 'service-connected'.[7] The principal reason for this approach by the Supreme Court was that to subject civilians to court-martial procedures for criminal offences was to deprive them of their constitutional right to be tried by jury. Civilians accompanying the United States forces in West Germany who commit criminal offences there will have to be tried by the West German authorities or be dealt with administratively by the military commander.[8]

There are about ninety-six thousand civilians based at any one time in BAOR and about four thousand in Cyprus. Of these over half will be the children of Servicemen, many thousand of whom will be teenagers. Until 1976 a delinquent teenager (or indeed his mother) could only be tried by court-martial, whose powers were limited to a fine or imprisonment. They might be dealt with summarily but the only punishment that could be imposed then was a fine of £25. The position in Cyprus was different because of the establishment of the Sovereign Base Area Court, which in 1975 tried seventy-two British civilians.[9]

In 1976 a completely new court was created to deal with civilians, subject to military law outside the United Kingdom, who were charged with a civil offence that might be tried by the magistrates' court in England and Wales. This was the Standing Civilian Court in which sits a civilian magistrate, nominated by the Judge Advocate General, and two assessors when the accused person is under the age of 17.[10] The court is modelled on the magistrates' courts and its powers to sentence to imprisonment or fine are the same. The real importance of the Standing Civilian Court is in the wide range of sentence that it can impose. Not only can it sentence the convicted civilian to an absolute or conditional discharge, but it can make a reception order whereby an offender under the age of 17 can be returned to the United Kingdom and placed in the care of a local authority. This sentence is only available where the young person has committed an offence which would normally attract a term of imprisonment had he been older. In such a case the Service authorities would normally give consideration to the posting back to the United Kingdom of the offender's parents. The court can also impose a community supervision order on an offender of any age which is a mixture of a probation order, community service and supervision orders and has no direct equivalent in the magistrates' court in England. Under this order an offender is placed under the supervision of a social worker and he may be required to perform some community work.[11] The type of offender who might attract this sentence would be a civilian over the age of 21 who has been convicted of an offence of dishonesty, such as shoplifting. Roughly one in ten orders passed by the Standing Civilian Courts since their inception in 1977 has been a community supervision order and of all offenders so dealt with only two have reappeared in court charged with further offences.[12] In one or two cases a year a civilian under the age of 17 is found guilty of a serious offence for which a reception order would not be appropriate since that involves him in being returned to the United Kindom and placed in the care of a local authority. The Armed Forces Act 1986 now permits a Standing Civilian Court to sentence a male offender between the ages of 15 and 21 to a custodial sentence. This power is similar to a sentence of youth custody introduced by the Criminal Justice Act 1982.[13] The court may also impose a compensation order against him or his parents or impose a fine on them.[14] The court has no power to suspend a sentence, but it can now defer passing sentence for up to 6 months in order to see what progress the offender makes in the meantime.[15] A civilian convicted by the Standing Civilian Court may appeal to a court-martial. Like an appeal from a magistrates' court in England, the appeal is by way of a rehearing and, like an initial trial by court-martial, it is subject to confirmation. There is further appeal to the Court-Martial Appeal Court. A civilian who wishes to preserve the option to appeal to the latter court would normally elect to be tried by court-martial rather than by the Standing Civilian Court, and he has the right to do so. In this case the court-martial possesses all the powers of the Standing Civilian Court, but the court will be comprised of five or three members, depending on whether it is a general or a district court-martial. The Armed Forces Act 1976 introduced a major reform to the procedures where a civilian was to be tried by a court-martial. Instead of the court being composed solely of officers of the armed forces, it permitted two civilians to be members of a general court-martial and one to be a member of a district court-martial. Since, however, a court-martial finding is by a majority vote it can be seen that the officer members of the court are a majority group (assuming, for the sake of argument only, that they vote in the same way).

Once convicted by court-martial the civilian has the same opportunity as the convicted soldier to have the finding or sentence set aside, or amended, by the confirming officer or on review. Should these not prove satisfactory to him he may appeal to the Court-Martial Appeal Court, which, it will be recalled, is comprised of civilian judges who are eligible to sit in the Court of Appeal (Criminal Division). He has the same rights of appeal as the convicted soldier except that he can appeal against his sentence, which the Serviceman cannot do.[16] Further appeal, as in the case of a person initially convicted by a Crown Court in the United Kingdom, can be taken to the House of Lords.

With a large number of civilians accompanying the armed forces abroad problems of a different nature might arise. The military authorities may become aware that the child of a person subject to military law is being ill-treated or is otherwise in danger from its parents. The Armed Forces Act 1981 gave commanding officers the power to order the removal of a child to a place of safety, but the Armed Forces Act 1986 now enables the child to be removed to the United Kingdom where it will be received by a local authority and proceedings can then begin to have the child placed in care. The commanding officer may also order that a civilian, who is subject to military law, be detained in a hospital upon the written recommendation of two medical practitioners. The patient may then be transferred to the United Kingdom.[17]

The Liability of Civilians to Trial by Court-Martial within the U.K.

Civilians will not generally be liable to be tried by court-martial within the United Kingdom unless very exceptional circumstances occur. During the Second World War legislation was prepared to empower the military authorities to try by court-martial, civilians who committed certain offences in the event of this country being invaded.[18] The legislation never came into force and it is hoped that neither will the Emergency Powers (No. 3) Bill. This would have draconian effects in time of war. One member of Parliament described its powers in graphic form. 'It does away with the existing legal system, allows for summary courts-martial (*sic*) and trials, including provision for the death penalty, and provides for many and varied regulations to be enforced.'[19]

Finally, it should be mentioned that in a state of martial law the 'normal processes of law and justice have broken down and the military exercise *de facto* authority over the public at large'.[20] Martial law was imposed in certain areas of Ireland in the early 1920s and during this period civilians were tried, convicted and sentenced to death by court-martial.[21] It has not been employed as a means of maintaining order in Northern Ireland where statutory powers have been conferred on members of the armed forces to arrest and detain suspects, to search property and to close roads. It may be that, as in Northern Ireland, emergency powers will be imposed by statute and not through the concept of martial law but it has been suggested that martial law could 'prove particularly relevant to the aftermath of a nuclear war'.[22]

Notes

1. Articles of War of 1748 brought 'settlers and retainers to a camp and all persons whatsoever serving within our armys in the field' within the ambit of military law; see generally, *Manual of Military Law, Part 1 . . . Civilian Supplement*, London, H.M.S.O. (1977), p. 1.
2. Section 209(1) of the Army Act 1955 applies to those who are employed by or accompany the armed forces. 'Active service' means that the armed forces are 'engaged in operations against an enemy or . . . engaged elsewhere than in the United Kingdom in operations for the protection of life or property or . . . in military occupation of a foreign country', s. 224 of the Army Act 1955. 'Active service' was declared by the Secretary of State for Defence in 1981 in relation to the South Atlantic, H.C. Deb. vol. 29, col. 258, 25 October 1983.
3. See also Civilians (Application of Part II of the Army Act 1955) Regulations 1956, which lists the organisations whose members will come within the terms of the Fifth Schedule.
4. For a complete list of military offences to which civilians may be liable, see s. 209 (the proviso) of the Army Act 1955.
5. Professor (now Sir Gordon) Borrie, *Courts-Martial, Civilians and Civil Liberties* (1969) 32 M.L.R. 35, 52.
6. *Kinsella v. Singleton* 361 U.S. 234 (1961) and see Weiner, *Civilians under Military Justice, The British Practice Since 1689*, University of Chicago Press (1967), pp. 237-240.
7. *O'Callaghan v. Parker* 395 U.S. 258 (1969). Justice Douglas, speaking for the majority, said, at p. 266, 'military law has always been and continues to be primarily an instrument of discipline and not justice'. But Everett in *Military Justice in the Wake of Parker v. Levy* (1975) 67 Mil. L.R. 1 says 'the change in the (Supreme) Court's approach to military justice that has occurred in the past five years is striking'.
8. Draper suggests that, 'amendment of the (U.S.) Constitution would be necessary to regain the military jurisdiction over the civilians. Such an amendment is not feasible for the foreseeable future', *Civilians and the NATO Status of Forces Agreement*, Leyden Sijthoff (1966), p. 187.
9. Select Committee on the Armed Forces Bill (1976) H.C. 429, p. 129.
10. See sections 6-8 and Schedule 3 of the Armed Forces Act 1976.
11. For the details of its operation see the Select Committee on the Armed Forces Bill (1986)

H.C. 170, p. 50. The social worker is an SSAFA employee and will be professionally qualified. These social workers also prepare social inquiry reports for the Standing Civilian Court. Prior to the Armed Forces Act 1986 there was an age limit of 21 years, above which the order could not be made. Community work is, however, rarely made part of the sentence. The maximum number of hours work that may be ordered is 90. In the civilian courts a community service order may require a maximum of 240 hours.

12. See the Select Committee on the Armed Forces Bill (1986) H.C. 170, para. 199. The figures were 61 community service orders out of a total of 602 cases.

13. The Standing Civilian Court can impose a maximum sentence of 12 months on males aged 15 or 16 years, but there is no power to so deal with young female offenders under the age of 17 years. In 1983 one young offender and in 1982 two young offenders received a custodial sentence by a Standing Civilian Court; Select Committee on the Armed Forces Bill (1986) H.C. 170, para. 233.

14. To impose a fine or compensation order on the parents or guardian the offender must be under the age of 17.

15. Section 9 of the Armed Forces Act 1986; see, generally, *R. v. George* (1984) 3 All E.R. 13. A court-martial has power to suspend a sentence on appeal from a Standing Civilian Court; s. 12 of the Armed Forces Act 1986.

16. An independent right of appeal is given to the parent or guardian against whom an order has been made by the court-martial, section 8 of the Courts-Martial (Appeals) Act 1968.

17. Section 13 of the Armed Forces Act 1981. An interesting question arose in the course of the Select Committee on the Armed Forces Bill 1975-76, H.C. 429, para. 431, as to the legality of the order of a commanding officer, prior to the 1976 Act, to a Serviceman to place his child or wife in a designated hospital; see Rowe; *Armed Forces Act 1981* (1981) 44 M.L.R. 693, 696.

18. See the Emergency Powers (Defence) (No. 2) Act 1940, s. 1.

19 Mr. McNamara, M.P., H.C. Deb. vol. 87, col. 445; 21 November 1985.

20. Wade and Bradley, *Constitutional Law*, London, Longmans, 10th edn (1985), p. 41.

21. Compare Evelegh, *Peacekeeping in a Democratic Society: The Lessons of Northern Ireland*, London, Hurst & Co. (1978), pp. 32-34. In Northern Ireland the statutory powers are contained in the Northern Ireland (Emergency Provisions) Act 1978.

22. See Bonner, *Emergency Powers in Peacetime*, London, Sweet & Maxwell (1985), p. 10, and see Wade and Bradley, *op. cit.*, pp. 251-252.

4

Military Intervention in Civilian Affairs

'Soldiers are sometimes faced with legal difficulties to be solved in a flash which could take a trained lawyer hours to consider,' Lord Lowry C. J. in *R. v. McNaughton* (1975) N.I.

It will be recalled that Parliament, fearing a standing army as a potential threat to liberty, enacted in 1688 the Bill of Rights which directed that the raising and keeping of a standing army in time of peace could only be with its consent. The use of the Army as an engine of tyranny was at that time not unforeseeable. Control over the Army (and later the Navy and the Royal Air Force) passed into the hands of Parliament, but only as to their creation and maintenance. The actual use or disposition of the armed forces is a matter of the prerogative and is exercised by the Secretary of State for Defence.[1] However, since he is answerable to Parliament, and not to the courts, for the exercise of these powers, parliamentary control over actual deployment of the armed forces is, in theory, safeguarded.[2] In addition, it will be seen, legislation in the form of the Emergency Powers Acts 1920 and 1964 deal with what might be described as the more common situation in Britain of the armed forces being employed to fill a gap created by striking workers or through some other emergency. The actual deployment of the armed forces is therefore based squarely on a wide-ranging prerogative power and on more limited statutory powers.

To call upon the armed forces to perform some task normally undertaken by civilians is an unusual event. It departs from the traditional role of the armed forces, to meet an external threat or aggression against the United Kingdom. Whilst it would be unusual to deploy the Army frequently on such tasks, it would not be illegal to do so, since, as discussed above, there are no statutory limitations on the part of the Crown, acting through the appropriate minister. However, merely to deploy the Army may not be sufficient for the proposed task. It will often be necessary to give to soldiers powers additional to those possessed by a civilian, and these will have to be given by statute.

The armed forces possess a number of highly desirable qualities that fit them well for this role. They are characterised by a high degree of organisation and mobility. Their members are subjected to a strict system of discipline, and they can bring to bear upon a problem ample manpower and, if necessary, the benefits of their particular form of training and weapons.

38

In some roles they may be highly efficient. In others they may be quite unable to cope.[3] There would be little difficulty, for instance, in the Army organising itself to provide a basic fire service in the face of striking firemen, even if this action were required to be mounted throughout the country. It would be an entirely different matter for the Army to take over the task of keeping the railways operating to their normal schedules, or the hospitals open.[4] In a similar way, sporadic outbreaks of violence or even terrorist activity in a limited area might be contained, but civil disturbance on a large scale would obviously be more difficult.

The armed forces then can perform only a limited role in civilian matters. It is for the minister (or Cabinet) to judge the necessity and scope of their action and to answer to Parliament for it. The main types of activity upon which the armed forces have been employed in this connection are military aid to the civil ministries and to the civil community and military aid to the civil power.[5] In each of these activities an order given to a soldier by his superior will not be unlawful merely because it involves work of an entirely different nature from that for which he was trained. It might also run counter to the soldier's political sympathies, especially in relation to strike activity,[6] but it will nevertheless be an order that he must obey. Should he be ordered to commit an unlawful act, it will be seen that whilst a defence would exist to a charge under s. 34 of the Army Act 1955 (disobeying a lawful command) it would not necessarily apply to a prosecution under civilian law.

While acting in one of the roles mentioned above, the relationship of the soldier to the police officer is brought into sharp focus. In particular, the question arises of whether a soldier can be given a lawful order by a police officer and whether the police can come under the command of the military authorities. It seems clear that a police officer can require a soldier to do that which he can order a civilian to do or refrain from doing. So in relation to road traffic offences a soldier has no immunities *qua* soldier,[7] nor would he have if he creates an obstruction on the highway, for instance. This is a consequence of the legal position of the soldier as 'a citizen in uniform'. Unless he is given statutory powers greater than those possessed by a civilian, his authority and his immunities are no different. Yet he is subject to military law, which, of course, the civilian is not, and as a result he may be ordered by his military superiors to comply with the orders of a particular police commander and a refusal to carry out these orders would be an offence under the Army Act.[8] It is, however, unlikely that the military authorities would in this way subordinate themselves to the police in a matter calling for a 'military solution', that is, one requiring the use or deployment of military weapons. Where no such order has been given by a soldier's military superior, there can be no question of a soldier coming under the command of the police, unless an ordinary citizen would be liable for a failure to assist the police if called upon to do so.[9]

The police, on the other hand, cannot be controlled by the government, but only by the chief officer of police of the particular force.[10] Indeed, within the limits of his discretion the chief constable's actions cannot even be challenged in the courts.[11] So a chief constable who refused to prosecute an individual for an alleged criminal act cannot be forced to do so by the courts. Of course, it would be a different matter if he decided not to uphold the law at all, for instance by not bringing proceedings against any alleged thieves. It may be interesting to speculate whether the government could indirectly control police actions by placing a particular police force under the command of the Army, which it could then control quite legitimately. In the same way as discussed above, it would seem that any police force could in theory be placed by its chief constable under the command of the Army.[12] Each police officer, like each soldier, would retain any obligations he possessed under the law which would prevail over his service obligations. This course of action was followed in Northern Ireland in 1969 when the British government 'transferred overall responsibility for security and public order matters to the G.O.C., including full control of the deployment and tasks of the Royal Ulster Constabulary when operating in this capacity'.[13] The events in Northern Ireland were of course highly unusual, and it is unlikely that in Britain a chief constable would order his men to take their orders from the military authorities unless for a limited operation during which the co-operation of the police and Army was envisaged.[14] In most cases it would simply be sufficient that both Army and police acted together but on separate tasks, so that no question of 'who is in command' arises. But there have been occasions in which the armed forces and police have acted together during a joint operation unconnected with terrorist activity. During the air traffic controllers dispute in 1977 military fuel tankers, accompanied by police, were able to enter an air traffic control centre despite the presence of pickets. It should be said that the use of the armed forces for tasks normally performed by civilians can be a matter of great political significance.

A limited and successful deployment is more likely to be acceptable politically than one that drags on for some time. Experience has shown that in Britain the armed forces have not been used extensively in industrial disputes and, apart from Northern Ireland, not since 1919[15] in a public order capacity. To this extent their popularity as an institution has not suffered.[16] In marked contrast with a police force, the Army does not seek to play an impartial role in any of its activities. It is seen and understood as an arm of the government of the day.

Strikes and other Emergencies

The consequences of a strike may affect only the employer and his business or it might cause a national emergency, depending upon the industry concerned. In the former situation an employer might request of the military authorities assistance in order to carry on his business. It would seem that men could legally be made available by the Ministry of Defence on condition that their services are paid for by the employer concerned.[17] It is by no means uncommon for a request to be made of the police by a football club for the attendance of extra police officers during a particular game.[18] Military bands may also be 'borrowed', but in each case a charge is made by the police authority or the Ministry of Defence. There is nothing illegal in this practice providing that the relevant authority was not under a duty to provide that particular service. This point is well illustrated by *China Navigation Co. Ltd. v. Attorney-General* in 1932.[19] The plaintiffs, an English trading company, operated ships in the China seas, an area in which pirates also operated. In order to provide protection to their passengers and crew, the plaintiffs requested the Crown to provide armed guards to travel on board their ships. This request was granted on terms that the service should be paid for by the plaintiffs. The Court of Appeal held that since the Crown was under no obligation to afford military protection to British subjects abroad, it could at their request enter into an agreement by which the service would be paid for. 'I know of no authority', stated Lawrence L. J., 'which prevents the Crown, if so minded, from employing any available soldiers in time of peace as well as in time of war in rendering services to private individuals, or from demanding and receiving remuneration for any services so rendered.' Whether the Minister of Defence would consent to the use of troops on this basis to replace striking workers is, it is thought, highly unlikely.

There is a hierarchy of industries in which a total strike, or even a go-slow, would have the most serious repercussions on the nation as a whole, or a particular section of it. Attempts to place various industries in this hierarchy and the effects of industrial action within them has been the function of various contingency planners. High on this list there would without doubt appear electricity supply workers, oil tanker drivers, firemen and health service workers. A government could not stand idly by and see essential services crippled by industrial action. The armed forces may be the only body standing between a civilised society and an abyss, and no one would doubt their function of defending the State.[20] Whelan shows that betwen 1945 and 1983 'service personnel have replaced striking employees in at least 30 disputes ... twelve of these 30 disputes occurred since 1970. ... These figures became more significant ... if one adds to them the number of disputes in which the military have been standing-by, ready to intervene, within 72 hours. Since 1970, the military have been standing by in 15 disputes ....'[21] The type of activities in which the armed forces have been involved range from replacing dock workers, railwaymen, dustmen, firemen, to oil tanker drivers, air traffic assistants and prison officers.

It has been shown that the prerogative power to deploy the armed forces yields to a relevant statute. It will be the statute that lays down the terms upon which the armed forces can be employed and the powers of Parliament control their use.

There are two major statutes which can involve use of the armed forces in industrial disputes, although, strictly, they are wide enough to cover other emergencies, including public disorder.

The Emergency Powers Act 1920

This Act, which was amended in 1964, provides in s. 1(1) that:

'If at any time it appears to Her Majesty that there have occurred, or are about to occur, events of such a nature as to be calculated, by interfering with the supply and distribution of food, water, fuel or light, or with the means of locomotion, to deprive the community, or any substantial portion of the community, of the essentials of life, Her Majesty may, by proclamation ... declare that a state of emergency exists.'

A proclamation remains in force for up to one month, but it may be renewed; the average time for the continuance of a proclamation would appear to be one month.[22] Following the issue of a proclamation of emergency, Her Majesty in Council may issue detailed regulations[23] giving powers to those who act on behalf of the government. Parliament must be informed of any proclamation and, in addition, regulations made under the Act are subject to the affirmative resolutions of both Houses. This statutory obligation to inform Parliament of a proclamation contrasts with other occasions on which the armed forces may be deployed, where there is no such requirement. When, for instance, troops were placed on duty at Heathrow Airport in 1974, in order to guard against the threat posed by armed terrorists, Parliament was not at the time informed. A statement was made subsequently by the government in the House of Lords, but only in answer to a question put by a member of that House. There is an inherent danger in any emergency that a government will accrue to itself draconian powers by regulation and that these will be drawn up in terms wider than are strictly necessary for the particular occasion. Lord Pearce had this danger in mind when he said, 'the flame of individual right and justice must burn more palely when it is ringed by the more dramatic light of bombed buildings'.[24] It has been shown that regulations will not possess any force of law unless both Houses pass affirmative resolutions concerning them, but there are further limitations contained in the Act itself.[25] So, regulations cannot be drafted which would have the effect of imposing compulsory military service; it would not be lawful under the 1920 Act to conscript strikers into the armed forces. In a similar way, it is not permissible to draft regulations that would make it a criminal offence to be on strike or to alter existing procedure in criminal cases or to confer any right to punish by fine or imprisonment without trial.

If we pause here to consider the powers granted by s. 1(1) to issue a proclamation of emergency, we see that the section is an enigma. First, the 'event' must interfere with 'the supply and distribution of food, water, fuel or light, or with the means of locomotion'. What of a fireman's strike or a strike by local authority refuse collectors?[26] Secondly, the 'event ... must deprive the community, or any substantial portion of the community'. When is 'a substantial portion' affected? What of a strike by bus drivers (the means of locomotion) in Liverpool or by all transport drivers in London? Finally, it is by no means clear what is meant by 'the essentials of life'.[27] Presumably it refers to the deprivation of food, water, etc., but what of medicines?

Proclamations of emergency have been made on twelve occasions since 1920, five of which were during the period 1970-74.

The Emergency Powers Act 1964, s. 2

The Defence Council may:

'authorise officers and men of Her Majesty's naval, military or air forces ... to be temporarily employed on agricultural work or such work as may be approved in accordance with instructions issued by the Defence Council as being urgent work of national importance, and thereupon it shall be the duty of every person subject to the Naval Discipline Act, military law or airforce law to obey any command given by his superior officer in relation to such employment, and every such command shall be deemed to be a lawful command within the meaning of the Naval Discipline Act 1957, the Army Act 1955, or the Air Force Act 1955, as the case may be.'[28]

It should be noticed that there is no requirement of a proclamation to be made in order to invoke s. 2 of this Act, and Parliament need not be informed. Any detailed orders to units of the armed forces will be the sole province of the services themselves, subject only to challenge in Parliament. Power is given to the Defence Council in respect of 'agricultural work or such work as may be approved', a term much wider than that provided in the 1920 Act. It might be seriously questioned whether s. 2 of this Act is a tautology. The prerogative of the Crown extends to the deployment of the armed forces in whatever place or manner the Crown thinks fit. If the Crown considers it expedient to place members of its armed forces in agricultural or other work of national importance, it need only give the order, which could not be challenged in the courts. An individual Serviceman could hardly be permitted to say that such an order would be unlawful and one that he need not obey. The Defence Council could, in theory order a Serviceman to do anything that was not contrary to law, providing it had some military purpose. Arguably, 'urgent work of national importance' would, in peacetime as well as in war, have some military purpose. In any event, a directive from the Defence Council itself would, *ex hypothesi*, be for a military purpose. The very practical effect of s. 2 is that it prevents a Serviceman, who has disobeyed such an order, from challenging its lawfulness under military law. Finally, the Act requires a decision to employ the armed forces in such work to be made by the Defence Council, and not, for example, merely by a commanding officer.

There is no provision in the 1964 Act enabling the armed forces to requisition vehicles. This could, however, be achieved either through regulation made under a proclamation within the terms of the 1920 Act or by virtue of s. 165 of the Army Act 1955. This latter section may be invoked whenever it appears to the Secretary of State that the public interest so requires, but he must report his action to Parliament, which may extend it beyond its initial period of one month.[30] Requisitioning of vehicles does not seem to have played any part in those disputes where it might have been useful, for example, the ambulance drivers strike in 1979 and the firemen's strike of 1978. In both cases service vehicles were used, no doubt due to the real practical problem of getting past pickets in order to requisition civilian ambulances or fire-fighting appliances.

Whelan records that the 1964 Act has been 'invoked on at least ten occasions between 1970 and 1983. Indeed, with the exception of the dockers dispute in 1972, and the industrial civil servants disputes in 1978 and 1981, all military intervention in industrial disputes since 1970 has been authorised by this statute.'[31]

Public Disorder

Public disorder on a large scale in the past has generally been a consequence of strike action[32] or political agitation and until fairly recently the Army, and to some extent the Navy, had been the natural force to call upon in the absence of a well-organised, well-disciplined and effective police force which required support. The last occasion on which the Army and the Navy were involved in public order duties was during the strike by the Liverpool police force in 1919. This was a classic example of troops being used as a substitute police force.[33]

Although public disorder has erupted on a number of occasions and even on a scale that might presage the 'military option' to control it, it has been the local police force, at times supplemented by other forces, that has borne the brunt of maintaining order. This has largely been due to an awareness by government that a properly trained and equipped police force is able to cope with most situations that might foreseeably arise. The creation of a 'third force', or paramilitary police force like the C.R.S. in France or the former 'B' Specials in Northern Ireland, is not politically a realistic alternative to the use of the police or the Army. Since containment of disorder by minimum force is considered to be a basic tenet of maintaining order, it would set a dangerous precedent to employ, at the outset, a paramilitary force. Far better, it is thought, to hold in reserve the Army to be used if minimum force used by the police proves obviously to be inadequate.

The legal controls over the use of the armed forces to assist the civil power (or MACP) are by no means clear. Since no statute governs the matter, it is left to vague generalisations drawn from constitutional principles, such as the prerogative, from judicial opinion and from statements of government law officers. That it has never been entirely clear who possesses the legal power to direct the armed forces to assist the civil power is due, in part, to the absence of a written constitution. In West Germany, for instance, the constitution places limits on the use of the armed forces for this purpose. Britain, on the other hand, has always taken a rather pragmatic approach, with the 'right solution' being either to give control to the government or the civil power, depending on the view taken at a particular time in history.[34] One thing is certain. In the exercise of their prerogative powers, ministers of the Crown can direct that the armed forces be deployed in a particular area in which public disorder is occurring. Since this involves a particular exercise of the prerogative and not a statutory power, the ministers are answerable to Parliament and not to the courts.[34a]

The dispatch of troops would be considered by the Home Secretary following a request by the chief officer of police to him. The Secretary of State for Defence, in consultation with the Home Secretary (and probably the Prime Minister), would then decide whether to respond.[35]

The older authorities spoke of the Army being called out by the local magistrate, whose duty it was to read the proclamation contained in the Riot Act 1714. Moreover, it was a criminal offence for the magistrate to fail to call upon the Army when the urgent need arose and also for him to call upon the Army when there was no justification at all for doing so.[36] Whether an Army commanding officer was bound by law to respond to this request is to some extent unclear, since no military commander appears to have been prosecuted for not coming to the assistance of the magistrate upon his order.[37] The *Manual of Military Law* takes the view that 'a soldier must come to the assistance of the civil authority where it is necessary for him to do so but not otherwise' and further that they must 'judge for themselves whether to intervene'.[38] There are recorded occasions in which a request by a magistrate to call out a locally based battalion was rejected by the chief constable[39] and the whole thrust of Queen's Regulations is that a commanding officer should report a request 'from a source other than the chief officer of police' to him and to his superior.[40] Whether at any time magistrates have been able, on their own initiative, to call out the Army whose duty it was to obey, can hardly now be a credible position. The chief officer of police has, for all intents and purposes, replaced the magistrate as the authority responsible for law and order within a particular area. With this demise of the magistrates goes the power of the courts to investigate and control his actions.

This position has, however, been complicated by a further duty which, it is argued, applies to soldiers. The reasoning runs along the following lines. A citizen in whose presence a breach of the peace is being committed or reasonably appears to be about to be committed has a duty to 'take reasonable steps to make the person who is breaking or threatening to break the peace refrain from doing so'.[41] But this duty is one of 'imperfect obligation'; in other words, the citizen is not expected to risk unreasonably his own life or limb in the exercise of this duty.[42] If we add to this syllogism the principle that a soldier 'differs from the ordinary citizen in being armed and subject to discipline but his rights and duties in dealing with crime are precisely the same as those of the ordinary citizens,'[43] we can then conclude that a soldier attracts the same duty as the civilian. If this is correct, and there is considerable authority to support it,[44] a soldier is under a duty to prevent a breach of the peace, independently of any orders from a magistrate, chief officer of police, or indeed the Secretary of State for Defence acting through the Defence Council. A moment's reflection suggests that this would produce bizarre consequences as shown by Evelegh in the following passage: 'A corporal, with ten privates in a lorry, who happened to drive through an area when a crowd of demonstrators had burst through a police cordon and were attacking an embassy, would have not merely a right to intervene and suppress the disorder with lethal weapons if necessary, but an absolute duty to do so, in spite of anyone from the Prime Minister to the senior policeman on the spot telling him not to.'[45]

It is suggested that the law does not require this conclusion. First, it is open to doubt whether the common law really imposes a duty on a citizen to intervene, as opposed to providing him with a defence if he does so.[46] There is no recorded case of a person ever being prosecuted for failing to act on his own initiative. In addition, the House of Lords has stated that the judges have no inherent power to create criminal offences.[47] Secondly, even if a duty to intervene does exist, it is by no means clear that it applies to soldiers in a body, compared with a soldier as an individual. No quarrel can be made of the fact that once on the ground a soldier's rights and obligations are precisely those of the citizen; he has no greater immunity merely because of his status as a soldier.

A soldier, like a citizen, may, on the other hand, be under a duty to come to the assistance of a constable if called by him to do so. In *R. v. Brown* (1841)[48] the defendant was convicted of a common law misdemeanour in refusing, without lawful excuse, to assist a constable who had requested him to assist in putting an end to an illegal prize fight. It would be necessary, for a conviction, for the prosecution to show a 'reasonable necessity' for calling upon the citizen and the absence of a lawful excuse or the physical impossibility of the task allotted. This case could hardly be argued to be a precedent for a constable to call out on his own initiative a locally based battalion. The defendant in *Brown* was at the scene of the illegal prize fight when it was occurring and could reasonably be called upon to assist the constable.

It would appear then that the ultimate decision whether to deploy the armed forces when public disorder is occurring to such an extent that the police force along with any other force drafted in is unable to contain it rests squarely with ministers of the Crown under the royal prerogative. In theory, a request by the local chief constable would not be an essential prerequisite to involvement, but in practice it will be. Neither a magistrate, nor police officer (of whatever rank) can compel the armed forces to assist them,[49] nor is there an independent duty imposed by common law on the soldiers themselves to intervene.[50] This conclusion leads to the view that the only control existing to prevent an improper use of the armed forces is in Parliament itself. The courts are *functus offico*.

The special circumstances of the deployment of the Army in Northern Ireland,[51] along with legal controls over their operations against terrorists or suspected terrorists, will now be considered. It is then proposed to consider those incidents involving the deployment of Army units at Heathrow Airport and to deal with specific terrorist sieges. Finally, the legal aspects of guarding military establishments will be considered.

Use of the Armed Forces in Northern Ireland

The population of Northern Ireland is about one and a half million, with an approximate split of one million Protestants and half a million Roman Catholics. The majority of the total population support the constitutional link with the United Kindom, but it is perhaps true to say that the Roman Catholics 'generally favour the reunification of Ireland'.[52] Northern Ireland was granted a unique constitutional status by the United Kingdom in 1920 when the Government of Ireland Act was passed. This provided for a Parliament at Stormont and the right to enact laws 'for the peace, order and good government' of the Province.[53] Certain matters, such as defence, foreign affairs and taxation, were reserved to the United Kingdom government. The courts were to administer those laws passed by the United Kingdom Parliament which were expressly stated to apply to Northern Ireland, laws passed by the Stormont Parliament, and the common law, in so far as it was not inconsistent with these statutes. Final appeal from the Court of Appeal in Northern Ireland is taken to the House of Lords.

In 1969 trouble between the two communities escalated into serious civil disorder which the Royal Ulster Constabulary felt unable to contain. On 14 August the Inspector-General of the Royal Ulster Constabulary requested the Army to assist the police in Londonderry where serious rioting was taking place. The request was made to the Northern Ireland government, who in turn requested the government of the United Kingdom to make the troops available. Within a very short time the General Officer Commanding in the Province received orders to deploy troops in that city.[54] It was considered at the highest level that the common law required the request for military assistance to come directly from the police authorities and in order to comply with this the Inspector General formally requested of the General Officer Commanding that the troops be deployed.

These events were the beginnings of the military involvement in Northern Ireland. The statistics tell their own story. Hutton J. in *Lynch v. The Ministry of Defence*[55] illustrated the tactical importance for the security forces of being able to stop vehicles and question their occupants when he said; 'In Northern Ireland during the past fourteen years since 1st January 1969 the IRA and other terrorist organisations, republican and loyalist, have murdered 676 members of the security forces and 1613 civilians and have injured 8266 members of the security forces and 17,355 civilians and have destroyed and damaged millions of pounds worth of property.'[56]

Emergency Legislation

Political violence has on several occasions erupted during the relatively short existence of the State of Northern Ireland, and it is therefore not surprising to find a local emergency law to deal with it. The Civil Authorities (Special Powers) Act (Northern Ireland) 1922, which at one moment created very vague offences[57] but yet was inadequate to cope with the scale of violence that erupted in 1969. There were no general powers given to soldiers to arrest and detain in order to question persons who might be terrorists.[58] In his Report, which led to the passing of the Northern Ireland (Emergency Provisions) Act 1973, Lord Diplock[59] explained that it 'is only when his identity has been satisfactorily established that it is possible to be reasonably certain of the particular ground on which he was liable to arrest and to inform him of it' and hence the need for a power to detain a person for questioning.

General powers were given in the 1973 Act to members of the armed forces on duty to arrest and detain a person suspected, *inter alia*, of being about to commit *any*[60] offence and the only ground for the arrest that need be given by the soldier was that he was effecting the arrest as a member of Her Majesty's forces. Powers were also given to search premises and persons, to stop and question any person, to stop vehicles, to enter premises during the course of operations and to close a highway.

Through its generation of fear in those who do not actively support a terrorist organisation and sympathy from those who do, the trial of terrorist suspects imposes an intolerable strain on the normal criminal process. For these type of offences trial by jury was hardly possible. The 1973 Act therefore provided for trial by judge alone when an accused was charged with a schedule offence (broadly, an ordinary criminal offence, but with terrorist implications). A confession would be admissible providing that it was not obtained by torture or by inhuman or degrading treatment, a much wider ground than in 'ordinary' trials where the common law imposes very strict tests for the admissibility of a confession.[61]

The Northern Ireland (Emergency Provisions) Act 1978 now codifies all the emergency[62] statute law including the 1973 Act, but the main provisions described above have been retained.

Use of Weapons

Legal control over the use of weapons against suspected terrorists is to be found in the 'ordinary' law and under military law. Emergency legislation is silent on the point, although, it will be seen, the conditions for arrest and therefore a possible condition precedent for the actual use of force is contained in this legislation. It may seem strange to the observer that this emergency legislation should fail to lay down precisely when, in particular, lethal weapons might be used. The result is that in a situation far from ordinary, the 'ordinary' law, designed for peaceful times, is the prevailing law. In addition, the soldier, as it has been shown, is also subject to military law, which itself may impose more detailed orders restricting the actual use of weapons.

Where a soldier uses force, his actions will be judged *ex post facto* to determine whether he has 'hit the exact line of his duty'.[63] An unjustified use of force may result in a criminal prosecution or in an action for damages against the Ministry of Defence in which the soldier's alleged tort will be the basis of the action. Decisions over the former proceedings are made by the Director of Public Prosecutions in which, of course, individual members of the public have no right to participate, whilst in an action for damages the victim of the soldier's actions, or his family, will decide whether to bring proceedings. Since 1974 there have been seven reported cases of actions for damages against the Ministry of Defence involving the use of firearms, whilst the number of reported cases involving criminal prosecutions in the same period was four. It will be seen that in both types of action the soldier's response is tested against the same criteria, but there is an important difference in relation to the burden of proof. In a criminal case the burden rests firmly on the prosecution, who will have to provide that the use of force was unreasonable. If there is any reasonable doubt about this, the soldier must be acquitted. However, in an action for damages it is the defendant, the Ministry, who will have to establish the reasonableness of the soldier's actions,[64] and if it cannot establish this the plaintiff will succeed. For these reasons, at least, the action for damages appears to have replaced criminal prosecution as the usual means of holding the user of weapons accountable in law in cases where a criminal prosecution is not obviously required.

The limits of permissible force are laid down in s. 3 of the Criminal Law Act (Northern Ireland) 1967 as follows:

'A person may use such force as is reasonable in the circumstances in the prevention of crime, or in effecting or assisting in the lawful arrest of offenders or suspected offenders or of persons unlawfully at large.'

In proposing this enactment, the Criminal Law Revision Committee considered that a judge would in attempting to assist the jury in its meaning draw their attention in particular to 'the nature and degree of force used, the seriousness of the evil to be prevented, and the possibility of preventing it by other means'.[65] But the section did not say this, and indeed there is doubt whether it is even permissible for a court to use such a device as a means of statutory interpretation.[66] Since Parliament remained silent on detail in the section, the gap could only be filled by judicial interpretation. Lord Diplock in *Attorney-General for N.I.'s Reference (No. 1 of 1975)*[67] attempted to draw out the salient points in the following passage:

> 'The form in which the jury would have to ask themselves the question
> . . . would be: are we satisfied that no reasonable man (a) with knowledge
> of such facts as were known to the accused or reasonably believed by him
> to exist (b) in the circumstances and time available to him for reflection
> (c) could be of opinion that the prevention of the risk of harm to which
> others might be exposed if the suspect were allowed to escape, justified
> exposing the suspect to the risk of harm to him that might result from
> the kind of force that the accused contemplated using?'

It will be noticed that Lord Diplock's approach was general rather than specific. This followed from his lordship's conclusion that 'reasonable force in the circumstances' was a question of fact for the jury and not one of law for the judge. In consequence, the courts cannot lay down, *a priori*, a fixed set of guidelines for those who may have to use force; that would be to usurp the function of the jury. To the question from a soldier, 'When can I open fire?', a commander could only repeat the general words of the section as explained by Lord Diplock (if this was available to him). What was needed was some administrative guidance, if the courts could not be more accommodating. This came in the form of the yellow card issued to each soldier, spelling out in more detail the occasions on which fire could be opened.[68] This document can have no greater status than a set of printed orders emanating from a superior authority, but it has been commented on judicially and extra-judicially. Lord Lowry, C.J. in *R. v. MacNaughton*[69] in stressing the overriding duty of the soldier to obey the civil (non-military) law, said;

> 'There was, of course, at the same time in existence what is called the
> yellow card; something the contents of which, it seems are largely
> dictated by policy and are intended to lay down guidlines for the security
> forces but which do not define the legal rights and obligations of
> members of the forces under statute or common law.'

The question of what is 'reasonable force' has been the central focus of a number of cases that have been decided by the courts in Northern Ireland. Section 3 of the 1967 Act applies whether the case involves a criminal prosecution or an action for damages and it has been discussed in both contexts. However, in many of these cases the trial has been before a judge without a jury[70] and it is therefore possible to see how the judge has interpreted this phrase. Unlike a judge, a jury does not give reasons for its decisions and so in a jury trial it is never possible to go behind the verdict; neither is it possible for the judge to guide the jury specifically on how to interpret the section.[71]

It will also be noticed that many of the cases exhibit at least two common features. These are the almost total conflict of evidence between the accused or defendant and the victim or plaintiff as to the events in question and the group loyalty shown by those soldiers called as witnesses. The judge is therefore left with the task of totally rejecting the evidence of one of the parties.

It is proposed now to look in some detail at the judicial interpretation of section 3 of the 1967 Act. One must, however, bear in mind that the actual decision in any individual case may depend upon whom the burden of proof rests. It will be recalled that in a criminal case it will be borne by the prosecution and in an action for damages by the defendant, in practice the Ministry of Defence.

(a) 'A person'

This section does not draw any distinction between a private citizen and a member of the police or armed forces. It may to some appear strange that the terrorist, ordinary criminal and the soldier can use the same degree of force, even although the latter is armed with a lethal weapon by the State with the role of protecting it, and its citizens, from the former.[72] This is, however, a superficial interpretation since the section directs the court to consider the circumstances, in which the purpose of using force will be a very relevant consideration.

The section only protects the actual person who uses the force. It does not therefore provide a defence, in crime or in tort to the person who gave the orders as to when to use force. This point arose in a novel form in *Farrell v. Secretary of State for Defence*[73] where a number of soldiers had shot and killed the husband of the plaintiff believing that he was about to place a bomb in the night safe of a bank. Before the Court of Appeal in Northern Ireland it was sought to prove that the officer, who had planned the operation had been negligent in not providing for means other than by firing to arrest those suspected of the offence. The House of Lords held the section had application only to the person who had used the force and that the 'circumstances' could not be taken to incorporate other persons.[74]

(b) 'In the prevention of crime'

Whilst few would doubt that it was reasonable to use lethal force to prevent a serious crime such as murder there may be strong difference of opinion in relation to other less serious offences. Suppose the only offence that a soldier suspects a person of is membership of the IRA, a proscribed organisation, and that person fails to stop at a road block. Or take the case of a teenager who has taken a car for a joy ride without the owner's consent. Is the soldier justified in opening fire in either or both of these cases? The obvious answer would seem to be in the negative, since the maximum punishment, should the offender be arrested, would be a relatively short term of imprisonment. The logic of this would then take us to the conclusion that it is only permissible to use lethal force to prevent a crime as serious as the act committed by the soldier, i.e. murder. There would therefore appear to be no justification for using lethal force to prevent the mere destruction of property, however valuable it might be.[75] It follows also that looters could not be fired upon.

The whole position is, however, altered if the soldier is permitted to take into account any *future crimes* that the suspected person may commit. To fire upon a person merely suspected of belonging to the IRA could be considered as in the prevention of terrorist crime that that person may commit in the future. This, it may be argued, reflects no more than reality. A member of that organisation is required to commit acts that frequently result in the death of members of the security forces as well as civilians. Lord Diplock in the *Reference* case took the view that the jury (or, in Northern Ireland, the judge) could assess 'the kind of harm to be averted by preventing the accused's escape as even greater—the killing or wounding of members of the patrol by terrorists in ambush, and the effect of this success by members of the Provisional IRA, in encouraging the continuance of the armed insurrection and all the misery and destruction of life and property that terrorist activity in Northern Ireland has entailed'.[76] In *Farrell* Viscount Dilhorne did not consider as crucial whether or not the men had succeeded in placing the bomb in the bank. 'If they had not', his lordship explained, 'then it might be said that the force used was in the prevention of crime, for it could not be assumed that the bomb or device would not be used elsewhere'.[77]

This approach would seem to be understandable in the type of case under consideration. Whether it is correct is a matter of judgment, since in the absence of an *immediate* threat posed by the suspected terrorist speculation becomes the test of whether action should be taken. It would clearly not be a relevant consideration where the force is used against an ordinary criminal whose pattern of crime is sporadic and variable.

(c) 'In effecting or assisting in the lawful arrest of offenders or suspected offenders'

For the soldier to act effectively in an environment like Northern Ireland he must have powers to arrest greater than those possessed by the ordinary citizen. A consequence of the common law view of the soldier as merely 'a citizen in uniform' was that his power to arrest suspected offenders was limited to this status. Following the Northern Ireland (Emergency Provisions) Act 1973, members of Her Majesty's forces on duty were given powers to arrest and detain wider than the ordinary citizen, but narrower than those possessed by a police officer. Section 12[78] of that Act gives the general power of arrest and section 16[79] permits a soldier to 'stop and question any person for the purpose of ascertaining the person's identity and movements ... (and) what he knows concerning any recent explosion or any other incident endangering life ...'. It will be appreciated that to open fire at a person believed to be a member of the IRA and fleeing, whether on foot or in a car, from a soldier can be justified more readily as a 'prevention of (future) crime' than in order to effect the 'lawful arrest of' an offender. For the latter justification the soldier will need to know more than merely that that person is suspected of being a member of a prescribed organisation. He will need reasonably to suspect that he has committed an offence which justifies him in using that degree of force.[80]

In any event, it is somewhat unrealistic to contemplate a soldier opening fire at a fleeing person in order to 'arrest him'. Given that the yellow card permits only the firing of aimed, and therefore not warning, shots and that soldiers are trained to fire at the centre of the target it can be assumed that they have the necessary intent to kill, or at least to cause grievous bodily harm.[81]

Finally, it is not at all clear whether a soldier may open fire at a person in order merely to exercise his right to stop and question him under section 16 where there are no circumstances pointing to involvement in a proscribed organisation.[82]

(d) 'Or of persons unlawfully at large'

A person may be unlawfully at large if he has been lawfully arrested or has been dealt with through the legal process and he escapes. In *R. v. MacNaughton*[83] the accused, an Army sergeant, shot and wounded a man whom he had lawfully arrested when that man tried to escape from his custody. He was charged with attempted murder and relied upon section 3 of the 1967 Act to justify his actions. His trial was before Lord Lowry C.J. sitting without a jury and in giving his reasons for acquitting the accused we have a valuable insight into the interpretation of the section and the factors considered to be relevant in deciding that the soldier's action was reasonable. His lordship stressed the point that once the escape had occurred there was no other viable course of action that the accused could take. To run after the man would be folly; the patrol, of which the accused was the commander, was operating in 'hostile country' and there was the danger of booby traps. His lordship concluded that, 'This created a situation quite different from the escape of a person from prison or an escape in some place where conditions were comparatively peaceful, apart from the escape itself.' But the prevention of future crime seems to be the real basis of the judgment, as can be seen from Lord Lowry's statement that, 'Present to his mind must have been the likelihood that if (the man) escaped he would undertake terrorist acts.'

Typical Instances where Soldiers have Opened Fire

It has been shown that soldiers 'are sometimes faced with legal difficulties to be solved in a flash which could take a trained lawyer hours to consider',[84] but solve them they must. It is proposed now to consider the most typical types of case where soldiers have opened fire and where they have either been prosecuted or an action for damages has been brought on the basis of their conduct. It has only been possible to consider those cases that have been reported and which are therefore available for study.

(a) Road Blocks

The motor car is as useful to the terrorist as a weapon or bomb. With it he can move men, arms, ammunition and explosives to his chosen locations and be virtually indistinguishable from the civilian population. Any anti-terrorist operation must be able to control this movement, and in order to do so the Army must possess the legal and physical power to stop vehicles. Section 18 of the 1978 Act, it will be recalled, gives members of Her Majesty's armed forces on duty the power to stop and question in certain circumstances, whilst section 20 gives a general power to stop and search any vehicle.

Can a soldier ever be justified, under section 3 of the 1967 Act, if he opens fire at an unknown driver of a car who fails to stop at a road block? It will be assumed that the activities of the soldiers constitute unequivocally a road block and that no reasonable person could be under any other impression. In these circumstances a person who deliberately failed to stop at the soldier's signal could hardly complain if he were taken to be a suspected terrorist.[85] Firing at him could therefore be considered as the use of reasonable force to prevent a (future) crime. In giving judgment in *Donaghy v. The Ministry of Defence*,[86] MacDermott J. considered the argument that other means should have been adopted to deal with those who deliberately fail to stop at road blocks but concluded that, 'In the circumstances the only practical option was to do nothing or use the only available weapon—the S.L.R. rifle.' In such a situation, his lordship opined, immediate action is necessary and it would prove futile, for instance, to radio for assistance to seal off the area since in the time taken to achieve this the suspect vehicle could be anywhere. In addition, where the driver is known, or reasonably suspected of being a person who has committed a very serious crime, it may be possible to justify the soldier's actions in opening fire at him as being in order to effect an arrest.

Hutton J. in *Lynch v. The Ministry of Defence*[87] dealt with the argument of counsel that instead of opening fire at the driver of the car the soldiers could have fired at its tyres. His lordship rejected this argument in the following passage: 'I consider that where a car is being driven fast and in a determined manner, firing at the tyres might well be ineffective to stop the vehicle, and in any event, if the soldiers were not permitted to fire at the driver of the car, the driver might often escape from a foot patrol with any weapons or explosives which he might be carrying, even if the car were eventually stopped by bullets striking a tyre or tyres.'

(b) Observation Posts

An observation post is here taken to refer to any place where soldiers are able to observe without being seen directly. In such a position they may be very vulnerable once they are spotted and in a number of the cases fire is opened because the soldier concerned believed that he was about to be shot at. The reported cases show that often he has made a mistake about this, but the effect that such a mistake can have on liability will be discussed below.

The main grounds of justification advanced in these cases is self-defence and section 3 of the 1967 Act, both of which depend on the use of reasonable force and, it would appear, little is to be gained from a separate treatment of those two grounds.[88] In a criminal case *R. v. Bohun and Temperley*[89] the trial judge found the accused not guilty of murder in circumstances where two soldiers opened fire on a youth who had approached a graveyard wherein a cache of arms had been discovered by the Army and which they were keeping under observation. Here the soldiers concerned believed that they had been spotted by the youth who had turned round and was about to fire at them. However, in *Doherty v. The Ministry of Defence*[90] and in *McGuigan v. The Ministry of Defence*[91] the Ministry were unable to prove that the soldier opened fire either in self-defence or by virtue of section 3 of the 1967 Act and in both cases substantial damages were awarded to the plaintiff.

In both *Doherty* and *McGuigan* it was for the defence to prove that reasonable force had been used by the soldiers concerned and these cases do illustrate the difficulty of doing this when the soldier has made a mistake and has shot an innocent person and especially where that person has been under observation, perhaps for some time.[92]

Special Problems of Law

(a) The Soldier Who Makes a Mistake

In virtually all the cases in which damages were sought, the plaintiff alleged that he had been an innocent person and that the soldier had mistaken him for a terrorist. Two questions arise here. First, can a mistake of fact excuse and secondly, does the mistake have to be a reasonable one?

A mistake of fact can lead the individual soldier to believe that circumstances existed that made it reasonable for him to open fire. It would appear, at least from judgments in the courts of Northern Ireland, that the belief of the soldier must be a reasonable one. The trial judge in *McGuigan v. The Ministry of Defence* found in favour of the plaintiff, who had been shot by a soldier from an observation point, and stated that, 'the defendant has failed to prove on the balance of probabilities that the soldier had reasonable grounds on which to believe that the plaintiff was about to fire at him or at other members of the security forces'. The House of Lords in the *Reference Case*[93] postulated a reasonable belief but it may be argued at least in a criminal case that a merely honest belief will suffice.[94] The latter approach would seem to be preferable, since if a soldier honestly believes that a person is about to fire at him he clearly believes in circumstances in which it would be reasonable for him to open fire.[95] Of course, the more unreasonable the belief, the less likely will it be that it is believed by the judge (or jury) but to deny the 'defence' to the soldier in these circumstances is to do so because of his negligence in forming an unreasonable (although honest) belief. Was the trial judge in *McGuigan* really saying that he did not believe the soldier when he explained why he opened fire or that in an action for damages a belief must be reasonably held?

(b) Superior Orders

In a sense every order that the private soldier receives is a superior order, whether it be in a printed form as in the yellow card or in the *Manual of Military Law* or in an oral form. His duty under military law is to obey all lawful commands,[96] in other words, orders from a superior that have a military purpose and do not contravene either military or civil law. Where the soldier is ordered to do something that is contrary to the civil law, a potential conflict between the two systems arises. What is the legal position of the soldier who is given the order, 'shoot that man' in circumstances in which the soldier does not believe that he is justified in doing so? The *Manual of Military Law*, whilst recognising that the matter is not free from doubt, states 'the better view' to be that a superior order 'can never of itself excuse the recipient if he carries out the order, although it may give rise to a defence on other grounds'.[97] There is authority for two schools of thought on this issue. The *Manual* represents what might be called the 'non defence' school whilst other authorities suggest that a superior order may be a defence if the order given was not manifestly illegal.[98] Legal writers appear to prefer the *Manual* stance, since it subordinates military law to the civil law[99] and illustrates the status of military command as being subject to the law of the land. The theoretical difficulty of a soldier challenging his orders on the ground of perceived illegality is answered by the law's insistence that each man is responsible for his own actions, in the light of the facts as he perceived them to be. When the *Manual* states that a superior order may provide a defence on other grounds, it can only be referring to a mistake of fact. So an order to 'shoot that man' may lead a soldier (and possibly, a reasonable soldier) to believe that the man at whom he is ordered to open fire is a suspected terrorist and that the force he is about to use is reasonable to prevent a future terrorist crime.

(c) Actions for Damages

It will be recalled that the majority of the reported cases in the field under consideration are actions for damages by those who have been shot by soldiers. It has been explained how the burden of proof rests upon the Ministry of Defence to prove that the force used was reasonable in the circumstances. If the jury is left in doubt, they will find for the plaintiff. There are two particular torts that might be invoked by a plaintiff in these circumstances. The tort of negligence imposes liability on those who owe a duty to the plaintiff not to be negligent and who breach this duty, causing damage. The relevant duty is owed to those who can reasonably be foreseen as being at risk from a potential defendant's acts or omissions.[100] However, in certain circumstances the courts, for reasons of policy, have taken the view that no duty in negligence should be owed.[101] In the type of case under discussion no decision has yet been made by the courts as to whether a soldier owes to a terrorist or suspected terrorist a duty of care in negligence. It was argued in *Farrell v. Secretary of State for Defence*[102] that the officer who had planned the operation had been negligent in not providing for means other than by firing upon those suspected of placing a bomb in the bank in order to arrest them. The House of Lords held, however, that as negligence against the officer had not been pleaded by the plaintiff, the House could not consider this aspect of the claim. It will therefore be noticed that the tort of negligence has the potential to range far beyond those who actually used the force itself.

The tort that has succeeded on all occasions where a plaintiff has secured an award of damages is the tort of trespass to the person, in particular, assault and battery. Here the plaintiff merely needs to show that he has been shot intentionally[103] by someone for whom the defendant is liable. It is then necessary for the latter to prove that there was some lawful justification for the action of the soldier. This might be that the shooting was in self-defence or was justified by section 3 of the 1967 Act. This tort is a simple one compared with negligence since there is no requirement to show a duty of care, which, as shown above, is a matter of public policy and in relation to which there are powerful arguments in favour of denying such a duty.

Having flirted with the tort of negligence, the courts in Northern Ireland seem to have taken the line that the primary issue in these cases is the justification for the shooting and this would be so in either tort claim.

Negligence as a cause of action therefore appears to have been dropped, and along with it the additional problem of the standard of care expected of the soldier in using a legal weapon. In *Doherty v. The Ministry of Defence*,[104] for instance, O'Donnell J. stated that he would also have held the soldier liable in negligence since 'his marksmanship fell below the standard which was desirable or reasonable in anyone discharging a lethal weapon'. Upon appeal to the House of Lords, that court considered the statement to be wrong but did not give any reasons for its conclusion.

Two particular defences to an action for damages have also been raised by the Ministry of Defence to defeat the claims brought against it. These are the defences of *ex turpi causa* and *volenti non fit injuria*, each of which would strictly only be relevant if the court had determined that the force used had not been reasonable.

These defences were raised by the defendant in *Lynch v. The Ministry of Defence*[105] where the plaintiff had stolen a car and, it was alleged, had attempted to drive at soldiers and thereby cause them injury. The defence of *ex turpi causa non oritur actio* had been considered by Lord Lowry C.J. in *Farrell v. The Ministry of Defence*[106] and his lordship explained that the doctrine 'depends on the proposition that a plaintiff cannot maintain a cause of action which is based on his own criminal or immoral act' and that '*ex turpi* does not mean that a plaintiff who is guilty of a crime cannot recover from a defendant whose tort is independent of the plaintiff's crime'. Indeed to apply the maxim at all would mean that a person who used more force than was reasonable would never be liable if the person shot was a terrorist, in which case 'excessive force would be excusable'. The defence, in fact, has only succeeded where the plaintiff and defendant are joint participants in a crime and the latter injures the former or where the plaintiff's criminal conduct is the direct cause of his injury.[107]

The defence of *volenti non fit injuria* may succeed where the plaintiff has agreed, 'expressly or impliedly, to waive any claim for any injury that may befall him due to the lack of reasonable care by the defendant'.[108] Merely to run, with full knowledge, the risk involved will not be sufficient. In practice it would be very difficult to show that even a terrorist, who appreciates fully the risks of driving through an Army road block, has consented to waive any claim against the Ministry if the force used against him turns out to have been excessive.[109]

In theory, also, it would be possible to reduce the damages awarded where the use of force by a soldier had been excessive on the ground that the plaintiff had been contributorily negligent, in respect of his injury. This point was argued but rejected, before the Northern Ireland Court of Appeal in *Farrell*.[110] McGonigal L.J. considered that the risk of excessive force being used against him was not a risk to be reasonably anticipated by the plaintiff. It should be remembered that these defences will only be relevant where the force used against the plaintiff is not justifiable by section 3 of the

1967 Act and in the light of earlier discussion of this section it is clear that an unusual situation will have to occur before any of them could apply. It is therefore only section 3 (or self-defence) that stands between an award of damages against the Ministry of Defence and no award at all.

An employer is vicariously liable for the torts of his employees (quaintly described as servants) or agents, and hence it is the Ministry of Defence that is actually sued. In strict law there are a number of difficulties with this position. First, vicarious liability arises only where there is the relationship of master (or employer) and servant. In certain limited cases the law provides that an agent may make his principal liable. The soldier is not, however, employed under a contract of service, the hallmark of a servant.[111] His engagement to the Crown is based not on contract but at the prerogative of the Crown. He cannot sue for his wages nor complain if he is dismissed summarily.[112] Secondly, there is some authority pointing to the non-applicability of vicarious liability to the tort of trespass to the person.[113] Whatever the theoretical position it is clear that the Ministry of Defence will continue to be the defendant where it is alleged that a soldier has committed a tort in the course of his employment.

The Role of International Law

It is, perhaps, not surprising that unsuccessful plaintiffs, or indeed those who seek a determination of the legality of government action, whether through its use of the military or civil authorities, should invoke the international obligations of the United Kingdom. The European Convention of Human Rights and Fundamental Freedom is not a part of English law[114] and so a claim that the Convention has been infringed must be brought, in the first instance, before the European Commission, and the applicant must show that he cannot get satisfaction of his claim in his own country.

By Article 2 of the Convention, a State guarantees to everyone within it the 'right to life', but it also goes on to provide that a killing may be justified if it is 'absolutely necessary' in (a) defence of any person from unlawful violence, (b) in order to effect a lawful arrest or to prevent the escape of a person lawfully detained, (c) in action lawfully taken for the purpose of quelling a riot or insurrection. Might it be argued that reasonable force in section 3 of the 1967 Act permits of wider action on behalf of the security forces than 'absolutely necessary' under the Convention?[115] A number of such claims have been brought by residents of Northern Ireland against the United Kingdom, but so far as is known, none has been successful.[116]

Whether the IRA or a member of any other such organisation in Northern Ireland is entitled to be treated as a prisoner of war has been a matter of some debate. The Geneva Conventions of 1949 do not apply, since the 'troubles' in Northern Ireland are not an international conflict nor do the members of these organisations comply with the four conditions of Article 4. The *Manual*

of Military Law[117] interprets the requirement that irregulars must carry
arms openly as follows; 'if it is found that their sole arm is a pistol, hand-
grenade, or dagger concealed about the person, or a sword stick, or similar
weapon, or if it is found that they have hidden their arms on the approach
of the enemy' they will not be entitled to prisoner of war status. Moreover,
Article 3 of the Third Convention of 1949 has no application either, since it
is dependent on there being an 'armed conflict not of an international
character'. An 'armed conflict' would seem to imply a level of intensity of
activity greater than riots or banditry or other acts merely of a criminal
nature.[118]

At the time of writing, the United Kingdom has not ratified the two 1977
Protocols to the 1949 Convention, both of which deal with the problem under
discussion. Protocol 1 applies only to international conflicts but it does also
provide for those 'peoples' who 'are fighting against colonial domination and
alien occupation and against fascist regimes in exercise of their right of self-
determination'.[119] It is not at all clear whether the IRA, or any other such
organisation, represents a 'people', as opposed to a group of defined religious
(or other) sect. In any event, the whole population of Northern Ireland has,
for many years, had the right, through the ballot box, to exercise its right of
self-determination and has expressed its wish to remain part of the United
Kingdom. The Second Protocol is designed to cover non-international
conflicts, but its applicability depends upon an intensity of activity greater
than 'situations of internal disturbances and tensions, such as riots, isolated
and sporadic acts of violence and other acts of a similar nature'.[120] Even if
this condition could be met, and it is very unlikely that it could, the IRA,
or other such organisation, would need to be able to show that it was a
'dissident armed force or other organised armed group which, under
responsible command, exercised such control over part of its territory as to
enable (it) to carry out sustained and concerted military operations'.[121] To
exercise 'such control over a part of a territory' would suggest more than
merely to operate in a territory, control of which is either in the hands of the
lawful government or is actively contested on a regular basis.

Army Units at Heathrow Airport

Following a request by the Metropolitan Police Commissioner to the
government, Army units were deployed at Heathrow Airport in order to
deter potential foreign terrorists from making attacks either on aircraft using
the airport or on passengers. To achieve this purpose, it was necessary to
show those who might be minded to carry out such attacks that they would
be met with determined opposition. Firearms would thus have to be carried
openly. Only the army was equipped and trained to do this.

In order to check on the occupants of vehicles within the airport complex,
it was obviously essential to be able to stop vehicles. A police officer has

power to do so—but does a soldier? Viscount Colville, in making a statement in the House of Lords on behalf of the government, stated: 'In this case the military assisted police at road blocks and check points and by undertaking general patrols ... but some of the troops engaged in the operation did question drivers and search vehicles. When they did so they were ... acting in support of the police, and there would generally have been a police officer at the scene ... had anyone (refused to have his car searched) the soldier would have referred the matter to the police.'[122] A soldier in these circumstances has, it was admitted, no greater powers to stop vehicles or to arrest than those possessed by a civilian. It will be recalled that in Northern Ireland he was given statutory powers in 1973 which included these two rights. In the absence of statutory powers we are thrown back to the common law, which treats the soldier as a 'citizen in uniform'. The legal lacuna is not solved by employing military police, since their authority generally attaches only to those subject to military law.

Suppose, however, that soldiers are instructed to stop vehicles or arrest suspected terrorists on the orders of a police officer who is present with them, as occurred at Heathrow Airport. It has been shown that if a soldier is ordered by his military superior to carry out the orders of a police officer the latter's order can be a lawful one, and failure to obey it would be an offence under the Army Act. Yet if by stopping vehicles or arresting a person on the orders of a police officer a soldier acts contrary to the law he can only be relieved of liability if the orders of a police officer provide a lawful excuse. But they do not merely because they are issued by a police officer.[123]

The Northern Ireland experience shows that a power to detain rather than arrest those who might be involved in terrorist plans or who might have valuable information is a useful weapon in the armoury of those acting on the State's behalf. Police officers possess some powers under the Prevention of Terrorism (Temporary Provisions) Act 1976, but soldiers do not. On the other hand, soldiers, civilians and police officers are subject to the same limits on the use of force, contained in s. 3 of the Criminal Law Act 1967.

In strict law, then, a soldier has limited legal powers; those of a police officer are greater. The evidence suggests that despite this divergence police and Army have been able to co-operate satisfactorily in the task of protecting the airport. The visible display of arms to deter the potential terrorist has, however, since January 1986, also been in the hands of special units of the police.[124]

Terrorist Sieges

The action by members of the S.A.S. at the Iranian Embassy in 1980 ended the siege in a matter of minutes and left most of the terrorists dead. Some commentators spoke of a deliberate policy of killing rather than of arresting the terrorists and bringing them to trial. In reply the Attorney-General stated in a letter to *The Times*:[126] 'I can assure (a previous correspondent) that the Director of Public Prosecutions and myself in considering whether to institute criminal proceedings against members of the S.A.S. applied the same criteria which we apply generally and that there was no question of special rules for the S.A.S.'

In other words, each individual member of the S.A.S., like any other soldier, the police or a civilian who uses force, is to be judged by the same criteria, the reasonableness of the force in the circumstances. Clearly, the use of firearms by S.A.S. soldiers in the Embassy was the only realistic course open to them in the light of the dangers to the hostages and the known fact that the terrorists were armed.

Defending Defence Property

Where there is a risk of interference with property under the control of the Ministry of Defence, military armed guards may be stationed there to protect it from civilian interference. In the normal course of events in peacetime civilians will become involved in this type of activity only where they wish to make a protest against a particular form of defence policy, such as the stationing there of nuclear weapons. It is an offence under s. 1 of the Official Secrets Act 1911 to enter a prohibited place such as a military base and those apprehended may be prosecuted, as in *Chandler v. D.P.P.*[127] Suppose, however, that at the Greenham Common and Molesworth bases where Cruise missiles are, or will be stored, large number of protesters succeed in breaking through the perimeter fence. The first line of defence is likely to be unarmed British Servicemen or police. By overcoming this thin brown and blue line demonstrators may then come up against armed members of the British and American forces. Would the use of firearms against them be justified?

It will be recalled that the pertinent area of law is s.3 of the Criminal Law Act 1967. This is complicated by the fact that the soldiers (or airmen) would be defending property and would not necessarily be using force to safeguard life or limb. No *a priori* assumption can be made as to the legality or otherwise of such actions. This is because the question of whether a particular use of force was reasonable or not is a question of fact for a jury, should a person be prosecuted. Smith and Hogan[128] show the elusive nature of this problem by posing, without being able to give a categoric answer to any of the following questions; 'Is it reasonable', they ask, 'to kill in order to prevent ... robbery, when the property is very valuable. ... How much force may be used to prevent the destruction of a great work of art?'

Should a protester be shot and killed by one of the guards, a jury would have to determine whether by opening fire the accused was acting reasonably and they would have to take into account the consequences of a protester being successful in damaging, destroying or removing a missile. An order by his military superior to shoot anyone who came within close proximity to the missile would not, for the reasons discussed above, by itself relieve the defendant of liability.

The fact that military forces of the United States are stationed at these bases adds to the legal difficulties involved. Under the NATO status of Forces Agreements (discussed in Chapter 6), United States forces are responsible for the security of the bases they occupy.[129] There exists, therefore, the possibility that a British citizen, who has penetrated the outer limits of the base, will be shot and killed by an American guard. It would appear, however, that, 'U.S. security personnel follow the same basic principles as U.K. personnel . . . they are required to use the absolute minimum force necessary in a situation.'[130] Indeed, if they use force, their actions will be judged on the basis of s.3 of the Criminal Law Act 1967.

Notes

1. Supperstone, in *Brownlie's Law of Public Order and National Security* (1981), 2nd edn, p. 210, states that the 'decision to call in the military will be taken by the Home Secretary'. Compare Wade and Bradley, *Constitutional Law* (1985), 10th edn, p. 210, and Rowe and Whelan (eds.), *Military Intervention in Democratic Societies* (1985), p. 90, both of which conclude that the appropriate minister is the Secretary of State for Defence. It may well be the case that so long as the decision is made by a minister of the Crown it matters not which one.
2. However, a minister may refuse to answer a question relating to operational matters; see 1971-2 H.C. paper 393 at Appendix D.
3. See, generally, S. E. Finer, *The Man on Horseback, The Role of the Military in Politics* (1975), 2nd edn, chap. 3.
4. Rowe and Whelan, p. 101.
5. See, generally, *The Queen's Regulations for the Army* (H.M.S.O.), chap. 11.
6. Straining the loyalty of members of the T.A. would be 'improper and probably counter productive', Rowe and Whelan, *op. cit.*, p. 107. See also *The Times*, 26 September 1978, letter concerning blockade of Beira.
7. R. Evelegh, *Peacekeeping in a Democratic Society* (1978), p. 98, draws attention to the case of the military driver who was prosecuted for ignoring traffic lights during a 'battle' in Northern Ireland.
8. See Viscount Colville (1974) H.L. Deb. vol. 348, col. 1051, relating to military-police relations at Heathrow Airport, discussed *infra*; Rowe and Whelan, p. 74. Compare Evelegh, p. 13.
9. *R. v. Brown* (1841) Car. & M. 314, discussed *infra*.
10. See, generally, Wade and Bradley, *op. cit.*, p. 364, 'the hierarchy of command within a police force runs from the police constable on the beat to the chief constable, and no further'. In *R. v. Metropolitan Police Commissioner, ex p. Blackburn* (1968) 1 All E.R. 763, 771, Salmon L.J. opined that 'Constitutionally it is clearly impermissible for the Home Secretary to issue any order to the police in respect of law enforcement.'
11. *R. v. Chief Constable of the Devon and Cornwall Constabulary, ex p. Central Electricity Generating Board* (1981) 3 All E.R. 826.
12. Lord Denning M.R. in *R. v. Metropolitan Police Commissioner, ex p. Blackburn* stated at p. 769, 'It must be for him (a chief constable) to decide on the disposition if his force. . . . No court can or should give him direction on such a matter.'
13. See S. Greer, *Military Intervention in Civil Disturbances: The Legal Basis Reconsidered* (1983) Public Law, 573, 588.
14. Rowe and Whelan, p. 91 (former Metropolitan Police Commissioner), p. 74 (former Chief of Defence Staff).

15. Although to act as a possible deferrent troops were deployed in London during the General Strike of 1926.
16. Haldane, *Evidence to Select Committee on Employment of Military in Cases of Disturbance*, H.C. paper 236 (1908), para. 143: 'We want the Army to be a popular institution and not a menace to civil liberty.'
17. *Manual of Military Law*, vol. 2, para. 31; *China Navigation Co. Ltd v. Attorney-General* (1932) 2 K.B. 197, Lawrence L.J. at pp. 230-232.
18. Section 15 of the Police Act 1964; *Glassbrook Bros. Ltd v. Glamorgan C.C.* (1925) A.C. 270.
19. (1932) 2 K.B. 197.
20. Lord Scarman in talking about the riots in Brixton said; 'If that thin blue line had been overwhelmed ... there is no other way of dealing with it except the awful ultimate requirement of calling in the Army, and to turn the military inwards on British people is not something which our tolerant and free society can possibly accept.' H.L. Deb. vol. 428, col. 1006.
21. Rowe and Whelan, p. 110.
22. Bonner, *Emergency Powers in Peacetime* (1985), p. 225.
23. Emergency Powers Act 1920, s. 2(2). Regulations remain in force for 7 days, but may be renewed. See, for example, Emergency (No. 2) Regulations, 1973, S.I. 1973, No. 2089.
24. *Conway v. Rimmer* (1968) A.C. 910, 982.
25. Section 2(3).
26. See H.C. Deb. vol. 729, col. 37, where the Prime Minister indicated that a proclamation of emergency was made during the seamen's stike of 1966 because of the difficulty caused to the import of raw materials and its effect on 'our export trade'.
27. Morris, *The Emergency Powers Act 1920* (1979) Public Law 317, 310.
28. This was formerly Regulation 6 of the Defence (Armed Forces) Regulations 1939 (S.R. & O. 1939, No. 1304).
29. It would be wide enough to cover any activity covered by the 1920 Act.
30. Section 174 of the Army Act 1955.
31. Rowe and Whelan, *op. cit.*, pp. 115-116. See also *Statement on Defence Estimates*, (1985), vol. 1, chap. 6, and vol. 2, p. 59.
32. See for example, *Report on the Featherstone Riot*, Parl. Papers 1893-1894, c. 7234, where a riot occurred at the Acton Hall Colliery.
33. See also note 15 *supra*.
34. See, generally, Radzinowitz, *A History of English Criminal Law* (1968), vol. 4, p. 153 et seq.
34a. See *Council of Civil Service Unions et al. v. Minister for the Civil Service* (1984) 3 W.L.R. 117 and Chapter 1.
35. *The Queen's Regulations for the Army*, chap. 11 and note 1 *supra*.
36. *R. v. Kennett* (1781) 5. Car. & P. 282; *R. v. Pinney* (1832) 3 B. & Ad. 947; *R. v. Eyre* (1868) Fin. Sp. Rep. 58.
37. Though see the Report on the Featherstone Riot, note 32 *supra*, and Lord Tindal C.J. in his charge to the *Bristol Grand Jury* (1832), 5 Car. & P. 262. Lord Tindal refers to the statute 1 & 2 Will. IV C.41 which is now repealed. Lord Tindal's charge to the *Bristol Grand Jury* was invoked as authority that an Army officer, like a civilian, had a duty at common law to suppress disorder and thus justified the imposition of a curfew: *R. v. McBurney* (1970) Belfast Telegraph, 8 September. Two officers were charged under military law for neglect of duty as a result of the situation in Bristol in 1832; see Radzinowitz, *op. cit.*, vol. 4, p. 148.
38. *Manual of Military Law*, Part 2, paras. 3 and 4.
39. See note 16 *supra*.
40. *The Queen's Regulations for the Army*, chap. 11, para. 11. 002.
41. *Albert v. Lavin* (1982) A.C. 546, 565, *per* Lord Diplock. His lordship was not referring to riotous and tumultuous assemblies, see note 44.
42. *Attorney-General for Northern Ireland's Reference (No. 1 of 1975)* (1976) 2 All E.R. 937, 946, Lord Diplock.
43. Opinion of law officers on duty of soldiers called upon to assist the police (1911), Appendix in Section v of *Manual of Military Law*, Part 2.
44. *Burdett v. Abbott* (1812) 4 Taunt. Rep. 449, Lord Mansfield C.J.; *Charge to the Bristol Grand Jury* (1832) 5 Car. & P. 261, Tindal C.J.; Report of the Committee on Featherstone

Riot, 1893-4; *Manual of Military Law*, Part 2, section v; notes 41, 42, 43 *supra*. Scarman (1975), Cmnd 5919, para. 26; cf. *R. v. Chief Constable of the Devon and Cornwall Constabulary ex parte C.E. G.B.* (1981) 3 All E.R. 826, 832.

45.   Evelegh, p. 8.
46.   In *R. v. Atkinson* (1869) XI Cox C.C. 330, Kelly C.B. said, 'the mere presence of a person among the rioters, even though he possessed the power and failed to exercise it of stopping the riot, did not render him liable'. In any event, the accused was not prosecuted for failing to intervene to prevent the riot. If such a criminal offence existed, this would be the more appropriate charge. It is interesting that in *R. v. Dytham* (1979) 3 All E.R. 641 the Court of Appeal did not discuss this alleged common law offence, but instead invoked an alternative common law offence of misconduct in a public office (police officer). This offence requires the neglect to be wilful and not inadvertent and there must be no reasonable excuse or justification.
47.   *Knuller (Publishing, Printing & Promotions) Ltd. v. Director of Public Prosecutions* (1973) A.C. 435.
48.   (1841) Car. & M. 314. See also Smith and Hogan, *Criminal Law* (1983), 5th edn, p. 715.
49.   Unless the situation is covered by *R. v. Brown*. They would be liable for neglect if they remained supine in the face of public disorder. Criminal liability may be imposed by virtue of *R. v. Kennett* (1781) 5. Car. & P. 282 or *R. v. Dytham* (1979) 3 All E.R. 641. See also s. 23(2) of the Reserve Forces Act 1980.
50.   It may be argued, however, that a soldier is a 'public officer' and would be liable for his neglect under the principle in *R. v. Dytham* (1979). If this is so, he is not then 'merely a citizen in uniform'? In *Attorney-General for New South Wales v. Perpetual Trustee Co. Ltd* (1955) A.C. 457, 489, Viscount Simonds stated: 'Their lordships share the opinion entertained by all the judges of the High Court that the case of the constable is not in principle distinguishable from that of the soldier.' See also the *Manual of Military Law*, Part 2, para. 3, where it is stated that a duty is imposed on soldiers (and not, therefore, on civilians) by virtue of Queen's Regulations. No objection can be made of this statement; it merely confirms the existence of a prerogative power possessed by the Crown to deploy armed forces where it so desires.
51.   For a definition of 'terrorist' see s. 31(1) of the Northern Ireland (Emergency Provisions) Act 1978.
52.   Boyle, Hadden and Hillyard, *Ten Years on in Northern Ireland* (1980), Cobden Trust, p. 8.
53.   Section 4.
54.   See S. Greer, *Military Intervention in Civil Disturbances* (1983) Public Law 573, 587.
55.   (1983) 6 N.I.J.B.
56.   The Annual Report of the Chief Constable of the Royal Ulster Constabulary (1984) indicates that Army fatal casualties in 1984 were nine; *The Times*, 17 April, 1985.
57.   See, in particular, s. 2(4): 'If any person does any act of such a nature as to be calculated to be prejudicial to the preservation of peace or maintenance of order in Northern Ireland and not specifically provided for in the regulations, he shall be deemed to be guilty of an offence against the regulations.'
58.   The Northern Ireland Minister for Home Affairs purported to make regulations under the Civil Authorities (Special Powers) Act (Northern Ireland) 1922 which would have given powers to members of H.M. Forces to disperse an assembly of more than three persons. In *R. (Hume et al.) v. Londonderry Justices* (1972) N.I. 91, the High Court of Northern Ireland held these regulations to be void. The Northern Ireland Act 1972 retrospectively restored the legal position prior to *R. (Hume et al.) v. Londonderry Justices*.
59.   Report of the Commission to Consider Legal Procedures to Deal with Terrorist Activities in Northern Ireland (Lord Diplock), Cmnd 5185 (1972), para. 45.
60.   This is wider than the power of a constable. Note this Act applies only to Northern Ireland. In the rest of the U.K. members of the armed forces do not possess such a power. The military police have no greater powers of arrest over civilians than is possessed by the ordinary civilian. Ministry of Defence police officers possess the legal powers of a constable in the field of their responsibilities; see Ministry of Defence Police Act 1987, s. 2.
61.   See s. 76 the Police and Criminal Evidence Act 1984 (which does not extend to Northern Ireland). The common law will continue to apply; see *Ibrahim v. R.* (1914) A.C. 599.
62.   Other relevant legislation designed to deal with those who interfere with the operation of

the armed forces include the Incitement of Disaffection Act 1934; S. 193 of the Army Act 1955 (offence to obstruct a soldier in the exercise of his duty); Prevention of Terrorism (Temporary Provisions) Act 1976. The Baker Committee has recently proposed changes to the 1978 Act; *Review of the Northern Ireland (Emergency Provisions) Act 1978*, Cmnd 9222 (1984).

63. *R. v. Pinney* (1832) 5 C. & P. 254. The special (and unlikely) situation of martial law is discussed in de Smith, *Constitutional and Administrative Law* (1985), 5th edn, pp. 523 et seq. A member of H.M. forces is permitted to carry weapons while on duty, s. 54 of the Firearms Act 1968.

64. This is identical to the Criminal Law Act 1967 which prevails in England and Wales.

65. Seventh Report, *Felonies and Misdemeanours* (1965), Cmnd 2659, para. 23.

66. See D. S. Greer, *Legal Control of Military Operations—A Missed Opportunity* (1980) N.L.I.Q. 151, 154.

67. (1976) 2 All E.R. 937, 947.

68. For a discussion of some of the terms in the yellow card, see *Report of the Tribunal to Inquire into Events of 30 January 1972 which led to loss of life* (1972) H.C. paper 220 (Lord Widgery), paras. 89 et seq. For the equivalent set of instructions issued to the police, see *The Times*, 30 September 1985.

69. (1975) N.I. 203, 206.

70. A 'scheduled offence' under the Northern Ireland (Emergency Provisions) Act 1978 is tried by a judge alone. See generally, Boyle, Hadden and Hillyard, *Ten Years on in Northern Ireland* (1980), Cobden Trust, chapter 6.

71. This follows from the decision of the House of Lords in *Attorney-General for Northern Ireland's Reference (No. 1 of 1975)* (1976) 2 All E.R. 937 that 'reasonableness' is a question of fact for the jury.

72. See Wakerley (1975) Crim. L. Rev. 186 (letter); letter to *The Times*, 17 February 1981 by Attorney-General concerning the Iran Embassy siege.

73. (1980) 1 All E.R. 166.

74. The House of Lords refused to consider the alleged negligence of the officer concerned on the ground that this had not originally been pleaded.

75. See Smith and Hogan, *Criminal Law*, Butterworths, 5th edn (1983), pp. 328-329. Suppose, however, the property to be protected is highly dangerous if it fell into the hands of terrorists. It is hard to imagine that this would not be a relevant circumstance justifying the use of lethal force.

76. (1976) 2 All E.R. 937, 947.

77. (1980) 1 All E.R. 166, 172-173.

78. Now s. 14 of the 1978 Act.

79. Now s. 18 of the 1978 Act. At common law no such right is given to a police officer, *Rice v. Connolly* (1966) 2 Q.B. 414.

80. See *Lynch v. Ministry of Defence* (1983) 6 N.I.J.B.; *Attorney-General for Northern Ireland's Reference (No. 1 of 1975)* (1976) 2 All E.R. 937, 947 (the *Reference Case*).

81. The Widgery Report (note 26), para. 93; *R. v. McNaughton* (1975) N.I. 203, 204.

82. But it may be argued that a person who deliberately chooses not to stop can hardly complain if he is treated as a suspected terrorist, see *infra*.

83. (1975) N.I. 203.

84. *Ibid.*, p. 208. In *R. v. Robinson* (1984) 4 N.I.J.B., McDermott J. said, 'while policemen (or soldiers) are required to act within the law they are not required to be "supermen" and one does not use jewellers' scales to measure what is reasonable in the circumstances'.

85. See McGonigal L. J. in *Farrell v. Secretary of State for Defence* (1980) N.I. 55, 72.

86. Quoted in *Lynch v. Ministry of Defence* (1983) 6 N.I.J.B.

87. *Supra*.

88. See Smith and Hogan, *op. cit.*, p. 326.

89. Unreported, Judgment, 4 July 1979.

90. Unreported, House of Lords, 1980. See Rowe (1981) 44 Mod. L.R. 466.

91. (1982) 19 N.I.J.B.

92. Just as the shortness of time in which to make a decision whether to open fire or not is a relevant consideration (see Lord Diplock in the *Reference Case*), so must the length of time.

93. (1976) 2 All E.R. 937, 947.
94. This seems to be the view of McGonigal L.J. in the *Reference Case* (1976) N.I. 169, 186. See also Williams, *Textbook of Criminal Law*, Butterworths, 2nd edn, (1983), p. 137. The Divisional Court in *Albert v. Lavin* (1981) 1 All E.R. 628 would require the belief to be a reasonable one, but cf. *R. v. Williams* (1984) Crim. L.R. 163.
95. If this view be correct a soldier will incur no criminal liability if, while acting *bona fide* in the course of his duties, he fires at, and kills, any person.
96. Section 34 of the Army Act 1955.
97. Part I, paras. 156-157; see, for example, *McKee v. The Chief Constable for Northern Ireland* (1985) 1 All E.R. 1.
98. *R. v. Smith* (1900) extracted in Keir and Lawson, *Cases in Constitutional Law*, 6th edn (1979), pp. 180-182; *Keighley v. Bell* (1866) 4 F. & F. 763, 790. See, generally, Nichols, *Untying the Soldier by Refurbishing the Common Law* (1976) Crim. L.R. 181.
99. See, generally, Sir David Hughes-Morgan, *Disobedience to a Lawful Military Command* (1977) 122 R.U.S.I. Jo. 9; *R. v. Trainer* (1864) 4 F. & F. 105; *R. v. Thomas* (1816) 4 M. & S. 41; *R. v. Taylor* (1940), quoted in Keijzer, *Military Obedience* (1978), Sijhoff, p. 175.
100. *Donoghue v. Stevenson* (1932) A.C. 562.
101. See, for example, *Rondel v. Worsley* (1969) 1 A.C. 191.
102. (1980) 1 All E.R. 166.
103. Liability may be imposed in a case where a soldier fires at A and hits B, *Livingstone v. Ministry of Defence* (1984) 15 N.I.J.B.
104. See note 90.
105. (1983) 6 N.I.J.B.
106. (1980) N.I. 55.
107. See *Ashton v. Turner* (1981) Q.B. 137; *N.C.B. v. England* (1954) A.C. 403; *Lane v. Holloway* (1967) 3 All E.R. 129.
108. *Nettleship v. Weston* (1971) 3 All E.R. 581 per Lord Denning M.R. at p. 587.
109. Compare *Dann v. Hamilton* (1939) 1 K.B. 509.
110. See note 106.
111. See, generally, Hogg, *Liability of the Crown in Australia, New Zealand and the United Kingdom* (1971). See also *Attorney-General for New South Wales v. Perpetual Trustee Co.* (1955) A.C. 457, 489.
112. Manual of Military Law, Part 2, p. 353. However, in *Lavery v. Ministry of Defence* (1984) 7 N.I.J.B., Kelly L.J. treated a soldier as a 'servant of the government' for the purpose of awarding exemplary damages.
113. *Re Tuffnell* (1876) L.R. 3 Ch. D. 164; *Leaman v. R.* (1920) 3 K.B. 663; Cowan, *Armed Forces of the Crown* (1950) 66 L.Q.R. 478, 483 et seq. See Rowe (1981), 44 Mod. L.R. 466, 469.
114. *Malone v. Commissioner of Police of the Metropolis (No. 2)* (1979) 2 All E.R. 620. The European Court of Human Rights cannot compel a State to prosecute those who breach the Convention, *Ireland v. The United Kingdom* Eur. Court H.R. Series A, Judgment of 18 January 1978.
115. See D. S. Greer, *op. cit.*, p. 153.
116. See *Farrell v. The United Kingdom* (Application no. 9013/80). The European Commission held admissible a complaint based on Article 2; it was subject to a 'friendly settlement'. Bonner, *Emergency Powers in Peacetime*, pp. 13-14.
117. Part III, para. 94.
118. Greenspan, *The Modern Law of Land Warfare* (1955), p. 625.
119. Article 1 (4).
120. Article 1 (2). See the U.K. Declaration (a) to the Protocols of 1977.
121. Article (1).
122. H.L. Deb. vol. 348, col. 1052. See also (1974) Crim. L.R. 141.
123. See, however, *McKee v The Chief Constable for Northern Ireland* (1985) 1 All E.R. 1.
124. See also Aviation Security Act 1982, sections 26 and 28.
125. *The Times*, 9 January 1986.
126. *The Times*, 17 February 1981.
127. (1964) A.C. 763. See, generally, Report on the Ministry of Defence Police Review Committee (1986), Cmnd 9853, esp. para. 109.

128. *Criminal Law* (1983), 5th edn, p. 325, and see note 75. See also Widgery (1971-72), Cmnd 220 at para. 92.
129. Article VII (10).
130. *The Physical Security of Military Installations in the U.K.* (1985), Cmnd 9422, para. 17. See also Parliamentary Under-Secretary of State, Home Office in H.C. Deb. vol. 51, cols. 103-108; 19 December 1983; Secretary of State for Defence, H.C. Deb. vol. 64, col. 248; 18 July 1984; (U.S. Servicemen) 'enjoy the same power (as British Servicemen) to deal with trespassers, including the right to use reasonable force to remove them if they refuse to leave when asked and to arrest an individual for breach of the peace'.

5

The Security of Defence Information

'It is important to prevent the disclosure of information about defence matters which would be damaging to national security. The law provides penalties for such disclosure but the practical difficulty is to know precisely where the line should be drawn between what is damaging and what is a legitimate matter for public discussion.' Third Report from the Defence Committee, 1979-80.

In a democratic society defence security sits uneasily on the borderline between the free disclosure of information by a government and censorship and between the rights of individuals and the protection of the State itself. How this issue is resolved in the United Kingdom is the purpose of this chapter to explore.

Official Secrets

The purpose of the Official Secrets Acts 1911, 1920 and 1939 is to protect the State against espionage and sabotage, but it is much wider than this, as the discussion of section 2 will show. The offences contained in the Act are, moreover, of extra-territorial effect and can therefore be committed by a British subject anywhere in the world. The trial of eight Servicemen at the Old Bailey in 1985 on charges under the Acts alleged to have been committed in Cyprus is an example of this wide-ranging jurisdiction. It may be usual for those who deal with sensitive material that is protected by the Acts to 'sign the Official Secrets Acts', but there is no legal importance attached to this activity. It may serve to remind a person of his obligations under the Acts, but it will certainly not be a bar to a prosecution of a person who had not 'signed' them.

The Attorney-General must consent to a prosecution and the statistics show an average of at least one prosecution every year since the Second World War.[1] There have been a number of attempts to replace the Official Secrets Acts with a Freedom of Information Act, but no general agreement has yet been possible on how much information should be disclosed and what must be kept secret.

Section 1 of the Official Secrets Act 1911

Section 1 is entitled 'Penalties for Spying', and it is in the following terms: 'If any person for any purpose prejudicial to the safety or interests of the State (a) approaches, inspects, passes over or is in the neighbourhood of, or enters any prohibited place (which is defined in section three); or (b) makes any sketch, plan, model, or note which is calculated to be or might be or is intended to be directly or indirectly useful to an enemy; or (c) obtains, collects, records, or publishes or communicates to any other person any secret official code word or password or any sketch, plan, model, article, or note, or other document or information which is calculated to be or is intended to be directly or indirectly useful to an enemy' he shall commit an offence, the maximum sentence for which is imprisonment for 14 years.

This section will clearly catch the person who passes information to a potential enemy (which is assumed to be any of the Warsaw Pact countries and possibly other countries as well).[2] Geoffrey Prime was convicted in 1982 after pleading guilty to passing documents related to his work at the Government Communications Headquarters to the Russian Intelligence Service and was sentenced to imprisonment for a total of 35 years.[3] Michael Bettaney, an employee of the counter-espionage section of the security service, was convicted in the following year after collecting information which he hoped to be able to pass on to the agents of the U.S.S.R.[4] A lance-corporal who pleaded guilty to an offence under section 1 in taking a highly classified document with the intention of passing it on was sentenced to imprisonment for 4 years in 1983.[5] Eight Servicemen stationed in Cyprus were prosecuted, but acquitted, at the Old Bailey in 1985 for offences alleged to be contrary to this section. In the Aubrey, Berry and Campbell case of 1978[6] the trial judge expressed his dislike of the use by the prosecution of this section where the facts did not disclose either spying or sabotage and in consequence the section 1 charges were dropped. In this case there was no suggestion that the information which the two journalists (Aubrey and Campbell) received from Berry, a former soldier, was to be passed on to a potential enemy. To be convicted, the accused must intend to do any of the acts mentioned in the section, but in addition he must have a purpose prejudicial to the interests of the State. The case of Chandler v. Director of Public Prosecutions in 1962[7] goes some way to explain the meaning of this phrase. The six accused, members of the Committee of 100, wished to protest about the use of R.A.F. Wethersfield as a base from which aircraft capable of carrying nuclear weapons were operated by the United States Air Force for the defence of the United Kingdom and its NATO allies in Western Europe. The object of their protest was to immobilise the base by preventing the aircraft from taking off. They were charged with a conspiracy to commit and to incite others to commit a breach of section 1 of the 1911 Act. The accused were clearly not spying and the House of Lords held that the section was not limited to this type of activity but could also cover sabotage.

The heart of the case involved the claim of the accused that their purpose was not prejudicial to the interests of the State because they believed that the aircraft involved 'used nuclear bombs and that it was not in the interests of the State to have aircraft so armed at that time there'.[7a] What was their real purpose? It could be none other than to immobilise the base. This is what they intended and desired as the consequences of their action. Why they wished to act in this way (to argue that it was beneficial to the interests of the State to immobilise these aircraft) was immaterial, since it was merely their motive. Given that the purpose of the accused's action was to immobilise the base, the next question was whether this was prejudicial to the interests of the State? The answer must, said the court, be in the affirmative. It can hardly be within the interests of the State that a military air base is immobilised. The opinion of the accused was not all relevant on this issue. Finally, it has been shown that the House of Lords was not prepared to hear argument that the policy of the Crown was wrong in permitting the United States Air Force to use the base. The disposition of the armed forces is within the prerogative of the Crown and cannot be challenged in a court. The opposite finding would have opened the door to the type of argument that defence counsel sought to pursue in this case. This was along the lines of the effect of exploding a nuclear bomb and 'reference was made to the possibility of accident or mistake, and other reasons against having nuclear bombs ... and to the basic wrongness of the conception of a deterrent force and the likelihood of it attracting hostile attack'.[8] A court of law is clearly not the right place to argue such a matter.

The Wrongful Communication of Information

Section 2 of the Official Secrets Act 1911 is very wide-ranging in its effect and covers all official information which a person has 'obtained or to which he has had access owing to his position as a person who is or has held office under Her Majesty'.[9] To commit the offence a person must do any one of a number of acts. These are, without authority (a) to communicate the information to any person, other than a person to whom he is authorised to communicate it, or a person to whom it is in the interest of the State his duty to communicate it, or (b) to use it for the benefit of any foreign power or in any other manner prejudicial to the safety or interests of the State, or (c) to retain the information in his possession or control when he has no right to retain it, or (d) to fail to take reasonable care of the information or to conduct himself as to endanger the safety of the information.[10]

It is also an offence to receive such information knowing or having reasonable grounds to believe that it was communicated in contravention of the Act. In these circumstances the burden of proof is placed upon the accused to prove that the communication was 'against his desire'. This will in practice be very difficult to prove, since the information that is protected by the Act need not be secret or even confidential as long as it is 'official information' obtained in the course of the employment of a Crown servant. It certainly need not be information that affects national security, as the Ponting case in 1985, discussed below, showed. In *Fell*[11] the Lord Chief Justice confirmed that a section 2 offence was 'committed whatever the document contains, whatever the motive for disclosure is and whether or not the disclosure is prejudicial to the State'. A soldier who disclosed to his mother that there was a green filing cabinet in the guard room would therefore commit an offence, but the requirement of the consent of the Attorney-General to a prosecution is some measure of protection against 'technical' prosecutions.

The opinion of the Lord Chief Justice in *Fell* is sufficient to show that to convict an accused under this section the prosecution need prove nothing other than an intentional act of communicating or receiving the protected information. The nature of the section is well illustrated by the Ponting case of 1985 when Clive Ponting, an assistant secretary at the Ministry of Defence, was charged with an offence under section 2. The details of the charge were that he communicated official information to a person (Mr Tam Dalyell M.P.) who was not a person to whom he was authorised to communicate it, nor was he a person to whom it was in the interest of the State his duty to communicate it. The documents sent to Mr Dalyell related to the sinking of the Argentine cruiser the *General Belgrano* in 1982 during the Falklands War.

The heart of the case was whether Mr Dalyell was a person to whom it was in the interest of the State Ponting's duty to communicate the information, since the former was not authorised to receive it. Ponting's defence set out to show that it was indeed in the interest of the State his duty to communicate it.[12] This involved establishing two main points. First, that as he believed Parliament was being deceived by ministers he had a moral or civic duty to Parliament to correct statements made to it, and secondly, that the interest of the State was not synonymous with the interests of the government of the day. On both points the trial judge ruled against the defence. The word 'duty' in the section referred only to an 'official' and not a moral or civic duty and Ponting clearly did not have an official duty to pass on the information to a member of Parliament. He also summed up to the jury on the basis that the interest of the State was synonymous with the interest of the 'policies of the government of the day'. Moreover, there was no need, ruled the trial judge, for the jury to consider whether Ponting honestly believed that it was his duty to pass on the information to a member of Parliament. One commentator has expressed the view that 'It was probably deemed appropriate that civil servants and others found leaking official information should be penalised whether or not it can be shown that they had *mens rea*, thereby rendering them strict liability offences.'[13]

It is well known that the jury acquitted Ponting of all charges laid against him, but what conclusions can be drawn from this case? If we assume that the rulings on the law made by the trial judge are correct, a person who is in Crown service, say in the armed forces, will commit an offence under this section if he discloses any information obtained in his employment where he has no official duty to pass it to another. It will be no defence for him to argue that it is in the public interest that he should disclose it to an unauthorised person. He may, for instance, believe that his superior officer is taking bribes[14] or that defence contractors have been charging exorbitant prices for items of equipment that are sub-standard. There is no defence to the offence created by the section that the public ought to know. This may be so in law but the Ponting case highlights the role of the jury in prosecutions under the Official Secrets Act. Despite the rejection of Ponting's argument by the trial judge he was acquitted by the jury as was Aitken, a journalist, who received a report on the supply of British arms to the Nigerian government during the Biafran conflict. He, in turn, passed it to the *Sunday Telegraph* and argued that 'it was his duty in the interests of the State to show that Ministers may have been deceiving Parliament'.

There have been many attempts to reform section 2 of the 1911 Act. In 1972 the Franks Committee recommended an entirely new Act that would cover only the unauthorised disclosure of classified information instead of catching any official information. The 'blunderbuss (would be) replaced by the Armalite'.[15] Both Labour and Conservative governments have attempted to alter radically the effects of section 2. In 1976 the Home Secretary, Merlyn Rees, told the House of Commons that a person should only commit an offence where serious damage to the national interest had been caused by his unauthorised disclosure of information, and that this would normally only occur where security, intelligence, defence and international relations were damaged.[16] The road to reform is, it seems, a long and difficult one. Should the public have a right to obtain official information? Should the Ombudsman have the obligation to enquire into allegations of unreasonable secrecy? Should there be a defence that the accused believed that his disclosure was in the national interest, as did Ponting, Berry, Aitken and Sarah Tisdall?[17]

The trial judge in the *Aitken Case* went so far as to say of the section that, it may 'well alert those who govern us at least to consider . . . whether or not section 2 . . . should be pensioned off'.[18] That statement was made in 1971, but no alteration has yet been made to the section.

It seems that the most common way for a person, who is in possession of official information, to bring it to national attention is to send it to a newspaper. This is what Berry, Aitken and Tisdall did. It will often be essential that the leaked document should be returned to the appropriate Ministry in order to discover who was responsible for its disclosure. In the Tisdall case the Secretary of State for Defence sought return of the document relating to the delivery of cruise missiles at R.A.F. Greenham Common and eventually the Court of Appeal ordered *The Guardian* to return it. Whilst the ownership of a document taken from the Ministry of Defence can hardly be in doubt, nice questions of law arise as to the ownership of a photocopy. The view of the Court of Appeal was that *The Guardian* had no right to retain a copy of a leaked document.[19]

A trial under the Official Secrets Act may be held partly *in camera* where the Crown seeks to protect from disclosure some of the evidence given. In the Ponting case this procedure was adopted when evidence was being given of the so-called 'crown jewels'. It is also not uncommon for the jury to be vetted by the prosecution in order to discover whether they have previous convictions or in some way might be objected to by the Crown. The jury was vetted in the ABC case in 1978 and in the Ponting case.[20]

Prohibited Place

All defence establishments will be prohibited places within the Official Secrets Acts and it is quite common to see a notice to this effect at R.A.F. stations. Section 3 of the 1911 Act defines a prohibited place very widely so as to cover virtually all Crown property having some connection with defence and to property that belongs to others if the Secretary of State declares it to be a prohibited place. This might be a private factory making weapons or defence equipment, an electricity generating station or a place used by the Atomic Energy Authority. Such a declaration can only be made if information relating to that place, or its destruction or interference with it, would be useful to an enemy. It will be recalled that section 1 of the 1911 Act makes it an offence for a person to approach, inspect, pass over or be in the neighbourhood of or enter a prohibited place as long as he has a purpose for so doing that is prejudicial to the safety or interests of the State. In *Chandler v. Director of Public Prosecutions* the six defendants were convicted of a conspiracy to enter a prohibited place, R.A.F. Wethersfield. Various offences under the Official Secrets Act 1920 relate to the guarding of a prohibited place. A person who uses false pretences for the purpose of gaining admission, such as by wearing a uniform to which he is not entitled or by forging a pass, or a person who interferes with, or impedes a police or armed forces guard in the vicinity of, or indeed inside, a prohibited place, would commit offences under the 1920 Act.[21] There is no legal reason why the peace protesters at Greenham Common or at Molesworth might not be charged with these offences.

Attempts and Preparatory Acts

In keeping with the normal rules of the criminal law it is an offence to attempt to commit an offence under the Official Secrets Acts, but the 1920 Act goes further than this by including preparatory acts, which would not attract criminal liability in other spheres. The case of *R. v. Bingham* in 1973 is one that attracted considerable attention in the media when the wife of a lieutenant in the Royal Navy started to tell about the background to her husband's conviction under the Official Secrets Act 1911. It was she who had approached the Russian Embassy, she boasted, on behalf of her husband with a view to offering them secret information in return for money. At her subsequent trial she argued that she never intended any secrets to pass, but that she had planned to trick the Russians into giving her money for innocuous information. The jury at her trial obviously did not believe this and the Court of Appeal dismissed her appeal against conviction. When she approached the Russians with her proposal her belief must therefore have been at least that the passing of secret information to them was possible. She would equally have been guilty of this offence even if nothing more had happened; by approaching the Russian officials with this belief she had, at that moment, committed the offence of doing a preparatory act. She would have had to do an act that was more than merely preparatory to be guilty of an attempt to commit an offence under the Official Secrets Acts.[22]

'D' Notices

While prosecution under the Official Secrets Acts might be considered as acting after the horse has bolted, the 'D' notice system is designed to prevent the horse from bolting. It is an attempt to prevent the publication of information that would be damaging to national security. A purely voluntary arrangement between the government, press and broadcasting bodies exists in the form of the Services, press and broadcasting committee headed by a retired senior officer of the armed forces as secretary. The notices issued by the committee, of which there are now eight, cover such matters as defence plans, the state of readiness and training, defence equipment and nuclear weapons and equipment.[23] They are sent to the press, the broadcasting bodies and relevant publishers and advice about whether publication can be made of any particular item can be obtained by an editor from the secretary to the committee. This occurred during the Falklands War when the secretary received a number of queries from editors and in the Suez crisis of 1956 informal guidance was given to editors requesting them not to publish certain types of information.

Since the 'D' notice system is a form of voluntary censorship, publication in the face of a notice is not an offence as such, but it may well be a breach of the Official Secrets Acts. On the other hand, compliance with a notice cannot guarantee immunity from prosecution as did the stamp 'Passed for Publication' by the wartime censor, but in practice it normally would. However, uncertainty may be caused when the piece which it is intended to publish is not covered by a 'D' notice. In both the *Daily Express* story by Chapman Pincher in 1967 about 'cable vetting' and in the *Aitken* case of 1971 no such notices applied directly to the matters published. In both cases the newspapers approached the secretary to the committee and were told that there were no specific notices relating to the issues involved. In the latter, but not in the former case, a prosecution under the Official Secrets Acts was brought. The Radcliffe Committee in 1962 explained the value of the system as follows: 'Breaches of the terms of "D" notices do occur from time to time, but it seems to be agreed that nearly every breach that has occurred has been attributable to inadvertence, and a deliberate refusal to comply with a "D" notice is extremely rare. If it were otherwise, the system . . . would have long since broken down.'[24]

Public Interest Privilege

In non-criminal cases each party to a contested case must disclose to the other relevant documents that he has in his possession or control. On occasion these documents might, if they were disclosed, reveal information that the government would wish to keep from disclosure. In these circumstances it can apply to the court to order that the document need not be made available to the other party. This is what occurred in *Duncan v. Cammell Laird & Co. Ltd.*[25] when relatives of submariners sued the shipbuilders for negligence in the construction of the submarine *Thetis* which sank on its maiden voyage. The defendants were requested by the Admiralty to object to the production of the plans of the submarine, since their disclosure in time of war was not in the national interest. The House of Lords upheld this request and made it plain that once a request for non-disclosure was made by a government minister the courts could not challenge it. But in *Conway v. Rimmer* in 1968 the House of Lords altered its position on this issue and decided that it was for the court to weigh the minister's request with the public interest that all relevant information should be disclosed.[26] The minister's view would normally be accepted if the document raised matters of national defence, but not where it merely related to the welfare of members of the armed forces.[27]

In similar circumstances the government may attempt to prevent the publication of material which it considers not to be in the interests of national security. In 1986 the British government applied to a court in Australia to prevent a former member of the British security services from publishing a book about the service. The author could not be prosecuted under the Official Secrets Acts since he could not be brought within the jurisdiction of the English courts, but he had received in confidence the information which he sought to publish.

Disclosing Information to the Enemy

British subjects, whether civilians or members of the armed forces, will remain subject to the Official Secrets Acts during war or other armed conflict. But each may in turn have additional obligations to avoid passing information to the enemy. The soldier is bound by the Army Act 1955 neither to communicate with nor give intelligence to the enemy. Moreover, he will also commit an offence if he discloses information which would or might be useful to an enemy.[28] It will be recalled that the term 'enemy' is defined widely enough to include all persons engaged in armed operations against any of Her Majesty's forces.[29] In *R. v. Murphy* the accused, a soldier, was convicted by court-martial of disclosing information (contrary to section 60 of the Army Act 1955) to police officers posing as members of the IRA.[30]

In the aftermath of the Falklands War in 1982 concern was expressed both by journalists at what they saw as censorship by the military authorities during the conflict and also by the government over the risks of disclosing useful information to the enemy in the coverage of news reporting. In 1983 the Secretary of State for Defence appointed a study group under the chairmanship of Sir Hugh Beach to consider the problems raised.[31] This concluded that in a major conventional war censorship would be necessary and that wide-ranging regulations, similar to those which applied in the Second World War, should be adopted. The committee further suggested that an accreditation bargain might be struck with war correspondents so that in return for facilities offered by the armed forces, such as access to sensitive areas, confidential background briefings and so on, war correspondents would submit their material for vetting. If they refused, their accreditation would be revoked.

Notes

1. There were twenty-three prosecutions under section 2 of the Official Secrets Act 1911 between 1947 and 1972 and twenty prosecutions under section 1 of the Act; the Departmental Committee on Section 2 of the Official Secrets Act 1911 (the Franks Report), Cmnd 5104 (1972), App. II. For the Attorney-General's criteria for prosecution see (1983) 127 Sol.Jo.134, esp. para. 9(a) where the likely penalty is a relevant factor. For the history of the Acts see Thompson, *The Committee of 100 and the Official Secrets Act 1911* (1963) Pub. L.201, 203-211 and App. 3, the Franks Report.

2. The term 'enemy' as used in the Act clearly covers also a potential enemy, *R. v. Parrott* (1913) 8 Cr. App. Rep. 186. The accused communicated information about the position and movement of warships to persons in Europe. Phillimore J. described a potential enemy as a state 'with whom one might some day be at war' (p. 192).

3. *R. v. Prime* (1983) 5 Cr. App. Rep. (S) 127; see also the Report of the Security Commission (1983), Cmnd 8876 which recommended that 'a pilot scheme should be undertaken with a view to testing the feasibility of polygraph security screening in the British intelligence and security agencies' (at para. 9.14).

4. *R. v. Bettaney* (1985) Crim. L.R. 104.

5. See the Report of the Security Commission (1984), Cmnd 9212. Aldridge held a restricted PV (positive vetting) certificate, but was permitted to handle top secret documents. For detail on PV see memorandum by the Ministry of Defence to the House of Commons Defence Committee (1982-83) H.C. 242. A compendious account of the above cases, and much else, is contained in Bailey, Harris and Jones, *Civil Liberties, Cases and Materials*, London, Butterworths, 2nd edn (1985), chap. 7. Sentences of imprisonment of longer than 14 years (the maximum sentence) are due to the judge passing consecutive sentences on

different charges. The passing of consecutive sentences 'must be exercised with care', *R. v. Britten* (1976) 1 All E.R. 517, 519 *per* Davies L.J. who also commented that the accused's acts of passing documents to the Russian agent was 'absolutely certain to interfere with and handicap the defences of this country and might ... in certain events be disastrous to us all'.

6. See, Nicol, *Official Secrets and Jury Vetting* (1979) Crim. L.R. 284, 287. Bailey, Harris and Jones, *op. cit.*, give short accounts at p. 327 of others convicted of section 1 offences. These include Fuchs, Blake and Vassall.

7. (1964) A.C. 763.

7a. Lord Reid, (1964) A.C. 763, 788. See also the comments of Professor Smith concerning *R. v. Bettaney* in (1985) Crim. L.R. 104-105.

8. *Ibid.* See also Smith and Hogan, *Criminal Law*, London, Butterworths, 5th edn (1983), pp. 789-890. Considerable criticism might be levelled at this decision on the ground that it paid scant regard to the general principles of the criminal law. A more satisfactory approach, it is suggested, would have been for the House to consider whether the accused *believed* their purpose (to immobolise the base) was prejudicial to the interests of the state. In this case the accused believed their purpose was beneficial. They might, however, still be convicted of other offences, such as under the Official Secrets Act 1920 or section 193 of the Army Act 1955 and the Air Force Act 1955.

9. It also covers those who hold or have held a 'contract made on behalf of Her Majesty as a person who is or has been employed under a person who holds or has held such an office or contract'. The section also includes any information that has been entrusted to any person in confidence by any person holding office under Her Majesty.

10. Section 2 also makes it an offence to communicate directly or indirectly with any foreign power, or in any other manner prejudicial to the safety or interests of the state, information concerning munitions of war.

11. (1963) Crim. L.R. 207.

12. See, generally, Thomas, *The British Official Secrets Acts 1911-1939 and the Ponting Case* (1986) Crim. L.R. 491, 497; Ponting, *The Right to Know, The Inside Story of the Belgrano Affair*, London, Sphere Books Ltd. (1985), p. 4.

13. Thomas, *op. cit.*, p. 501. Compare *R. v. Cairns, Roberts and Sunday Telegraph* (1971) quoted in Thomas, *op. cit.*, at p. 495.

14. Nichol, *Official Secrets and Jury Vetting* (1979) Crim. L.R. 284, 290, 289, n. 24. The trial judge allowed the jury to consider this argument. Jonathan Aitken had been charged with unauthorised receipt of the information and with unlawfully communicating it to the newspaper. In the *ABC Trial* (Aubrey, Berry and Campbell) of 1978, on the other hand, Berry, a former soldier with experience of the Government Communications Headquarters, argued that he 'believed it was his duty in the interest of the State to communicate information to Campbell because he feared some of (Government's) activities were either highly dangerous or illegal and needed to be exposed', Thomas, *op. cit.*, p. 499. He was convicted. In 1939 Duncan Sandys M.P. obtained information concerning the state of preparations against air attack, while serving as an officer in the T.A. He sought to ask a question in the House of Commons on this matter and, it was alleged, was threatened with prosecution under the Offical Secrets Act 1911. Ultimately the issue revolved around parliamentary privilege and a select committee concluded that a member of Parliament had a privilege to speak about matters governed by the Official Secrets Act in Parliament, see R.S.T.C. (1938) 2 M.L.R. 163.

15. Merlyn Rees M.P., H.C. Deb. vol. 919, col. 1887. The Franks Committee made a large number of recommendations including the retention of the offence of using official information for private gain and failure to take reasonable care of official information. Mr. Rees M.P. was a member of the Committee.

16. *The Times*, 23 November 1976. For a comprehensive review of the attempts to reform section 2, see Ponting, *op. cit.* (note 12), chap. 1, and Bailey, Harris and Jones, *Civil Liberties, Cases and Materials*, London, Butterworths, 2nd edn (1985), pp. 322-323; Supperstone, *Brownlie's Law Relating to Public Order and National Security*, London, Butterworths, pp. 256-259.

17. See letter to *The Times* of 3 November 1978, Anthony Lester Q.C.; Thomas, *op. cit.*, p. 508. Sarah Tisdall believed that the Secretary of State for Defence was acting improperly

with regard to his proposed announcement in the House of Commons of the delivery of cruise missiles to R.A.F. Greenham Common. She pleaded guilty to the offence under section 2. In this case the material which she passed to *The Guardian* was classified as SECRET. She received a 6 months' prison sentence. See also Cripps, *Disclosure in the Public Interest: The Predicament of the Public Servant Employee* (1983) P.L. 600, where the author shows that an employee who is sued by his employer for breach of confidence can rely on the defence that the public has an interest in receiving the information. See the case of Trevor Brown (at pp. 602-603) who criticised in a TV programme some of the safety precautions at the Atomic Research Establishment. He was not prosecuted under the Official Secrets Acts, but dealt with by civil service disciplinary procedures. Cripps also deals with the disclosure by officials and the Official Secrets Acts, at pp. 614 et seq.

18. Quoted in Bailey, Harris and Jones, *op. cit.*, p. 318.
19. *Secretary of State for Defence v. Guardian Newspapers Ltd.* (1984) Ch. 156. The view of the Master of the Rolls was that the original document was Crown property and so would be a photocopy of it that was prepared in the Ministry of Defence. But the copy would also belong to the Crown, by virtue of the Copyright Act 1956, if it was made outside the M.O.D. The markings on the document would also be copyright (see p. 164).
20. Nicol, *op. cit.*, at p. 285, and Ponting, *op. cit.*, p. 203.
21. See *Adler v. George* (1964) 2 Q.B. 7, where the accused obstructed a member of H.M. forces engaged on security duty while inside R.A.F. Marham. He could also have been charged with section 193 of the Air Force Act 1955.
22. (1973) 2 All E.R. 89. The offence is created by section 7 of the Official Secrets Act 1920. The Court of Criminal Appeal had decided in *R. v. Oakes* (1959) 2 All E.R. 92, that for a person to be guilty of an act preparatory to the commmission of an offence he need not also aid or abett the offence. Were it otherwise, Mrs Bingham would not have been guilty if she had not been present when her husband committed an offence. Lance Corporal Aldridge (see note 5 above) pleaded guilty to an offence under section 7 of the Official Secrets Act 1920 when he admitted the unauthorised abstraction of a highly classified document.
23. For a comprehensive review of the 'D' Notice system, see *Third Report from the Defence Committee 1979-80; The D Notice System*, H.C. 773, para. 9. The contents of various D notices are discussed at pp. 96-99. See also Report of the Committee of Privy Councillors Appointed to Inquire into the 'D' Notice System (1967), Cmnd 3309 (the Radcliffe Committee), which considered the publication of a story by Chapman Pincher in the *Daily Express* in 1967 about 'cable vetting'. It concluded that the newspaper had not broken a 'D' notice (para. 81).
24. The Radcliffe Report, *ibid.*, para. 7.
25. (1942) A.C. 624; *Asiatic Petroleum Co. Ltd. Anglo-Persian Oil Co. Ltd.* (1916) 1 K.B. 822. See, generally, Hogg, *Liability of the Crown*, chap. 3 (1971).
26. (1968) A.C. 910.
27. *Broome v. Broome* (1955) 1 All E.R. 201.
28. See sections 25 and 60 of the Army Act 1955.
29. Section 225 of the Army Act 1955.
30. (1965) N.I. 138. The Court-Martial Appeal Court affirmed his conviction. The accused had passed on information about the security of a particular Army barracks.
31. *The Protection of Military Information Report of the Study Group on Censorship (Sir Hugh Beach) (1983)*, Cmnd 9112. The Report reprints the Defence (General) Regulations 1939, Regulation 3(1), to which the Committee referred.

6

The Stationing and Movement of Forces Abroad

'You are ordered abroad as a soldier of the king. . . . It will be your duty not only to set an example of discipline . . . but also to maintain the most friendly relations with those whom you are helping in the struggle.' Earl Kitchener, A Message to the Soldiers of the British Expeditionary Force, 1914.

Until comparatively recent times British forces were sent out of the United Kingdom only on active service when they were governed by the Articles of War. No question arose over any conflict of jurisdiction between the military authorities and the criminal law of the foreign State that the Army occupied or against whom it fought. At the end of the nineteenth century British forces were on occasion stationed in the territory of a foreign friendly State. It then became 'customary for HM Government to retain by treaty jurisdictional rights over members of the forces and accompanying civilians alike'.[1]

It was during the two World Wars that large numbers of allied Servicemen were stationed in the United Kingdom and British forces were engaged in operations in the territory of allied powers. The issue of whether these foreign forces could hold courts-martial in the territory of an ally and whether they were subject to the jurisdiction of the receiving State needed an urgent solution. In the absence of a treaty between the States concerned, customary international law attempted to provide the answer, but the direction in which it pointed was not entirely clear. Marshall C.J. in the United States Supreme Court decision in 1812 of *The Schooner Exchange v. McFaddon* made the point that one sovereign was 'in no respect amenable to another' and that each was bound not to 'degrade the dignity of his nation, by placing himself or its sovereign rights within the jurisdiction of another'. He then went on to explain that, 'A third case in which a sovereign is understood to cede that portion of his territorial jurisdiction, is where he allows the troops of a foreign prince to pass through his dominions . . . the grant of a free passage therefore implies a waiver of all jurisdiction over the troops during their passage and permits the foreign general to use that discipline and to inflict those punishments which the government of his army may require.'

This judgment seems to suggest the answer to both questions, namely, whether the receiving State retains jurisdiction over the visiting force and whether the sending State can hold courts-martial in the territory of the receiving State. Such an easy solution to the problem was not, however, accepted by all jurists. The practice of States was not uniform; Marshall C.J. had not referred at all to the civilian component or the dependents of a visiting force and the pedant might argue that the Chief Justice was only referring to troops passing through, and not staying, within the jurisdiction.[2]

During the two World Wars a number of treaties were entered into to make it clear that the visiting force might hold its courts-martial in the territory of the receiving State, but in general the question of liability to the criminal law of the host State was more difficult. Even if the treaty referred to the matter, this would not have any effect in English law unless it was expressed in a statute. In *R. v. Aughet* (1918) a Belgian Army officer had shot and wounded a Belgian soldier in England and subsequently he had been acquitted by a Belgian court-martial. Although there was in existence an Anglo-Belgian Agreement which granted immunity from the jurisdiction of the English courts, this was not reproduced in an English statute. The Court of Criminal Appeal decided, however, that 'it would be contrary to the true intent and meaning of the Convention to subject the man to punishment here for an offence for which he has been in jeopardy and has been acquitted in accordance with Belgian law'.[3]

Large numbers of foreign forces stationed in the United Kingdom during the Second World War led to the passing of the Allied Forces Act 1940 which permitted courts-martial to be conducted by the various visiting forces, but it went on to provide no immunity from the English criminal law. Members of the visiting force were therefore liable to the jurisdiction of the English courts for crimes committed, even if against a member of the same force within the confines of their camp.[4] When the United States entered the war they took a completely different view about the liability of their troops to the jurisdiction of the English courts. In their opinion the judgment of Marshall C.J. in the *Schooner Exchange* case led to the conclusion that international law granted immunity to the troops of a foreign State that had been granted permission to be in the territory of another State. Draper explains that the 'United States authorities presented strong arguments to the British Government, based upon a combination of diplomatic, political, constitutional, military and morale factors, that the members of the armed forces of the United States present in the United Kingdom should remain wholly and exclusively subject to United States military jurisdiction.'[5] Section 1 of the United States of America (Visiting Forces) Act 1942 stated that no criminal proceedings were to be prosecuted in the United Kingdom against a member of the naval or military forces of the United States.[6]

It was to remain in force until the Visiting Forces Act 1952 which gives effect to the NATO Status of Forces Agreement 1951.

The Modern Position

The NATO Status of Forces Agreement of 1951 became an essential part of the postwar arrangements for that part of Germany in which the armed forces of the allied powers were stationed. Separate treaty arrangements between the individual States about the status of their armed forces was not seen as the most appropriate answer to what was to be a long-term arrangement. The solution was the Treaty of 1951[7] to which has been added the Supplementary Agreement of 1959.[8] The States party to these treaties are Belgium, Canada, France, Netherlands, West Germany, United Kingdom and the United States, while the Warsaw Pact countries have entered into bilateral agreements.[9]

It will be recalled that the 1951 Agreement required accompanying civilians and dependants of members of the armed forces to become subject to military law and this was achieved by the Fifth Schedule to the Army Act 1955.[10] There are about 90,000 British civilians in West Germany who are subject in this way to military law.[11]

The NATO Status of Forces Agreement applies to all those who are subject to the military law of their own State. Hence, it will not apply to accompanying civilians and dependants of members of the armed forces of the United States, since they are not subject to the military law of the United States.

The 1951 Agreement covers a wide range of matters of concern between the receiving and the sending States (the terms used in the Agreement to refer to the respective States concerned) such as the validity of driving licences, the wearing of uniforms and the carrying of weapons on duty, but Article VII deals with the matter of jurisdiction over members of the visiting force. This provides that 'the military authorities of the sending State shall have the right to exercise within the receiving State all criminal and disciplinary jurisdiction conferred on them by the law of the sending State over all persons subject to the military law of that State'. British courts-martial and standing civilian courts may therefore exercise jurisdiction within the territory of the Federal Republic of Germany, or indeed any other State party to the Agreement. Instead of conferring exclusive jurisdiction on the sending State, the receiving State retains its jurisdiction over all offences punishable by its law. The British Serviceman and civilian (who is subject to military law) is therefore bound by his own law, but also that of the host country.

Where an offence is committed by a person subject to military law but which is not an offence against the law of the receiving State, there can be no possible conflict of jurisdiction and the British military authorities are free to deal with the matter as they consider appropriate. This situation would occur where a soldier is charged with an offence under section 69 of the Army Act 1955 of conduct to the prejudice of good order and military discipline or, indeed, with any purely military offence.[12]

In the vast majority of all cases where a soldier commits a crime, jurisdiction will be concurrent between the sending and receiving States and the Agreement resolves this conflict by a system of primary rights. The military authorities of the sending State will have the primary right to try an offence committed solely against the property or security of that State or against a person subject to its military law. So, if a British soldier committed an assault against another British soldier in a bar in Dortmund and no other damage or injury was caused the British military authorities would have the primary right to deal with the offence. This is also the case where the offence arises 'out of any act or omission done in the performance of official duty'.[13] The reason for this grant of a primary right of jurisdiction is, no doubt, that the permission of the receiving State to allow foreign troops on its territory brings with it an understanding that it will not interfere with the force while it is operating as a military force, in other words, while its members are on duty.

In all other cases the receiving State has the primary right to try members of the visiting force for crimes committed against its law, but by the Supplementary Agreement of 1959 the Federal Republic of West Germany has granted a waiver of this jurisdiction to the British military authorities. The waiver may be 'recalled' if the 'competent German authorities hold the view that, by reason of special circumstance in a specific case, major interests of German administration of justice make imperative the exercise of German jurisdiction'.[14] Between 1981 and 1986 there were eighteen cases where the Federal Republic recalled its waiver. The offences concerned were murder, manslaughter, rape, armed robbery, grievous bodily harm and various assaults.[15] The accused Serviceman has no right at all to elect under which system of law he will be tried and, indeed, if the military authorities decide not to charge him they must notify the receiving State so that it may exercise its jurisdiction, if it so desires.[16]

The authorities of both the receiving and sending States are bound to assist each other in the arrest of persons subject to the military law of the sending State and to hand them over to whichever of them will subsequently exercise jurisdiction.[17] Article VII also deals with the infliction of the death penalty and provides that it 'cannot be imposed if the legislation of the receiving State does not provide for such punishment in a similar case'.[18] The Federal Republic has abolished the death penalty completely, although the United Kingdom retains it for five offences.[19] The effect of this is that a court-martial in Germany could not pass the death sentence on a Serviceman convicted of one of the five offences that continue to attract this penalty.

Since jurisdiction is concurrent between the receiving and sending States, the Agreement provides that a person who has been tried by one State may not be tried subsequently for the same offence by the other. But there is no bar to, say, the British military authorities charging a soldier under section 69 of the Army Act 1955 following his conviction by a German court, since this offence relates to discipline only.[20] Should he be prosecuted under the laws of the receiving State, the Serviceman is entitled to the minimum standards of trial contained in the Agreement, including legal representation and to the services of a competent interpreter. The question arose in 1978 whether the accused was bound to pay for the services of an interpreter when a British soldier had been convicted by a West German court of a traffic offence and was required to pay the interpreter's fee. He brought a case that eventually reached the European Court of Human Rights, which came to the conclusion that the wording of Article 6(3)(e) of the European Convention on Human Rights was clear in granting an accused the right to have the 'free assistance of an interpreter'.[21]

The NATO Status of Forces Agreement provides the model for similar agreements made between the United Kingdom and other States outside the NATO region. British forces come within an identical regime while serving in Belize by a treaty of 1981,[22] in Brunei by a treaty of 1984,[23] and in Kenya by a treaty of 1985.[24] Those serving in Cyprus are also subject to jurisdictional arrangements similar to the NATO agreement, but in addition there are two sovereign base areas with their own courts to deal with any offence committed within them.[25]

The United Kingdom as a Receiving State

It will be recalled that allied forces stationed in the United Kingdom during the Second World War could be tried by British courts as well as by court-martial of their own force, and that an exception was made for the armed forces of the United States. The United States of America (Visiting Forces) Act of 1942 gave to the American armed forces total immunity from local jurisdiction and therefore exclusive jurisdiction to their courts-martial. The NATO Status of Forces Agreement 1951 eschews immunity from local jurisdiction and instead provides a system of primary rights to both the receiving and sending States. The Visiting Forces Act 1952 incorporates the 1951 Agreement into English law and governs visiting armed forces from not only the NATO allies but also from many other countries.[26]

There are about thirty thousand members of the armed forces of other States at any one time in the United Kingdom, the majority of whom are from the United States.[27] The use by the United States forces of bases and facilities within the United Kingdom is the result of an agreement reached in 1951 by the British Prime Minister and the American President and reaffirmed in 1952.[28]

The Visiting Forces Act 1952 enables the visiting force (which is defined as a body of the armed forces for the time being present in the United Kingdom at the invitation of Her Majesty's government) to hold courts-martial and to deal with those subject to its military law.[29] In keeping with the 1951 Agreement, the death penalty cannot be carried out in this country if it is imposed by a court-martial of a visiting State unless a sentence of death could have been passed in a British court-martial.[30] It has been shown in

Chapter 3 that only members of the armed forces of the United States are subject to its military law, with the result that civilians and dependants are not and cannot therefore be tried by court-martial. British jurisdiction is, in consequence, exclusive.

In the vast majority of cases where a crime has been committed by a member of the visiting force, jurisdiction between the British courts and the military authorities of the visiting force will be concurrent. Section 3 of the 1952 Act confirms that the British[31] courts will not deal with a member of a visiting force who is charged with a crime solely against another member of the visiting force or against the property of that force or which arose out of and in the course of his duty. Once a member of the visiting force has been tried by court-martial for an offence, he cannot subsequently be tried in a British court. In all other cases the British courts may assume jurisdiction and appear to do so in serious cases. Between 1981 and 1983 there were twenty-seven instances of serious violence committed against United Kingdom citizens by members of the armed forces of the United States and all were tried in British courts.[32]

Where a visiting serviceman causes injury or damage to a British citizen he can be sued in the normal way and, if he does not admit liability, the British courts will decide the matter. Where liability is admitted, or is found by the court, damages are paid by the Ministry of Defence who may then recover an amount from the authorities of the visiting State.[33]

Warships in the Waters of a Foreign State

Oppenheim considered that 'men of war are State organs just as the armed forces are, a man-of-war being in fact a part of the armed forces of a State', but he equated a warship as a 'floating portion of the flag State'.[34] If this view is correct, there is no scope at all for concurrent jurisdiction where a crime is committed on board a warship of one State in the waters of another. The warship is treated as an island of its flag State to which all its laws apply exclusively. This view was, however, criticised in *Chung Chi Cheung v. The King* (1939) by the Judicial Committee of the Privy Council who considered that customary international law did not support the theory of extra-territoriality. Lord Atkin demonstrated the fiction of this theory by taking as an example the case of a civilian who went on board a warship and stole something there. His conclusion would have to be that 'the local courts would have no jurisdiction because the crime would have been committed on foreign territory'.[35] Instead, the Judicial Committee favoured the view that permission to allow a warship into its waters carries with it an implied waiver by the coastal State of its jurisdiction. The practical effect of this is that the crew of a warship, unlike the members of visiting armed forces on land, are immune from the local criminal law in respect of crimes committed on board the ship, although, as in the *Chung Chi Cheung* case itself this immunity may be waived.[36]

A further consequence of the rejection of the extra-territoriality theory is that English law applies, by virtue of the Naval Discipline Act 1957, only to the sailors on board but not to any visiting British civilian. When Ronald Biggs, a fugitive from British justice, went on board a British warship visiting Brazil he could not lawfully have been arrested because he was not then on English territory.

The *Chung Chi Cheung* case was not concerned with a sailor who committed an offence against the local law whilst ashore. It seems that international law would permit the coastal State to exercise jurisdiction over a sailor who brawled with one of its citizens in a bar on land, but not where the sailor committed a traffic offence while on shore to collect provisions for his ship, since he would then be acting in the course of duty.[37]

Suppose the warship intrudes into the territorial waters of a State and there engages in gathering information? This is what happened in the so-called 'whisky on the rocks' case in 1981 when a Soviet Whisky class submarine entered Swedish internal waters, without authority, and got into difficulties. When the submarine was raised to the surface, the captain was questioned by the Swedish authorities who then released him, the crew and the submarine. Even in these circumstances international law treats the warship as immune from the laws of the coastal State, in this case Sweden.[38]

The Movement of Military Forces

Unlike the armed forces of some states, British forces serve in many different parts of the world and the ability to move them quickly and expeditiously or to reinforce a small garrison in an emergency is a prerequisite of British defence and foreign policy. International law requires the consent of the State through which the military forces of another State are to pass by land or in the air, but the movement of forces by sea only requires such permission in very limited cases.

Movement by Sea

The sea is considered as an international highway, but it consists of distinct zones in which the coastal State has certain rights and the high seas over which no State has any jurisdiction. On the high seas, therefore, warships and other ships operated by a State for non-commercial purposes are immune from the jurisdiction of any other State.[39]

They can go as they please without interference, although other States do have a right to use parts of the high seas for naval exercises or weapons testing providing their use is not unreasonable. The British view is that 'Many States, including the United Kingdom, have in recent years engaged in rocket and other weapons tests on the high seas. In British practice the tests are suspended if a vessel enters the range. This does not constitute a claim to close an area of the high seas and would not contravene (Article eighty-eight of the Law of the Sea Convention 1982 which reserves the high seas for peaceful purposes).'[40]

A coastal State may claim a territorial sea, in which its jurisdiction will extend, to a maximum width of 12 nautical miles[41] drawn from its baselines, usually the low-water line along the coast.[42] The United Kingdom government has recently extended the width of its own territorial sea to 12 nautical miles,[43] but for other States that have not done so the traditional width of 3 nautical miles will continue to apply.

The effect of coastal States extending the width of their territorial seas to 12 nautical miles is to bring within the territorial jurisdiction of coastal States parts of what were formerly the high seas. The rights of navigation, whilst curtailed in these new areas to some extent, are nevertheless preserved by the right of innocent passage. The Geneva Convention on the Territorial Sea 1958 confirms that 'passage is innocent so long as it is not prejudicial to the peace, good order or security of the coastal State',[44] while the Law of the Sea Convention 1982, which is not yet in force, attempts to outline acts that would make passage non-innocent.[45] These include passage in which a ship uses force, or the threat of force, against the sovereignty, territorial integrity or political independence of the coastal State; any exercise or practice with weapons of any kind; any act aimed at collecting information to the prejudice of the defence or security of the coastal State; any act of propaganda aimed at affecting the defence or security of the coastal state; the launching, landing or taking on board of any aircraft or military device.

The 1958 Convention requires submarines to navigate on the surface and to show their flag,[46] requirements that may inhibit a nuclear armed submarine, which operates on the basis of the secrecy of its movements, from traversing the territorial sea of another State. The coastal State may take steps to prevent passage that is not innocent and if a warship does not comply with the regulations of the coastal State concerning passage it may be required to leave the territorial sea.[47] A particular problem to both Norway and Sweden is the activities of unidentified submarines operating within their territorial seas. In 1981 a Russian Whisky class submarine ran aground whilst submerged near the Swedish naval base at Karlskrona in Swedish internal waters. The activities of the submarine were clearly in breach of international law but what could the Swedes do when they assisted the submarine to the surface? It has been shown that the crew remained immune from the criminal process of the coastal State and so the only action that they could take against the government of the U.S.S.R. would be at the diplomatic level.[47a]

Whether warships have the right of innocent passage without prior authorisation of the coastal State is a matter upon which States differ. A number of countries do require prior authorisation.[48] Swedish law, for instance, requires prior authorisation by a statute of 1982 which provides that 'Admission is granted to foreign state vessels for passage through the Swedish territorial sea. Prior notification of such passage shall be made through diplomatic channels.'[49] The British government take the view that 'there is no basis in international law for requesting prior authorisation or notification to the coastal state of the intended passage of warships through the territorial sea'.[50] On occasions a particular navy may feel that it should assert what it considers to be its rights under international law. The United States Navy has recently asserted its rights to sail warships in the territorial sea of the U.S.S.R. when the cruiser *Yorktown* and the destroyer *Caron* sailed within 6 miles of the Russian Crimea coast in March 1986[51] and in the same month its Sixth Fleet commenced exercises in the Gulf of Sirte, which it claimed to be the high seas.[52]

In 1946 the Royal Navy had sailed through the Corfu Channel to assert the right of innocent passage through straits and had suffered casualties when two destroyers were mined in the channel.[53] The incident came before the International Court of Justice in 1949 which decided that warships had the right of innocent passage through straits without the prior authorisation of the coastal State.[54]

An extensive claim by a coastal State to territorial seas will have the effect of appropriating what other States consider to be the high seas in which they have the freedom of navigation and use. This may cause problems to the warships of other States as it did in two particular incidents. In the first, the United States Naval vessel *Pueblo* was seized by the North Koreans 15 miles from its coast in what the United States government believed to be the high seas, but which the North Koreans claimed to be their territorial seas. The seizure could not be justified in international law, since even if the North Korean claim to a territorial sea of 15 miles had been valid, the *Pueblo*, as a warship, was immune from capture by the coastal state and could only be ordered to leave the territorial sea.[55] The second incident was when the United States Sixth Fleet carried out exercises in the Gulf of Sirte in March 1986. The Libyan government had claimed the Gulf to be its internal waters after it had purported to draw a line across it and to encompass all the waters on its coast side as internal. Had this claim been valid in international law, the Sixth Fleet would, of course, have had no right in international law to sail into this area. However, the Libyan claim has no basis in international law[56] and so the Gulf is within the high seas, except for that part which Libya may lawfully claim as its territorial seas. The Sixth Fleet could therefore sail within 12 miles of the Libyan coast without leaving the high seas. Straits connect one part of the high seas with another[57] and can have considerable strategic importance. The *Corfu Channel* case of 1949 shows that warships have the right of innocent passage through straits, but the Law of the Sea Convention 1982 gives in addition all States the right of transit passage through straits.[58] This right of transit passage is wider than the right of innocent passage through the territorial sea of a coastal State; the list of prohibited activities is shorter and there can be no suspension of transit passage.[59]

Movement by Air

The use of aircraft during the First World War showed the considerable risk that they posed to the territory of any State and by 1919 there had developed a rule of customary international law that each State had exclusive sovereignty over the airspace above its territory. This was confirmed by the Chicago Convention on International Civil Aviation 1944 in Article 1 which applies both to the airspace above the land territory and the territorial sea of a State. This means that there is no right of innocent passage through the airspace, unlike the territorial sea, of a State.[60] Military aircraft must therefore seek permission to fly through the airspace of another State and since this is also a rule of customary international law it will apply irrespective of whether the State concerned is a party to the 1944 Convention It was for this reason the United States F111 aircraft that took off from the bases in the United Kingdom in 1986 to attack targets in Libya could not fly through the airspace of France who refused permission for them to do so.

There have been a number of instances where military aircraft have flown over the territory of another State without permission and have been shot down. During the Second World War Sweden, as a neutral State, was compelled to act in this way when both German and allied aircraft overflew its territory in order to carry out military operations in the territories of each other. In 1952 the U.S.S.R. shot down a Swedish military aircraft that had entered its airspace without authority. Both the United States and Sweden argued that the U.S.S.R. had, in these circumstances, a right merely to warn off the intruding aircraft, but in the U2 incident in 1960 the United States did not protest when the U.S.S.R. shot down its reconnaisance aircraft over Russian territory. The pilot, Gary Powers, ejected from the aircraft and was subsequently sentenced by a Russian court to a period of imprisonment.

The flight of the U2 was clearly in breach of international law, since it did not have the permission of the Soviet authorities to overfly their territory. It was quite beside the point that the U.S.S.R. was not a party to the Chicago Convention of 1944, since this Convention reflected customary international law. The aircraft had been flying at 60,000 feet and could only be brought down by a ground-to-air missile; it was unrealistic to say that the Soviet authorities should only have escorted it out of their airspace.[61]

All aircraft have the right to overfly the high seas.[62] In August 1981 United States naval exercises took place in the Gulf of Sirte in what the United States (and most States) considered to be the high seas. Two United States F14s were attacked by two Libyan fighters at a distance of 60 miles from the Libyan coast. They returned fire and succeeded in shooting down the Libyan aircraft. It has been argued in this chapter that the status of the Gulf of Sirte is that of the high seas and in consequence the F14s had every right to fly in the airspace above it and to defend themselves if attacked.[63]

Environments Prohibited for Military Purposes

Advances in technology have opened up the possibility of stationing military forces or weapons in environments that are not subject to the jurisdiction of any State. The Treaty on Outer Space 1967[64] prohibits State claims to sovereignty over outer space, including the moon and other celestial bodies. Military bases, installations and fortifications, the testing of any type of weapons and the conduct of military manoeuvres on celestial bodies is forbidden; the moon is to be used exclusively for peaceful purposes.[65] The moon itself is now the subject of a treaty in 1979 which prohibits the establishment of military bases, installations and fortifications, the testing of weapons and so on.[66] Restrictions also exist to prevent a State from placing nuclear weapons or any other weapons of mass destruction as well as structures and installations for their storage, testing or use, on the deep sea bed more than 12 miles from its coast.[67] However, the placing of listening devices on the deep sea bed for the purpose of detecting submarines is not caught by the 1970 Treaty.

The Antarctic is also subject to restrictions about military activities. The Antarctic Treaty of 1959 is a multilateral treaty that applies to the area south of latitude 60 degrees and in which some States, including the United Kingdom, claim sovereignty.[68] The treaty asserts that 'Antarctica shall continue forever to be used for peaceful purposes' and it prohibits 'measures of a military nature' and nuclear explosions. The treaty does not prevent the use of military personnel or equipment for scientific research or for peaceful purposes and it does permit other parties to it to inspect each other's installations, stations and equipment.

Notes

1. *Manual of Military Law, Part I, Civilian Supplement*, London, H.M.S.O. (1977), p. 3.
2. For a very sound discussion of the position under customary (or non-treaty) international law (derived from the practice of States which is considered by them to be part of international law) see Barton, *Foreign Armed Forces, Immunity From Supervisory Jurisdiction*, (1949) 26 B.Y.I.L. 380; *Foreign Armed Forces, Immunity From Criminal Jurisdiction*, (1950) 27 B.Y.I.L. 186; *Foreign Armed Forces; Qualified Jurisdictional Immunity* (1954) 31 B.Y.I.L. 341. Barton argues that it is 'too facile a way of dismissing the case (*Schooner Exchange v. McFaddon*)' to say that it refers only to passage and not to the stationing of foreign troops. See also Lazareff, *Status of Military Forces*, ... chapter 1, who argues that, 'the problem in the *Schooner Exchange* was not to find out which court had jurisdiction over members of a force, but to determine whether a force, as such, could be brought before an American court. The purpose of the action was to prove that the vessel did not belong to France (it was seized by a French man-of-war), it was not to determine the status of members of the French Navy in the United States.' See also Draper, *Civilians and the NATO Status of Forces Agreement*, Leyden, Sijthoff (1966), chap. 3.
3. (1918) 34 T.L.R. 302, 304 *per* A. T. Lawrence J.
4. See *R. v. Novratil* (1942) Unrep., discussed in Barton, (1950) 27 B.Y.I.L. 186, 198, where Cassels J. explained that if the Czech military authorities had sole jurisdiction, 'it would mean that whenever there were foreign armed forces stationed in this country, there could be committed within the lines of their camp every conceivable offence against our law, which our courts would be quite unable to entertain at all. That is not so.'

5. *Civilians and the NATO Status of Forces Agreement*, Leyden, Sijthoff (1966), p. 89.
6. The constitutional argument put forward by the U.S.A. was that the U.S. Constitution 'guaranteed to the members of their forces that they would, when outside the limits of the United States, be subjected exclusively to the United States Articles of War and that they were entitled to the benefits of that Constitution in all places', Draper, *op. cit.*, p. 39. Mr Webster, the Secretary for Foreign Affairs of the United States at the time of the *Caroline* incident (see Chapter 7), confirmed that McLeod, who had been a member of the British armed force which had set fire to the *Caroline*, ought not to have been amenable to the United States courts. If this was the position when the British armed force had not been invited on to U.S. territory, *a fortiori* ought it to be the case if the force had been invited.
7. 199 U.N.T.S. 67; Cmnd 9363 (1951)
8. 481 U.N.T.S. 262; Cmnd 852 (1959)
9. See generally, Draper, *op. cit.*, note 5, chap. 9. In particular, see the Agreement between the U.S.S.R. and the German Democratic Republic 1957.
10. See Chapter 3.
11. A breakdown of the figures is given in the Select Committee on the Armed Forces Bill 1975-76, H.C. 429, p. 74.
12. Article VII(i)(b) enables the receiving State to exercise its jurisdiction where the offence committed by a person subject to military law is an offence solely by the law of the receiving State. A soldier who breaks the law of the receiving State may, *ipso facto*, also be in breach of section 69 of the Army Act 1955 in which case jurisdiction is concurrent, see *R. v. Bissett* (1980) 1 W.L.R. 335. Compare, however, the position of the civilian or dependant, neither of whom is subject to section 69.
13. Article VII(3)(a)(ii). A certificate provided by the sending State that a Serviceman was on duty shall be issued to the receiving State authorities. In 'exceptional circumstances' this certificate may be challenged, by diplomatic means, Article 18 of the Supplementary Agreement 1959. This requirement of 'performance of official duty' cannot, of course, apply to a dependant of a member of the armed forces.
14. Article 19(3) of the Supplementary Agreement 1959.
15. See Select Committee of the Armed Forces Bill 1985-86, H.C. 170, p. 199.
16. Article VII(3)(c). Given the very wide-ranging effect of section 69 of the Army Act 1955, this is unlikely to arise in practice.
17. Article VII(5). They shall also co-operate in investigation, sub-Article (6).
18. Article VII(7).
19. See Select Committee on the Armed Forces Bill, 1985-86, H.C. 170, pp. 84, 91.
20. Article VII(8).
21. *Luedicke et al. v. Federal Republic of Germany* (1979-80) 2 E.H.R.R. 149; Judgment of 28 November 1978. See also Lt. Col. A. Rogers, *Human Rights Interpreters Fees*, (1979) XVIII Revue de Droit Pénal Militaire et de Droit de la Guerre, p. 189.
22. Exchange of Notes Concerning the Continuing Presence in Belize After Independence of United Kingdom Armed Forces, 17 U.K.T.S. (1981), Cmnd 8250, Article 12.
23. 31 U.K.T.S. (1984), Cmnd 9207, Article 15.
24. 10 U.K.T.S. (1985), Cmnd 9446, Article 3.
25. See the Treaty of Establishment 1960 4 U.K.T.S. (1961), Cmnd 1252, Annex C, Section 8, and section 2(i) of the Cyprus Act 1960. There are about 4000 U.K.-based civilians in Cyprus who are normally tried by the Sovereign Base Area Court, see Select Committee on the Armed Forces Bill 1975-76, H.C. 429, p. 129. See also the Select Committee on the Armed Forces Bill 1980-81, H.C. 253, paras. 146, 148, where the Sovereign Base Area Court is described as a 'colonial court'.
26. By section 1 of the 1952 Act and by Order in Council to the forces of any designated country. Both the Allied Forces Act 1940 and the U.S.A. (Visiting Forces) Act 1942 are repealed. Military and civilian members of headquarters and defence organisations are subject to the regime of the 1952 Act; see The International Headquarters and Defence Organisations Act 1964, section 1(2).
27. H.C. Deb. vol. 57, col. 431 (Written Answers), 2 April 1984.
28 H.C. Deb. vol. 995, col. 401, 10 December 1980.
29. Section 2.

30. A court-martial held under the Army Act 1955 can pass a sentence of death upon conviction for one of five separate offences; see sections 24, 25, 26, 31, 32. The Select Committee on the Armed Forces Bill 1985-86, H.C. 170, was informed that the death sentence would not in practice be imposed in peacetime, *ibid.*, para. 452. However, section 2 of the Visiting Forces Act 1952 permits a visiting force to carry out the death penalty if a 'sentence of death could have been passed in a similar case'. A soldier of a visiting force could, in theory, be executed in the United Kingdom for an offence similar to the five mentioned above.

31. This refers to a court anywhere in the United Kingdom. The British courts can only assume jurisdiction if the military authorities of the sending State do not intend to prosecute, section 3(3)(a). 'Waiver is therefore treated, in United Kingdom law, as an administrative, and not a legal, matter', Draper, *op. cit.*, note 5, p. 95.

32. H.C. Deb. vol. 51, cols. 103-108, 19 December 1983. British courts may also order deserters and those absent without leave to be returned to the visiting force, or, indeed, to the armed forces of any State to which the 1952 Act applies; *R. v. Thames Metropolitan Magistrate, ex p. Bindle* (1975) 1 W.L.R. 1400, where the applicant was a deserter from the U.S. Army when stationed outside the U.K. See also section 187 of the Army Act 1955.

33. A case that does not proceed to trial is considered by a claims commission, section 9 of the 1952 Act. The NATO Status of Forces Agreement 1951, Article VII(5), provides that 75 per cent of the amount awarded is to be recovered from the sending State. Between 1978 and 1983 'the claims commission has handled about 430 claims a year against the United States service men, all of which have involved road traffic accidents. In each year about 15 cases have involved personal injury, but not more than two fatal injuries. The majority of cases are settled amicably out of court', H.C. Deb. vol. 51, col. 106, 19 December 1983. For a different point of view see *ibid.*, cols. 90-94.

34. *International Law*, vol. 1, London, Longmans, 7th edn, 1952, pp. 851 and 853. A warship is defined in Article 8(2) of the Geneva Convention on the High Seas 1958 as 'a ship belonging to the naval forces of a state and bearing the external marks distinguishing warships of its nationality, under the command of an officer duly commissioned by the government and whose name appears in the Navy List, and manned by a crew who are under regular naval discipline'. See also Article 29 of the Law of the Sea Convention 1982. Warships have complete immunity while on the high seas, Article 9 of the 1958 High Seas Convention.

35. (1939) A.C. 160, 174.

36. The accused was a British subject, who had killed the captain of the ship (also a British subject) in Hong Kong waters (a British colony). The ship was a Chinese State ship. There was therefore immunity from Hong Kong jurisdiction, but the Chinese permitted the Hong Kong authorities to exercise jurisdiction.

37. Oppenheim, *op. cit.*, p. 855; Delupis, *Foreign Warships and Immunity For Espionage* (1984) 78 A.J.I.L. 53, 56. It is not a relevant consideration that a sailor was, or was not, on duty if the crime was committed on board the warship. Section 42 of the Naval Discipline Act 1957 incorporates the whole of English criminal law into the 1957 Act.

38. See Delupis, *supra*, pp. 71 and 74. Had the submarine been engaged in espionage, the immunity may have been lost, *ibid.*, p. 71. Espionage involves a disguise or the use of false pretences. There was no evidence that the submarine had acted in any of these ways. Consider, however, the rights of the coastal State to act in self-defence, see Chapter 7.

39. Article 9 of the Geneva Convention on the High Seas 1959 and Article 32 of the Law of the Sea Convention 1982. For the freedoms of the high seas, see Article 2 of the 1958 Convention. A State may create security zones around its installations on the high seas (e.g. oil rigs in the North Sea), Article 5 of the Continental Shelf Convention 1958.

40. H.L. Deb. vol. 388, col. 842, 1 February 1978. *The Nuclear Test Cases* (1974) I.C.J. Reps. 253 and 457 (Australia v. France and New Zealand v. France respectively), did not decide whether the use of the high seas for testing nuclear weapons was contrary to international law. The Nuclear Test Ban Treaty of 1963 prohibits testing of nuclear weapons, *inter alia*, on the high seas or within the territorial waters of a coastal State. France is not a party to the Treaty.

41. Article 3 of the Law of the Sea Convention 1982. This Convention is not yet in force. The Geneva Convention on the Territorial Sea and Contiguous Zone 1958 was silent on the

width of the territorial sea. The majority of States, however, now claim a territorial sea of 12 nautical miles, see H.L. Deb. vol. 440, cols. 993-994, 21 March 1983; Booth, *Law, Force and Diplomacy at Sea*, London, Allen & Unwin (1985), p. 217; Churchill and Lowe, *The Law of the Sea*, Manchester U.P. (1985), p. 42. See, generally, Articles 3-13 of the Geneva Convention on the Territorial Sea and Contiguous Zone 1958 and Articles 4-16 of the Law of the Sea Convention 1982.

43. H.L. Deb. vol. 448, col. 283, 15 February 1984. See Territorial Sea Act 1987.

44. Article 14. Passage means, 'navigation through the territorial sea for the purpose either of traversing that sea without entering internal waters, or of proceeding to internal waters, or of making for the high seas from internal waters'.

45. Article 19(2). Although the Convention is not yet in force, it is likely that the activities listed in the Article would be considered by most States to render passage non-innocent.

46. Article 14(6).

47. Article 23 of the Geneva Convention on the Territorial Sea and Contiguous Zone 1958. The coastal State may not enforce its criminal law against the crew of a warship (see above, note 37), but its right of self-defence is not impaired (see Chapter 7).

47a. See, generally, Booth, *op. cit.*, note 41, pp. 130-136; Delupis, *op. cit.*, note 37. For the municipal law of Sweden see *infra*, note 49, sections 8 and 10. A state may refuse permission, for example, for a nuclear powered or nuclear armed ship to enter its harbours. A case in point is New Zealand.

48. See (1978) 49 B.Y.I.L. 395 for a list of such States. These include the U.S.S.R., Denmark, China, Libya (in the Gulf of Sirte).

49. Swedish Code of Statutes 1982: 755, section 3. Notification is not required for passage through the Swedish territorial sea in Öresund (the waterway between Denmark and Sweden which provides the means of passage from the Baltic to the North Sea).

50. See note 48 above. The Minister for the Armed Forces stated in Parliament that, 'Soviet vessels enjoy the right of innocent passage through the territorial seas of the United Kingdom,' H.C. Deb. vol. 57, col. 664 (Written Answers), 5 April 1984.

51. *The Times*, 21 March 1986. The U.S.S.R. claims a territorial sea of 12 nautical miles, see (1983) 54 B.Y.I.L. 496.

52. *The Times*, 26 March 1986.

53. For details of the mining of H.M.S. *Saumarez* and H.M.S. *Volage* in October 1946 with the loss of 44 lives, see Leggett, *The Corfu Incident*, London, New English Library, 1976.

54. *U.K. v. Albania*, I.C.J. Reps. (1949), p. 4. One further reason for the passage through the straits in October 1946 of a number of British warships was to dissuade Albania from firing on ships in passage, which it had done in May 1946.

55. Article 23 of the Geneva Convention on the Territorial Sea and Contiguous Zone 1958. If it be assumed that the *Pueblo* was on the high seas, it was immune from seizure by Article 8 of the Geneva Convention on the High Seas 1958. See, generally, Rubin, *Some Legal Implications of the Pueblo Incident* (1969) 18 I.C.L.Q. 961. The crew was eventually released after the *Pueblo's* captain had signed a confession admitting that the ship had been in North Korean territorial waters. The captain, upon signing, did so only in order to secure the release of his crew. See (1969) 8 I.L.M. 198 for details.

56. Article 7(4) of the Geneva Convention on the Territorial Sea and Contiguous Zone 1958 permits a coastal state to draw a line between the natural entrance points of a bay if they do not exceed 24 miles. Waters enclosed within the landward side become internal waters. The Gulf of Sirte is 275 miles across and could not therefore come within Article 7(4), which is repeated by Article 10 of the Law of the Sea Convention 1982. Neither is the Gulf of Sirte an historic bay to which the above rules do not apply (see Article 7(6) of the 1958 Convention), since Libya first made its claim in 1974.

57. They can also connect one exclusive economic zone with another; Article 37 Law of the Sea Convention 1982. For the rights of the coastal State in the exclusive economic zone see Article 56 of the 1982 Convention. Generally, the coastal State has sovereign rights for the purpose of exploring and exploiting, conserving and managing the natural resources contained therein.

58. Article 38 which defines transit passage as, 'the freedom of navigation and overflight solely for the purpose of continuous and expeditious transit of the strait between one part of the high seas (or exclusive economic zone) and another part of the high seas (or exclusive economic zone)'.

59. See Articles 39 and 44 of the 1982 Convention. In addition, aircraft also possess the right of transit, but not innocent, passage.
60. Note the right of overflight of straits by aircraft in transit passage, *ibid*. See also Article 53 of the Law of the Sea Convention 1982 concerning the right of aircraft to fly in archipelagic sea lanes passage.
61. See, generally, Wright, *The U2 Incident*, (1960) 54 A.J.I.L. 836. The U.S.A. did not seek to argue that Powers, as a member of its armed forces, was immune from the criminal jurisdiction of the U.S.S.R. Even if he had been (which is doubted, because a military aircraft does not possess the immunity of a warship), it might be argued that his immunity had been lost, since his activities could be considered as espionage. Unlike the Soviet whisky class submarine that penetrated Swedish internal waters in 1981, the U2 had no external markings and Powers was not wearing uniform; see Delupis, *op. cit.*, note 37. See also the *Case Concerning Military and Paramilitary Activities in and Against Nicaragua (Nicaragua v. United States of America)* (1986) 15 I.L.M. 1023, at para. 251 of the judgment: 'The principle of respect for territorial sovereignty is also directly infringed by the unauthorized overflight of a State's territory by aircraft belonging to or under the control of the government of another State. The Court has found ... that such overflights were in fact made.'
62. Article 2 of the Geneva Convention on the High Seas 1958. The general lack of protest would seem to have validated the right of a coastal State to require aircraft flying over the high seas to identify themselves if they are headed for its territory. These are the so-called Air Defence Identification Zones; see Hailbronner, *Freedom of the Air and the Convention on the Law of the Sea* (1983) 77 A.J.I.L. 490, 515-519. The standard work is Murchison, *The Contiguous Airspace Zone in International Law* (1955) Ottawa.
63. Had the F14s been returning from an attack on Libyan territory, there would be difficulty in accepting that the Libyan aircraft could fire on them over the high seas. There is no right of hot pursuit into the airspace above the high seas by aircraft. Ships (and aircraft) have such a right, Article 23 of the Geneva Convention on the High Seas 1958, but only against a ship (see also Article 111 of the 1982 Convention). The only possible legal justification that could be invoked by the Libyans in the scenario would be by way of self-defence, as to which see Chapter 7.
64. Treaty on Principles Governing the Activities of States in the Exploration and Use of Outer Space, Including the Moon and Other Celestial Bodies, 610 U.N.T.S. 205 (1967). The U.K., U.S.A., U.S.S.R. are all parties to the treaty.
65. Article 4.
66. Article 3 of the Agreement Governing the Activities of States on the Moon and Other Celestial Bodies, (1979) 18 I.L.M. 1434. The treaty entered into force in 1984; see Christol, *The Moon Treaty Enters into Force* (1985) 79 A.J.I.L. 163. Neither the U.S.A. nor the U.S.S.R. is a party to this treaty. The U.K. is also not a party to it. The 1979 Treaty reiterates many of the principles to be found in the 1967 Treaty.
67. Treaty on the Prohibition of the Emplacement of Nuclear Weapons and Other Weapons of Mass Destruction on the Seabed and the Ocean Floor and in the Subsoil Thereof (1970). There is no restriction on a State placing such weapons on the seabed of its territorial sea.
68. The other States that claim territorial sovereignty are Australia, Argentina, Chile, France, New Zealand, Norway. One-sixth of Antarctica has not been claimed by any State as part of its sovereign territory. See, generally, (1982) 53 B.Y.I.L. 459-466.

7

Legal Controls on the Use of Force by States

'Any nation that uses (war) intelligently will, as a rule, gain superiority over those who disdain its use.' Von Clausewitz (1832).

Thomas Hardy may well have been right when he said that 'war makes rattling good history; but peace is poor reading'. Many would agree that the history of Europe is anything but poor reading. War was seen both as a means of self-help in a world that lacked any organisation to police it, or indeed, any body of international law to govern it, and as a way in which the balance of power in Europe might be maintained.

The latter part of the nineteenth and the early part of the twentieth centuries saw an international concern with some of the methods and means of warfare and it was not unnatural to expect some States to give thought to the question of whether aggressive war might be outlawed.[1] The First World War was styled 'the war to end all wars' and one might have been forgiven for thinking that the rush to enter into treaties prohibiting aggressive war that followed the Armistice in 1918 would have spelt an end to war. There was, of course, the Covenant of the League of Nations in 1920 in which states accepted the obligation not to resort to war, but if a 'rupture' should occur they were to submit the dispute to an organ of the League and undertook not to go to war until a period of 3 months from its decision. The Locarno Treaty in 1925 was a non-aggression pact between Germany, France and Belgium, with guarantees from the United Kingdom and Italy. It was of little consequence; a 'harmless drug to soothe nerves'.[2] The major achievement of the period was the Kellogg-Briand Pact of 1928 in which States condemned 'recourse to war for the solution of international controversies, and renounce(d) it as an instrument of national policy'.[3] Almost the whole of the international community at the time became a party to it and remained so at the time of the outbreak of the Second World War.

Were these attempts to control war doomed from the start? In one sense they were. Any international lawyer of the day could have seen enormous gaps in the law which his political masters might later wish to exploit. The very term 'war' was a subjective notion which States at their discretion could ascribe or deny to a conflict in which their armed forces were engaged. The bombardment and subsequent occupation of Corfu by the Italians in 1923, for instance, was not seen by either Greece or Italy as giving rise to a state of war.[4] Where the use of armed force was limited or merely threatened, a State could argue that it was not in breach of the Pact. The most promising justification for the use of armed force, self-defence, was not mentioned by the Pact at all, although many of the signatories made it plain that they reserved the right to act in self-defence. The Pact did, however, have a profound effect on thinking at the time. Taylor considered it as part of a 'golden age' when 'hatred for the Germans was forgotten'[5] but it also led, despite many setbacks, to acceptance of the principles both that aggressive war was, in itself, contrary to international law and that the use of armed force outside a State's borders was a matter of concern for the whole world community. In 1946 the International Military Tribunal at Nuremberg went so far as to say that even before the outbreak of war in 1939 the prohibition of aggressive war was 'demanded by the conscience of the world' which had found expression in the various treaties to outlaw it.[6]

The United Nations Charter 1945

The origins of the United Nations lie with the Dumbarton Oaks Conference of 1944 when the United States, the United Kingdom, the U.S.S.R. and China agreed on the major structure of what was to become the United Nations.[7] The United Nations Charter now provides for a Security Council composed of five permanent members and ten elected members[8] which has 'primary responsibility for the maintenance of international peace and security'[9] and a General Assembly in which all member States have a right to vote. The Security Council, under Article 39 of the Charter, has the right to determine the existence of any threat to the peace, breach of the peace or act of aggression and to make recommendations, which it does occasionally. In Resolution 502 the Security Council determined that there existed a breach of the peace in the region of the Falkland Islands in April 1982 and called for an immediate withdrawal of all Argentine forces from the islands and for the governments concerned to seek a diplomatic solution.

The prohibition of the use of force by States is contained in Article 2(4) of the Charter. It directs that 'All members shall refrain in their international relations from the threat or use of force against the territorial integrity or political independence of any State, or in any other manner inconsistent with the purposes of the United Nations.'[10] The idea behind this article is simple enough to grasp, but it lacks the precision of a statutory rule and so it gives scope for debate as to whether a particular action infringes it. Does 'force' mean only 'armed force'? Can it cover 'economic force' in the form of a boycott of an essential product, such as oil? The International Court of Justice in *The Case Concerning Military and Paramilitary Activities in and Against Nicaragua (Nicaragua v. United States of America)* in 1986 took the view that, 'while the arming and training of the *contras* can certainly be said to involve the threat or use of force against Nicaragua, this is not necessarily so in respect of all the assistance given by the United States Government. In particular, the Court considers that the mere supply of funds to the *contras*, while undoubtedly an act of intervention in the internal affairs of Nicaragua ... does not in itself amount to a use of force.'[10a] What of a use of force in the territory of another State that does not affect its territorial integrity or political independence? This was the basis of an argument by the Israeli government when it bombed the Iraqi nuclear reactor in 1981. It might be suggested that 'a use of the territory—to construct a nuclear reactor—was interfered with but the territory remained integral'.[11] Again, would a State be in breach of Article 2(4) if it used force for a purpose that it argued was not inconsistent with the purposes of the United Nations, such as in rescuing its nationals from another State? In a national legal system one would expect to find a detailed interpretation of a statutory provision in the form of case law, but in the international sphere it is perhaps not surprising that the answers to the questions posed have not benefited from extensive judicial analysis. The reasons are not hard to find. The Security Council is not a court able to issue a judgment solely on the basis of international law, even if it could do so. Different groupings of States may view the use of force in some circumstances as justifiable, whilst others would condemn it. Through problems of jurisdiction the International Court of Justice has not been able to play the active role it was intended to play. The *Corfu Channel Case* in 1949 and the *Nicaragua v. United States of America Case* in 1986 stand as isolated legal beacons. The judgment in the *Corfu Channel Case* is of great interest to those who would take a wide view of the prohibition on the use of force. The court could 'only regard the alleged right of intervention (by the British in sweeping the mines from the channel) as the manifestation of a policy of force, such as has, in the past, given rise to most serious abuses and such as cannot ... find a place in international law. ... Between independent states, respect for territorial sovereignty is an essential foundation of international relations.'[11a] The court in 1986 considered that in laying mines, attacking Nicaraguan ports and arming and training *contras* the United States had infringed the prohibition on the use of force and had unlawfully intervened in the affairs of a sovereign State.

The major contribution to an understanding of Article 2(4) has been made by the General Assembly in a number of important resolutions. Both the Declaration on Principles of International Law Concerning Friendly Relations Among States in 1970 and the Resolution on the Definition of Aggression in 1974 were adopted without a vote and add considerable detail to the customary international law concerned with the use of force.[12] The 1974 Definition of Aggression goes a long way to spell out what would clearly amount to aggression, which it, more or less, equates with an infringement of Article 2(4).[13] So, the first use of armed force by a State in contravention of the Charter will constitute *prima facie* evidence of an act of aggression. The Definition goes on to enumerate acts of aggression, such as the attack by the armed forces of a State on the territory of another and the bombardment or use of any weapons against the territory of another State, but it also leaves the door open for the Security Council to determine that any act not within the Definition may also be considered to be aggression. Both resolutions make it clear that the acquisition of territory by aggression will not give the aggressor a good title to that territory, although it once did.[14]

Some recent examples of the use of force by States will help to illustrate the uncertainties of this basic rule of international law. It should be noted, however, that in most instances emphasis is placed by the governments concerned on the legal justification for their actions, a matter that will be discussed later in this chapter.

The Falkland Islands 1982

On 2 April 1982 the Argentine forces occupied the Falkland Islands asserting their right to do so on the basis of a long-standing claim to sovereignty over the islands.[15] The British representative at the Security Council argued that by its action Argentina was in breach of Articles 2(3) and 2(4) of the Charter, had committed an act of aggression within the 1974 Definition of Aggression and by occupying the islands by military force was in breach of the 1970 Declaration on Friendly Relations. He also dealt with a very interesting Argentine argument. This was that the Charter provisions did not apply to a dispute that had arisen before it came into existence in 1945. Admittedly there was an active dispute over the islands between the two governments since 1832, but to accept such an argument would throw into confusion the stability of many different territories. The British representative explained that 'the roots of many problems under consideration by the United Nations stretch back years, decades, centuries before the Charter was adopted in 1945 ... there was no foundation in the Charter for such a dangerous doctrine'.[16]

Grenada 1983

In October 1983 armed forces of the United States, along with those of other Caribbean countries, landed in Grenada, engaged in fighting local troops and finally withdrew in early November 1983. There were a number of different justifications given for the incursion, which will be discussed later in this chapter, but of overwhelming importance was the request by the Governor-General of Grenada to the Organisation of Eastern Caribbean States to intervene militarily to restore law and order. That organisation, in turn, requested the United States for military assistance.[17]

Legal Justification for the Use of Force

There are occasions recognised by all legal systems when the use of force is permitted. To legislate otherwise is to wander into unrealism; a man who is attacked is hardly likely to submit to the blows merely because the law denied him the opportunity to defend himself. Those who uphold the law must also be able to use some degree of force in order to discharge their obligations. International law can be no different if it is to be respected by States.

The broad scheme of the Charter of the United Nations was that the use of force by an individual State would no longer be acceptable, unless its action could be justified as self-defence. Instead, the Charter provided that disputes should be solved peaceably, but if they were not, the matter should come before the Security Council who, in turn, could take action through military force under Chapter VII of the Charter or authorise a regional arrangement to do so on its behalf under Chapter VIII. Matters did not, however, work out in such a tidy fashion. The Security Council found itself unable to act on a number of occasions through the power of veto possessed by the permanent members, and the special agreements by states with the United Nations, by which they would make forces available to the Security Council, were never made.[18]

The Charter has been likened to a 'wild west' town in the nineteenth century when a sheriff arrives to enforce the law. No longer will the townspeople have to carry guns or to use force to protect themselves or their property; the sheriff will act on their behalf. What happens when the sheriff is seen to be ineffective is that the people once more arm themselves and are prepared to use force if necessary.[19] The result is that a number of the townspeople will use force and attempt subsequently to justify it on the basis of what is most advantageous to them. It would be rare for an individual to use force in this way and not seek to justify what he had done. States are no different, as discussion of the justifications given for the use of force will show.

Self-Defence

The Charter attempts to spell out in Article 51 the limits of the right of States to use force in self-defence. Like Article 2(4), it is an imprecise formulation and it has therefore given considerable scope to those who might wish to argue either its width or its limits. It is in the following terms: 'Nothing in the present Charter shall impair the inherent right of individual or collective self-defence if an armed attack occurs against a Member of the United Nations, until the Security Council has taken measures necessary to maintain international peace and security.' It then goes on to provide that measures taken under the Article shall be reported to the Security Council, whose authority and responsibility for the maintenance of international peace and security, is not affected.

The essential problem with Article 51 is whether it contains within it the whole of the law of self-defence, so that a State must bring itself within the exact limits of the Article, or whether it sweeps in the pre-existing customary international law of self-defence. If the latter is the right interpretation, scope for argument over the limits of self-defence in international law is inevitable.

If Article 51 does indeed mark the limits of self-defence, the right can be seen to be a very narrow one. This, it may be argued, is no bad thing, since it curtails the right to engage in the use of force on an individual basis, one of the main purposes of Chapter VII of the Charter.[20]

There is no point in prohibiting the use of force in Article 2(4) and then permitting wide exceptions to it later in the Charter. The exceptions must be construed narrowly on the twin principles that that was the intention behind the Charter itself and that exceptions to a general principle should themselves be narrowly construed. The right, under this interpretation, is only permissible if an 'armed attack' occurs, and here lies the difficulty. Apart from the extremely difficult question in present conditions of intercontinental and other missiles of when an armed attack begins (is it when the missile is about to be fired, is fired, or strikes home?), it is by no means certain what constitutes an armed attack. In the Second World War conditions it was relatively easy; the *Blitzkrieg* could hardly be mistaken for a more peaceful avocation. But the infiltration of small numbers of men across a frontier is less clear. The International Court of Justice in the *Nicaragua v. United States of America* case has recently seen no reason 'to deny that, in customary law, the prohibition of armed attacks may apply to the sending by a State of armed bands to the territory of another State, if such an operation, because of its scale and effects, would have been classified as an armed attack rather than as a mere frontier incident had it been carried out by regular armed forces'.[21] The other main difficulty with this approach is in what it denies to States and whether in so doing it is open to the charge of unrealism. Since it requires an armed attack to trigger off the right to act in self-defence, it precludes a State from acting first in order to prevent an attack upon itself, or anticipatory self-defence. Does this mean, therefore, that a State will have to await an attack upon it before it can legitimately take action in self-defence? In the missile age a first strike could be decisive and prevent the attacked State from being in a position to respond, although the two superpowers possess a second-strike capability. Would a State really wait when it has incontrovertible evidence that an attack upon it is imminent? To deny a legal justification for such action is to run the danger of States, just like the townspeople in the 'wild west' town, cocking a snook at the law. The International Court of Justice in the *Nicaragua Case* of 1986 asserted that, on the facts alleged, it was not necessary for it to consider this point.

The other side of the coin presents a wholly different picture. Instead of accepting that Article 51 contains the whole of the right of self-defence, the wider view of it is based on relying on customary international law, which, it is argued, is swept into Article 51 by the words 'Nothing in the present Charter shall impair *the inherent right of . . . self defence.*' The inherent right of self-defence must refer to customary international law which had established such a right, a right which was relied upon by the International Military Tribunal at Nuremberg.[22] If this view is correct, and it is supported by the International Court of Justice in the *Nicaragua Case* of 1986, then customary international law tells us not merely that all States have an inherent right of self-defence but also the extent of the defence, in terms of necessity and proportionality. If an armed attack occurs, one might argue, nothing can impair the right of self-defence, but if there is no actual armed attack, there may still be a right under customary international law to act by way of defence. There is much to be said for this wider view. On a policy level it seems to reflect the wishes of States themselves in a world where the sheriff is not always effective in preventing the unlawful use of force.

The *locus classicus* of the position under customary international law is the *Caroline Case* which resulted in diplomatic exchanges between the British and the United States governments in 1841. 'It was', wrote Professor Jennings, 'in this case that self-defence was changed from a political excuse to a legal doctrine.'[23]

To bring itself within the *Caroline* principles a State will need to show 'a necessity of self-defence, instant, overwhelming, leaving no choice of means and no moment for deliberation'. The act must be 'justified by the necessity of self-defence, must be limited by that necessity and kept clearly within it'. This principle, it will be noticed, does not require anything actually to occur to the State that purports to act in self-defence; it merely has to believe that there is a need to act in self-defence.

Those who would argue that the *Caroline* principles have been incorporated into the Charter have to accept that the use of force may the more readily be justified by States; that a State may perceive the need to act in defence of its vital interests. These might range from protection of its territory to the protection of its own and even another State's nationals abroad or the protection of its property abroad. Some examples serve to make the point although all have drawn fierce criticism from some States, which detracts from their value as setting a precedent in the flourishing field of customary international law. In 1956 the Lord Chancellor gave three reasons for British (along with French forces) invading the Suez Canal area. These were 'the danger to our nationals . . . the danger to shipping in the Canal itself (and their crews); and the danger to the enormously valuable installations of the Canal itself'.[24] The Entebbe incident in 1976 is also a well-known instance of armed force being used, in this case by Israel on the territory of Uganda, to rescue its nationals who had been taken hostage. In the ensuing action a number of Ugandan soldiers were killed. The Israeli representative speaking in the

Security Council debate on the raid asserted that 'The right of a State to take military action to protect its nationals in mortal danger is recognized by all legal authorities in international law', but the representative of the United States limited this to cases where 'the State in whose territory they are located is either unwilling or unable to protect them'.[25] In this case there was some evidence that the Ugandan authorities actually co-operated with the hijackers, which, of course made it that much less difficult to justify the Israeli action. Although the United States action in Grenada in 1983 was based to a large extent on the protection of the lives of about one thousand of its citizens there, a notable difference was the request of the Governor General of Grenada to the Organisation of Eastern Caribbean States for assistance.

In two other incidents the United States claimed that it had been acting in self-defence through its attempts to rescue and to protect its citizens abroad. In the abortive attempt in 1980 to rescue its citizens taken hostage in Iran, the United States claimed that it had the right to use force in Iran to try and rescue them,[26] and it used the same argument to justify its air raids on Tripoli and Benghazi in 1986. It is, however, difficult to bring these air raids into any established view of self-defence. The ostensible reason given was the need to protect United States citizens, not in their own country, nor in Libya, but throughout the world from terrorist action inspired by Libya. It is difficult to accept that 'the need was instant or overwhelming' or that there was 'no choice of means or moment for deliberation'. It might also be questioned whether the raids were proportionate to the injury inflicted to United States nationals, but if its real justification was on the basis of anticipatory self-defence, it illustrates only too clearly the dangers of accepting that States have such a right in international law.[27]

One of the consequences of leaving the concept of self-defence obscure is that it becomes almost impossible to draw a clear line between permissible self-defence on the one hand and a reprisal on the other. The use of armed force by way of a reprisal cannot be justified under the Charter. It is a clear breach of Article 2(4) and it is one of the forms of self-help that the Charter was designed to eliminate. The problem of distinguishing between anticipatory self-defence and a reprisal is well brought out in the 1986 air raids on Libya. Were the raids really a reprisal for the bomb attack in Berlin shortly before, or were they a genuine attempt to prevent such action by the Libyans in the future? The action looks more like a reprisal than one in which armed raiders from one State attack another and then escape to their own territory, where they are attacked in turn in order to prevent them launching further action across the border.[28]

Collective Self-Defence

It will be recalled that Article 51 of the Charter speaks of individual or collective self-defence and without defining the latter term throws up another conundrum. Does each State that uses force have to be acting in defence of itself so that each State does together what it could do separately or can a State that is acting in self-defence call upon another to assist it? The actual practice of States seems to favour the wider approach, that a State acting in self-defence may call upon any other State to join it in resisting aggression even though the intervening State is under no direct threat itself. In practice, however, it is likely that such a possibility will have been foreseen and States that have a common interest in a particular area will have entered into a treaty to provide such military assistance. The NATO Treaty of 1949 and the Warsaw Pact of 1955 are examples of European treaties that provide for collective self-defence. The NATO Treaty requires the parties to consult together whenever, in the opinion of any of them, their territorial integrity, political independence or security is threatened and in Article 5 they agree 'that an armed attack against any one or more of them in Europe or North America shall be considered an armed attack against them all'. Should this occur, 'each of them, in exercise of the right of individual or collective self-defence recognized by Article 51 of the Charter of the United Nations, will assist the Party or Parties attacked'. An attack by Warsaw Pact countries on Norway would therefore bring into play the collective self-defence provisions of the NATO Treaty and would give a direct right, for example, to the United States, to take military action to assist in the defence of Norway.

It was on the basis of collective self-defence with the Republic of Vietnam that the United States justified its military activity in Vietnam and for its limited incursion into Cambodia in 1970.[29] But the claim by the United States to be acting in collective self-defence with Nicaragua's neighbours, none of whom had asked for United States assistance to meet an armed attack, was rejected by the International Court of Justice in 1986. The court considered that there was 'no rule in customary international law permitting another State to exercise the right of collective self-defence on the basis of its own assessment of the situation. Where collective self-defence is invoked, it is to be expected that the State for whose benefit this right is used will have declared itself to be the victim of an armed attack.'

Self-Defence and the Security Council

Article 51 requires States to notify the Security Council of the United Nations of the actions that they take by way of self-defence, a matter that was scrupulously observed by the United Kingdom during the Falklands War, but was not observed by the United States in its claim to be acting in collective self-defence against Nicaragua. The Falklands conflict also showed that the right of self-defence is not placed in abeyance merely because the Security Council has been able to pass a resolution calling for one of the parties to a conflict to withdraw. It will be recalled that Resolution 502 called for the Argentine forces to withdraw from the islands, but their refusal to do so had no effect on the right of the United Kingdom to act in self-defence under Article 51.

Regional Arrangements

It is natural that States within a region should be primarily concerned with preventing attempts from outside, or indeed inside the region, to disturb its peace and security. Chapter VIII of the United Nations Charter permits States to enter into regional arrangements, such as the Organisation of American States, but it directs that if enforcement action is to be taken within the region the approval of the Security Council must be obtained. The region is, in other words, permitted to 'police' itself under powers delegated by the Security Council. Two actions of the United States show the way in which Chapter VIII of the Charter has been applied. The first was the Cuban missile crisis of 1962 when United States forces stopped ships on the high seas as a measure of 'quarantine' to prevent the installation of missiles on Cuban territory. The legal justification for this action was not on the basis of self-defence but on Chapter VIII, and in particular on the Rio Treaty of 1947, a treaty made under the umbrella of the Charter of the Organisation of American States 1948. Both Cuba and the United States were parties to both of these treaties. The decision to set up the quarantine was made by the Organ of Consultation under the Rio Treaty (in effect, a decision of the Organisation of American States), but any use of force had to be with the consent of the States concerned. It was on this basis that the United States was able to argue that the quarantine action was not enforcement action calling for the prior approval of the Security Council; there was no decision of the Organ of Consultation that was to be enforced by force by all States party to the Treaty.[30]

The intervention by forces of the Organisation of Eastern Caribbean States and the United States in Grenada in 1983 is a further example of the use of force alleged to be carried out under a regional arrangement. The major difference between the Cuban and Grenadian incidents was the request by the Governor General of Grenada to the Organisation of Eastern Caribbean States for assistance. The Grenada incident could be seen therefore as a 'regional peacekeeping action for the purpose of restoring order and self-determination at the request of lawful authorities or in a setting of breakdown of authority' as envisaged under Chapter VIII of the United Nations Charter.[31] No prior approval of the Security Council was required, since the action was not enforcement action.[32] There is a difference of opinion, however, on the issue of whether the action was permitted by the relevant treaties, the Charter of the Organisation of American States and the Organisation of Eastern Caribbean States Treaty.[33] What is clear is that neither the Cuban nor the Grenadian action were based on self-defence but rather on ensuring the *status quo* of the region was not altered by the communist bloc.[34]

United Nations Forces

It will be recalled that the original scheme of the Charter was that the Security Council would determine the existence of a breach of the peace or act of aggression and that it could decide whether to take military or non-military action in response to it. States had agreed to be bound by the decisions of the Security Council and to enter into agreements with the United Nations to provide armed forces for use of the Security Council. No agreements were ever entered into, but nevertheless the United Nations has been able to call upon States to provide armed forces to carry out its policies.

The first such action was in 1950 when forces of North Korea crossed the border into South Korea. The Security Council was able, through the absence of the representative of the U.S.S.R., to determine that the North Korean action amounted to a breach of the peace. It later recommended that 'all members provide military forces and . . . make such forces . . . available to a unified command under the United States'.[35] Altogether, sixteen members of the United Nations sent forces to Korea, although the contingent from the United States was by far the largest. In the following month the representative of the U.S.S.R. returned to the Security Council and imposed his veto on further action of the Council. Matters then passed to the General Assembly which resolved that if the Security Council was, through lack of unanimity, unable to act, the General Assembly would do so.[36] Eventually the General Assembly approved of the force, that it now controlled, crossing the thirty-eighth parallel to engage North Korean forces.

Debate has centred around the question of whether the force that was assembled in Korea was a United Nations force or whether it was really an instance of a number of States acting in collective self-defence with South Korea. Some have argued that under the Charter the Security Council may make recommendations (which it did in this particular case) or decide whether to take military action under Article 42 (which is made subject to the agreements to supply military forces under Article 43 and which have not been made). Since the Security Council made only a recommendation in its resolution of 7 July 1950 there was no authority to create a United Nations force. Adherents to this view would say that the force was really a United States one since that country supplied not only the commander who took his orders from Washington but also about 93 per cent of the armed forces involved. On the other hand, the force did use the United Nations flag and United Nations medals were awarded, facts that led Professor Bowett to regard the 'Korean action as an enforcement action authorized by recommendations under Article 39' of the United Nations Charter.[37]

The Korean episode has been the only one where the United Nations has taken action against a State by military force without the consent of the State concerned and it can properly be described as enforcement action. Of much greater importance since has been the creation of United Nations forces to act in trouble spots around the world. This has taken the form of supervising a cease-fire or disengagement (as in Egypt in 1956, Cyprus in 1964 and the Lebanon in 1978) or maintaining law and order (in the Congo in 1960). These forces are not designed to go on the offensive but merely to use force, where necessary, in self-defence. In addition, the United Nations has established unarmed observation groups to report on movement across a particular area. In 1974, for instance, the Security Council set up a Disengagement Observation Force following Israeli withdrawal from Syrian territory (the Golan Heights) that it had occupied in 1967 and 1973.

The emphasis of this chapter is clearly on the use of force by States and not by the United Nations. This is only a reflection of how States themselves have perceived the role of the United Nations. Some have consistently refused to pay any contributions towards the expenses of establishing United Nations peacekeeping forces while the legal basis for their establishment has been by no means clear. The International Court of Justice has advised that it was within the power of the General Assembly to establish the force in Egypt in 1956 and in the Congo in 1960.[38] Since then the Security Council has retaken the leading role in creating and renewing the mandates of each force, but it has never clearly explained whether they have been created under Chapters VI or VII of the Charter. Perhaps the real answer is that the Charter has been modified by the practice of the Organisation and it has adapted to a world where the use of force by the United Nations to enforce a decision, although perceived in 1945 as the means to end the scourge of war, is not now seen as a realistic option but the creation of a peacekeeping force is.

In Conclusion

The use of force by States has not been effectively eliminated as the United Nations Charter had envisaged. But that is not to say that the Charter has been a failure. Article 2(4) has succeeded in creating a norm of international law that the use of force by a State outside its borders will have to be justified, not only to the world community but also on the national political scene. The difficulty is that to an international lawyer the gaps in the law appear to be extremely generous to a State which, for policy reasons, is minded to use armed force. To argue that what is not expressly prohibited is permitted and that Articles 51 to 54 of the Charter grant extensive rights to States is to argue for a wide latitude of action, outside the control of the United Nations. Whether one believes that Article 2(4) is dead and that the exceptions to the rule in Articles 51 to 54 have triumphed over the rule itself or whether the Charter provisions provide the only practical answer in the real world is essentially a matter of judgment.[39]

Notes

1. See, generally, Oppenheim, *International Law*, vol. II, Longman, London, 1952, chap. 3; Brownlie, *International Law and The Use of Force by States* (1963), Oxford, Clarendon Press.
2. Taylor, *English History 1914-18*, Clarendon Press, Oxford, 1965, p. 222.
3. General Treaty for the Renunciation of War, 1928.
4. The League itself was not anxious to condemn it as 'war' either because it acted as a limitation on the conduct of the State or because a finding of 'war' would illustrate the impotence of the League. See, generally, Brownlie, *International Law and The Use of Force by States*, chap. XXIII.
5. See note 2, p. 260. Among the other non-aggression pacts that may be noted are those of January 1934 between Germany and Poland, May 1939 between Germany and Denmark and August 1939 between Germany and the U.S.S.R.
6. (1947) 41 A.J.I.L. 172, 220. The United Kingdom was not in breach of the Kellogg-Briand Pact when it declared war on Germany in 1939 because of the invasion of Poland by Germany, see Oppenheim, *International Law*, vol. II, p. 183.
7. See Churchill, *The Second World War*, vol. VI, Cassell & Co., London, 1954, p. 181 and pp. 182 et seq. for the problems of voting in the proposed Security Council. The background to the drafting of the Charter is well described in Brownlie, *International Law and the Use of Force by States*, chap. XIII.
8. The permanent members are China, France, U.S.S.R, U.K. and U.S.A.
9. Article 25 U.N. Charter.
10. Article 2(3) requires all members to 'settle their international disputes by peaceful means'. Article 2(4) would now reflect customary international law. The article is probably also an example of *jus cogens*; a treaty is void in so far as it conflicts with a rule of *jus cogens*. See Article 53 of the Vienna Convention on the Law of Treaties 1969. The purposes of the United Nations can be found in Article 1 of the Charter.
10a. (1986) 15 I.L.M. 1023, para. 228.
11. D'Amato, *Israeli Air Strike upon Iraqi Nuclear Reactor* (1983) 77 A.J.I.L. 584; Shoham, *The Israeli Raid upon the Iraqi Nuclear Reactor and the Right of Self-Defence* (1985) 109 Mil. L.R. 109. The raid was condemned, however, by the Security Council G.A. Resolution 36/27, 13 November 1981. See also the 1974 Definition of Aggression (*infra*), Article 3(6). The British government also argued along these lines concerning Operation Retail in the *Corfu Channel Case* (1949) I.C.J. 4, but the judgment of the court did not support it; see Brownlie, *International Law and The Use of Force by States*, p. 266, and see also p. 268 'if there is an ambiguity the principle of effectiveness should be applied'.
11a. (1949) I.C.J. Reps. 4, 35.
12. G.A. Resn. 2625(XXV)(1970) and G.A. Resn. 3314(XXIX) 1974.
13. The definition is not on all fours with Article 2(4). It does not, for instance, mention a *threat* of force and it speaks of 'sovereignty' along with territorial integrity or political independence. For a criticism, see Stone, *Hopes and Loopholes in the 1974 Definition of Aggression* (1977) 71 A.J.I.L. 224.
14. This was at a time when international law considered the use of force by States in an entirely different light. The British government totally rejected the unilateral action by Israel to change the status of the Golan Heights and considered that Israel was bound by the Fourth Geneva Convention of 1949 in respect of all the territories seized by it since 1967. Statement in Security Council, January 1982 (1982) 53 B.Y.I.L. 530-531. A treaty by which the victor compelled the vanquished to transfer to it parts of its territory would be void; Article 52, Vienna Convention on the Law of Treaties 1969.
15. For an analysis of this claim based on a derivitive right through Spain and Argentine actions from the early nineteenth century, see Rubin in Coll and Arend (eds), *The Falklands War*, Allen & Unwin, Boston, 1985, chap. 2. See also the views of the British government in (1982) 53 B.Y.I.L. 432; (1983) 54 B.Y.I.L. 453-454. A very full statement was made in a letter to the President of the Security Council by the British representative, see (1983) 54 B.Y.I.L. 456-461, and for further comment, *ibid.*, pp. 461-468. For an account of the Argentine case, see Acevedo, *The U.S. Measures Against Argentina Resulting from the Malvinas Conflict* (1984) 78 A.J.I.L. 323. The history of South Georgia is quite

different. For an early essay, see Waldock, *Disputed Sovereignty in the Falkland Islands Dependencies* (1948) 25 B.Y.I.L. 311. The British government offered to refer the dispute to the International Court of Justice, but Argentina declined, H.C. Deb. vol. 21, col. 481, Written Answers, 8 April 1982.

16. Debate, 21 May 1982, Security Council. See (1982) 53 B.Y.I.L. 350-351. The British also argued that the Argentine action was contrary to the rights of self-determination of the inhabitants of the Falkland Islands, was contrary to Article 73 of the Charter and was in breach of the Rio Treaty of 1947. Their continued presence on the islands, it was argued also, was a breach of Resolution 502 of the Security Council which called for a withdrawal of Argentine forces.

17. For a very detailed account see Dieguez, *The Grenada Intervention: 'Illegal' in Form, Sound as Policy* in Redden (ed.), *Modern Legal Systems Cyclopedia*, vol. 7, Hein & Co., New York, 1985, p. 277. See also Vagts, *International Law under Time Pressure: Grading the Grenada Take-Home Examination* (1984) 78 A.J.I.L. 169, and compare Boyle *et al.*, *International Lawlessness in Grenada* (1984) 78 A.J.I.L. 172. For a general account, see Gilmore, *The Grenada Intervention, Analysis and Documentation* (1984), Mansell Publishing Ltd, London.

18. The veto power is granted by Article 27(3) of the Charter. The Security Council was able to mount a campaign against North Korea in 1950 due to the absence of the representative of the U.S.S.R. from the Security Council. On his return the veto was used and the issue passed to the General Assembly.

19. Reisman, *Coercion and Self-Determination: Construing Article 2(4)* (1984) 78 A.J.I.L. 642 and for comments on this model, see Schacter, *The Legality of Pro-Democratic Invasion* (1984) 78 A.J.I.L. 645, and D'Amato, *The Legal Basis for the U.S. Position* (1985) 79 A.J.I.L. 659.

20. See Brownlie, *International Law and the Use of Force by States* (1963), pp. 269-280. See also Article 1 of the U.N. Charter which lists as the first purpose of the U.N. the maintenance of international peace and security. See also Article 5, General Assembly Definition of Aggression 1974 (note 12 above).

21. *Ibid.*, p. 279. See also Meeker, *Memorandum on the Legality of United States Participation in the Defence of Vietnam* (1966) 60 A.J.I.L. 565.

22. Judgment of the International Military Tribunal (1947) 41 A.J.I.L. 172, 205.

23. During the Canadian rebellion in 1837 the rebels were supported by an American ship, the *Caroline*. The British seized the ship whilst she was in an American port, set her on fire and sent her over the Niagara Falls. A national of the United States was killed. Subsequently, the American authorities arrested one McLeod, a British national, for taking part in the *Caroline* incident. The exchanges between Webster (U.S.A.) and Fox (U.K.) gave rise to the famous formulation of self-defence in international law. For an account of the history of the event, see Jennings, *The Caroline and McLeod Cases* (1938) 32 A.J.I.L. 82.

24. H.L. Deb. vol. 199, col. 1358.

25. See (1976) 14 I.L.M. 1224 et seq. For the general principle see Bowett, *Self-Defence in International Law* (1958), Manchester U.P.

26. See the *Mayaguez* incident of 1975 in Paust, *The Seizure and Recovery of the Mayaguez*, 85 Yale L.J. 774.

27. For a good discussion of the alleged right of intervention to protect nationals, see Riggs, *The Grenada Intervention: A Legal Analysis* (1985) 109 Mil. L.R.1. For a discussion of the competing views in respect of anticipatory self-defence, see Shoham, *The Israeli Raid Upon the Iraqi Nuclear Reactor and the Right of Self-Defence* (1985) 109 Mil. L.R. 191. For an analysis of the Libyan raid in 1986, see Thornberry, *International Law and its Discontents: The U.S. Raid on Libya* (1986) VIII Liverpool L.R. 53. For an analysis of the principle of non-intervention see the *Nicaragua v. United States Case* at para. 202.

28. See Bowett, *Reprisals Involving Recourse to Armed Force* (1972) 66 A.J.I.L.1. A useful table of incidents is included in the paper at pp. 33-36.

29. See Meeker, *The Legality of United States Participation in the Defence of Vietnam* (note 21 above) and Stevenson, *United States Military Action in Cambodia Questions of International Law*, in Falk, *The Vietnam War and International Law*, vol. 3 (1972), Princeton, Princeton University Press, p. 23.

30. Moreover, there was, it was argued, a difference between action being taken by the U.N. and by regional agencies. See, generally, Wright, *The Cuban Quarantine* (1963) 57 A.J.I.L.

and by regional agencies. See, generally, Wright, *The Cuban Quarantine* (1963) 57 A.J.I.L. 546, and Owen, *The Politics of Defence* (1972), Jonathan Cape, London, chap. 3. For a detailed analysis and for the Memorandum of the Department of State, *Legal Basis for the Quarantine of Cuba*, see Chayes, *The Cuban Missile Crisis* (1974), Oxford, O.U.P.

31. Moore, *Grenada and the International Double Standard* (1984) 78 A.J.I.L. 145, 153.

32. For an interpretation of 'enforcement action', see *Certain Expenses of the United Nations* (1962) I.C.J. Rep. 151 (Advisory Opinion). See also Akehurst, *Enforcement Action by Regional Agencies* (1967) 42 B.Y.I.L. 175, who discusses the Cuban Missile Crisis and the legality of the quarantine at pp. 197-203.

33. Compare Vagts, *Legal Basis for the OECS Mission*, (1984) 78 A.J.I.L. 753 with Boyle *et al.*, *International Lawlessness in Grenada* (1984) 78 A.J.I.L. 172. See also Dieguez, *The Grenada Intervention: 'Illegal' in Form, Sound as Policy* (1984) (see note 17 above), who shows that the constitutional position of the Governor General was by no means clear.

34. Whether NATO is a regional arrangement within Chapter VII of the United Nations Charter has given rise to debate. See, generally, Baxter, *Constitutional Forms and Some Legal Problems of International Military Command* (1952) 29 B.Y.I.L. 325 at 337 et seq.

35. Security Council Resolution of 7 July 1950.

36. This resolution has become known as the Uniting for Peace Resolution 1950.

37. Bowett, *United Nations Forces* (1964), London, Stevens & Sons, also deals with the arguments of those who deny to the force the imprimateur of the United Nations, see chap. 3. For the definitive account of U.N. peacekeeping, see Higgins, *United Nations Peacekeeping*, 4 vols. (vol. 4, 1981), Oxford U.P.

38. *Certain Expenses of the United Nations* (1962) I.C.J. Reps. 151. It should be noted that 'peacekeeping forces' may be established outside the framework of the United Nations. The Multinational Force in Lebanon created in 1981 by agreement between Lebanon and the participating countries (including now, the United Kingdom) is an example.

39. See Franck, *Who Killed Article 2(4)? (1970)* 63 A.J.I.L. 809, and Henkin, *The Reports of the Death of Article 2(4) Are Greatly Exaggerated* (1971) 65 A.J.I.L. 544. Perkins expresses the view that 'Most Americans I believe, have concluded that an action that flouts international law is likely to be a foreign policy disaster ... there is a power in law, and for lack of that power an action may fail', *The Prudent Peace, Law as a Foreign Policy* (1981), Chicago, Univ. of Chicago Press.

8

The Methods and Means of Warfare

'The laws of war belong to a past age and except for a few minor matters of no consequence, it is futile to attempt to revive them ... War has got beyond the control of law.' Fenwick (1949).

If 'war' is properly described as 'a contention between two or more States through their armed forces, for the purpose of overpowering each other and imposing such conditions of peace as the victor pleases',[1] then it might be asked, why should they not unleash their full might against each other so as to enable the strongest to win? If a State were to hold back from using its undoubted military muscle at a particular time, it might be thought, it runs the risk of losing or at the least it is doing nothing more than prolonging the suffering. Modern warfare is rarely so simple and the development of the idea that the fighting man himself was not to be wholly sublimated to the cause for which he fought led to the adoption of certain restraints in the conduct of war. There is no doubt that these owed something to the concept of chivalry, practised by those of a higher status than the common soldier, which finds its expression today in the restriction of perfidious and treacherous action and in the emergence of a humanitarian concern for the victims of war.[2]

The 'just war' theorists had preached a harsh doctrine, one in which the supposed ends had justified the means and where the adversary was seen as not only an enemy of the State but also of God. The demise of this doctrine paved the way for a fresh approach to the way that war should be fought and the standards adopted were to be applicable to all belligerents, no matter what the cause of the conflict. What had really been achieved, therefore, was a separation of the cause of war from the conduct of war, the *jus ad bellum* from the *jus in bello*.

The very first Geneva Convention in 1864 was concerned with the wounded and sick in battle but it was closely followed by the St. Petersburg Declaration of 1868, which opened with the words 'Considering that the progress of civilization should have the effect of alleviating as much as possible the calamities of war'. It then went on to declare that 'the only legitimate object which States should endeavour to accomplish during war is

110

to weaken the military forces of the enemy'.[3] 'This object', it continued, 'would be exceeded by the employment of arms which uselessly aggravate the sufferings of disabled men, or render their death inevitable' and that the use of such arms would 'be contrary to the laws of humanity.'

In short compass, therefore, the St. Petersburg Declaration had concentrated the minds of those seeking to place restraints on the actual conduct of war on the object of the whole business, to weaken the military forces of the enemy, but that the power to do so was not an unlimited one. The varied attempts to keep within these parameters illustrates the place of law as a means of restraining belligerents from conduct, the pursuit of which may have very distinct and direct military advantages. The measure of the task can be compared with Geneva law which is concerned with the protection of those who can have no further, or indeed any, part to play in the conflict, the wounded and sick, prisoners of war and civilians. Law-making in this field is comparatively easy, since there is usually no desire on the part of combatants to kill or injure these people and the law can therefore lay down fairly detailed regulations for their treatment. By and large, Geneva law is respected by the belligerents, not least because of the element of reciprocity and, in a world where war is a major news item, an unwillingness, in propaganda terms, to shoot oneself in the foot. Hague law (which is taken to refer to the law concerning the methods and means of warfare), on the other hand, must take into account military necessity if it is not to be totally unrealistic. Before the First World War some German writers spoke of the doctrine of *Kriegsraeson*, by which the necessities of war overrode the laws of war. This meant, in other words, that if the object of war could be achieved by illegal means, it was permissible to use them. A moment's reflection will show the danger of such a view and how it could be totally destructive of all attempts to limit the conduct of warfare.[4] This was also the view of various war crimes tribunals in which it was accepted that Hague law had already taken into account military necessity in formulating the rules of warfare and there was therefore no scope for it to be invoked as a defence to a breach of the law.[5] To kill those *hors de combat* in order to avoid being subsequently found and captured, could not be justified by military necessity, unless one was prepared to grant merely conditional protection to the victims of war. To shoot the survivors of a ship sunk by a submarine so that they could not be rescued could not therefore be justified by the military necessity of keeping the presence of a submarine in that area secret.[6] But in relation to property the Fourth Hague Convention of 1907 expressly permits destruction if it be 'imperatively demanded by the necessities of war' and it thereby permits an accused to argue that the destruction he caused was justified by military necessity.[7]

Restraints on the Conduct of Combatants

The basic principles of the actual conduct of combatants towards each other is to be found in Articles 22 to 28 of the Regulations annexed to the Hague Convention IV of 1907 along with Part III of the First Protocol 1977. Article 22 provides what is probably the overriding norm, that 'the right of belligerents to adopt means of injuring the enemy is not unlimited' and Article 23 goes on to declare, *inter alia*, that it is forbidden to 'employ arms, projectiles, or material calculated to cause unnecessary suffering'.[8] In so far as these articles are relevant to the type of weapons that are prohibited by the laws of war, they will be discussed later.

Article 23 proscribes killing or wounding treacherously, declaring that no quarter will be given and making improper use of a flag of truce, of the national flag or of the military insignia and uniform of the enemy, as well as the distinctive emblem of the Red Cross, while the following Article expressly permits ruses of war. In practice, the boundary is between the ruse of war, which is permissible, and perfidious action, which is not.[9] Clear instances of the ruse of war are the use of camouflage, constructing dummy airfields, transmitting bogus signals and so on, but the use of treachery would not be. The *Manual of Military Law* gives the following graphic example: 'Do not fire, we are friends', and then firing.[10] The feigning of protected status by, for example, shamming death or injury, and then using weapons when the enemy has been induced to believe that this is the true state of affairs, is described in the First Protocol of 1977 as perfidy. A certain measure of good faith as between combatants is therefore required.

Wearing the uniform of the enemy can be a very effective way of infiltrating his lines, but the question that arises is whether it is prohibited by the laws of war as perfidy or whether it is legitimate ruse. The Regulations annexed to the Fourth Hague Convention prohibit the *improper use* of the uniform of the enemy, but do not attempt to define what would be considered as improper. The First Protocol 1977 does by prohibiting the use, *inter alia*, of uniforms of adverse parties while engaging in attacks or in order to shield, favour, protect or impede military operations (Article 39(2)). This is probably no more than a restatement of what would have been considered to be customary international law; that those engaged in actual military operations should wear uniform not only to distinguish themselves from the civilian population but also as between themselves.[11] Where the enemy's uniform is worn merely in order to escape, there would seem to be no improper conduct, but where it is used to obtain information this could be considered as spying. These issues were raised in the case of Otto Skorzeny. Otto Skorzeny was in charge of a number of German soldiers who broke through the United States lines in the Ardennes in 1944, while wearing American uniforms (along with German parachute overalls) and driving captured American vehicles. Following capture, some of Skorzeny's men were shot summarily and Skorzeny himself was later captured and tried for committing by this action a war crime, but he was acquitted.[12] This case well illustrates the legal difficulties posed if members of the armed forces wear the enemy's uniform; the men summarily shot were illegally executed, since if considered to be spies they were entitled to a trial and Skorzeny's acquittal suggests that the particular use he made of the enemy's uniform was not 'improper'.[12a] Had he used any weapon while so disguised, there would hardly have been any doubt as to his guilt.

During or at the conclusion of a battle the use of a white flag to indicate that one belligerent wishes to negotiate with another is an accepted procedure and is dealt with in the Regulations annexed to the Fourth Hague Convention of 1907. The bearer of the flag is entitled to protection, along with his entourage, but he need not be received by the other belligerent. It has become common practice that the hoisting of a white flag is synonymous with the desire to surrender and its use to lure an enemy into believing falsely that this is the case would be considered as perfidy.[13]

Restraints on the Use of Particular Weapons

It will be recalled that arms which cause unnecessary suffering or superfluous injury are proscribed by the Regulations annexed to the Hague Convention of 1907 and by the First Protocol 1977. The 1907 Convention draws particular attention to the employment of poison and poisoned weapons, but it is in other conventions that international law has made its most valiant attempts to control the use of particular weapons.

Gas Weapons

The use of poisonous gas during the First World War led to sustained calls for its prohibition, which was achieved, along with a ban on bacteriological methods, by the 1925 Geneva Gas Protocol. Whether this was effective or not, it is clear that gas was not used as a weapon during the Second World War. A. J. P. Taylor considers it most likely that this was because of the simple calculation that, 'weight for weight, high explosive was more effective than gas in killing people'.[14] Be this as it may, the United Nations reported that in 1986 Iraq had used toxic gas against Iranian targets and it is believed that this is the first time that a country has actually been named for violating the 1925 Gas Protocol.[15] Bacteriological weapons are of a much more hazardous nature, since they have scope to affect the civilian population indiscriminately and would therefore be contrary to the laws of war for this very reason.

It does seem somewhat surprising that the whole field of chemical and bacteriological weapons should be on such a loose legal footing. A literal reading of it would throw up difficulties over whether it applied to any weapon giving off toxic or asphyxiating gases, such as high explosives, or whether it applied to biological agents that affect only animals or vegetable matter. The answer would seem to be that these are covered by the Protocol, but there is scope for disagreement.[16] The Vietnam War showed the use by the United States of defoliants and herbicide sprays on a large scale, but the legality of this practice was doubtful, since in sufficient concentration it could prove hazardous to the health not only of combatants but also to the civilian population. Again, a number of States, including the United Kingdom, entered reservations to the 1925 Protocol to the effect that they would not consider themselves bound by it if their adversaries used such weapons against them. As a counter to this some would say that the 1925 Gas Protocol merely reflects customary international law and it is therefore binding on all States as a result, but this still leaves unclear the status of those weapons said to be prohibited on a wide interpretation of the Protocol. The real answer to the problem of chemical, or gas, weapons would be to secure a ban on their manufacture, stockpiling or acquisition, a move that has already been made, to great effect, with bacteriological weapons.[17]

Fire Weapons

Flamethrowers would appear to be an horrific weapon if used against combatants, but against property their use would seem to call for little atttention. It seems clear that by analogy with existing legal controls to use a flamethrower against a human target would produce unnecessary suffering or superfluous injury. Added to this is the likelihood that the death of the victim will be rendered inevitable and his suffering will be prolonged.[18] The use of napalm, a form of jellied petroleum which adheres to the skin as it burns, was widespread in the Vietnam War (it was also discovered in the Argentinian arsenal captured by the British in the Falklands War) and, it is suggested, its use was contrary to the 1925 Gas Protocol,[18a] either because it came within the proscription of all 'analogous liquids' or because it also produced an asphyxiating effect on the victim. In addition, the same analogies could be applied as with flamethrowers, and there could, of course, be no justification for deployment of napalm either directly or indiscriminately against civilians.[18b]

Nuclear Weapons

There is no specific treaty banning the use of nuclear weapons with the result that any argument supporting its illegality must be by way of analogy with existing controls on the use of weapons. The argument that if nuclear weapons are ever used it will have been a purely academic exercise to consider beforehand their legality in international law must be put to one side, since an all-out nuclear exchange is not the only possible scenario. The use of such a weapon against a limited target such as a ship, for instance, would raise many of the same issues. A 'nuclear weapon' is defined in Article 5 of the Treaty of Tlatelolco 1967 as 'any device which is capable of releasing nuclear energy in an uncontrolled manner and which has a group of characteristics that are appropriate for use with warlike purposes'. The main effects will be blast, heat and radiation of both short and long-term effect, as was shown by the bombs dropped in Japan in 1945. It may seem strange that someone injured by the atomic bombs dropped on Hiroshima and Nagasaki should be able to sue the Japanese government, but such a claim, known as *the Shimoda Case*, was brought in the Tokyo District Court in 1955.[19] It is of particular importance, since it is the only time that a court, whether national or international, has had to consider directly the question of the legality of the use of such weapons. Although the court held that the Japanese government was not liable, as a matter of national law, to the claimants, it came down firmly to the view that the use of the atomic bomb against its cities in 1945 was a breach of international law. There exists the temptation to read into this decision that it declared illegal the use of nuclear weapons in any circumstances, but it clearly did not since it was concerned only with the facts before it. These facts suggested that the two cities were undefended, were not military objectives and were populated mostly by civilians. The court gave 'short shrift' to the argument that the bombing was legitimate and was necessary to bring the war to an end and that it saved the lives of Allied servicemen who would have suffered if an invasion of Japan had been necessary. To accept such a view would have been to move towards the concept of total war and to approve of any belligerent act that would bring a war to an end. Military necessity would have triumphed over the attempts to restrain the conduct of war.

A number of authors argue, by drawing upon existing conventions, such as the St. Petersburg Declaration 1868, the Hague Rules of 1907, the Geneva Gas Protocol 1925, the Genocide 1948, and the Geneva Conventions 1949, that the use of nuclear weapons would clearly infringe international law.[20] The General Assembly has also condemned their use as a violation of the United Nations Charter[21] and there would seem to be little doubt that they are tainted with illegality although there may be some conceivable situations in which their use might be condoned. The first and most obvious case is in response to a nuclear attack. This does not get us any further with the issue of legality, since a State that uses a nuclear weapon by way of retaliation, kind for kind, may either claim that it is legal to do so or that, although illegal, it is justified as a reprisal (assuming that it does not attack indiscriminately the civilian population).[22] The view of the British government is that the NATO alliance would not use nuclear weapons unless attacked,[23] and if attacked by a non-nuclear weapon State it would not reply with nuclear weapons, unless the attacker was acting in association with a nuclear weapon State.[24]

A further ground of justification put forward by Oppenheim for using a nuclear weapon would be if an enemy violated 'the law of war on a scale so vast as to put himself altogether outside the orbit of considerations of humanity and compassion'. He gives the example of Nazi Germany and suggests that if it 'had become established beyond all reasonable doubt that Germany was engaged in a systematic plan of putting to death millions of civilians in occupied territory, the use of the atomic bomb might have been justifiable as a deterrent instrument of punishment'.[25] One of the difficulties with this position is that the separation of truth from propaganda in time of war is notoriously difficult, with the truth really only emerging at the end of a war when individual incidents are pieced together. In any event, such action could only realistically be contemplated against a non-nuclear State and one might well wonder how the effects of using it could be confined to those responsible for the alleged atrocities. Would an atomic bomb dropped on the centre of Berlin have prevented the crimes for which it was dropped and have brought respect for the laws of war?

The omission of a reference to nuclear weapons in conventions dealing with the laws of war reflects no more than *realpolitik*, and it is a realisation that while they exist a treaty to ban them in the event of war would be meaningless. Even a treaty to ban their first use is unlikely to be supported. The British view is that 'no reliance could be placed on the provisions of such a treaty. Verification would be impossible. It is better to reduce the number of nuclear weapons.'[26]

Environmental Damage

Damage to the environment during warfare became a reality when artillery was first used, but the wars of this century have produced damage on a vast scale. From the battlefields of the First World War to the deliberate laying waste of large areas in the Vietnam War, the path of progress of military technology threatens the environment as much as it does those who have to live in it during and after the war has ended. The Vietnam War is an example of how military attention was focused towards the environment as a direct, and not merely an incidental, target. This happened because of a combination of factors. First, the United States found themselves fighting a guerrilla-type enemy who could merge into the surrounding countryside with ease and who often failed to distinguish themselves from the civilian population. Secondly, the use of massive firepower to strike at what was perceived to be the enemy was extremely economical for United States forces. It was clearly not acceptable to allow American casualties to continue increasing at a time when the war was proving very unpopular and so the answer seemed to be in the weapons that would 'clear the ground' rather than by using troops to do so.

Whatever the reasons, there is clear evidence that American forces used various means to achieve this object. There was, for instance, the 'Daisycutter', a large bomb dropped in South Vietnam to establish clearings for fire-base helicopter landing areas and which had the effect of deforesting an area of about a quarter of a mile radius and, of course, large-scale bombing, the craters from which caused much arable and timber land to be destroyed. The use of chemical herbicides (Agents Orange, White and Blue, depending on whether the target was forest vegetation, or rice) was extensive, but clearing the land of vegetation by the so-called 'Rome Plows' may have produced even more extensive destruction. Finally, there were attempts to modify the weather by seeding clouds to increase dramatically the rainfall and thereby to cause flooding of 'the network of roadways constituting the Ho Chi Minh trail'.[27] It is interesting to note that at the time there were no specific treaty provisions to prohibit any of these activities, although it is difficult to argue that any of them is a legitimate method of warfare. Chemical herbicides could easily be brought within the regime of the 1925 Geneva Gas Protocol, particularly in the light of the 1969 interpretation given to it by the General Assembly,[28] while the others could be considered objectionable in so far as they attack indiscriminately the civilian population. At the end of the Vietnam War it was not surprising to hear a chorus of pleas, from the United States Senate as much as from anyone else, for the international community to get down to the task of creating a legal framework to deal with this new method of warfare.

The result of this concern was the adoption of the United Nations Convention on the Prohibition of Military or Any Other Hostile Use of Environmental Modification Techniques 1977. The convention is very short and it requires those States that are parties to it to undertake not to engage in military or any other hostile use of environmental modification techniques having widespread, long-lasting or severe effects.[29] The whole basis of the convention is the prohibition on using the environment as a weapon and as such it would now catch actions such as the American attempts to modify the weather in Vietnam, assuming that the effects of that activity were widespread, long-lasting or severe. It would also catch an attempt to modify the weather, or in any other way, to produce a drought or an earthquake.

The methods and means of war that actually cause damage to the environment are dealt with in the First Protocol 1977 Additional to the Geneva Conventions 1949. Article 35(3) prohibits the employment of methods or means of warfare which are intended, or may be expected, to cause widespread, long-term and severe damage to the natural environment. It may well be that some or all of the American practices against the environment in Vietnam described above would now come within the parameters of this article.

It is difficult to imagine circumstances by which a strategic nuclear bomb would not cause widespread, long-lasting and severe damage to the natural environment, especially if it has the effect of producing the so-called nuclear winter.[30]

Other Conventional Weapons

Following the First Protocol of 1977, the United Nations sought international agreement to ban certain types of conventional weapons and success was achieved with the 1981 Conventional Weapons Convention. Protocol I to this Convention prohibits the use of any weapon, the primary effect of which is to injure by fragments that escape detection by X-rays in the human body; it is a good example of a weapon that can cause unnecessary suffering. The main significance of this convention is in its attempt to control certain weapons that have the effect of injuring soldier and civilian alike and it is discussed later.

New Weapons

The laws of war have achieved much since 1977 in establishing some framework to the principles in the Hague Rules that the means which belligerents might choose of injuring the enemy are not unlimited and that they must not employ weapons that cause unnecessary suffering. The whole problem of controls on the use of weapons is that a horrifying weapon of today is usually outpaced by a weapon of tomorrow; the atomic bomb dropped on Hiroshima in 1945 can stand no comparison with the nuclear weapons of today.[31] Argument that a new weapon is covered by the terms of a convention, drawn up at a time when that particular weapon could not have been foreseen, invariably leads to disagreement over interpretation. It is therefore of considerable significance that the First Protocol 1977, in Article 36, directs attention to new weapons. States are required to consider, when they develop or acquire a new weapon or adopt a new means or method of warfare, whether, if they used it, they would be in breach of international law. By drawing attention not only to a new weapon but also a possible new use to which an existing weapon is to be put (a new method or means of warfare), both sides of the problem are considered. It was, after all, not the use of new weapons that caused such damage to the environment in Vietnam, but the use to which existing weapons were put. This article has the merit of requiring States to consider, in advance, the effect of their new developments, but, of course, if it does not do so, there is little that the international community can do.[31a]

Target Restraints

It was a clear rule of customary international law, stemming at least from the St. Petersburg Declaration of 1868, that the civilian population and individual civilians were not to be attacked and that combatants should direct their attacks only against military objectives. In the nature of things, however, military objectives are rarely located so conveniently that civilians and non-military property are at no risk from the attack. In reality, therefore, the laws of war have had to call upon belligerents to respect the principle of proportionality, that incidental damage caused should be in proportion to the military advantage gained. The greatest danger faced by civilians was in the aerial bombing of towns and cities, but a war fought in a highly populated area could pose problems no less serious.

The Regulations annexed to the Fourth Hague Convention 1907 pinpointed one problem, that of bombarding undefended towns and buildings, which it prohibited. In a sense this was an easy rule to adopt, since the undefended place would not be in the immediate battle area and therefore a restraint on a belligerent would hardly hamper his immediate military plans. It might also be considered that there is no military necessity to attack an undefended town; military necessity can be seen here to be a factor in limiting, rather than in justifying, an action. It was on this ground, *inter alia*, that the *Shimoda Case* based its decision, that the bombing of Hiroshima and Nagasaki was contrary to international law.

When it comes to imposing restraints about what belligerents may or may not attack, the laws of war are taken to the outer limits of their ability to control the conduct of war. It is here that the cry of military necessity is the strongest and the claims of humanity the weakest. The First Protocol 1977 and the Conventional Weapons Convention 1981 make considerable advances in limiting the right of belligerents to select targets, the destruction of which would have a disproportionate effect on the civilian population or in using a particular weapon that would harm soldier and civilian alike. The general importance of these conventions is that they impose restraints in the battle, or front-line area, and not merely at the rear.

The First Protocol of 1977 has much to say about restraint where the target is located on land. Article 52 makes it plain that attacks are to be limited to military objectives, which it then goes on to describe as objectives that make an effective contribution to military action and, where they are put out of action, a definite military advantage would have been gained. An ammunition dump, for instance, would clearly be a legitimate target, but so also would be a building in which a sniper was operating, if there were no other feasible means to stop him. On the other hand, a building that is making no effective contribution to military action and where there are no military advantages to be gained from its destruction should not be attacked; there is no need to do so. What, though, of a retreating army that destroys buildings in order to prevent their use by its adversary? Examples of this tactic can be found in the practice of the retreating German Army in Russia and Norway. What has to be borne in mind here is proportion; the buildings may, in these circumstances, amount to military objectives, but the Fourth Geneva Convention 1949 permits such destruction only if it is rendered absolutely necessary by military operations (Article 147, and see Article 23(g) Hague Rules 1907). If the destruction had been committed by the British

Army in 1940 along the south coast of England in order to prevent the Germans being able to use the buildings, had they invaded, the matter would be entirely different, since international law is generally silent on the rights of a State to undertake warlike activities within its own boundaries.[32]

The civilian population must not be attacked indirectly, by attacking objects indispensable to their survival, such as agricultural areas for the production of foodstuffs or their livestock with the deliberate aim of starving them or of making them move away.[32a] These provisions are closely linked with those dealing with weapons that cause damage to the environment, discussed above, and would now make the conduct of a Vietnam-type war difficult unless those involved make a deliberate decision to flout the laws of war (or are not a party to this 1977 Protocol).

The 'Dam Busters' is a popular story of the air raids that took place during the Second World War against the Mohne and Eder Dams, which 'supplied the industries of the Ruhr, and fed a wide area of fields, rivers, and canals'.[33] Such a raid would now be contrary to Article 56 of the First Protocol 1977, concerned with works and installations containing dangerous forces. There was no doubt but that the German dams were military objectives, but the effect of attacking them was, as the Protocol graphically puts it, to release dangerous forces and so to cause severe losses among the civilian population. The same arguments would apply, of course, to attacks upon nuclear power generating stations, the modern equivalent of the Mohne and Eder Dams.

If we assume that an army takes its obligation seriously under the laws of war and refrains from attacking civilians or their property, there is one more basic rule that its commanders must obey, which is that indiscriminate attacks are prohibited.[34] Here lies a real problem for the commander. He must press home his military objectives but at the same time he must weigh up the consequences to the civilian population and their property. If some civilian damage is almost certainly going to result, the question of when it becomes unacceptable is a value judgment. A commander may therefore be faced with the problem of weighing up the destruction of an enemy tank against civilian lives, a problem by no means new. The law attempts to solve the conundrum by relying on the concept of proportionality. Let us assume in the example given above that to destroy the tank, the town in which it is located is totally destroyed by artillery fire. Here the incidental damage to civilians and their property clearly outweighs the concrete and direct military advantage gained (destruction of the tank). The attack would therefore be prohibited by the 1977 Protocol and the commander involved, who has a duty under Article 57 to take precautions before an attack to avoid such an effect, would have committed a grave breach of it.[35]

When fighting in an area in which injury to civilians cannot be discounted, a further problem arises. This concerns the effects of particular weapons which cannot distinguish between combatant and civilian, such as a mine.

The mine may be a very useful addition to the soldier's armoury in defending territory from a surprise attack, but its use, along with certain other weapons, is now controlled by the 1981 United Nations Convention on Prohibitions or Restrictions on the Use of Certain Conventional Weapons (Protocol II).

The 1981 Convention supplements the First Protocol of 1977 by concentrating on the use of certain weapons that have a potentially indiscriminate effect, such as the mine, booby trap and incendiary weapon, in so far as they cause injury to civilians but not combatants. Mines and booby traps must not be used indiscriminately; for example, where the mine cannot be directed at a specific military objective or, if it can, the incidental loss of civilian life would outweigh the concrete and direct military advantage anticipated. Where these weapons are used all feasible precautions are to be taken to protect civilians from their effects. The Convention draws a distinction between combat zones and hinterlands and directs its attention only to the latter. A consequence of this approach is to offer little protection to civilians who happen to be in an area in which combat between ground forces is taking place.[36] One can only assume that this is because the drafters of the Convention assumed that civilians would not stay in such an area and that they wished to give proper regard to military necessities. Remotely delivered mines, i.e. those dropped by an aircraft or by an artillery shell, can only be used within military objectives and then only if their location can be accurately recorded and they have been fitted with a device that neutralises them after a period of time.

The Falklands War showed very clearly the menace to civilians that mines can cause if their location has not been accurately recorded. Large tracts of land have had to be placed out of bounds and the risks in clearing them are considered to be too great. A moment's reflection serves to illustrate the problems that would have been caused had they been laid in a highly populated area. It was for this reason that the 1981 Convention imposes an obligation on those who lay mines, or booby traps, to record their location and to pass on this information to those who, like the British in the Falklands, seek to make the area safe.

Another aspect of the protection offered to civilians in the zone of military operations was also seen in the Falklands War. This was the neutralised zone which is intended to shelter civilians and the wounded and sick from the hostilities taking place around them. The battle for Port Stanley clearly posed a considerable risk to the civilian population, since there were few places in which they could seek shelter, not only from the fighting but also from the South Atlantic winter. The International Committee of the Red Cross proposed to the British and Argentine governments the creation of a neutralised zone in an area of about 5 acres around the cathedral in Port Stanley; the zone was established in June 1982.[37]

The modern laws of war place great emphasis upon separating combatant from civilian and providing protection to the civilian and those members of the armed forces who, because they are prisoners of war or are wounded and sick, are no longer able to take any part in the hostilities. That combatants should not make civilians a target in war has been shown, but what of the supposed right to attack protected persons by way of a reprisal?

A reprisal is, in essence, a retaliation by one belligerent against another for an alleged breach of the laws of war and is in itself an act contrary to those laws. It has been argued that its adoption, or threat of adoption, by a belligerent is a means of enforcing the laws of war,[38] but there can be little doubt that such means soon degenerate into general lawlessness. Strategic bombing by the R.A.F. of Germany and the conduct of unrestricted submarine warfare during the Second World War were both claimed to be justified as acts of reprisal, with the result that from all sides the law was placed in abeyance.[39]

Even if it is accepted that under customary international law proportionate reprisals are permitted as between combatants, the Geneva Conventions of 1949 and the 1977 Protocols to them prohibit the taking of reprisals against all those protected under their terms. There is, therefore, no right in international law to kill prisoners of war, the wounded, sick and shipwrecked or civilians merely because one's adversary has done so, and indeed such acts would amount to grave breaches of the conventions.[40] It might be thought that all would applaud this protection of those who are not involved in the fighting, but consider the following problem. State A, which is at war with State B, in defiance of the laws of war bombs B's capital city causing considerable loss of life among the civilian population. It repeats this activity on a nightly basis and calls are made by the inhabitants of B to retaliate and to bomb A's capital city. The government of B asks its legal adviser whether the laws of war permit it to act by way of a reprisal against A's capital city (it being assumed that both States are parties to the Geneva Conventions and to the First Protocol of 1977). The answer would seem to be in the negative, because to bomb the city would be an illegal act (Article 51 of the Protocol directs that the civilian population shall not be the object of attack). It could not be justified as a reprisal, because of Article 33 of the Fourth Geneva Convention 1949 and Article 51(6) of the Protocol which prohibit reprisal attacks against the civilian population and individual civilians. State B is therefore placed in a dilemma; whether to ignore the laws of war and to bomb A's city, and thereby hope to deter A from continuing its bombing campaign, or to abide by the prohibitions, watch its city being bombed and hope to strike at A by an alternative but legitimate means.

Air Warfare

The development of air warfare as a means of bombing enemy cities was clearly foreseen by H. G. Wells in *The Shape of Things to Come* published in 1933, but it also occupied the minds of those who, after the First World

War, saw its potential as a major weapon of war. Aircraft had, of course, been used in that war, but not as part of a large bomber fleet. With its appearance, the possibility of total war was born in which wars would be fought by whole nations rather than merely between their armed forces. The use of bomber aircraft is perhaps the most likely way in which the civilian population will become victims of war, but it is an activity in which the law (certainly until the First Protocol of 1977) remained virtually silent although not without efforts by the International Committee of the Red Cross. One only needs to consider the statistics from the Second World War. From air raids there were about a quarter of a million British casualties, of whom 60,000 were killed, a figure that represents roughly 15 per cent of all those killed during the war.[41] The Germans lost more than this in one raid, on Dresden in 1945, but the human cost in aircrews was also immense; Churchill puts the losses of both British and American aircrews at over 140,000.[42] Whether it was all worthwhile in bringing the defeat of Germany, has been the subject of much controversy,[43] but of more pressing concern is the legality in international law of the bombing campaigns.

The major characteristic of bombing from the air, which really sets it apart from other means of warfare, is its indiscriminate effect. This need not only be a deliberate policy, where it is really nothing less than terror bombing, but in the state of the art during the Second World War, where bombing was largely conducted at night (except by the Americans) it was virtually inevitable. Indeed, it was clear policy that 'the undermining of the morale of the German people to a point where their capacity for armed resistance is fatally weakened' was one of the main objects of the Allied bombing campaign.[44] The attack on Dresden in February 1945 was to change thinking about the morality of the type of strategic bombing that had led to the destruction of that city. Dresden was to conventional bombing as Hiroshima was to atomic bombing.

Although the Hague Rules of 1907 had made passing reference to air war-fare, it was at The Hague in 1923 that an attempt was made to draw up limits on the use of aircraft in war. The result was what has become known as the Hague Draft Rules of Air Warfare. They never came formally into effect as a treaty, but the *Shimoda Case* in 1955 treated them as reflecting customary international law at the time the atomic bomb was dropped on Hiroshima. Neither Germany nor the Allies took the stand that the indiscriminate bombing of each other's cities was permitted by international law. Rather, the justification was either that the attacks were directed against military objectives and it was regrettable that civilian casualties should occur, or they were by way of reprisal.[45] Articles 22 and 24 of the Draft Hague Air Rules represent an attempt to control bombing of civilians. Article 22 prohibits bombardment for the purpose of terrorising the civilian population or of injuring non-combatants, while Article 24 requires the attack to be limited to a military objective. It goes on to deal specifically with the town or city in which there are military objectives and directs that if they cannot be bombarded without the indiscriminate bombardment of the civilian population, the aircraft must abstain from bombardment. The Casablanca Directive of 1943 showed the morale of the German people to be one of the aims of the Allied bombing campagn, an aim that is at the outer limits of legitimate warfare. Take two possibilities. The first is that 'sleepy villages' and the second is that munitions factories are bombed. In the first case none would doubt that to attack morale in this way would be contrary to international law, but in the second the munitions factory is a military objective since its destruction would constitute a distinct military advantage to the side that bombed it. This case is much more difficult because the air raid has at least the presumption of legitimacy and to bomb the area around the munitions factory would, at the least, deprive the factory worker of his accommodation and, it may be hoped, his desire to be a factory worker.[46]

The modern law of air warfare, such as there is, is now contained in certain provisions of the conventions relating to war on land; the 1925 Gas Protocol, the Geneva Conventions of 1949 (particularly in their banning of reprisals against civilians); and the 1954 Hague Convention for the Protection of Cultural Property. All have some measure of influence, but it is the First Protocol of 1977 that marks the major achievement in regulating this type of warfare. Article 49 makes it plain that the Protocol applies to all attacks from the air against objectives on land, but not otherwise; so, air-to-air combat is not controlled by it. The most relevant parts of the Protocol are those which proscribe the mounting of indiscriminate attacks, which would now include so-called 'saturation bombing', reprisal raids, attacks on civilian objects and on those works and installations containing dangerous forces. In addition, Protocol III to the 1981 United Nations Conventional Weapons Convention spells out very clearly that it is prohibited to make any military objective located within a concentration of civilians the object of attack by air-delivered incendiary weapons.[47] Time alone will tell whether this new law of air warfare will offer any greater protection to the civilian population than did the Hague Draft Air Rules or whether individual governments will perceive the weapon as being of too great a value to its war aims to comply with this new law. The issue, in other words, will revolve around the question, whether sufficient account has been taken of military necessity. It is salutory to note that in very recent times air attacks have taken place against Beirut, Tripoli, and against cities in the Iran-Iraq War with, to some extent, limited objectives, but it is clear that civilian casualties have been caused.

Sea Warfare

Where the law of land warfare, some might argue, has been over-exposed to the lawyer, the conduct of sea war is governed largely by customary international law developed from the practice of States. A number of the conventions drawn up at the Hague in 1907 are concerned with this type of warfare, but their appearance was in advance of the development of the submarine as a weapon of war. The Second Geneva Convention 1949 admittedly deals with the wounded, sick and shipwrecked, which the First Protocol 1977 supplements, but all these treaties are silent about sea-to-sea attacks.[48]

The regime of the seas has recently been the subject of a major revision at the Law of the Sea Conference sponsored by the United Nations. The result of 9 years' bargaining and concessions led to the Montego Bay Convention 1982 which will come into force when there are at least sixty States party to it. It adds, and makes amendments, to the 1958 Geneva Conventions on the Law of the Sea, the Territorial Sea and Contiguous Zone Convention, the High Seas Convention and the Continental Shelf Convention. It is likely that the 1958 Conventions will remain binding on those States that are parties to them for some considerable time, although customary international law has its part to play in recognising that the law does not always remain static. For present purposes the two most important constituents of the law of the sea are the high seas and the territorial sea. The high seas encompass all parts of the sea that are not included in the territorial sea or the inland waters of a State and all States have in the high seas, *inter alia*, the right of freedom of navigation.[49] The territorial sea is that part of the sea adjacent to its coast over which a State may extend its sovereignty.[50] Although the Montego Bay Convention of 1982 permits a coastal State to claim a territorial sea of up to 12 miles in width, many States, including the United Kingdom, have already done so (Territorial Sea Act 1987).

Warships and Merchant Ships

A warship is a ship belonging to the naval forces of a State and bearing the external marks distinguishing warships of its nationality, under the command of an officer duly appointed by the government and whose name appears in the Navy List, and manned by a crew who are under regular naval discipline.[51] A merchant ship can be converted into a warship and so take the benefit of that status if it complies with the main requirements for a warship.[52] Ships of the Royal Fleet Auxiliary Service remain merchant ships, because they are neither commanded by a commissioned officer nor are they manned by a crew subject to naval discipline.[53]

Warships may attack the warships of an adversary, but may not attack an enemy merchant ship, unless it refuses to stop for the purposes of visit and search, is actively resisting, is armed offensively or is acting as an enemy auxiliary. The reason for this right of visit and search is that the high seas are an international highway and neutral states have the right of navigation in order to carry on their trade. Belligerents will wish to assure themselves that the neutral merchant ships they stop on the high seas are not assisting their enemy by carrying contrabrand (goods that each belligerent specifies as being subject to seizure).[54]

Enemy mechant ships may, instead of being attacked, be seized, along with contraband in neutral ships and be brought before a prize court of the captor's State for a judicial decision as to whether the captor is entitled either to the ship itself, or in the case of a neutral, to its cargo.[55] As a general rule the captor is not entitled to sink an enemy merchant ship unless there is virtually no alternative because, for instance, a prize crew cannot be spared or the prize is not seaworthy. In this case the crew and the ship's papers must be placed in safety. This particular aspect of sea warfare is of considerable importance in relation to submarines and is discussed below.

It was common practice during both World Wars for merchant ships to be armed and to resist capture. Indeed, Churchill expressed the view, when discussing the merchant aircraft-carrier, that the 'merchant ship had now (in 1943) taken the offensive against the enemy instead of merely defending itself when attacked. The line between combatant and non-combatant ship, already indistinct, had almost vanished.'[56] The crews of these merchant ships were to be treated, upon capture, as prisoners of war, and not as *francs tireur*, even though they may have engaged in hostilities.[57] This favourable treatment should be compared with the position in land warfare where a civilian (who is not a member of an organised resistance movement) will be treated as an unprivileged belligerent, that is, not entitled to prisoner of war status if he takes part in hostilities. The crew of a merchant ship, on the other hand, remain in private employment, although their employers may be subject to considerable government control and despite the offensive action taken by such ships they do not merely because of that become naval vessels.

Immunity of Certain Ships from Capture

The most important category of ship that is immune both from attack and from capture is the hospital ship. It will be shown in Chapter 12 that a hospital ship may not be used for any military purpose, other than collecting and caring for the wounded, sick and shipwrecked, and that it must not hamper the movements of the combatants. Should these strictures be flouted, a hospital ship even then may not be attacked unless a warning has been given by an adversary and has gone unheeded.[58] Other ships that are immune from attack by warships include coastal fishing boats and small boats employed in local trade, unless they take any part in the hostilities, small craft used for coastal rescue operations, so far as operational requirements permit and ships charged with religious, scientific or philanthropic missions.[59] Mail ships are subject to a special regime, the effect of which is that postal correspondence of neutrals or belligerents is inviolable and if the ship is detained the correspondence must be sent on with the least possible delay.[60]

Submarines

The advent of the submarine as a weapon threw much of the law of sea warfare into confusion. Here was a weapon that could attack without being seen and one which could only with great difficulty rescue the crew and passengers of any merchant ship that it attacked. The international lawyer may well have been asked at the time whether it really was a legitimate weapon and if so were there any limitations on its use? Certainly there were attempts to have it outlawed, with the United Kingdom in the vanguard, starting with the Hague Peace Conference of 1899 and continuing until the London Naval Conference of 1930. The struggle over the submarine conveniently illustrates one major theme in the laws of war, the appearance of a new really effective weapon. Those States which would be most vulnerable to the submarine, such as the United Kingdom with a large surface fleet, were keen to see it outlawed. Those with a relatively small surface fleet opposed the attempt. The final result was really a compromise. The submarine was to be treated no differently from any other naval vessel if it should attack a merchant ship. It had to ensure, if it sank the ship, that the passengers, crew and ship's papers were placed in safety, but putting them in the ship's boats would not be considered to be a place of safety unless they could be rescued quickly by a surface ship or they were near land.[61]

Taken literally, the submarine would have been emasculated as a weapon in economic warfare, although it was quite free to attack naval vessels. It is, however, common knowledge that the submarine played a major role in attacking convoys during the Second World War and sinking merchant ships.[62] Was this because the law was totally ignored or was it because belligerents had found a way around it? The truth lies somewhere in the middle.

It was not difficult to argue that a particular merchant ship was in reality armed and taking an active part in hostilities and so was not entitled to the protection of the 1936 London Protocol. Alternatively, the law might be deliberately disregarded. In this regard Admiral Doenitz was charged with waging unrestricted submarine warfare contrary to the London Protocol. His defence was broadly that he had not infringed the Protocol, since the British Admiralty had, in 1938-39, armed its merchant vessels, placed them in convoys with armed escort, ordered them to radio the position of submarines and to ram them whenever possible. In the light of these facts the International Military Tribunal at Nuremberg was not prepared to find Doenitz guilty. However, he was convicted of ordering the sinking, without warning, of neutral ships found within operational zones and of a further breach of the Protocol in ordering that the submarines under his command should not attempt to rescue shipwrecked survivors. The Tribunal brushed aside the argument that the security of the submarine was paramount and explained its view that 'if the commander cannot rescue, then under (the Protocol) he cannot sink a merchant vessel and should allow it to pass harmless before his periscope'.[63]

The sinking of the cruiser *General Belgrano* by H.M.S. *Conqueror* during the Falklands War illustrates the importance of the long-range nuclear-powered submarine as an effective weapon against a surface warship. The effect of the sinking was to bottle up the Argentine Navy in port and so to neutralise it as a threat to the task force. It is interesting to note here that it was not a submarine that put the Argentinian submarine the *Sante Fé* out of action, but British helicopters as it attempted to enter Grytviken harbour.

Mines

The mine is a weapon that is particularly liable to be indiscriminate, affecting belligerent and neutral shipping alike. For this reason, automatic contact mines have been the subject of control since the Hague Convention VIII of 1907.[64] Although this convention was strictly only concerned with the automatic contact mine, it is believed to reflect the legal position about all mines.[65] This Hague Convention forbids a State to lay unanchored automatic contact mines, except when they are so constructed as to become harmless one hour at most after the person who laid them ceases to control them. It also lays down conditions for the adoption of anchored automatic contact mines as a means of warfare and, in a very ambiguous form, prohibits the laying of automatic contact mines off the coast and ports of the enemy with the sole object of intercepting commercial shipping.[66] There is a requirement in Article 5 of the Convention to notify the State off whose coast automatic contact mines are anchored, but international law would probably now require that notification be given in all cases so as to protect innocent shipping.[67] However, where the mines are put in place but not armed, as they might be in a period of international tension and in order to prevent the passage of submarines should hostilities develop subsequently, there would appear to be no requirement that any other State be notified.

Naval Bombardment of Coastal Targets

In the same way that mines may strike at the belligerent and the innocent alike, so naval bombardment of coastal targets can have the same effect. The Hague Convention IX of 1907 expressly forbade the bombardment of undefended ports, towns and buildings but not naval establishments or military works that could be utilised for the hostile fleet or army. In the same way, the shelling of warships in harbour was confirmed as a legitimate target for naval guns. The general principles to be followed in modern conditions are those previously discussed and, in particular, the obligation imposed on a belligerent by the First Protocol of 1977 to distinguish between military and civilian objectives and to attack only the former. In addition, it will be recalled, belligerents have an obligation not to mount an indiscriminate attack.[68]

Operational and Exclusion Zones

Since the high seas are an international highway, a State that creates a zone in which neutral shipping is barred or is put at risk from attack clearly has an obligation to justify such action. Professor O'Connell posed the dilemma clearly when he wrote: 'If all shipping could be excluded from an operational area, or around a convoy or task force, the designation of a contact as potentially hostile would be easier, and that would tend to solve the problem of identification.'[69] Any ship, in other words, that ventured into this area would have made a positive decision to offer a challenge to its adversary who, in return, would be in a much better position to argue that its actions were motivated solely by self-defence considerations. The declaration of such a zone also has the merit of warning innocent shipping to stay away and so to separate belligerent from neutral shipping.

The creation of these zones is, however, liable to abuse. Their creation does not establish a kind of no-man's land in which the laws of war are silenced. The International Military Tribunal at Nuremberg considered that the orders of Admiral Doenitz to sink neutral shipping within the declared zone around the British Isles was a breach of the London Protocol of 1936. The Tribunal justified this decision by recalling that operational zones had been adopted during the First World War and States that had become bound by the London Protocol must have realised that the Protocol had made no exceptions for them. But this is not to suggest that all operational zones are illegal. A State may be able to create such a zone and, providing it is no more than a reasonable restriction of the right of navigation on the high seas, argue that it is necessary in the exercise of its right of self-defence. Such was the case during the Falklands War in 1982.

The overriding consideration in the creation of the Maritime Exclusion Zone was the need to protect the British task force from attack by submarine, where the problem of identification was greatest, surface ships and, at a later stage, aircraft. The zone was of a radius of 200 miles from the centre of the Falkland Islands. It declared that, from its establishment, 'any Argentine warships and Argentine naval auxiliaries found within this zone will be treated as hostile and are liable to be attacked by British forces', but it also went on to make it clear that the creation of the zone was 'without prejudice to the right of the United Kingdom to take whatever additional measures may be needed in exercise of its right of self-defence, under Article 51 of the United Nations Charter'.[70] The latter part of this declaration was to become of crucial importance when the cruiser *General Belgrano* was torpedoed when it was outside the zone.

Later in the same month the British declared, in the same area, a Total Exclusion Zone. This brought within its ambit all ships, whether naval or merchant, operating in support of the Argentine forces on the Falkland Islands and it applied, alike, to all aircraft.[71] The effect was that any ship or aircraft, other than British, found within the zone would be presumed to be acting in support of the Argentinian forces and so a potential target.

Apart from the crippling of the Argentine submarine the *Sante Fé*, the first attack by British forces against an enemy ship was the sinking of the *General Belgrano* by H.M.S. *Conqueror*, a nuclear-powered submarine, outside the Total Exclusion Zone. The task force commander feared that the Argentine cruiser would be able to evade the British submarine as it ran over a shallow bank and so pose a real threat to the task force surface vessels. He requested of the British government permission to change the Rules of Engagement in order to attack the *General Belgrano* outside the Total Exclusion Zone. The necessary permission was forthcoming, H.M.S. *Conqueror* fired her torpedo and sank the cruiser.[72] The sinking subsequently caused a political storm; a civil servant was prosecuted under the Official Secrets Act 1911 for disclosing documents relating to the event to a member of Parliament and the issue was aired both in and outside Parliament for some time. If the political wisdom of the action is removed, the question that remains is whether the sinking was justified under international law? The answer would seem to be that it was. There is no rule of customary international law (in the absence of a treaty obligation) that an enemy warship can only be attacked on a declared zone and not outside it.[73] Although the British government claimed that the sinking had been executed in the exercise of the inherent right of self-defence under Article 51 of the United Nations Charter, this is not the only ground on which such an action could be legally justified. If it was the only grounds then the sinking of the *General Belgrano* would be difficult to place within it. If it is assumed that Article 51 incorporates the *Caroline* concept of self-defence, and there is evidence that the British government believes that it does,[74] the need to use armed force must be 'instant, overwhelming, leaving no choice of means, and no moment for deliberation'. It is difficult to believe that the Argentine cruiser posed such an immediate threat to the task force, but that is not to say that the sinking was contrary to the laws of war. There was a military necessity, while the *General Belgrano* was still under the surveillance of the task force commander, to neutralise the threat that the ship possessed and there can be no doubt but that the ship was a lawful military objective. The submarine, H.M.S. *Conqueror*, did not stop to pick up survivors[74a] but her commander did know that the *General Belgrano* was being escorted by two destroyers which could take the survivors on board.

The Impact of the Montego Bay Convention 1982

Neither the United Kingdom nor the United States is a party to the 1982 Convention, which, through an insufficient number of ratifications, has not yet come into force, but its impact cannot be ignored. Some of its provisions clearly reflect customary international law, whilst others may have such an effect in time to come. The Convention deals, *inter alia*, with the establishment of exclusive economic zones, archipelagic waters and the right of transit passage through straits. The combined effect, in particular, of the increase in width of the territorial sea to 12 miles and the assumption by coastal States of exclusive economic zones has been to reduce the area of the high seas on which sea battles have traditionally taken place. Whether all of this will seriously affect a belligerent in relation to a neutral coastal State is to be doubted. Although a belligerent must not carry on the fight into the territorial waters of a neutral, it will probably be justifiable to engage other warships within the exclusive economic zone of a neutral coastal State, providing sufficient regard is paid to the rights of that State. This is because the exclusive economic zone is not part of the territorial sea of a coastal State; its rights over it are limited and the rights of other States to use it for lawful purposes is expressly preserved.[75]

Neutrality in Sea Warfare

The right of neutral States to make use of, and to be free from attack on, the high seas is well established, but in return they have a duty of impartiality towards the belligerents. If a neutral State were to permit the warships of one belligerent to enter its ports to take on stores or ammunition but to deny this to another, it could hardly be said to be impartial. The Hague Convention XIII of 1907 sets out a detailed scheme of permitted and prohibited acts on the part of neutrals in naval warfare, but it must be remembered that although some of the details involved have been overtaken by the passage of time, the principles may be said to reflect customary international law and to that extent they are binding on all States.[76]

The neutral State is bound to see that only repairs that are absolutely necessary to make a belligerent warship seaworthy are carried out and that they are not rearmed. Neither may they take on fresh crews, but they are permitted to refuel so as to reach the nearest port in their own country. If a belligerent warship does take on fuel in a neutral port it cannot return to any port of that neutral for a further period of 3 months.

A warship that is pursued by an adversary might attempt to seek shelter in the port of a neutral State, as did the *Graf Spee* in December 1939. The German pocket battleship had been engaged off the coast of South America by three British cruisers and had been severely damaged. It made for the harbour of Montevideo in Uruguay and sought permission to remain there for 15 days in order to effect repairs. As already noted, the Convention permits the neutral to allow the warship to remain for the purpose of effecting repairs that are absolutely necessary to render it seaworthy, but not for the purpose of adding to its fighting force. In so far, therefore, that Captain Langsdorff of the *Graf Spee* sought to put his ship in a condition to enter into battle with the British cruisers that were waiting for it to leave harbour, he would be infringing the neutrality of Uruguay. In the event, the Uruguayan authorities offered Langsdorff permission to stay in Montevideo harbour for only 72 hours and he scuttled the ship after placing its crew on a German merchant ship in harbour at the time.[77] Had the *Graf Spee* refused to leave within the time limit the Uruguayan authorities could have interned her and her crew.[78] The auxiliary to the *Graf Spee*, the *Altmark*, escaped, carrying on board the crews of a number of ships sunk by the pocket battleship and it was to reappear in another incident, also involving a neutral, shortly afterwards.

Article 25 of the 1907 Convention requires the neutral 'to exercise such surveillance as the means at its disposal allow to prevent' breaches of the convention. Suppose the Uruguayan authorities had allowed the *Graf Spee* to effect such repairs so as to put her in a better fighting condition to meet the British ships that lay in wait for her. Can a belligerent take action to prevent a neutral from performing un-neutral service? The answer would revolve around the view one took of the *Altmark* incident. In February 1940 the *Altmark*, the former auxiliary to the *Graf Spee*, had arrived in Norwegian territorial waters and claimed to be an innocent tanker. She was being escorted under Norwegian escort through Norway's territorial sea when the British Admiralty became aware of the presence of the German ship and its cargo of Allied seamen. Eventually, the crew of a British warship were able to board the *Altmark* and rescue the prisoners of war aboard her. The incident had occurred in the internal waters of Norway and Professor O'Connell concluded as a result that the *Altmark* incident was really no different from the *Graf Spee* in Montevideo.[79] The difference between the two is, however, based on the legality in international law of the Norwegian action in permitting the *Altmark* to continue her passage. The Uruguayan authorities had not been in breach of their obligations as a neutral, but if the Norwegians had been there is some justification for the British action.[80]

Notes

1. Oppenheim, *International Law*, vol. II, Longmans, 1956, 7th edn, p. 202. The term 'war' is used in this and subsequent chapters as being synonymous with an armed conflict although, strictly, 'war' as such is no longer a legal concept in the absence of a declaration of war.
2. An excellent account of the development of the laws of war can be found in Best, *Humanity in Warfare, The Modern History of the International law of Armed Conflicts*, Methuen, London, 1983. For a shorter account, see Pictet, *The Need to Restore the Laws and Customs Relating to Armed Conflicts* (1979) 1 Review of the International Commission of Jurists 22.
3. Moltke opposed this view and laid emphasis on involving all the resources of the hostile government. A successful land war, he considered, of itself destroys the greater part of the enemy's commerce during the war. Naval warfare has its particular weapons adopted to this purpose. See Nippold, *Development of International Law After the Great War*, Oxford, Clarendon Press, 1923, p. 121.
4. For the history of the concept see Best, *op. cit.*, and Oppenheim, *op. cit.*, p. 231. The German view can be found in *The German War Book* (with an introduction by Morgan), John Murray, London, 1915, p. 4.
5. See Preamble to the Hague Convention (IV) of 1907, including the Martens Clause and

common Article 1 of the four Geneva Conventions of 1949. For a composite view of the various war crimes tribunals see Dunbar, *Military Necessity in War Crime Trials* (1952) 29 B.Y.I.L. 442. Necessity is no defence under English law, *R. v. Dudley & Stevens* (1884) 14 Q.B.D. 273. If a British soldier killed a person contrary to the laws of war, he could be tried by court-martial for an offence under s. 70 of the Army Act 1955.

6. *The Peleus Trial* (1947) 1 War Crimes Reports 1, discussed by Dunbar (see note 5) at pp. 447-448. There is some evidence that the safety of the submarine could have been secured without such drastic action. *Quaere* if killing the survivors was the only way of enabling the submarine to escape.

7. Article 23(g) of the Regulations annexed to the Hague Convention IV of 1907. See also Article 53 of the Fourth Geneva Convention of 1949. An accused must still justify his actions, see *List et al.* (1949) 8 War Crimes Reports, 34.

8. See also Article 35 of the First Protocol 1977, which adds, 'superfluous injury'.

9. See Article 37 of the First Protocol 1977, which gives some examples of the ruse.

10. Part III, H.M.S.O., London, p. 101.

11. See, generally, Jobst, *Is Wearing the Enemy's Uniform a Violation of the Laws of War?* (1941) 35 A.J.I.L. 437, and Chapter 10, where the case of *Mohamed Ali v. Public Prosecutor* (1968) 3 All E.R. 488 (P.C.) is discussed. Compare the position with respect to warships; see O'Connell, *The International Law of the Sea*, vol. 2, Clarendon Press, Oxford, 1984, p. 1140.

12. 9 War Crimes Reports 90. See also Barker, *Behind Barbed Wire*, Batsford, London, 1974, p. 23. He could not have been tried for spying because he had before falling into American hands regained his lines, see Article 31 of the Regulations annexed to the Hague Convention IV 1907. For an account of the law concerned with spying see Chapter 10.

12a. See Article 39(2) of the First Protocol 1977.

13. The white flag was used in the Falkland War when the local British and Argentinian commanders met to conclude the surrender of the latter at Goose Green, *The Times*, 31 May 1982. See the Hague Rules, Article 23(f); Article 37(1)(a) of the First Protocol 1977.

14. *English History, 1914-1945*, Oxford, Clarendon Press, 1965, p. 428. Added to this is the unique feature of these weapons, that they are 'highly dependent upon weather variables such as wind, temperature, humidity and precipitation', Thomas and Thomas, *Development of International Legal Limitations on the Use of Chemical and Biological Weapons*, 5 Methodist Univ. School of Law Press, Dallas, 1968, p. 28. Note there had been attempts in 1899 and 1922 to ban the use of poisonous gas. See also McFarland, *Preparing for What Never Came; Chemical and Biological Warfare in World War II* (1986) 2 Defence Analysis 107, 'Germany never developed plans to use the V-weapons for CB warfare' (p.111).

15. *The Times*, 17 March 1986. The 1925 Geneva Protocol for the Prohibition of the Use in War of Asphyxiating, Poisonous or Other Gases, and of Bacteriological Methods of Warfare, specifically bans, apart from the activities included in its title, the use in war of all analogous liquids, materials or devices.

16. Compare, Thomas and Thomas, *op. cit.*, pp. 76-77, with Greenspan, *The Modern Law of Land Warfare*, Univ. Calif. Press (1959), p. 359, n. 186, on the question of the use of tear gas. The British view is that tear gas is not prohibited by the 1925 Protocol; see, H.C. Deb. vol. 795, col. 18, written answers, 2 February 1970. Note also the interpretation given to the 1925 Protocol by the General Assembly Resolution of 16 December 1969 (G.A. Resol. 2603A (XXIV)) which declared that 'chemical agents of warfare ... which might be employed because of their direct toxic effects on man, animals or plant and any biological agents of warfare' were contrary to the 1925 Geneva Gas Protocol. Both the United Kingdom and the United States abstained in the vote. For an account of the use of chemical weapons in Vietnam, see D'Amato *et al.*, *The Vietnam War and International Law*, vol. 3, Princeton Univ. Press (1972), pp. 407, 443 et seq.

17. Convention on the Prohibition of the Development, Production and Stockpiling of Bacteriological (Biological) and Toxic Weapons and on their Destruction 1972. The United Kingdom government has 'approved plans to produce a new generation of chemical weapons', *The Times*, 29 April 1986.

18. See Article 23(e) Hague Rules 1907; Article 35(2) of the First Protocol 1977; the St. Petersburg Declaration 1868 and the Geneva Gas Protocol of 1925.

18a. The United States did not become a party to the 1925 Gas Protocol until 1975.

18b. Its use against civilians would be contrary to the 1981 *U.N. Convention on Prohibitions or Restrictions on the Use of Certain Conventional Weapons which may be Deemed to be Excessively Injurious or to have Indiscriminate Effects*, Protocol III.

19. See, generally, Falk, *The Shimoda Case: A Legal Appraisal of the Atomic Attacks on Hiroshima and Nagasaki* (1965) 59 A.J.I.L. 759. The plaintiffs were able to bring their action against the Japanese government as a consequence of Article 19 of the Peace Treaty between Japan and the Allies by which Japan waived all claims of itself and of its nationals against the Allied powers.

20. See the excellent article by Brownlie, *Some Legal Aspects of the Use of Nuclear Weapons* (1965) 14 I.C.L.Q. 437; Menon, *Legal Limits on the Use of Nuclear Weapons in Armed Conflict*, (1979) XVII Revue de Droit Pénal Militaire et de Droit de la Guerre 11; Singh, *Nuclear Weapons and International Law* (1959); Schwarzenberger, *The Legality of Nuclear Weapons*, Stevens & Sons, London (1958). The First Protocol to the Geneva Conventions 1977 would also be relevant to the debate.

21. G.A. Resol. 1653 (XVI) (1961). There were other Resolutions in 1966 and 1972.

22. The question of reprisals is considered below.

23. The Secretary of State for Foreign and Commonwealth Affairs, H.C. Deb. vol. 42, cols. 777-778, 11 May 1983.

24. *Ibid.*

25. *Op. cit.*, p. 351.

26. Minister of State, Foreign and Commonwealth Office, H.C. Deb. vol. 29, col. 70 Written Answers, 19 October 1982. Even the International Law Commission in 1984 was unable to reach a decision as to whether the proposed Code of Offences Against the Peace and Security of Mankind should contain a reference to the use of atomic weapons.

27. A very full account of these matters is given by Falk in *The Vietnam War and International Law*, vol. 4, Princeton (1976), at pp. 292-299. The Rome Plows (*sic*) were heavily armoured bulldozers with a 2.5 ton blade which could cut 'a swath through the heaviest forest', *ibid.*, p. 294. Falk proposed an international convention on the crime of ecocide, *ibid.*, p. 300.

28. See note 16. It should be noted that the United States did not ratify the 1925 Gas Protocol until 1975.

29. 'Environmental modification techniques' is defined in Article 2 as any technique for changing—through the deliberate manipulation of natural processes—the dynamics, composition or structure of the earth, including its biota, lithosphere, hydrosphere and atmosphere or of outer space. The terms 'widespread, long-lasting or severe' are subject to rather vague understanding as to their meaning (which applies only to this Convention). 'Widespread' means encompassing an area on the scale of several hundred square kilometres; 'long-lasting' means lasting for a period of months, or approximately a season; 'severe' involves serious or significant disruption or harm to human life, natural and economic resources or other assets. This Convention may assume greater significance as scientific knowledge and capabilities increase.

30. A serious flaw in this article must be its use of the words 'widespread long-term and severe damage.' It does not define them and it thereby gives a golden opportunity to government legal advisers to argue that the article has not been infringed. Note the use of the word 'and' rather than 'or' (in the Environmental Modification Convention 1977). See also Article 2(4) of the 1981 Conventional Weapons Convention (Protocol III).

31. The various Conventions that prohibit the use of specific weapons are the St. Petersburg Declaration 1868 (explosive projectiles under 400 grammes weight); the Hague Declaration of 1899, No. 2 (asphyxiating gases); No. 3 (expanding or dum-dum bullets); Geneva Gas Protocol 1925; 1981 U.N. Conventional Weapons Convention.

31a. Although see Articles 86, 89 and 91 of the First Protocol 1977.

32. See also Articles 49(2) and 54(5), First Protocol 1977. Article 52(3) of the Protocol creates a presumption that a building usually used for civilian purposes is not a military objective. Article 53 deals with the protection of cultural objects and places of worship.

32a. See Article 54 of the First Protocol 1977 and note, in particular, Article 54(2).

33. Churchill, *The Second World War*, vol. V, Cassell & Co., London, 1952, p. 63.

34. Article 51(4) of the First Protocol 1977.

35. Article 85(3)(b) of the First Protocol 1977. This would also be the case if a combatant

treated as a single military objective a number of clearly separated and distinct military objectives located in a defined area, Article 51(5)(a).

36. See Rauch, *Attack Restraints, Target Limitations and Prohibitions or Restrictions on Use of Certain Conventional Weapons* (1979) 18 Revue de Droit Pénal Militaire et de Droit de la Guerre 53. Rauch questions whether the 1981 Convention and Article 49(3) of the First Protocol 1977 are reconcilable on this issue. See, generally, Article 31 of the Vienna Convention on the Law of Treaties 1969.

37. The neutralised zone is set out in Article 15 of the Fourth Geneva Convention 1949. For the terms of the I.C.R.C. proposal see (1982) 53 B.Y.I.L. 523 and for the British response H.C. Deb. vol. 25, col. 611, 14 June 1982. It is some measure of its success that there were only three civilian casualties in the whole of the War; *Protection of the Victims of Armed Conflict, Falkland-Malvinas Islands* (1982) I.C.R.C. (1984), p. 33. See the more limited protection offered to civilians in hospital and safety zones, Article 14, Fourth Geneva Convention 1949, and for the establishment of non-defended and demilitarised zones see Articles 59 and 60 of the First Protocol 1977.

38. *Manual of Military Law* Part III, H.M.S.O., 1958, p. 184; Oppenheim, *International Law*, vol. II, Longmans, London (1952), p. 562; Greenspan, *op. cit.*, p. 408; Kalshoven, *Belligerent Reprisals*, Sijthoff & Geneva, Leyden (1971).

39. There were no convictions at the International Military Tribunals at Nuremberg and Tokyo for these acts, largely because of the problem of separating illegitimate acts from reprisals. Had the I.M.T. accepted the pleas of military necessity and superior orders as justification for infringement of the laws of war, there would be little left of those laws; see Greenspan, *op. cit.*, p. 409.

40. See, for example, Articles 13 and 130 of the Third Geneva Convention 1949. See also the related problem of hostage-taking and collective punishments discussed in Chapter 10.

41. Taylor, *op. cit.*, p. 411. The total number of British killed was about 400,000 (see p. 599). There were about half a million Germans killed as a result of air raids (see p. 591, n. 2).

42. *Op. cit.*, vol V, p. 469. See generally chap. XXIX.

43. For a review of the literature see Blix, *Area Bombardment: Rules and Reasons* (1978) 49 B.Y.I.L. 31, 60. See also Taylor, *English History 1914-1945*, Clarendon Press, Oxford, 1965, p. 592. The definitive work is Webster and Frankland, *The Strategic Air Offensive Against Germany*, 1939-45, H.M.S.O., 1961, 4 vols. Churchill considered that the 'German people endured more than we thought possible', *The Second World War*, vol. VI, Cassell & Co., London (1953), p. 471.

44. The Casablanca Directive, February 1943; See Churchill, *The Second World War*, vol. V, Cassell & Co., London (1952), p. 458. For an excellent account of the topic see Johnson, *Rights in Air Space*, Manchester U.P.O., 1965, chap. IV.

45. The German V1 and V2, flying bomb and rocket respectively, were so called because the 'V' represented the German word *vergeltungswaffe* meaning 'vengeance' or 'reprisal'. Although State practice during the Second World War was to engage in this type of bombing, it did not create a rule of customary international law that such bombing was permitted, since no State argued that it was legal to do so.

46. The whole matter is well discussed by Blix, *Area Bombardment: Rules and Reasons* (1978) 49 B.Y.I.L. 31, at pp. 44-45 and 52-54.

47. Article 2(2). An incendiary weapon is defined in Article 1(1) of Protocol III of the Convention as a 'weapon or munition which is primarily designed to set fire to objects or to cause burn injury to persons'.

48. See Article 49(3) of the First Protocol 1977.

49. Articles 1 and 2 of the Geneva High Seas Convention 1958.

50. Article 1 of the Geneva Convention on the Territorial Sea and the Contiguous Zone 1958.

51. Article 8 of the Geneva High Seas Convention 1958. See also Article 29 of the Montego Bay Convention 1982. The use by belligerents of privateers, or privately owned ships, to capture enemy vessels was abolished by the 1856 Paris Declaration Respecting Maritime Law.

52. See the Hague Convention VII Relating to the Conversion of Merchant Ships into Warships 1907. It is unclear whether they can be reconverted while hostilities continue.

53. See, generally, O'Connell, *The International Law of the Sea*, vol. 11, Clarendon Press, Oxford (1984), p. 1106.

54. To avoid the delays caused by a search of cargoes the 'navicert' system developed in which neutral shipping carrying non-contraband goods was given a certificate which could be presented to the captain of a warship. See, generally, O'Connell, *ibid.*, p. 1147, and Tichie, *The 'Navicert' System During the World War*, Carnegie Endowment for International Peace, Washington, 1938. See also Draper, *The Times*, 23 January 1986, for the right of a belligerent to search a neutral ship. Professor Draper was concerned with the Iran-Iraq War.

55. See the 1856 Paris Declaration Pespecting Maritime Law, paras. 2 and 3, for the position of enemy goods in a neutral ship and neutral goods in an enemy merchant ship. With the exception of a contraband, neither is liable to capture merely because of its status. For the position of enemy public goods see O'Connell, *ibid.*, p. 1114. A prize-court may go behind the flag of convenience to discover the real nationality of a merchant ship. O'Connell, *ibid.*, states at p. 1113, 'In a future conflict the working of the rule is likely to lead to the condemnation of vessels which are ostensibly neutral.'

56. *The Second World War*, Cassell & Co., London, vol. V, p. 11, 1951.

57. See Hague Convention 1907 (XI) Relative to Certain Restrictions with Regard to the Exercise of the Right of Capture in Naval War, Article 8, and the Third Geneva Convention 1949, Article 4A(5). In the First World War the Germans executed one Captain Fryatt, master of a merchant vessel, for taking part in hostilities. See (1916) 10 A.J.I.L. 865.

58. Second Geneva Convention 1949, Articles 30 and 34.

59. Hague Convention 1907 (XI) (see note 57), Articles 3 and 4, and Article 27 of the Second Geneva Convention 1949. The *Narwal*, an Argentine fishing vessel, was sunk within the Maritime Exclusion Zone in May 1982 on the ground that it was spying on the British task force.

60. *Ibid.*, Articles 1 and 2. Whether this entitles belligerents, into whose hands the correspondence falls, to censor it to prevent intelligence being communicated to an enemy is unclear.

61. Procès-verbal Relating to the Rules of Submarine Warfare Set Forth in Part IV of the Treaty of London 1930; also known as the London Protocol of 1936. The Nyon Agreement 1937 provided that submarines which attacked non-Spanish warships during the Spanish Civil War were to be treated as pirates.

62. Churchill estimated the total loss of shipping by U-boats alone as fourteen and a half-million tons. The highest number of losses were in 1942 and early 1943. *The Second World War*, Cassell & Co., London (1952), vol. VI, pp. 473-474.

63. Judgment of the International Military Tribunal (1947) 41 A.J.I.L. 172, 304-305. See also the case of Admiral Raeder at p. 308; O'Connell, *The Influence of Law on Sea Power*, Manchester U.P. (1975), pp. 48 and 78, and Article 18 of the Second Geneva Convention 1949. See also Mallison, *Submarine Warfare and International Law*, U.S. Naval War College, LV III 111 (1966), for the statement of U.S. Admiral Nimitz. The background to the judgment in relation to Donitz is described in Tusa and Tusa, *The Nuremberg Trial*, Macmillan, London, 1983, p. 462.

64. Convention (VIII) Relative to the Laying of Automatic Submarine Contact Mines. I am indebted to Captain A. G. Y. Thorpe, R.N., Chief Naval Judge Advocate, who supplied me with a copy of his paper, *Mine Warfare At Sea: Some Legal Aspects of the Future*, first delivered at the British Institute of International and Comparative Law, London, in 1985.

65. See O'Connell, *The Influence of Law on Sea Power*, Manchester U.P. (1975), p. 96.

66. Articles 1(2), 3-5, and Article 2 respectively. The British reservation to the Hague Convention (VIII) stated that 'the mere fact that this Convention does not prohibit a particular act or proceeding must not be held to debar His Britannic Majesty's Government from contesting its legitimacy'. For the mining of Haiphong harbour during the Vietnam War, see O'Connell, *The Influence of Law on Sea Power*, Manchester U.P. (1975), pp. 94-96. Two issues are of considerable interest in this incident. The first relates to whether the Hague Convention (VIII) applied to unanchored accoustic mines and whether notification was required under Article 5. The International Court of Justice at the Hague in *Military and Paramilitary Activities in and against Nicaragua (Nicaragua v. U.S.A.) (No. 2)*(1986) XXV I.L.M. 1023, found that 'the laying of mines ... without notification was ... a breach of the principles of humanitarian law underlying the Hague Convention of 1907', para. 215 of the judgment.

67. See *Corfu Channel Case (Merits), U.K. v. Albania*, I.C.J. Reports (1949), p. 4. The court stressed that the obligation on the part of the Albanian authorities to warn of the minefield laid off its coast was based not on Hague Convention (VIII) but on 'certain general and well-recognized principles, namely: elementary considerations of humanity, even more exacting in peace than in war; the principle of the freedom of maritime communication; and every state's obligation not to allow knowingly its territory to be used for acts contrary to the rights of other States'. See also *Nicaragua v. U.S.A.* (1986) (note 66), where the court relied on this case.

68. Article 49(3) applies the First Protocol 1977 to all attacks from the sea against objectives on land.

69. O'Connell, *The International Law of the Sea*, Clarendon Press, Oxford (1984), vol. II, p. 1109.

70. For the full text see (1982) 53 B.Y.I.L. 539. The zone was established around British territory and could not therefore be considered as a blockade. A blockade would amount to aggression within the 1974 General Assembly Resolution on the Definition of Aggression (Resolution 3314 (XXIX)), Article 3(c).

71. The text can be seen in (1982) 53 B.Y.I.L. 542. It also closed Port Stanley airport. The Swiss government confirmed that notice of the zone had been received by the Argentine government. H.C. Deb. vol. 34, col. 602, Written Answers 22 December 1982. The Total Exclusion Zone has been replaced by a Protection Zone of 150 miles. The Argentine government also declared three zones around the islands, see Fenrick, *Legal Aspects of the Falklands Naval Conflict* (1985) 24 Revue de Droit Pénal Militaire et de Droit de la Guerre, 243, 250. An additional 'Defensive Area' was created around the task force itself and the British government also warned Argentina that any of her naval vessels or aircraft located more than 12 miles from her coast would be considered as hostile.

72. For an account of the facts see *The Falklands Campaign: The Lessons* (H.M.S.O.), Cmnd 8758, para. 110. See also Hastings and Jenkins, *The Battle for the Falklands*, Book Club Association, London, 1982, p. 147, for a much fuller account. This was the first occasion on which a nuclear-powered submarine was deployed offensively against a naval vessel. The Argentine government argued that in deploying a nuclear submarine in the area, the British were in breach of the Treaty of Tlatelolco 1967. The British replied that the treaty did not prohibit nuclear-powered vessels, see (1982) 53 B.Y.I.L. 535.

73. See Professor Draper, *The Times*, 7 April 1982. The sinking of the *General Belgrano* occurred on 2 May and it was on 7 May that the British government issued its statement that the Argentine ships located beyond 12 miles from home waters would be regarded as hostile, see (1982) 53 B.Y.I.L. 549. However, the Argentine government was warned on 29 April that 'all Argentine vessels ... apparently engaging in surveillance of, or intelligence-gathering activities against, British forces in the South Atlantic will be regarded as hostile ...', (1982) 53 B.Y.I.L. 544.

74. See the arguments of the U.K. representative to the International Civil Aviation Organisation when discussing the law concerned with the use of force against civil aircraft, (1984) 55 B.Y.I.L. 591. For the *Caroline Case* of 1837, see Jennings, (1938) 32 A.J.I.L. 82. For political reasons it was no doubt necessary to justify all such action as complying with Article 51, in the same way that the rules of engagement may have been draw up in more restrictive terms than the law actually required. Freedman concludes, that the sinking of the *General Belgrano* was a 'political defeat' and argues that 'any military action which is not self-evident for defensive purposes ... becomes an outrage,' (1982-83) 61 Foreign Affairs, 196, 209.

74a. See Article 18 of the Second Geneva Convention 1949.

75. See Article 58 of the 1982 Convention. The pre-existing right to transit passage through international straits (see the *Corfu Channel Case 1949* (note 67 above)) will also apply to archipelagic sea lanes (Article 54 of the 1982 Convention).

76. Hague Convention 1907 (XIII) Concerning the Rights and Duties of Neutral Powers in Naval War. The United Kingdom is not a party to it. The Convention also imposes obligations on belligerents. Article 2, for instance, prohibits 'any act of hostility ... by belligerent warships in the territorial waters of a neutral Power ...' and in Article 5 'belligerents are forbidden to use neutral ports and waters as a base of naval operations against their adversaries'. Whether the mere passage of belligerent warships through the

territorial waters of a neutral States is a prohibited act is unclear. Article 10 of the 1907 Convention directs that it is not, but the Montego Bay Convention 1982 defines 'innocent passage' more precisely, see Article, 19(2)(a).

77. For a very full account see O'Connell, *The Influence of Law on Sea Power*, Manchester U.P. (1975), chap. 3. For Churchill's account of the action, see *The Second World War*, Cassell & Co. (London), vol. 1, chap. XXIX. For the British attempt to keep the *Graf Spee* in Montevideo harbour until additional British ships could arrive, see O'Connell, *op. cit.*, p. 35. The attempt was based on Article 16 of the Convention which prohibited a belligerent warship to leave a neutral port less than 24 hours after the departure of a merchant ship of an adversary. British merchant ships were to be given orders to sail from Montevideo to postpone the departure of the *Graf Spee*.

78. Article 24 of the 1907 Convention. The German merchant ship transferred the crew to Argentine ships for passage to Buenos Aires where they were to be treated as shipwrecked sailors, see Oppenheim, *International Law*, Longmans, London, 7th edn, 1952, vol. II, p. 265, n. 6.

79. *The Influence of Law on Sea Power*, Manchester U.P. (1975), p. 42.

80. Compare O'Connell, *ibid.*, p. 44, with Waldock, *Release of the Altmark's Prisoners* (1947) 24 B.Y.I.L. 216. The view of the then British government was that 'the use of Norwegian territorial waters for hundreds of miles by a German warship for the purpose of escaping capture on the high seas and of conveying British prisoners to a German prison camp' was contrary to international law. The Norwegian view was that they had acted in accordance with international law, see Churchill, *The Second World War*, vol. I, p. 445. Churchill intervened directly on the issue, *ibid.*, p. 444. *Quaere* whether such action is compatible with the *Corfu Channel Case* (1949) I.C.J. 4, in which Operation Retail (sweeping mines from an international strait) was held to be illegal despite a finding by the court that Albania was required to notify shipping of the presence of the mines and had not done so. A neutral may lay mines around its coast, but in doing so it is bound by Hague Convention (VIII) 1907 in like manner as belligerents. For a similar situation in land warfare see Fried, *United States Military Intervention in Cambodia in the Light of International Law*, in Falk (ed) *The Vietnam War and International Law*, vol. 3, Princeton, U.P. 1972, p. 100. The use made by the United States of neutral countries during the Vietnam War is discussed at pp. 109-111. Neutrality in land war is governed by the Hague Convention (V) 1907.

9

The Geneva Conventions and Additional Protocols

'The way to international hell seems paved with good conventions.' Roling, *Hague Receuil des Cours* (1960).

The Geneva Conventions of 1949 are the beginning of the modern law of armed conflict. They are concerned with the victims of war while Hague law deals with the methods and means of war.[1] This division is, of course, a gross over-simplification, but it serves to emphasise the two main strands of this branch of international law, the conduct of warriors on the one hand and the plight of their victims on the other. The two could never be looked at in isolation, since civilians, in particular, are greatly affected by the methods or means of warfare adopted by the belligerents. To wage total or unlimited warfare generally creates more casualties among the civilian population than among the belligerents, as aerial bombing, particularly during the Second World War, has shown. To the extent that the First 1977 Protocol to the Geneva Conventions deals with both Hague and Geneva law, it is a realistic attempt to bring the laws of war into line with changes not only in world attitudes to the conduct of war but also with the continued development in weapons of war.

It was only to be expected that the end of the Second World War would usher in a new era; an era in which the rights of the individual, so abused in the war, would be placed on an improved footing. The first steps in this process were the international war crimes trials at Nuremberg and Tokyo in which the treatment of the inhabitants of occupied territory came in for close analysis. This was followed by frantic activity on the part of the nascent United Nations which led to the acceptance of the Nuremberg principles by the General Assembly in 1946, the Universal Declaration of Human Rights in 1948 and the Genocide Convention of the same year.[2] The year 1949 was therefore a good time to discuss the rights during time of armed conflict of the individual, rather than of States. The diplomatic conference called by the Swiss government met in the spring and summer of that year and produced four conventions. The first dealt with the Amelioration of the Condition of the Wounded and Sick in Armed Forces in the Field, the second with the Amelioration of the Condition of the Wounded, Sick and Shipwrecked

Members of Armed Forces at Sea, the third with the Treatment of Prisoners of War and the fourth with the Protection of Civilian Persons in Time of War, all of which are set out in the Appendix. It was no mean achievement and it is to be contrasted with the 3-year gestation period of the 1977 Protocols. To be fair, however, it should be remembered that there was a unanimity of purpose in 1949. The defeated States did not take part directly in the negotiations and the number of States then in existence was relatively small. In 1977 the world situation was entirely different. The developing nations possessed political power which they were not reluctant to use in the United Nations and it is therefore understandable that the 1977 Protocols were developed with the assistance of that body rather than solely through the International Committee of the Red Cross. Today, the Geneva Conventions are binding on all but eight States in the world and the 1977 Protocol concerned with international armed conflicts, on sixty-five out of a total of 171 States.[3] The United Kingdom has signed but has not, along with the United States, ratified the Protocols.[4] The Conventions of 1949 were essentially the product of hard bargaining between States who had fared differently in the recent war. Those States which had been subjected to occupation were keen to see enshrined in the Conventions a definite prohibition on the taking (let alone shooting) of hostages and of the carrying out of reprisals, whilst those with recent experience on being occupiers (Britain, for example, in Germany) wanted to ensure that they had sufficient legal powers to deal with those who took up arms against them. Along with these issues ran the parallel one of entitlement to prisoner of war status, or, in other words, who could be a lawful fighter and therefore entitled to the benefits of the third Convention and who was an unprivileged belligerent to be dealt with by the law of the occupier?[5] Concessions had to be made to both sides in the argument and, depending on which side you support, the Conventions are claimed in part to be unrealistic, with some taking the extreme view that they are fundamentally flawed and cannot thereby command respect by those engaged in armed conflict.[6] The fact that they have been accepted by virtually the whole world is a clear testament to their wide-ranging support, by nations of widely different cultures and religious backgrounds.

The 1949 Conventions contain a number of articles common to each and it is proposed now to consider these and then to discuss the main provisions of the 1977 Protocols and the effect that they will have on the conduct of warfare in the future.

Article 1 directs that the High Contracting Parties (the States that are bound by the Conventions) undertake to respect and to ensure respect for the Conventions *in all circumstances*. The imperative nature of this obligation cannot be understated. In one short sentence it gives short shrift to those who would argue that military necessity can justify a breach of the Conventions. Instead, the Conventions specifically provide when this justification can be pleaded.[7] Moreover, the Conventions will apply to all parties to them in an armed conflict whether they be guilty of aggression or acting in self-defence. They therefore applied as much to, and by, Argentina as they did to the British forces in the Falklands War. It is no argument to say that a State is relieved of its obligations under the Conventions because its adversary started the war and is therefore not entitled to its benefits.

It might be thought that Article 1 is directed at each individual State only if it is engaged in an armed conflict. But this is not so. First, because the Conventions require a State to apply certain of their provisions directly into its domestic or national law and this will have to be done in time of peace; the United Kingdom has done this, to some extent, in the Geneva Conventions Act of 1957, and second, because of the recently expressed view of the International Committee of the Red Cross. This view was expressed as a consequence of the frustration of the International Committee at the attitudes of both the belligerents in the Iran-Iraq War. It appealed to all parties to the Conventions to do what they could to ensure that the obligations of the Conventions were respected by the belligerents in that war. The way that they could do this would be by volunteering to act as a substitute protecting power, a matter discussed below.

Common Article 2 is the gateway to the Conventions and, as such, its applicability is often denied by States in an attempt to play down an incident or series of incidents. Take, for example, the Falklands War, a classic situation of this type. A relatively small proportion of the British armed forces was envisaged as being required; the operation was not reasonably expected to be long-lasting and the possible field of operations was limited by the size of the islands. A reasonably intelligent observer might have asked himself when the task force set sail, 'Are we at war with Argentina?' The issue of whether there was a war or not was, in fact, irrelevant. A gaze into history shows a number of cases where armed conflict was taking place between States but for political reasons the States concerned did not wish to characterise their conflict as a war.[8] A refusal to recognise that a war was in being prevented any of the laws of war from becoming operative. This might suit the political leaders of the States concerned, but at the best it only made the plight of the victims of the fighting uncertain. The 1949 Conventions eschew the concept of 'war', preferring instead to trigger off the law of Geneva when an 'armed conflict' occurs.[9] This is an entirely objective criterion; either there is, or there is not, an armed conflict taking place, and the views of the individual States concerned are certainly not decisive. The point arose during the Falklands crisis in April 1982 when the Prime Minister (wrongly) stated in the House that the captured members of the Argentinian forces on South Georgia were not being treated as prisoners of war since there had been no declaration of war.[10] The matter was subsequently corrected, although it was believed by all those involved and by commentators that there was no doubt but that the Conventions would apply.

The last paragraph of Article 2 was designed to avoid any argument that the Conventions did not apply when a non-party to them joined the conflict. It had been a feature of previous Conventions that a general participating clause had been inserted to emphasise the contractual nature of the agreements entered into by States.[11] This particular issue is of little relevance today, since many of the principal obligations to be found in the Conventions reflect customary international law and will, as such, be binding on all States and, in any event, most States of the world are now party to the 1949 Conventions.

Civil Wars

Whether the Conventions will apply in a civil war has always been a vexed question, simply because an established government will generally not wish to accord the status of belligerent to a group that it considers to be criminal. Common Article 3 is concerned with an armed conflict not of an international character, and it lays down very minimum standards of conduct. It requires those engaged in the fight to treat humanely those who have taken no part in it or those who have but who are *hors de combat*. In practice Article 3 has been of little direct significance, simply because it attempts to control the manner in which a State treats its own citizens in circumstances where the government concerned may be fighting for its very existence. In addition, a State may take the view that any trouble that it is having with armed groups intent on bringing down the government is really only criminal and that its laws are adequate to punish and to stamp out that activity. There is not, in other words, an armed conflict. This is the view taken by the United Kingdom in relation to the activities of the I.R.A. in Northern Ireland. The International Committee of the Red Cross was permitted to enter the 'H' block prison in Northern Ireland, but only on the express understanding that permission to do so did not carry with it any admission that the United Kingdom government admitted the applicability of common Article 3.[12]

Protocol 2 of 1977 takes up this theme and develops and supplements common Article 3. Article 1(4) of the First Protocol treats as international a conflict in which peoples are fighting against colonial domination and alien occupation and against racist regimes in the exercise of their right of self-determination. This type of conflict is therefore excluded from the category of civil war or non-international armed conflict. One might be forgiven for asking why this should be so. There are very few armed conflicts of this type today and in any event the same problem is faced here as with common Article 3 of the 1949 Conventions, namely that if the existing government does not recognise the struggle as being of this type, those who suffer in it will, in reality, be no better off. But does it represent the re-emergence of a doctrine long since discredited, the idea of the 'just war'?[13] Those who take up arms, it might be argued, to establish their right to govern themselves should no longer be considered as mere rebels. The advantage, it might be said, of this approach is that it brings this type of conflict into the main body of the laws of war whereas a civil war of the traditional kind is compartment-alised into a much smaller side-show. It might seem strange to many that what is perhaps the most common type of armed conflict in the world today, the non-international, should suffer from such a paucity of regulation compared with that accorded to the international armed conflict. This is due, no doubt, to the reluctance of States to bind themselves in their dealings with those who take up arms against them. This attitude can be shown by the very restricted gateway into the Second Protocol of 1977. The dissident armed forces (or other organized armed groups) must exercise such control over a part of the territory as to enable them to carry out sustained and concerted military operations. The Protocol will not apply to situations of internal disturbances and tensions, such as riots, isolated and sporadic acts of violence and other acts of a similar nature. These acts are not be considered as armed conflicts. The Protocol does not therefore cover the activities of the IRA in Northern Ireland, nor the Basque separists in Spain, since neither controls territory to the extent required in Article 1. The United Nations has, however, classified the struggle in El Salvador as one that is within the ambit of common Article 3 and of the Second Protocol of 1977,[14] but the government of that country has repudiated such an interpretation of Article 1 of the 1977 Protocol.[15] In these circumstances the intended beneficiaries of both common Article 3 and of the Second Protocol of 1977, that is those who do not take a direct part in the conflict, are left to the mercy of the combatants. When one adds to this that there is no machinery prescribed in either common Article 3 or in the Second Protocol of 1977 for the supervision of such conflicts by a protecting power,[16] and the fact that to date only 58 States are bound by the Second Protocol, one can see that this is perhaps the least successful area of the attempt by the international community to protect the victims of armed conflicts of whatever type. One of the reasons for the apathy of States in relation to non-international armed conflicts might well be that once they had classified wars of national liberation as coming within the First Protocol States lost interest in the Second Protocol.[17]

The Second Protocol of 1977 contains four main parts, the first of which is concerned with its applicability. Other parts deal with the obligation to treat with respect and humanely those who are not taking a direct part in the fighting and those who have ceased to take part in hostilities. It prohibits, *inter alia*, the taking of hostages, collective punishments, violence to life and health and any acts of terrorism (see Article 4). It also deals with the minimum conditions to be applied to those whose liberty has been restricted as a result of the armed conflict (see Article 5). It should be noted here that, unlike an international armed conflict, those captured as a result of the fighting are not considered to be prisoners of war. Captured members of the dissident armed forces (or other organized armed groups) can therefore be punished for offences against the national law committed in the course of the struggle.[18] Article 6 of the Protocol sets out the minimum standards of any prosecution and requires, for instance, that the accused is to be informed, without delay, of the offence with which he is charged and he is also to be afforded all the necessary rights and means for his defence.

The Protocol goes on, in Part III, to provide that the wounded, sick and shipwrecked are to be respected and protected even if they have taken a part in the armed conflict. This is in keeping with similar requirements in an international armed conflict, but the logistics of the dissident armed forces may not be in such a condition as to be able to offer much in the way of medical facilities to those *hors de combat*. The temptation to 'finish off' those who have been wounded is likely to be much stronger in this type of armed conflict, whilst the fear on the part of civilians that to help would render them liable either to retribution or to being charged with an offence under the national law of the State concerned cannot be underestimated. Article 10 of the Protocol addresses itself to this problem and, it must be stated, fails to offer much protection to those who assist the wounded and sick, mainly because of the role played by the national law of the State concerned. Suppose members of the dissident armed forces have been engaged in a fire-fight with government forces around a small village; a number of the dissidents have been wounded and in the safety of night they have been brought to the village for medical assistance. They are treated by two villagers, one of whom is a trained nurse on leave from her employment at a government hospital, whilst the other provides the dissidents with fresh clothing and food. They are threatened with death if they give any information about them to the authorities. Subsequently, the nurse is arrested by government forces. Is she entitled to the protection of the Protocol which directs that 'under no circumstances shall any person be punished for having carried out medical activities compatible with medical ethics, regardless of the person benefitting therefrom'? The answer would seem to be yes, assuming that this provision has found its way into the national law of the State concerned.[19] However, there is still the question of information acquired by the nurse and the activities of the other villager. They now know the condition of the wounded dissidents, their description, the number and condition of those who delivered them and so on. According to the Protocol the nurse is not to be penalised for refusing or failing to give information concerning the wounded and sick, but this is made subject to national law, which would probably make this an offence. The other villager is not protected at all and could be dealt with according to national law.[20]

The civilian population are not to be made the object of attack nor of acts or threats of violence, the primary effect of which is to spread terror. This sounds good until it is remembered that in this type of conflict a clear separation of combatants from the civilian population is not likely to occur with the result that from the government side, at least, all civilians may be at risk and that the protection offered to them will cease if they take a direct part in hostilities. The distinction between taking a direct or an indirect part in the hostilities may be far too subtle for the average government soldier faced with a civilian who has supplied food or shelter to members of the dissident forces.

In a non-international armed conflict the work of the International Committee of the Red Cross is vital, not only in conducting humanitarian activities (as shown in El Salvador) but also in making the various parties aware of the basic principles of the Protocol in the absence of a specific obligation on the part of the State concerned to instruct its armed forces. Members of the dissident armed forces are unlikely to accept the strictures of the government as to the way it conducts its operations against it, but they may well listen to the International Committee, if only because of their need for support from the outside world. Such support may well be put in jeopardy if the dissidents are shown to conduct their operations in such a way that would shock world opinion. This propaganda factor and the sanction of discipline from superiors in the dissident armed forces, are the only means by which the basic principles established in common Article 3 and in the Second Protocol of 1977 can be effectively enforced.[21]

Gaps in the Law

It is perhaps not unfair to say that the laws of war respond to the developments in the practice of warfare and in the use of particular weapons rather than being in the vanguard of military thinking. The cynic might say that it deals with all the problems faced in the last conflict and it is therefore in a state of perpetual obsolescence. This criticism is not a new one. In the Hague Convention of 1907, Martens, an adviser to the Tsar on international law, introduced a clause that was to bear his name and which was to have a profound effect on the structure of the laws of war. The Martens Clause begins by admitting that the Convention is not a complete statement of the laws of war and it then goes on to say that where there are gaps in it, 'the belligerents remain under the protection and the rule of the principles of the law of nations, as they result from the usages established among civilised peoples, from the laws of humanity, and the dictates of the public conscience'.

There were at least two profound consequences of this approach by Martens and his fellow delegates at the Hague in 1907. One was that at what was really the dawn of modern warfare the laws of war had not been cocooned in the thinking and practices of the nineteenth century. If they had been, all respect for the attempt to regulate warfare by international agreement would have been lost. The other was that the clause laid the ghost of a popular misconception, that what was not expressly prohibited in warfare was permitted. In his introduction to the German war book, Morgan graphically illustrates the point by saying that a hostess did not 'think it necessary to put up a notice in her drawing room that guests are not allowed to spit on the floor' and he concludes by wondering what we should 'think of a man who committed this disgusting offence, and then pleaded that there was nothing to show that the hostess had forbidden it'?[22] The argument surfaced again in relation to the use of nuclear weapons with the United States *Manual* taking the view that their use was not prohibited in the absence of an express prohibition,[23] but this rather simplistic view hardly represents the true legal status of these weapons, a matter which is discussed in Chapter 8. The First Protocol of 1977 reiterates the principle of the Martens Clause and provides confirmation, if that were required, that the influence of the laws of war extends beyond international agreements and into the shadowy realms of what a society considers to be acceptable conduct on the part of those who fight in its name.[24]

Non-Renunciation of Rights

Each Convention would fail to offer much protection to the victims of war if it permitted them to renounce their rights. It is not difficult to imagine pressure being put upon protected persons to renounce their status in return for some short-term benefit, such as food or medical supplies. It is interesting to note here that the rights under the Conventions are given to the individuals concerned and not merely to the State to which they belong and so any purported change by either their own country or by the State in which they are detained would be void. At the end of the Korean War a large number of North Korean prisoners of war did not wish to be repatriated but Article 118 of the Third Convention of 1949 stated quite categorically that 'prisoners of war shall be released and repatriated without delay after the cessation of active hostilities'. The solution to the problem involved the question of whether they could renounce their right to be repatriated and is discussed in Chapter 10.

Protecting Powers

The idea that a State neutral to the conflict should be able to accept a request for its services by a belligerent to supervise the treatment of its nationals is not a new one. There are examples of such a practice in the Boer War when the American Consul at Pretoria acted on behalf of British interests with the consent of the Transvaal government and in the Russo-Japanese war of 1904-06 when both the United States and France acted in this capacity.[25] The modern approach was formulated for the first time in the 1929 Geneva Convention dealing with prisoners of war and it was made a central part of all the 1949 Geneva Conventions. Each State was to request a protecting power to look after its interests and seek the approval of its adversary. As could be expected, difficulties arose over finding an acceptable neutral State and this, in part, led to the system of protecting powers falling into desuetude. The gap has, in practice, been filled by the International Committee of the Red Cross which has traditionally offered its services to the belligerents and who, under the First Protocol are, in certain circumstances, bound to accept its offer to act as a substitute protecting power.[26] The protecting power or its substitute, such as the International Committee of the Red Cross, has a right to go to all places where prisoners of war or other protected persons may be and it must be informed of various events in the treatment of such persons.[27]

During the Falklands War neither the United Kingdom nor Argentina appointed protecting powers under the regime of the Geneva Conventions, but each State did ask a neutral country to assist it by looking after the interests of its citizens. Switzerland acted for the United Kingdom, while Brazil undertook a similar mandate for Argentina. The International Committee of the Red Cross carried out its humanitarian role provided for in the Conventions with the assistance of the two appointed States and with the co-operation of Uruguay in whose territory repatriation of prisoners of war and the collection of the wounded and shipwrecked took place.

The 1977 Protocols

Jean Pictet, writing in 1969, called attention to the urgent need to revise the laws of war if they were not to be ossified to the period in which they were formulated. The methods and means of war, the so-called Hague law, dated from 1907 and had only been revised in a very piecemeal way since then. The principal achievements in this area had been the 1923 Hague Rules of Air Warfare, although they were never ratified, and the 1925 Geneva Gas Protocol. The International Military Tribunals at Nuremberg and Tokyo had drawn attention to methods and means of warfare that were considered to be unacceptable and to some extent these were etched into customary international law, whilst some canons had even found their way into the Geneva Conventions of 1949, notably, the provisions concerned with reprisals against protected persons and the taking of hostages. The law of Geneva had shown itself to be in need of an updating, largely, it might be said, because of the experience of the post-1949 wars, in the Middle East, in Nigeria and, of course, in Vietnam. The whole matter of revision was of concern to the United Nations, rather than being left to the sole initiative of the International Committee of the Red Cross as the 1949 Conventions had been. The laws of armed conflict were perceived by the United Nations as being part and parcel of the much wider field of human rights, a matter that much exercised it, and which had led to two international covenants concerned with human rights in 1966.[28]

The diplomatic conference that met between 1974 and 1977 to consider revision of the laws of war did so in a very different world from the one that had existed in 1949. The sixties had been a period of rapid de-colonisation and the principle of self-determination advanced by the General Assembly in 1960 had a momentum of its own;[29] so much so that delegates eventually agreed that a so-called war of liberation would attract the international laws of war and not merely the minimum standards laid down in common Article 3 of the 1949 Conventions.[29a] The development of new weapons, particularly those which had were indiscriminate in operation, affecting combatants and belligerents alike, and the effect that these new weapons could have on the environment were matters of the gravest urgency; the Vietnam War had shown that. But the concern was not merely over these weapons. No doubt some non-nuclear states were also hopeful that the Protocols would come down on the side of those who wished to see a declaration that nuclear weapons be outlawed. In addition, there was concern that what was perhaps the most frequent cause of suffering as a result of armed conflict, the civil war, was virtually unregulated.

Between the years 1974 and 1977 those States taking part in the diplomatic conference agreed on a major revision of the laws of war. Protection of the victims of war, especially civilians, was significantly increased. In the First Protocol the categories of those entitled to prisoner of war status were expanded to cover the guerrilla fighter, a major character in the war of liberation, while the mercenary was relegated to the status of an unprivileged belligerent. The civilian who became caught up in the fighting and who was wounded, sick or shipwrecked was to be entitled to the same protection as a combatant in a like condition and further protection was given to civilian medical personnel and transport. The journalist, who has played an increasingly important role in bringing home the realities of war and by so doing contributing, in no small way, to the way in which it is fought, is formally classed as a civilian with all the protection that that status entails.[30]

The protection of civilians from the direct effects of battle was one of the cornerstones of the First Protocol. Article 48 confirms what was originally a rule of customary international law that combatants are required to distinguish at all times between civilian and military objectives and to attack only the latter. It might be thought fairly obvious that a military commander should not shell a town which the enemy has abandoned or a church or a school, since there is no justification in terms of military necessity for such action. The greatest importance, it might be suggested, of the Protocol is that it directs attention to the indiscriminate attack; an attack that does have a military objective, but it is one in which, in the nature of things, the civilian population will also suffer. The Protocol draws upon the well-established principle of proportionality to solve this problem. An attack will be prohibited if injury to civilians or damage to their objects (such as the church or housing) would be excessive compared with the concrete and direct military advantage that would occur if the attack was made.[31] For the same reason the Protocol renders unlawful an attempt to destroy the sources of food and water supplies necessary for the survival of the civilian population or an attack in which widespread, long-term and severe damage is caused to the natural environment.

The Protocol requires States to consider all these matters seriously and in particular it imposes an obligation to ensure that legal advisers are available to advise military commanders on the application of the Conventions and to instruct members of the armed forces.[32] It is probably no exaggeration to say that unfamiliarity on the part of those actually engaged in military operations with the main principles of the Geneva Conventions and the Hague law has been the greatest cause of suffering not only to civilians but also to other combatants.[33]

Whilst the Geneva Conventions of 1949 are binding on most States of the world, the 1977 Protocols have only been accepted by about one-third of all States. Both the United Kingdom and the United States entered reservations, declared to be 'understandings', upon signing and in regard to the First Protocol, which is concerned with international armed conflicts, the British reservation stated that 'the new rules introduced by the Protocol are not intended to have any effect on and do not regulate or prohibit the use of nuclear weapons'. The United States, and the U.S.S.R. (when it agreed to participate in the Diplomatic Conference) entered similar reservations, whilst France was not a signatory State (although it has acceded to the Second Protocol). Only China amongst the nuclear weapon states is a party to the First Protocol.

It might well be argued that the British reservation is not valid, since the Vienna Convention on the Law of Treaties 1969 prohibits a reservation incompatible with the object and purpose of the (Protocol).[34] Part IV of the First Protocol is concerned with the general protection of the civilian population against the effects of war and in particular with prohibitions on the launching of indiscriminate attacks, attacks which damage civilian objects and those on the environment which cause widespread, long-term and severe damage to the natural environment. The use of nuclear weapons would almost certainly cause the type of damage that the Protocol was aiming to prevent, but whether the British reservation is rendered void by the Vienna Convention is really a matter of judgment. The lack of objections by other States would suggest that none wishes to make a serious issue out of this.[35] It is perhaps true to say that had the Protocol specifically prohibited the use of nuclear weapons during an armed conflict or had States objected to any reservation concerning these weapons, the United Kingdom, along with the United States, would not have signed it.

However, the legality, or otherwise, of the use of nuclear weapons is not based on the acceptability of the British reservation, but on the principles of customary international law and other treaty obligations. In any event, the reservation spoke of the '*new* rules' and this suggests that the British were not making the point that the laws of war did not prohibit the use of nuclear weapons.[36]

The 1977 Protocols are nevertheless a major achievement in bringing the laws of war into line with developments in the conduct of warfare itself. They transform areas of customary international law from mere assertion to reality and they will have a decisive effect in moulding thinking about the proper conduct of warfare not only by those States that are parties to them. The rules of customary international law that are enshrined in them bind all States alike. But perhaps the real practical value of, certainly the First Protocol, is that it merges the Hague with the Geneva law and it thereby enables the International Committee of the Red Cross to supervise, not only the treatment of the victims of war but also, in so far as it can, the methods and means of war. It should not be thought, however, that the International Committee has not hitherto been concerned with these matters. During the Iran-Iraq War, along with the United Nations Secretary-General, it has pointed out that the methods adopted by the belligerents have, at times, been at variance with the laws of war. In particular, concern has been expressed about the use of chemical weapons and the bombing of cities.

It may appear ungracious to question whether the Protocols have really been an advance in the laws of war or whether they reflect a common human trait of making laws for the conduct of war during times of peace and thereby wandering into unreality.[37] The danger is, of course, that once the new rules are perceived by those who have to carry them out as unrealistic, they, along with much else, will be abandoned. The question must therefore be asked whether the Protocols were too ambitious a project and whether, as a result, they will ever win worldwide acceptance in the same way as the 1949 Geneva Conventions did? The charge that various parts of the First Protocol are unrealistic has been made by a number of writers. Colonel Gonsalves put the position forcefully when he said that he had seen Article 56 (protection of works and installations containing dangerous forces, such as a dam or a nuclear power station) develop into an 'oversophisticated, unbalanced system of rules, which only attracts the laughter of military experts'. He concluded by saying that 'Many delegates left Geneva in July 1977, after signing the Final Act ... feeling that they had failed in grasping the opportunity to draft a really practicable and applicable system of new rules of humanitarian law and law of war.'[38] The same point is taken up by Professor Draper when he wrote: 'The essential balance in the Law of War has probably swung too far in the direction of humanitarianism. Insufficient attention has been paid to the nature of warfare and what commanders are trained to do.'[39]

Although these comments may be fair, they must be read in the light of subsequent developments. One of Professor Draper's main criticisms of the First Protocol was that it attempted to do indirectly that which it could not do directly. In other words, it did not prohibit specific conventional weapons but relied, instead, on formulating general principles. A separate conference was called by the United Nations in 1979 and this eventually led to the adoption of the 1981 Convention on Prohibitions or Restrictions on the Use of Certain Conventional Weapons, the main, although not the sole, purpose of which is to protect civilians during an armed conflict.

There may be many justifiable criticisms of the Protocols, and of the laws of war in general, not least of which is the difficulty in agreeing whether they apply or not,[40] but they are all we have and so the International Committee of the Red Cross must be right in its desire to see many more States accepting the obligations set out in the Protocols. Whether the principles embodied in the laws of war are adhered to depends, to some extent, on the type of armed conflict to which the parties have become involved. Two recent conflicts can be compared; the Falklands War and the Iran-Iraq War. In the former, breaches of the 1949 Geneva Conventions or of the general laws of war were few and of little consequence, whereas in the Iran-Iraq War the scale of the breach is much greater. Why should this be so? Both wars involved a limited conflict between two States in dispute over territory, fought by professional armed forces. One answer, and probably not the only one, is that the Falklands War was fought by both sides as a 'professionals war'; a mere test of strength between opposing armed forces in which there was no place for the involvement of civilians, as fighters or as targets. A clear winner was produced and the matter, as far as the military forces were concerned, was concluded. The Iran-Iraq War is one in which it is difficult to see how a winner could emerge, since both States seem quite prepared to accept high casualties and to win at any cost. It is really an example of the idealogical war, the type most likely to be fought with no holds barred. In these circumstances it is perhaps not surprising to learn that chemical weapons have been used and that the aerial bombing of cities has taken place.[41]

Where do the laws of war go from here? It is to be expected that the International Committee of the Red Cross will continue its task of keeping the laws of war not only in the forefront of world attention so that barbaric conduct is seen to be such, but also in line with developments in the practice of war itself. States will be actively encouraged to accept the Protocols and to consider additions to them. There is, for instance, an urgent need to explore the whole field of naval warfare and to assess the effectiveness of the existing law.

War Crimes

The legal difficulties involved in the trial of alleged war criminals have been considerably eased by the Geneva Conventions of 1949 and the two Protocols of 1977. Both World Wars had thrown up the problem of how to deal with those defeated Germans against whom it was alleged that crimes against the laws and customs of war had been committed. The Treaty of Versailles in 1919 had provided that the accused should be handed over to the Allies for trial. This was never accepted by the German government, who eventually agreed to try the alleged offenders themselves under German law at Leipzig.[42] The

Allies were not satisfied with the number of persons charged, nor with the low rate of convictions, but although they claimed the right to try such persons again in their own courts *in absentia* they did not in fact do so. During the Second World War the Allied powers made it their policy to try, at the conclusion of hostilities, war criminals and those who had ordered their acts.[44] The Charter of the International Military Tribunal to be held at Nuremberg asserted jurisdiction to try alleged offenders for crimes against the peace in planning, preparing, initiating or waging a war of aggression; war crimes, namely violations of the laws or customs of war; crimes against humanity committed against the civilian population. In 1946 the Tribunal announced its findings. Twenty-two defendants had been tried, of whom three were acquitted.

Considerable doubts were voiced by some as to the legality of the proceedings. It was argued that there was no basis in international law for the trial in their own State of individuals by a tribunal formed by a combination of other nations when the alleged crimes were committed in the territory of other States. Moreover, the judges of the Tribunal were drawn entirely from the victorious States.[45] The judgment of the Tribunal[46] was affirmed by the General Assembly of the United Nations in 1946 and the principles involved have found their way into various multilateral treaties, such as the Convention on the Prevention and Punishment of the Crime of Genocide in 1949 and the European Convention on Human Rights and Fundamental Freedoms 1951.

The effect of the war crimes tribunals in 1946 was to show that all States had jurisdiction to try a war criminal, whose crime, like that of the pirate, was *jure gentium*.[47] This principle was invoked by the District Court of Jerusalem in 1961 when it tried and convicted Adolf Eichmann of war crimes, 'crimes against the Jewish people' and of crimes against humanity. It should be noted that the State of Israel had not been in existence when Eichmann's crimes were committed, but the court based its judgment, *inter alia*, on the ground that all States had a universal jurisdiction to try those charged with these offences. The crimes charged were, in the judgment of the court, 'crimes, which struck at the whole of mankind and shocked the conscience of nations' and were 'grave offences against the law of nations itself'.[48] However, this analysis has not won the support of all writers where the charge is one of crimes against humanity as opposed to war crimes. The International Tribunal at Nuremberg drew a clear distinction between the two, and whilst universal jurisdiction may exist in respect of the latter, it is not clear whether it does in the former case.[49]

The approach of the Geneva Conventions of 1949 and the two Protocols of 1977 is to provide for the punishment of 'grave breaches' of the Conventions without adopting the old terminology of war crimes and crimes against humanity. All the 1949 Geneva Conventions list a number of grave breaches, which include wilful killing, torture or inhuman treatment, wilfully causing great suffering or serious injury to body or health.[50] It is one thing to define grave breaches of the Conventions, but it is also essential to provide some machinery for bringing to trial those accused of such acts. This is dealt with in each of the Conventions which requires each State to enact legislation to give itself the necessary jurisdiction to try those who come before its courts.[51] It would therefore be perfectly legitimate, in theory, for British courts to try a member of the armed forces of another State who committed a grave breach of one of the Conventions in an armed conflict in which the United Kingdom was not involved if the alleged offender happened to be within the jurisdiction of the British courts.[52]

The First Protocol of 1977 deals also with a problem that arose during some of the trials after the Second World War, the liability of the commander whose troops commit war crimes. General Yamashita was convicted by a United States Military Commission in 1946 of unlawfully disregarding and failing to discharge his duty as commander to control the acts of members of his command by permitting them to commit war crimes.[53] The four Geneva Conventions of 1949 impose the same obligations on all States to prosecute those who order grave breaches to be committed, and the First Protocol deals specifically with the liability of commanders in Article 87. Their obligation is to prevent, and where necessary to suppress and to report to competent authorities, breaches of the Conventions and the Protocol.[54]

Finally, a British soldier who commits a crime against English law while engaged on military duty can be prosecuted by court-martial and could be charged with a number of alternative offences, depending on the circumstances. The same would apply to the superior who ordered him to commit an unlawful act.[55]

Notes

1. Hague law also refers to other Conventions that bear a different name, such as the Declaration of St. Petersburg 1899 and the Geneva Protocol for the Prohibition of the Use in War of Asphyxiating, Poisonous or other Gases, and of Bacteriological Methods of Warfare 1925.
2. The Convention has become part of English law by the Genocide Act 1969. Both the Universal Declaration and the Genocide Convention were inspired by the General Assembly.
3. Figures are at 1 November 1986.
4. The reason commonly given for this attitude by the United Kingdom is that it will not ratify the Protocols whilst a major ally (i.e. the United States) has not. This country did not ratify the Geneva Conventions until 1957, but agreed to apply their principles in the Suez crisis of 1956. The Geneva Conventions Act 1957 incorporates the Conventions into English United Kingdom.
5. These issues are discussed in Chapter 10.
6. Roling, *Hague Receuil des Cours* (1960), points out some of the difficulties.
7. See, for example, Article 147 of the Geneva Fourth Convention 1949.
8. For a compendium of the various definitions of 'war', see McNair and Watts, *The Legal Effects of War*, C.U.P., 4th edn, 1966, p. 6, and for an account of the 'state of war' doctrine see Brownlie, *International Law and the Use of Force by States*, Oxford, Clarendon Press, 1963, pp. 26 et seq. A government minister replied by letter of 20 May 1982 to an M.P.

and repeated the government's view that it did 'not consider that there exists a state of war between this country and Argentina', (1982) 53 B.Y.I.L. 519 at p. 520.

9. Article 2 applies the Conventions to 'declared war or of any other armed conflict which may arise between two or more of the High Contracting Parties, even if the state of war is not recognised by one (*sic*) of them'. Oppenheim's view, which seems to have won general acceptance, was that Article 2 should have read, 'by one or both of them', *International Law*, vol. 2, Longmans, 7th edn, 1952, p. 369, note 6. Pictet, *Commentary* 1 to the Geneva Conventions (I.C.R.C.), Geneva, 1952, describes an 'armed conflict' as 'Any difference arising between two states and leading to the intervention of armed forces'.

10. See H.C. Deb. vol. 22, col. 609, 26 April 1982.

11. Examples would be the Hague Convention of 1907 and the 1925 Gas Protocol (fully described in note 1).

12. For a fuller discussion of the Northern Ireland situation see Chapter 4. There may also be considerable argument whether an armed conflict is an international one or not. The Vietnam War was perhaps a classic example of this problem. It may serve the interests of a State for it to argue that the conflict is an international one (the U.S. position in Vietnam) or that it is non-international and therefore no infringement of Article 2(4) of the U.N. Charter has occurred. The laws of war may have given too much latitude to a State to characterise its armed conflict.

13. For a compelling account of this doctrine see Keen, *The Laws of War in the Late Middle Ages*, Routledge & Kegan Paul, London, 1965. In the light of common Article 1 it cannot be invoked against an aggressor who has acted in breach of the prohibition in the U.N. Charter of the use of force.

14. See U.N. Document A/C 3/38/L.62 (6 December, 1983). See also Bothe, *Non-International Armed Conflicts* (1982) 31 The American University Law Review, 899, 905-908.

15. Monkllor, *Legal Status of Victims of Non-International Armed Conflicts: An Application of Protocol II in El Salvador*, in Redden (ed)., *Modern Legal Systems Cyclopedia*, Hein & Co., New York, vol. 7, 1985, pp. 219, 229.

16. Although the International Committee of the Red Cross may act under Article 3. It is active in El Salvador, See International Committee of the Red Cross, *Annual Report 1984*, pp. 32 et seq. The I.C.R.C. was able to visit government prisoners, but not those captured by the F.M.L.N. They were also able to assist in the release of wounded combatants. See also Article 18 of the Second Protocol of 1977.

17. See note 15 at p. 224. Note also Article 3 of the Second Protocol 1977, 'Nothing in this Protocol shall be invoked for the purpose of affecting the sovereignty of a state.' This may bring comfort to some States.

18. Captured members of the State's armed forces can not lawfully be prosecuted for any offence, since the dissident armed force has no authority to enact laws.

19. Under English law a treaty is not binding since it is not self-operating. The treaty 'remains irrelevant to any issue in the English courts until Her Majesty's Government has taken steps by way of legislation to fulfil its treaty obligations', Diplock L.J., *Salomon v. Commissioners of Customs and Excise* (1967) 2 Q.B. 116, 143.

20. See, for example, s. 4 of the Criminal Law Act 1967. The defence of duress might be available, see *Subramaniam v. Public Prosecutor* (1956) 1 W.L.R. 965.

21. See *International Herald Tribune*, 16 September 1985, reporting on civilian killings by both government and guerrilla forces in El Salvador.

22. *The German War Book, Being the Usages of War on Land*, with Introduction by J. H. Morgan, Murray, London, 1915, p. 6.

23. See, generally, *The New U.S. Army Field Manual on the Law of Land Warfare* (1957) 51 A.J.I.L. 388-396.

24. The Martens Clause was invoked by the International Military Tribunal at Nuremberg, (1947) 41 A.J.I.L. 172, 219. Since these Conventions do not represent the whole of the laws of war, a State that denounces them cannot escape from other obligations imposed by international law.

25. For a detailed treatment of the protecting power system, see Peirce, *Humanitarian Protection for the Victims of War: The System of Protecting Powers and the Role of the I.C.R.C.* (1980) 90 Mil. L.R. 89. For the basis of neutral States assisting foreign citizens

when diplomatic arrangements are withdrawn, see Article 45, Vienna Convention on Diplomatic Relations, 1961, U.K.T.S. 19 (1965).

26. See Article 5(4) of the Protocol. The main provisions are in Articles 8 and 10 of the First Geneva Convention of 1949 and in similar articles in the other 1949 Conventions. See also Resolution 2 of the Final Act of the Geneva Conference 1949.

27. A more detailed discussion of the protecting power system can be found in Chapter 13.

28. The International Covenant on Civil and Political Rights and the International Covenant on Economic, Social and Cultural Rights, both in U.K.T.S. 6 (1977).

29. See Declaration on the Granting of Independence to Colonial Territories and Peoples, G.A. Resolution 1514 (XV), 1960.

29a. See Article 1(4) of the First Protocol 1977.

30. Consider the important part played by *The Times* in exposing the incompetence of the British in the early stages of the Crimean War and those reporting the Vietnam War who showed the American people the tragic effects of that war. A war correspondent, who is authorised by his armed forces to accompany them, is entitled to be treated, upon capture, as a prisoner of war, Article 4(A)(4) of the Third Geneva Convention 1949.

31. This is, in reality, no more than an elaboration of the principle to be found in Article 35 of the Protocol that the right of belligerents to 'choose methods or means of warfare is not unlimited'. Compare Article 22 Hague Rules 1907 which spoke of a similar limitation in respect of 'injuring the enemy'.

32. See, generally, Hays Parks, *The Law of War Adviser*, (1979) 18 Revue de Droit Pénal Militaire et de Droit de la Guerre, 357, 405, who shows that the ratio of lawyers to personnel in the U.S. Army was 1:525 whilst in the British Army it was 1:3,667.

33. *Ibid.*, at pp. 389-393. Professor Adachi concludes his paper, *Unprepared Regrettable Events, a Brief History of Japanese Practices in Treatment of Allied War Victims during the Second World War*, The National Defence Academy, Yukosuka, 1982, p. 68, with the words 'Much more education and training among nationals is indispensable to attain humanitarian goal in the event of armed conflict.' The Japanese conduct was due to an 'overstressed sense of nationalism' and deviation from the traditional spirit of *Bushido*' (a code of honour and chivalry practised by warriors).

34. Article 19.

35. See, generally, *Reservations to the Convention on Genocide Case* (1951) I.C.J. 15 (Advisory Opinion) which deals with objection to a reservation by a party to a treaty. *Quaere* whether there would be objection if the U.K. did ratify whilst maintaining this reservation.

36. See, generally, Wortley, *Observations on the Revision of the 1949 Geneva Red Cross Conventions* (1983) 54 B.Y.I.L. 143. Other objections to ratification may well be due to unhappiness with the whole of the Second Protocol, the question of guerrilla warfare and what might be considered as unrealistic protection of the civilian population. See also Aldrich, *New Life for the Laws of War* (1981) 75 A.J.I.L. 764.

37. It is interesting to note that a number of States, in which there exists civil conflict, are parties to the First but not the Second Protocol. Examples are Angola, Mozambique, while surprisingly El Salvador is a party to both Protocols.

38. *Unbalance of the Rules, Unwillingness of the Commanders* (1984) 23 Revue de Droit Pénal Militaire et de Droit de la Guerre, 269, 272.

39. *The Emerging Law of Weapon Restraint* (1977) 19 Survival 9, 15. It is interesting to compare the First Protocol with the proposals for reform of the laws of war, put forward by Pictet in the *Need to Restore the Laws and Customs Relating to Armed Conflicts* (1969) 1 Review of International Commission of Jurists, 22 as an annex at p. 37.

40. Consider the Lebanon. Is this an international armed conflict to which the Geneva Conventions apply or is it a civil war to which only common Article 3 applies? The International Committee of the Red Cross is clearly of the view that the Fourth Geneva Convention of 1949 applies to the territory occupied by Israel. Israel does not; see Chapter 11.

41. A U.N. report accused Iraq of using toxic gas against Iranian targets contrary to the 1925 Geneva Gas Protocol, *The Times*, 17 March 1986. In the Falklands War steps were taken to assist those *hors de combat*. The Red Cross Box was instituted and healthy prisoners of war were repatriated while the hostilities continued.

42. The Allied powers reserved the right under Articles 228-230 of the Versailles Treaty to try offenders should the German trials not prove to be satisfactory.

43. Woetzel concludes that, 'Of the forty-five cases submitted by the Allies, twelve were tried by the Leipzig court, and six defendants were convicted. The Allied Powers were highly dissatisfied by this showing', *The Nuremberg Trials in International Law*, London, Stevens and Sons, 1962, p. 34.

44. See, generally, Tusa and Tusa, *The Nuremberg Trial*, London, Macmillan, 1983, chap. 4. The British government initially favoured summary punishment and were eventually persuaded by the U.S. government that a full trial should be held. Stalin's view at Yalta in 1944 was that the major criminals 'should be tried before being shot', *ibid.*, p. 63.

45. Woetzel, *op. cit.*, chaps. 3, 4 and 5. Woetzel concludes that 'the I.M.T. (International Military Tribunal) at Nuremberg was an international military tribunal with a firm basis in international law', at p. 93. The following 'defences' were rejected by the Tribunal, *nulla poena sine lege* (no punishment should be imposed which is not firmly based on law), *tu quoque* (the crime also has been committed by others), superior orders (although see Article 8 of the Charter of the Tribunal which states that superior orders may be taken in to account by way of mitigation), military necessity (unless specifically permitted in the laws of war, see Article 23(g) of the Regulations annexed to the Hague Convention (IV) of 1907).

46. See (1947) 41 A.J.I.L. 172. A Tribunal was also held in Tokyo and the various States also tried alleged war criminals before their own tribunals.

47. See *Manual of Military Law*, Part III, London, H.M.S.O. (1958), para. 637. The difference, of course, between the pirate and the war criminal is that the former, but not the latter, commits his offence beyond the jurisdiction of any State (usually on the high seas).

48. (1961) 36 I.L.R. 5, para. 12.

49. See Woetzel, *op. cit.*, p. 265. The International crime of waging aggressive war is also quite distinct, see also the General Assembly Resolution 2625 (XXV) October 1970, on Declaration of Principles of International Law Concerning Friendly Relations and Co-Operation Among States, 1970.

50. See Articles 50, 51, 130 and 147 of each of the four Geneva Conventions 1949 and Article 85 of the First Protocol 1977.

51. See the Geneva Conventions Act 1957. See, generally, Draper, *The Red Cross Conventions*, London, Stevens and Sons (1958).

52. There may be problems over extradition if a State with a better claim to try the alleged offender seeks his return from the United Kingdom, see Draper, *op. cit.*, at p. 106. See also Article 88(2) of the First Protocol 1977. A further problem would be whether the British prosecutors could gather sufficient evidence to convict in these circumstances.

53. 4 W.C.R. p. 1. See also the *Trial of S.S. Brigadeführer Meyer* in 4 W.C.R. p. 97, where the accused was convicted of inciting and counselling men under his command to shoot Canadian prisoners of war. See also the *German High Command Trial* 12 W.C.R. p. 1, esp. pp. 112-118. Consider also Article 86 of the First Protocol 1977.

54. See also Article 82 of the First Protocol 1977 dealing with the provision of legal advisers to advise military commanders and Article 90 concerned with an international fact-finding commission.

55. Each could be charged under section 70 of the Army Act 1955 with committing a criminal offence (such as murder, causing grievous bodily harm or rape). It is difficult to see of what value, in this context, are the Geneva Conventions Act 1957 or the Genocide Convention Act of 1969, since a person subject to military law can always be tried under the Army Act 1955. For examples of U.S. Servicemen convicted by their own courts-martial of war crimes, see Parks, *The Law of War Adviser*, (1979) XVIII Revie de Droit Pénal Militaire et de Droit de la Guerre, 359, 367 and esp. note 57 at p. 403.

10

Prisoners of War

'Today the prisoner of war is a spoilt darling.' Spaight.

Prisoners of war were often a valuable possession to their captor in the Middle Ages. Their safety in captivity was assured, however, only if they could be the subject of a ransom demand. Those who were of no economic value were entitled to nothing; their lives became the property of their captors.[1] Ideas about the status of prisoners of war altered inevitably with changing views about the status of man himself and with current ideas of chivalry. It came to be generally recognised by the eighteenth century that 'war captivity is neither revenge nor punishment, but solely protective custody, the only purpose of which is to prevent the prisoners of war from further participation in the war ... and that it was contrary to military tradition to kill or injure helpless people'.[2]

Attempts were made at the Hague conferences of 1899 and 1907 and by the Geneva Convention of 1929 to lay down a code for the treatment of prisoners of war, but the modern position is contained in the Geneva Convention 1949 (the Third Convention) which is supplemented by the First Protocol of 1977. Where one of these treaties is not strictly binding on a State, because it, or an adversary, is not a party to it, customary international law may impose obligations in respect of the fundamental principles contained in it. During the Second World War, for instance, the U.S.S.R. was not a party to the 1929 Geneva Convention. This relieved Germany of its obligations under the Convention, but the International Military Tribunal at Nuremburg held that Germany was not in consequence entitled to treat Russian prisoners of war as it wished. Customary international law pointed instead to a certain minimum standard of treatment.[3]

The question of who is entitled to prisoner of war status is closely linked to that of who can legitimately take up arms. The traditional punishment meted out to an unlawful belligerent has been death. He has been styled the *franc-tireur*, a term that originated during the Franco-Prussian War of 1870 to describe irregular troops employed by the French, many of whom were executed by the Prussians as criminals. Since most of the wars this century have involved the civilian population to an extent greater than hitherto, it is not perhaps surprising that the laws of war should take this into account and extend not only the status of prisoner of war but also, in the same breath, the categories of lawful belligerents (or combatants).[4]

157

Prisoner of War Status

The most obvious person entitled to prisoner of war status is a member of the armed forces of a party to the conflict.[5] Whether a volunteer corps or militia is part of the armed forces is dictated by national law; under English law it is the Service Discipline Acts that govern the matter. It is because members of the Palestine Liberation Organisation do not represent the armed forces of a State and therefore a party to the Convention that they are not entitled to the status of prisoner of war.[6] Article 4 of the Convention goes on to provide that persons who accompany the armed forces without actually being members, such as war correspondents and those responsible for the welfare of the armed forces, are also entitled to prisoner of war status providing they have been authorised to accompany the forces. In addition, members of the Merchant Navy are to be treated as prisoners of war, a clear recognition of the often decisive and active part that they play in modern warfare.

It has been a distinct feature of warfare in the present century that irregular fighters, partisans or guerrillas have become involved, operating usually in occupied territory. On one viewpoint they could be seen merely as *francs-tireur* rebelling against the *de facto* authority of the occupying power. On another, they could be viewed as legitimate combatants. The law of war has gradually steered a mid-course between these two and has come to recognise that in certain circumstances irregular fighters may be entitled to prisoner of war status if they are captured.

Inhabitants of a non-occupied territory who, on the approach of the enemy, spontaneously take up arms to resist the invading forces without having time to form themselves into regular armed units, are said to form a *levée en masse* and will be entitled to prisoner of war status on capture. 'The *levée en massse* created a new "irregular" but heroic type of combatant who could only be treated as unlawful (i.e., as a murderer or criminal) at the cost of shocking contemporary notions of patriotism and fair dealing.'[7] One obvious effect of a *levée*, along with all forms of irregular fighting, is that it obliterates the distinction between the armed forces of belligerents and the civilian population. Where an invading army cannot make this distinction, it will be the civilian population that will suffer. Should a *levée* occur, all the inhabitants are thereby rendered 'legitimate enemies until the place is taken'.[8]

Members of the *levée* must carry their arms openly and respect the laws and customs of war. To retain this status and to carry on the fight members of the *levée* will have to join the armed forces, or an organised irregular force, of a party to the conflict. Had the inhabitants of the Falkland Islands taken up arms spontaneously against the invading Argentinian forces in April 1982, they would have been entitled to prisoner of war status on capture. In the conditions of modern warfare it is more likely, however, that passive rather than active resistance will be offered by the civilian population against invasion forces.

Of much greater significance is the organised resistance movement which can operate inside as well as outside its occupied territory. The movement must belong to a party to the conflict so as to distinguish it from a criminal organisation, but in the confused circumstances of war, where a government exists only in exile when its territory is occupied, the movement may be taken under the command of an ally. This happened with the French Forces of the Interior in 1944 when they were taken under the command of General Eisenhower.

The requirement that the movement be organised is some guarantee that in return for the status of prisoner of war upon capture the movement will conduct its activities in accordance with the laws of war. It is the nearest one can get to the main characteristic of an army. The movement itself must possess the four following conditions. First, it must be commanded by a person responsible for his subordinates; in other words, there must be someone responsible to State authorities who can enforce discipline within the movement. Secondly, members of the movement must have a fixed distinctive sign recognisable at a distance. This takes the place of a uniform and is intended to distinguish combatant from civilian, but it will be seen it is a requirement with which it is difficult to comply if members of the movement are required to move about within occupied territory. Thirdly, arms must be carried openly. It has never been entirely clear whether this means that a member of the resistance movement must carry arms visibly or whether it merely means that he must not lead the enemy to believe that he is an unarmed civilian immediately prior to an attack.[9] Fourthly, the movement must conduct its operations in accordance with the laws and customs of war. This condition refers back to the requirements of organisation and discipline, since it places an obligation on the movement to instruct its members on the prohibited methods and means of warfare. 'It is necessary', suggests the *Manual of Military Law*, 'that they should have been warned against the employment of treachery, maltreatment of prisoners, wounded and dead, improper conduct towards flags of truce, pillage, and unnecessary violence and destruction.'[10]

An example of an organised resistance movement in England during the Second World War was the Home Guard, although its basis was the Regulations annexed to the Hague Convention IV of 1907.[11] All four conditions, described above, were clearly complied with. Its members would have been lawful combatants had England been invaded, despite the fact that they were only part-time soldiers.[12]

Serious difficulties with these four conditions led to their reappraisal at the Diplomatic Conference that produced the First Protocol of 1977. One might be forgiven for thinking that the plight of members of resistance movements operating within occupied territory was not an immediate priority for those aiming to bring the laws of war up to date. The issue was, however, brought to the front of the stage by the decision to treat an armed conflict in which peoples are fighting against colonial domination and alien occupation and against fascist regimes in the exercise of their right of self-determination as an international conflict and one to which the laws of war apply.[13]

In order to survive, guerrillas must be able to merge with the civilian population and be indistinguishable from it, certainly at all times other than when taking part in a military operation.[14] To wear a fixed distinctive sign recognisable at a distance and to carry arms openly was hardly compatible with these tactics. The First Protocol provides that combatants must distinguish themselves from the civilian population, but if they cannot comply with this the minimum requirement is that they carry their arms openly during each military engagement and during such time as the guerrilla is visible to his adversary while he is engaged in a military deployment preceding the launching of his attack. If he fails so to distinguish himself, he will forfeit his right to be a prisoner of war, although he is not to be treated as a common criminal (see Article 44(4)). It is a matter of judgment whether the balance has swung too far in favour of the guerrilla and whether the risks imposed upon the civilian population have now become unacceptable. Indeed, the adversary can take the fight to the guerrilla, since he remains a combatant and therefore a lawful object of attack. In this situation, however, there is no requirement, under the First Protocol, for the guerrilla to distinguish himself from the civilian population, unless a wide interpretation is given to the term 'military operations preparatory to an attack'.[15] It seems obvious that if an adversary cannot distinguish civilian from guerrilla, he will be tempted not to do so.

The problem of an unrecognised government is one to which the Conventions address themselves. The law would fail to offer protection to a member of the armed forces if the State into whose power he has fallen were to be permitted to withhold prisoner of war status on the ground that he was serving a government which the detaining power does not recognise.[16] One category of participant in hostilities which the law of war continues to treat as an outcast is the mercenary, a term that has proved very difficult to define. There have been a number of incidents in which the nationals of one State have volunteered to fight in the armed forces of another where their own State has remained neutral. United States nationals, for instance, joined the British armed forces before their own country declared war against Germany in the Second World War. The very essence, however, of the mercenary is that he is motivated to take part in an armed conflict for financial gain and he is not assimilated into the armed forces of that foreign State.[17] During the Falklands conflict in 1982 Argentina protested to the government of Nepal that a battalion of the Gurkha Rifles was to be sent to the islands. This protest was, no doubt, based on the understanding by Argentina that the Gurkhas were mercenaries. This is not the case, since the Gurkha battalions are a part of the British armed forces.[18]

The spy is one of the ancient offices of warfare, but the law of war takes an ambivalent view of his activities. The Regulations annexed to the Hague Convention IV of 1907 define a spy as a person (whether a member of the armed forces or not) who, acting clandestinely or on false pretences, obtains or endeavours to obtain information in the zone of operations of a belligerent, with the intention of communicating it to the hostile party.[19] It is clear from this definition that the spy carries on his activities *secretly* and so a member of the armed forces who attempts to acquire information about his adversary while wearing uniform is not considered a spy. The Whisky Class Russian submarine that penetrated the internal waters of Sweden and the naval base at Karlskrona in October 1981 could not be considered as being engaged in spying, although there is little doubt that its presence was for the purpose of acquiring information.[20] The U2 incident of 1960 was entirely different, since it was only through minute inspection of the aircraft that its country of origin could be discovered and the pilot was not wearing uniform.

Members of the armed forces who engage in spying forfeit, on capture, the right to be treated as a prisoner of war. 'The spy', wrote Spaight, 'is usually a soldier who has abandoned the recognised badge of his craft and his nation and adopted some disguise to shield his real character and intent. He has thrown away the insignia of his status, the evidence of his brotherhood among fighting men. ... The spy in modern war is usually a soldier who dons civilian dress, or the uniform of the enemy. ...'[21] This view is supported in the Privy Council case of *Mohamed Ali et al. v. Public Prosecutor* in 1968 in which the accused, a member of the armed forces of Indonesia, landed in Singapore wearing civilian clothes and proceeded to place a bomb in a civilian building. Following his capture shortly afterwards he was placed on trial for offences under local laws and claimed that he was entitled to be treated as a prisoner of war since he was a member of the armed forces of an adversary during an armed conflict between Indonesia and Malaysia (Singapore). The Privy Council held that he had forfeited his claimed status through his wearing of civilian clothes while participating in a military operation.[22] Mohamed Ali was not a spy, since he was not attempting to obtain information but the denial of prisoner of war status was based on the analogy with a spy. Merely to wear civilian clothes in the enemy's zone of operations is not, by itself, sufficient to render a member of the armed forces a spy. To illustrate this point the British *Manual of Military Law* takes the instance of a member of the aircrew who parachutes into the territory of an enemy belligerent after his aircraft has been disabled. He 'may disguise himself in order to avoid capture. If, however, he is captured, the burden of proof that he is not a spy rests upon him. The same applies to escaped prisoners of war who disguise themselves to avoid capture.'[23]

A spy who is captured is liable to be punished, but he is entitled to a trial and cannot be executed summarily. Although not condemned by international law, the spy is not protected by it.[24]

The law of war would fail to offer protection to combatants who are captured if it permitted their captors, by their own decision, to grant or to withhold prisoner of war status. Thus, whether a person is entitled to be treated as a prisoner of war, where a doubt arises, must be determined by a competent tribunal and not summarily.[25] He is entitled to be treated as a prisoner of war until it is decided to the contrary. A doubt arose in each of the following cases. In *Public Prosecutor v. Koi* (1968)[26] members of the Indonesian Army were captured in Malaysia during an armed conflict between the two countries. The Privy Council held that in so far as some of the captured were either citizens of Malaysia or owed allegiance to that State they were not entitled to prisoner of war status. In other words, a person who joins the forces of an enemy and is later captured by the State to which he owes allegiance is not entitled to the status of a prisoner of war. The other case was *Mohamed Ali et al. v. Public Prosecutor*, also in 1968, where, it will be recalled, a captured Indonesian soldier was denied prisoner of war status on the ground that he had carried out his military operations whilst wearing civilian clothes. As a result of the First Protocol an additional protection is given to the guerrilla who is captured. He cannot be denied the status of a prisoner of war merely because the organised resistance movement to which he belongs does not comply with the laws of war.

Little real protection would be offered to prisoners of war if the detaining power had the right to place them on trial for crimes that they may have committed before capture and, upon conviction, to withdraw their prisoner of war status. Three broad situations might be envisaged, although only in the third does the detaining power have a right under international law to try prisoners of war for offences committed before capture. First, take the case of a member of the armed forces of a party to the conflict who enters, by stealth, but wearing his uniform, the territory of the enemy and is captured whilst in possession of a firearm and explosives. This is likely to be an offence under the domestic law of the detaining power. Can he be prosecuted for this offence? The answer would seem to be that 'it would be an illegitimate extension of established practice to read (the domestic law) as referring to members of regular forces fighting in enemy country. Members of such forces are not subject to domestic law.'[26]

Secondly, the detaining power may have captured a prisoner of war whom it wishes to try for offences committed before the actual conflict, in which it is engaged, began. The case of Captain Astiz, who was the Argentinian commander of the Grytviken (South Georgia) garrison in April 1982 during the Falklands conflict, poses such a problem. The difference, that upon his capture by British forces the authorities of other States wished his extradition to stand trial for offences against their nationals committed during the so-called 'dirty war' in Argentina, would not appear to be decisive. Suppose, however, that the British authorities wished to try him for these offences. Could they do so? It is thought that there would be no legal basis for doing so, since British courts would lack jurisdiction.[27]

Finally, prisoners of war may be tried for offences either against the domestic law of an occupying power or for offences under international law; in particular, war crimes. Since, however, prisoners of war are 'privileged belligerents',[28] they cannot lose their status if convicted. Article 85 of the Third Convention provides that 'Prisoners of war prosecuted under the laws of the Detaining Power for acts committed prior to capture shall retain, even if convicted, the benefits of the present Convention.' There have been a number of reservations to this Article, in which States (mostly from the Eastern Bloc) have declared that they will not be bound by it.[29] Their view is that they have the right to try prisoners of war for war crimes and upon conviction to deprive them of their prisoner of war status. There is clearly a danger in accepting this position that a State will put on trial for war crimes a particular group of combatants, and upon conviction treat them as criminals. In 1942 the Japanese Army Ministry issued an instruction which directed that 'those captured airmen who violated the laws of war shall be punished as wartime felons through fair trials by military courts'.[30] An extreme approach was taken in relation to captured American aircrew during the Vietnam War when they were not accorded prisoner of war status at all. Article 85 clearly does not prohibit a trial by the detaining power, nor does it prohibit punishment, but it does require that the procedures laid down by the Convention be followed and to this extent prisoners of war are protected against arbitrary action by the detaining power.

Treatment of Prisoners of War

Article 13 declares that prisoners of war 'must at all times be humanely treated'. They are protected from the time that they fall into the power of the enemy until their final release and repatriation. It should be noted that the responsibility for the treatment of prisoners of war lies on the detaining power and not merely upon those individuals who effected the capture. In other words, a State cannot evade its obligations towards the treatment of prisoners of war by thrusting the responsibility upon the members of its armed forces, but neither do those individuals escape liability for any war crimes that they might commit against prisoners of war.[31]

Prisoners of war, like civilians in occupied territory and the wounded and sick, are protected persons. Wilful killing, torture or inhuman treatment, or causing great suffering or serious bodily injury, are styled 'grave breaches' of the Convention and give rise to individual liability, notwithstanding any plea of military necessity that might be raised. It would therefore not be permissible for the captors of prisoners of war to kill them because escorts could not be spared or food supplies were short. Other acts of violence, such as medical or scientific experiments and the use of reprisals against prisoners of war are all expressly prohibited. The duty to protect prisoners of war is clearly of a fundamental nature and a failure, for example, to prevent the civilian population from attacking them would be a war crime committed by the individuals responsible.[32] They are also to be protected against insults and public curiosity. Levie discusses the surrender of the Royal Marines at Port Stanley during the Falklands War and concludes that the taking of photographs of this event, with the Marines face down on the ground under guard, was probably not a breach of this Article of the Convention.[33]

The detaining power would fail to protect prisoners of war if it did not take steps to evacuate them from the combat zone or if it detained them in areas where they were exposed to the fire of that zone. The evacuation must be carried out in a humane fashion so that, for example, forced marches over long distances with inadequate supplies would be a breach of the Convention. It is perhaps interesting to note in this connection that the 1929 Geneva Convention placed a particular limit of 20 kilometres per day during an evacuation, but there is no specific mention of this in either the 1949 Convention or in the Protocol of 1977. A similar conclusion would follow if the detaining power attempted to render a military target, such as an ammunition depot, immune from attack by placing prisoners of war in its immediate vicinity. There may be cases, however, where prisoners of war cannot, because of the unusual conditions of combat, be evacuated. This may occur, for instance, where they have been captured at sea or in a jungle or desert. It would appear that under the customary laws of war 'the commander should supply the prisoners with that modicum of food, water and weapons as would give them a chance of survival', but the First Protocol of 1977 now specifically provides that they shall be released and that all feasible precautions shall be taken to secure their safety (Article 41(3)).

The detaining power may be very anxious to obtain from prisoners of war details of their units, formations and other military secrets, but it is expressly prohibited from using any form of coercion to secure this information. A prisoner of war may be asked about these matters, but he is not bound to answer beyond giving his name, rank, date of birth, and military unit number. It will be recalled that the British authorities were within their rights to question Captain Astiz on behalf of the French and Swedish governments, but in the face of his silence there was nothing further that they could do beyond repatriating him.

One of the dangers inherent in a conflict of ideologies is that prisoners of war are often subjected to ideological and political pressures. Nowhere is the problem so acute at present as in the Iran-Iraq War. This has led the International Committee of the Red Cross to comment forcefully about the treatment of Iraqi prisoners of war who are 'subjected to various forms of ideological and political pressure—intimidation, outrages against their honour, forced participation in mass demonstrations decrying the Iraqi government and authorities—which constitute a serious attack on their moral integrity and dignity'.[34]

The mental and physical welfare of prisoners of war is a matter of detailed provision in the Convention, since the effect of indefinite confinement on their mental condition cannot be underestimated. Prisoners of war are entitled to complete latitude in the exercise of their religious duties and the detaining power must encourage the practice of intellectual, educational, and recreational pursuits, games and sports.

The Convention spells out details of the conditions under which prisoners of war are to be detained, with the general principles being those of humane treatment in terms of the basic human needs, food, clothing, medical care and so on, and the standard of accommodation to be equal to the conditions enjoyed by the forces of the detaining power. A prisoner of war can hardly expect better. Article 22 of the Convention requires prisoners of war to be interned only in premises located on land. This would perhaps explain the unusual procedure adopted during the Falklands War of repatriating prisoners of war almost immediately upon capture. The islands were small and it was difficult to speak of an area outside the combat zone that would be suitable for the setting up of a prisoner of war camp. However, prisoners of war were put on freighters. There was no other place and the vessels provided more comfortable conditions than those available on land. The Argentine government was notified and the ships were kept away from battle areas. This was a technical breach of Article 22, but it was logical in the circumstances and was sanctioned by the International Committee of the Red Cross. A further course that might have been adopted would have involved the transfer of the prisoners of war to another State, in which they could more conveniently be accommodated. The Convention does not prohibit this providing the State which accepts the transfer is a party to the Convention and the transferring State has satisfied itself that the other is able and willing to apply it. Since a transfer may only be accepted by a State and not by an international organisation, such as the United Nations, NATO, or indeed the International Committee of the Red Cross, scope to place the care of prisoners of war outside the control of a State is extremely limited.

Work by Prisoners of War

Tensions associated with indefinite confinement may be relieved, to some extent, by the employment of prisoners of war in work that is not of a military character. The Convention permits the detaining power to utilise the labour of prisoners of war providing that they are fit to do so and directs that non-commissioned officers may only be required to do supervisory work, but that commissioned officers may not be compelled to work (Article 49). Article 50 attempts to spell out work to which prisoners may be put, such as agriculture, transport and handling of stores which are not military in character and domestic service. The conditions of work, including safety requirements and the duration of work, are set by the standard applicable to nationals of the detaining power (Article 51). They are entitled to a fair working rate of pay for the work that they do. This reference to the standards applicable to nationals of the detaining power is designed to prevent prisoners of war being employed as slave labour and the proscription of work of a military character is based on the principle that a prisoner of war must not be compelled to assist the enemy.

The use of prisoners of war 'by combat troops in combat areas for the construction of field fortifications' was condemned,[35] while the International Military Tribunal in its judgment found that Speer 'was also involved in the use of prisoners of war in armament industries'.[36] The removal of mines has been a long-standing problem and one on which some States have taken the view that captured members of the forces who laid the mines should be compelled to clear them.[37] Article 52 prohibits the employment of a prisoner of war on labour which is of an unhealthy or dangerous nature and it goes on to classify the removal of mines or similar devices as dangerous labour. There is no doubt that during the Falklands War Argentinian prisoners of war were involved in the clearing of mines, but it appears that they volunteered to do so. One of the Argentinians was killed and another injured during this exercise, but once the British authorities had conducted an enquiry into the death of the prisoner of war under Article 121, and no wrongdoing was found, their obligations were completed.

Finally, prisoners of war may be directed to work for private persons, but the detaining power in permitting such labour is not able to evade its responsibilities under the Convention (Article 57). In this way, prisoners of war may be employed by local farmers, but since they are not a form of slave labour the employer will have to pay for their services. German prisoners of war in England during the Second World War were employed on working parties and their employers were 'normally required to pay the military authorities the full value of the labour obtained according to the local civil labour wages rates, provided that such payments were not less than the payments required to be made to the prisoners of war by the military authorities'.[38]

Financial Resources of Prisoners of War

It has been shown that prisoners of war are entitled to a fair rate of pay for their labour and, in addition, they may receive money from their own State or from elsewhere, but the detaining power may specify an upper limit of cash which can be held by prisoners of war at any time. This is designed to ensure that prisoners of war do not have sufficient cash to make a successful escape more likely. The detaining power must grant to prisoners of war a monthly advance of pay, the amount of which may be agreed between the States concerned, although minimum amounts specified in Swiss francs are laid down. At the conclusion of the Second World War the British treated repatriated prisoners of war as having received 10 per cent of their pay from the German authorities and permitted them to claim the balance from their own force, less any sums that had been remitted during the period of their captivity. Adachi states that officer prisoners of war were to receive the same amount of basic pay as a Japanese officer,[39] but the British practice was to give repatriated British prisoners of war their pay in full, since 'no sums were considered to have been advanced to them in camp'.[40]

Information Bureaux

An important feature of any system of accountability of a State detaining prisoners of war must be a requirement to keep accurate records of those it holds. In addition, the families of prisoners of war can be kept informed of their condition. The Convention imposes an obligation upon States who hold prisoners of war to create a bureau[40a] to send details of transfers, releases, repatriations, escapes, admissions to hospital and deaths to the State to which the prisoners belong and to a central Prisoner of War Information Agency established in a neutral country. In practice, the latter function has been undertaken by the Central Tracing Agency of the International Committee of the Red Cross (acting as the Central Tracing Agency). It is one of the main concerns of the International Committee of the Red Cross that it has received notification of the names of no more than about 60 per cent of Iraqi prisoners of war held in Iran. The danger that the unrecorded prisoners may 'disappear' is a real one, and the uncertainty caused to their families a matter of grave concern. The First Protocol addresses itself to the problem of missing persons and directs that when circumstances permit or at the latest from the end of active hostilities, each party to the conflict is to search for those reported to be missing (Article 33).

Closely linked with the obligation upon the detaining power to communicate the names of prisoners of war is the right of a prisoner, within one week of arriving at a camp, to send a card to his family and to the Central Tracing Agency informing them of his capture, address and state of health (Article 70). The Convention goes on to provide a right for prisoners of war to communicate on a regular basis with their families (Article 71) and indeed stresses that they do not lose, upon capture, their full civil capacity; a prisoner of war who was so minded could therefore contract a valid marriage by proxy or draw up a will (Article 77).

The Maintenance of Discipline

It should be remembered that prisoners of war remain members of their own armed forces whilst in captivity and so will be subject to the discipline of their own superior officers, although the power to punish cannot be delegated to them.[41] They will also be under the authority of a commissioned officer of the armed forces of the detaining power, as a camp commandant and a prisoner of war becomes subject to the laws, regulations and orders in force of the armed forces of the detaining power (Articles 39 and 82). Thus, prisoners of war held in the United Kingdom become subject to the criminal law of England and Wales and to the military law of the British armed forces. It has been shown, in Chapter 2, that a member of the British armed forces may be tried for an offence against the Service Discipline Acts either in a military or a civilian court, depending on the offence committed. A prisoner of war may be entitled, by Article 84, to the same treatment, but if the detaining power has created an offence that can only be committed by a prisoner of war, such as attempting to escape, and not by a member of its own forces it can only impose disciplinary punishments which would, for example, exclude the death penalty (Article 82). Where a choice exists between trying a prisoner of war by disciplinary or by judicial means the former course should, whenever possible, be adopted (Article 83). The similarity of treatment with members of the forces of the detaining power is maintained in respect of punishments that may be imposed, so that a prisoner of war must not be subjected to a punishment that could not be imposed upon a member of the armed forces of the detaining power (Article 87). The detaining power must also take into account that a prisoner of war does not owe it a duty of allegiance and comes under its authority through circumstances beyond his control.

Article 89 sets out the disciplinary punishments that may be imposed on a prisoner of war, which range from a fine to confinement to last no more than 30 days (Article 90). Any confinement must be in accordance with the basic standards laid down by the Convention, and so it should not be served in harmful or dangerous conditions.[42] Formerly, it was permissible to punish by restricting the food rations of a prisoner of war, but Article 89, by omitting this, must be read as proscribing this form of disciplinary punishment. For serious offences the detaining power may wish to proceed against a prisoner of war by judicial rather than disciplinary procedures. One prisoner may have killed another or killed a guard or he may have committed what is clearly a criminal offence. Elementary principles of justice require that the offence the accused is alleged to have committed be one against the laws of the detaining power or against international law at the time it was committed (Article 99). The trial of prisoners of war for war crimes committed before capture is not prohibited, but as has already been shown, under Article 85 a person convicted of such an offence is entitled to retain the benefits of the Convention. A detaining power would not be entitled to place prisoners of war on trial for supposed war crimes that did not exist at the time that they were alleged to have been committed and, indeed, a number of post-war convictions for unlawful trials of prisoners of war were secured.

A safeguard for a prisoner of war subject to judicial procedures is that the protecting power must be notified at least 3 weeks before the opening of the trial; if it is not proved that the notice has been received, the trial must be adjourned (Article 104). This point was taken by the Privy Council in *Public Prosecutor v. Koi* in 1968 which decided that a failure to notify the protecting power of the trial of one of the accused, who claimed that he was entitled to the status of a prisoner of war, resulted in a mistrial.[43] This was by no means a straightforward case, since the appeal was based as much on the issue of whether the accused was entitled to be treated as a prisoner of war. Lord Hodson, in giving the Advice of the Board, outlined the position in cases of this kind. 'The court', he suggested, 'should have treated him as a prisoner of war for the time being and either proceeded with the determination whether he was or was not protected, or refrained from continuing the trial in the absence of notices (to the protecting power).' The main object of these provisions is not merely to inhibit (and, hopefully, to prevent) secret trials, but also to ensure that an accused is provided with the basic essentials of a fair trial, such as a defence advocate of his choice or one nominated by the protecting power. He is also entitled to call witnesses and, if necessary, to employ an interpreter. The detaining power must inform an accused prisoner of war of these rights in due time before the trial so that he might exercise them. Should the prisoner be deprived of the rights of a fair and regular trial, the detaining power will commit a grave breach of the Convention.[44]

The sentence imposed upon a prisoner of war will only be valid if imposed by the same courts and procedure as if the accused had been a member of the forces of the detaining power (Article 102). The death penalty cannot be carried out until at least 6 months have elapsed from the date the protecting power receives details of the sentence from the detaining power (Article 101). This delay will give the accused time within which to appeal (Article 106) or to take any further steps to have his case reviewed (or to request, if he is a prisoner of war in the United Kingdom, that the prerogative of mercy be exercised) and the protecting power time within which to make representations (Article 107).

Escapes

It may well be the duty of prisoners of war to escape, but it is equally the duty of the forces of the detaining power to prevent them. Article 91 deals with the question of when an escape is deemed to be successful and declares that it will be if the prisoner rejoins his own forces or those of an ally or he has left the territory of the detaining power or one of its allies (and has, for example, reached the territory of a neutral), or he has joined a ship of his own State (or an ally) in the territorial waters of the detaining power, the ship not being under the latter's control. The escaped prisoner of war, like the spy, is entitled to immunity once he has regained his lines (or those of an ally) and cannot thereafter be dealt with for that escape if at some subsequent time he is recaptured.

An unsuccessful escape will be visited with punishment by the detaining power, but a prisoner of war can be dealt with only under disciplinary rather than judicial proceedings even where it is not a first offence (Article 92). However, where the prisoner commits a criminal offence during the escape attempt he may be liable to judicial punishments (which alone can entail a death sentence) if the offence is a serious one. Article 93 outlines a number of offences that are not to be considered in this category. They include acts that do not entail any violence against life or limb, such as offences against public property, theft without intention of self-enrichment, the drawing up of false papers or the wearing of civilian clothing. Without this article a detaining power could treat almost every escapee as having committed a criminal offence in the attempt to make good his escape and could try him accordingly. It would not be difficult to imagine such criminal offences. They would range from theft, burglary, criminal damage or travelling on a train without a valid ticket.

The International Military Tribunal at Nuremberg considered the violation of the laws of war in the case of the Royal Air Force officers who had escaped from a prisoner of war camp and had later been recaptured. They had been shot on the direct orders of Hitler. 'It was not contended by the defendants', said the court, 'that this was other than plain murder, in complete violation of international law.'[45] It is permissible, however, to use weapons against prisoners of war, especially against those who are attempting to escape, but such action is to be considered as an extreme measure and must be preceded by warnings appropriate to the circumstances.[46] Under English law a soldier who shoots a prisoner of war would commit an offence unless he were to raise a reasonable doubt that he was justified in doing so. The death of any prisoner of war must be followed by an enquiry held by the detaining power under Article 121 and if this indicates guilt the detaining power is obliged to prosecute the person involved. During the Falklands War an incident occurred in which a British soldier shot and killed an Argentinian prisoner of war who was apparently attempting to sabotage the *Sante Fé*, a captured submarine, to prevent it from being moved. A Board of Inquiry was duly held and the soldier exonerated. In keeping with the obligations imposed by Article 121, the International Committee of the Red Cross (which had offered its services to both sides) was informed of the incident and the results of the Board.

The Protecting Power System

Forsythe comments that the protecting power system 'is one indication of the strength of the movement to guarantee that the law on the books does indeed become the applied law in war'.[47] Supervision by protecting powers of the nationals of another State is not a new concept, having a respectable history, but it was the advent of modern warfare that gave it impetus. During the Second World War Sweden and Switzerland acted for many of the belligerents and their activities were supplemented by the International Committee of the Red Cross. The 1949 Geneva Conventions had to take account of the possibility that there may be few neutral States in a future war and it therefore recognised that the International Committee of the Red Cross, or a different humanitarian organisation, would be likely in future conflicts to be appointed as a substitute protecting power. Article 10 of the Prisoners of War Convention stipulates that States may entrust the responsibilities of protecting power to the International Committee, or other humanitarian organisation, instead of to another State.[48] Independently of these arrangements, the International Committee has an automatic right to visit prisoner of war camps (Article 126). The First Protocol of 1977 strengthens the rights of the International Committee and enables it to carry out any other humanitarian activities in favour of the victims of war, subject to the consent of the parties to the conflict (Article 81(1)). Red Cross organisations are also to be granted facilities to enable them to carry out their functions in assisting the victims of war (Article 81(2), (3)).

Supervision of the Convention by the protecting power is achieved through inspections of prisoner of war camps, inspecting records of labour detachments and of disciplinary punishments (Article 96) and receiving complaints from prisoners of war, either directly or through the prisoners' representatives (Article 78). It has been shown that where the detaining power wishes to institute judicial measures against a prisoner of war, the protecting power must be informed and the importance of its role in the area cannot be underestimated. The protecting power also acts as the conduit for information about prisoners of war, including inquiries into the death of a prisoner, which is to be passed on to the State to which they belong (Article 121). Finally, the protecting power, or the International Committee of the Red Cross, may undertake to ensure the conveyance of relief shipments (such as foodstuffs, clothing, medical supplies, books and so on) to prisoners of war (Articles 72 and 73).

The protecting power system has not worked well, although the International Committee of the Red Cross has taken an active interest in all major conflicts. Protecting powers were appointed during the Suez crisis in 1956, although Egypt never accepted the choice of Israel nor the offer of the International Committee of the Red Cross which offered its services under Article 10 of the Convention. This episode illustrates one of the difficulties of the system: that it will only operate in practice if the parties to a conflict are willing to accept the choice of protecting power made by their adversary. The 1949 Convention made it mandatory, subject to certain conditions, for a party to the conflict to accept the offer of the services of the International Committee of the Red Cross, if no protecting power had been appointed. The difficulty with this arrangement in practice is that the International Committee may have to force itself upon a State that is unwilling to cooperate with it. From the view of the State concerned, issues of national sovereignty may arise. Intense debate on this matter took place in the Diplomatic Conference that produced the First Protocol in 1977. In Article 5 a duty is placed upon States to appoint protecting powers, but it then goes on to provide that the International Committee, without prejudice to the rights of similar organisations, can only act, as a substitute organisation, with the consent of the State, or liberation movement, concerned; in other words, there is no automatic appointment of the International Committee of the Red Cross. There is little doubt, however, that the International Committee will continue to act, if not as a substitute protecting power, as an unofficial overseer of State conduct towards the victims of war.

The United Kingdom appointed Switzerland as the protecting power for its interests during the Falklands War and the Argentine appointed Brazil. This marked a return to the scheme set out in the Conventions and a departure from the previous practice of States in not appointing protecting powers. Levie shows that 'there were ... no protecting powers in either Korea or Vietnam'[49] and certainly none has been appointed in the Iran-Iraq War. This is a matter upon which the International Committee of the Red Cross, varying from its usual practice, has spoken out. In 1984 it reminded all States of their obligation under Article 1 of the 1949 Conventions to ensure respect for the Conventions at all times. This has been interpreted to mean that States who are parties to the Conventions must take whatever steps they can to ensure that *other* States who are engaged in armed conflict abide by their obligations. The International Committee of the Red Cross has been performing its humanitarian duties under the Prisoners of War Convention, such as visiting camps in Iran and Iraq, but it has not always received the co-operation, especially from Iran, that it requires to carry out this function. It therefore appealed to all States and expressed a hope that discussions would be held to designate protecting powers willing to undertake the tasks encumbent on such states by the Geneva Conventions. Naturally, the I.C.R.C. would wish to work closely with the protecting powers.[50]

Repatriation of Prisoners of War

Prisoners of war must be released and repatriated without delay after the cessation of active hostilities (Article 118). Problems may well arise where there is no clear ending to the hostilities in the form of an armistice agreement and prisoners of war may become hostages to persuade the adversary not to recommence the conflict. A clear example of this attitude occurred in the India and Pakistan conflict of 1974 when India held Pakistani prisoners of war for 2 years after the conclusion of active hostilities. Following the surrender of Argentinian forces in the Falkland Islands the British authorities faced the problem of holding a large number of prisoners of war and a refusal by the Argentine government to declare an end to hostilities. Should the prisoners of war be repatriated in accordance with Article 118 or should they be held pending a determination of the intentions of their government? The British chose the former option and all prisoners were repatriated within a month of the surrender.

The whole tenor of Article 118 is that prisoners of war will be willing to be repatriated to the State to which they belong, but if they do not wish to be problems arise. In the first place, a British soldier who failed to return to his unit would commit an offence under s. 25 of the Army Act 1955 and whether he has a right to refuse to be repatriated is a matter of considerable doubt. At the conclusion of hostilities in the Korean War the North Koreans argued that Article 118 does not grant any discretion to the detaining power concerning repatriation, but the United Nations command took a different view. Its interpretation of the article suggested that repatriation could not be imposed upon an unwilling prisoner of war. To insist on repatriation might be to condemn a released prisoner to political persecution or, indeed, for a number of reasons, he may not wish to return home. An example might be the case of a soldier from Prague who, at the outbreak of the First World War, was an Austrian, but at the conclusion of hostilities, during which time he became a prisoner of war, his home was transferred to Czechoslovakia. Should he have the right to refuse repatriation to Austria?[51] It is fair to say that Article 118 can be interpreted as much in favour of compulsory repatriation as against it, but what will be crucial will be the attitude of the individual detaining power.[52] A Repatriation Commission was established by the Armistice Agreement of 1953, to whom all prisoners of war who had not been repatriated were transferred, but the results of this exercise were inconclusive.[53]

Repatriation can be delayed if a prisoner of war is being proceeded against for a criminal, but not a disciplinary, offence or if he is serving a sentence, but otherwise the actual repatriation must occur in conditions no less favourable than those applicable where a transfer of prisoners of war occurs while hostilities are still in progress (Article 119).

The detaining power need not wait until the end of hostilities before repatriating prisoners of war, since the Convention provides for compulsory repatriation, subject to certain conditions, of the seriously wounded and sick (Article 109). Article 110 goes on to require repatriation to their own State of the incurably wounded and sick, along with those who are clearly not fit to spend time in prolonged captivity, while the less serious should be accommodated in a neutral country, if this is necessary on medical grounds.[54] Nothing in the Convention prohibits the voluntary repatriation of *healthy* prisoners of war while hostilities are still in progress, but the experience of previous wars suggests that this is a rare phenomenon. It was, however, much in evidence during the Falklands War where neither side was willing to hold prisoners of war in the traditional way of establishing camps on the Second World War model. The consequence of this was the voluntary repatriation

of fit and healthy men and, in some cases, whole units. It will be recalled that
the Argentinian submarine, the *Santa Fé*, was captured at Grytviken. Very
shortly afterwards the crew were repatriated following a precedent established by Argentina which had repatriated the Marines captured on South
Georgia. This act of sending back the crew of the *Santa Fé* apparently
enraged the Royal Navy who thought that 'it was all very well returning a
few Marines, they could make no difference to the course of the conflict, but
to give the Argentines back a fully trained crew of submarine specialists
seemed the height of folly'.[55] The disadvantages of voluntary repatriation as
described above are that the returning combatant is able to provide his own
side with valuable information acquired during his, perhaps short, period of
captivity. In addition, a returned combatant could, as the apparent view of
the Royal Navy over the *Santa Fé* incident shows, return to the fight. The
scope of Article 117 of the Convention was much discussed when the Royal
Marines, who had been repatriated voluntarily from South Georgia, returned
to the Falklands Islands a short time afterwards. The article provides that
'No repatriated person may be employed on active military service.' Were
the Royal Marines so employed? They were clearly involved in active military
service; it would have been otherwise if they had merely been restricted to
a training role in the United Kingdom. The matter can only be resolved by
the view one takes as to the interpretation of the article. On the one hand,
it is a basic rule of construction that a treaty provision is to be interpreted
according to the context in which it is found, which in this case deals with
the voluntary repatriation of wounded and sick, and not healthy, prisoners
of war.[56] On the other hand, might one not argue that the purpose of the
Convention, which is designed to offer protection to prisoners of war, is more
than fulfilled by voluntary repatriation and that this is an action of the
detaining power to be encouraged? If it is, then it seems to follow that upon
repatriation the detaining power makes it an implied condition that those
who take the benefit of its actions should not become involved in active
military operations. An analogy might be drawn with the prisoner of war
released on parole under Article 21. Although the 1949 Convention does not
consider the consequences of his breach of parole, the Regulations annexed
to the Hague Convention (IV) of 1907 does. In Article 12 it deprives a person
released on parole of his right to be treated as a prisoner of war if he is
recaptured bearing arms against the government to whom he had pledged his
honour.[57] This must now be read subject to Article 85 of the 1949
Convention that prisoners of war are entitled to retain the benefits of the
Convention, even if convicted by the detaining power of offences committed
before capture. An exchange of prisoners of war is not very common, but it
has been a feature of the wars in the Middle East.

Notes

1. Keen, *The Laws of War in the Late Middle Ages*, Routledge R., Kegan Paul, London, 1965, pp. 156 et seq.
2. The Judgement of the International Military Tribunal at Nuremberg, (1947) 41 A.J.I.L. 172, 229.
3. See Draper, *The Red Cross Conventions*, Stevens, London, 1958, p. 12.
4. See Article 44(1) of the First Protocol 1977.
5. Article 4 of the Third Geneva Convention 1949 and Article 43 of the First Protocol 1977.
6. See *Military Prosecutor v. Omar Mahmud Kassem et al.* (1969) in (1971) 42 1.L.R. 470 and letter of Professor Draper, *The Times*, 16 July 1982.
7. Jones, *Status of the Home Guard in International Law* (1941) 57 L.Q.R. 212, 213. For the Swedish view see *Folkratlen I Krig*, S.O.U. 1984, vol. 56, Stockholm, p. 36.
8. Greenspan, *The Modern Law of Land Warfare*, Univ. Calif. Press, 1959, p. 63.
9. Greenspan, *op. cit.*, at p. 60, seems to prefer the first view; de Preux, *Commentary III to the Geneva Convention Relative to the Treatment of Prisoners of War*, I.C.R.C. (Geneva), 1960, at p. 61, prefers the second. See also First Protocol 1977, Article 44(3), and the U.K. understanding of the term 'deployment'.
10. Part III, H.M.S.O., 1958, para. 95. See also *Military Prosecutor v. Omar Mahmud Kassem et al.* (1971) 42 I.L.R. 470, at pp. 478-479.
11. Hague Rules (IV) 1907, Article 1. The conditions described in the text date back to the Hague Regulations 1899, Article 1.
12. Jones, *Status of the Home Guard in International Law* (1941) 57 L.Q.R. 212. Compare Bothe et al., *New Rules for Victims of Armed Conflict*, Martinus Nijhoff, The Hague, 1982, p. 252. For discussion of 'the farmer by day, assassin by night' concept, see Yingling and Ginnane, *The Geneva Conventions of 1949* (1952) 46 A.J.I.L. 393, 402.
13. Article 1(4) of the First Protocol 1977. Whether in practice many States will make the declaration required by Article 96(3) is unclear.
14. See Draper, *The Red Cross Conventions*, Stevens & Sons, London, 1958, p. 52; Baxter, *So-Called 'Unprivileged Belligerency': Spies, Guerrillas, Saboteurs* (1951) 28 B.Y.I.L. 353.
15. Article 44(3) of the First Protocol 1977. Upon signature the U.K. declared its understanding that 'the situation described in the second sentence of para. 3 of the Article can exist only in occupied territory or in armed conflicts covered by para. 4 of Article 1 ... the word "deployment" (will be interpreted as meaning) any movement towards a place from which an attack is to be launched'. If members of armed forces carry out operations behind enemy lines they must, to avoid being treated as unprivileged belligerents, distinguish themselves from the civilian population.
16. Article 4(3) of the Third Geneva Convention 1949. Members of the Palestine Liberation Organisation cannot seek the benefit of this provision, since 'it does not extend to the fighters of an organisation in relation to which there is no nexus with existing statehood', Draper, *The Times*, 16 July 1982.
17. Article 47, First Protocol 1977.
18. See (1982) 53 B.Y.I.L. 418; Levie, in Coll and Arend (eds.), *The Falklands War*, George Allen & Unwin, Boston, 1985, p. 74; for the background to Article 47 of the First Protocol 1977, see Devender, *Mercenaries at Geneva* (1976) A.J.I.L. 811. When it became known that a number of British subjects had been recruited into the F.N.L.A. forces in Angola, Lord Diplock chaired a Committee of Privy Councillors which looked into the recruitment of mercenaries in 1976. Its report recommended that there should be no offence in English law of merely serving in the armed forces of a foreign State, but that it should be an offence to be recruited into the armed forces of a State specified in an Order in Council (1976) H.M.S.O., Cmnd 6569. See, generally, Lynch, *British Subjects Involvement in Foreign Military Clashes* (1978) Crim. L.R. 257.
19. Article 29 of the Regulations annexed to the Hague Convention 1907; Article 46, First Protocol 1977.
20. Delupis, *Foreign Warships and Immunity for Espionage* (1984) 78 A.J.I.L. 53.
21. Spaight, *War Rights on Land* (1911), p. 203.
22. (1968) 3 All E.R. 488; 'He who adorns himself with peacock feathers does not thereby become a peacock', *Military Prosecutor v. Omar Mahmud Kassem et al.* (1971) 42 I.L.R. 470, 481.

23. Part III, H.M.S.O., 1958, p. 107, para. 330.
24. Stone, *Legal Controls of International Conflict* (1954), p. 549. Compare the *Quirin Case* (1942) 317 U.S. 31, where the Supreme Court stated that the spy was an unlawful belligerent. If this is so, why should Article 31 of the Regulations annexed to the Hague Convention 1907 expunge his guilt merely by rejoining his own forces?
25. Article 5 of the Third Geneva Convention 1949. See also *Mohamed Ali et al. v. Public Prosecutor* (1968) 3 All E.R. 488, and *Military Prosecutor v. Omar Mahmud Kassem et al.* (1971) 42 I.L.R. 470. See also Article 45 of the First Protocol 1977.
26. *Public Prosecutor v. Koi* (1968) 1 All E.R. 419, 427, Lord Hodson. Compare the dissenting views of Lord Guest and Sir Garfield Barwick at p. 432.
27. Meyer, *Liability of Prisoners of War for Offences Committed Prior to Capture: The Astiz Affair* (1983) 32 I.C.L.Q. 948; Dobson, Millar and Payne, *The Falklands Conflict*, Hodder & Stoughton, London, 1982, pp. 137 et seq.
28. See Baxter, *So-called 'Unprivileged Belligerency': Spies, Guerrillas and Saboteurs* (1951) 28 B.Y.I.L. 323.
29. See the declaration of ratification made by the United Kingdom concerning the reservation that some States had made to Article 85. The former position can be seen in the case of *Yamashita* (1946) 327 U.S. 1. See (1946) 40 A.J.I.L. at p. 442.
30. *Unprepared Regrettable Events, A Brief History of Japanese Practices on Treatment of Allied War Victims during the Second World War*, by Professor Adachi, National Defence Academy (1982), pp. 31-32. The instruction also listed a number of crimes, for example, 'bombing ... with the aim of terrorising, killing or injuring civilian population'. A total of 520 airmen were captured, 438 were interned as prisoners of war and the remaining were court-martialled' (at p. 32).
31. They may also be liable for an infringement of their own disciplinary code in domestic law. See, for example, s. 70 of the Army Act 1955 and the Geneva Conventions Act 1957.
32. The Judgment of the International Military Tribunal at Nuremberg, (1947) 41 A.J.I.L. 172, 226.
33. In Coll and Arend (eds.), *The Falklands War*, Allen & Unwin, Boston, 1985, p. 72.
34. International Committee of the Red Cross, Appeal to the Belligerents and to all State Parties to the Geneva Conventions, 7 May 1983.
35. See the *German High Command Trial* 12 W.C.R. 1.
36. (1947) 41 A.J.I.L. 172, 323. For a very detailed account of the labour of prisoners of war held by the Japanese, See Adachi, note 30 *supra*, pp. 34-44, who writes that the majority were employed in mining, followed by camp maintenance and shipbuilding.
37. Article 7 of Protocol II to the Conventional Weapons Convention 1981 requires minefields to be recorded.
38. See *Manual of Military Law*, Part III, H.M.S.O., 1958, p. 66, paras. 182 and 185.
39. Adachi (see note 30), p. 44.
40. *Manual of Military Law*, Part III, H.M.S.O., 1958, p. 62, para. 166.
40a. Articles 122 and 123 of the Third Geneva Convention 1949.
41. The British *Manual of Military Law*, Part I, states, 'During the time men are prisoners of war the ordinary relationship of superior and subordinate and the duties of obedience remain unaltered and (a soldier) who is guilty of insubordination or other breach of discipline ... or who commits any other offence against the Army Act 1955 is liable to be tried for his act or neglect after his release', para. 60. See also Article 96 of the Third Convention.
42. Article 98 of the Third Geneva Convention 1949. See also the Royal Warrant Governing the Maintenance of Discipline Among Prisoners of War 1958 (as amended), in *Manual of Military Law*, Part III.
43. *Public Prosecutor v. Koi* (1968) 1 All E.R. 419, 427; *Mohamed Ali v. Public Prosecutor* (1968) 3 All E.R. 488, 491.
44. Article 130 of the Third Geneva Convention 1949. The Convention does not deal with reimbursement of expenses incurred by a protecting power in providing legal assistance.
45. Judgment of the International Military Tribunal at Nuremberg (1947) 41 A.J.I.L. 172, 226.
46. Article 42 of the Third Geneva Convention 1949.
47. Forsythe, *Who Guards the Guards?: Third Parties and the Law of Armed Conflict* (1976) 70 A.J.I.L. 41; see also Peirce, *Humanitarian Protection for Victims of War. The System of Protecting Powers and the Role of the I.C.R.C.* (1980) 90 Mil. L.R. 89.

48. See also common Article 9 which confirms the pre-existing position that the Conventions should constitute no obstacle to the humanitarian activities of the I.C.R.C. or any other impartial humanitarian organisation.

49. In Coll and Arend (eds.), *The Falklands War*, Allen & Unwin, Boston, 1985, p. 69. For the attempts of the United States to secure the services of a protecting power in the Vietnam War, see Aldrich, *New Life for the Laws of War* (1981) 74 A.J.I.L. 764.

50. Second Memorandum from I.C.R.C. to States Party to the Geneva Conventions, 10 February 1984.

51. See Final Record IIA of the Diplomatic Conference at Geneva, (1949) Committee II, p. 462.

52. For the United States position see Baxter, *The Geneva Conventions of 1949 Before the U.S. Senate* (1955) 49 A.J.I.L. 554, and *The New U.S. Field Manual on the Law of Land Warfare* (1957) S1 A.J.I.L. 388 which declares that in its discretion the U.S. may offer such prisoners of war asylum in the U.S. See also Draper, *The Red Cross Conventions*, Stevens, London, 1958, p. 69, who takes the view that such a possibility was 'so remote that it did not justify an express provision in the Convention'.

53. *Quaere* whether transfer of prisoners of war to the Commission was, in itself, legitimate under the Convention, where transfer of prisoners of war can only be made to another State.

54. To be decided by Mixed Medical Commissions, Article 112. For the achievements of the Iran-I.C.R.C. and the Iraq-I.C.R.C. Mixed Medical Commissions, see I.C.R.C. *Annual Report 1985*, p. 67.

55. Dobson, Miller and Payne, *The Falklands Conflict*, Hodder & Stoughton, London, 1982, pp. 156-157.

56. Article 31, Vienna Convention on the Law of Treaties 1969.

57. The 1949 Convention is complementary to the relevant Regulations annexed to Hague Convention (IV) 1907 (see Article 135). A soldier who accepts parole may be in breach of his own military law, see *Manual of Military Law*, Part III, p. 82. Levie, in Coll and Arend (eds.), *The Falklands War*, Allen & Unwin, Boston, 1985, at p. 73, believes that the return of the Royal Marines was a violation of Article 117. Compare the *Manual of Military Law*, Part III, p. 86, para. 262. In addition, it might be argued that the situation that occurred in the Falklands War was not one envisaged by the drafters of the Convention, and hence there was no rule of international law prohibiting the return of the Royal Marines.

11

The Protection and Administration of Civilians in War

'The wounded and prisoners of war are human beings who have become harmless, and the state's obligations towards them are not a serious hindrance to its conduct of hostilities; on the other hand, civilians have not in most cases been rendered harmless, and the steps taken on their behalf may be a serious hindrance to the conduct of the war.' Pictet J. S.

During this century war has taken a dreadful toll of the civilian population, who, being non-combatant, have had little means to protect themselves. The problem has been intensified by the capacity of modern weapons to inflict great damage not only upon civilians but also upon their environment. Added to this is the hardship, and often danger, associated with the imposition of the authority of an occupying power. The laws of war that govern the protection of the civilian population during the conduct of hostilities have been considered in Chapter 8, and it is now proposed to consider the protection offered to civilians who are affected by an armed conflict and, in particular, those whose territory has been occupied.

It was the treatment of the civilian population in occupied countries in Europe during the Second World War that led to an urgent reconsideration of the need for protection of the civilian population in time of war. The scale of the problem was emphasised by the International Military Tribunal at Nuremberg in the following passage: 'The territories occupied by Germany were administered in violation of the laws of war. The evidence is quite over-whelming of a systematic rule of violence, brutality and terror.'[1]

In a sense, much of national law is concerned with striking a compromise between the needs and aspirations of opposing interests. The tort of nuisance, for instance, balances the right of a person to use his land in whatever way he chooses with the rights of his neighbours not to suffer harm to the use and enjoyment of their property as a result. There is a reciprocity of interest between neighbours, since neither wishes to suffer at the hands of the other and, in consequence, the law can be clearly formulated, although what amounts to an unreasonable use of land in any individual case may be difficult to predict.

The law of belligerent occupation, in contast, is predicated on a simple basis. This is that the occupying State has imposed its will over the inhabitants of the territory concerned. There can, in most cases, be no question of the consent of the inhabitants to this state of affairs. The most that the law can do is to place limits on the physical power of the occupant and to give some rights to the inhabitants. It is perhaps not surprising that the laws of war place more limits on the occupier than the inhabitants, since the latter will have little power except to strike clandestinely at the occupation forces.

The Diplomatic Conference that led to the Geneva Convention of 1949 was composed of some States that had been occupied and some who had been occupiers, and it was normal that each should strive to deal with the problems it faced during periods of occupation. The laws of belligerent occupation are therefore largely a compromise of the demands of each basic group, just as the extension of prisoner of war status, first to include the *levée en masse* and then the guerrilla fighter, had been. So, rights to a fair trial, limits on the imposition of the death penalty, prohibitions on the taking of hostages and engaging in reprisals on the one hand clearly benefit the inhabitant, while on the other, the right of the occupier to treat a person, who is definitely suspected of hostile activities as not entitled to the benefits of the Geneva Civilians Convention 1949 gives considerable legal power to the occupier.

The Fourth Geneva Convention of 1949, which has been added to by the First Protocol 1977, establishes a regime for the protection of two classes of civilians. Protected persons are those who find themselves in the hands of a party to the conflict or an occupying power of which they are not nationals.[2] They are the main object of the Fourth Convention and their position can be contrasted with the more limited protection offered to other civilians.

Protection of the Whole Population

It has been shown that a belligerent may create hospital, safety and neutralised zones for the protection of those who are not involved in the fighting and, further, that civilian hospitals may not be the object of attack.[3] These are all part of an attempt by the Convention to draw particular attention to the risks posed by the conflict to the civilian population. Moreover, all parties to the Convention must allow the free passage of medicines, hospital stores and objects necessary for religious worship, if they are intended only for the use of civilians, even if they are enemy civilians. States must also permit the free passage of essential food-stuffs, clothing and tonics if they are intended for children under 15, expectant mothers and maternity cases. The First Protocol of 1977 goes further in imposing duties on States to permit relief actions which are humani-tarian and impartial in character and which are designed primarily to benefit children, expectant and nursing mothers and maternity cases. So, in an armed conflict between States A and B (assuming they are parties to the 1949 Convention and to the Protocol) both would be obliged to allow and facilitate rapid and unimpeded passage that had been organised by States C and D of all relief consignments and personnel destined for the civilian population, even though it is intended for enemy civilians. The consignment may consist of food, bedding, clothing and means of shelter.[4] The combined effect of these provisions is to render an economic blockade of the essentials of life described above, and intended only for the civilian population or part of it, unlawful. The matter can be seen to work quite clearly during a naval blockade. The blockading State may, however, take the view that the relief shipment is, in reality, intended for the use of enemy combatants. In this case it can refuse to permit passage.

Children, under the age of 15 years, and women, are in particular need of protection, both from assaults and from the general effects of war. So, children are to be prevented from taking a direct part in the hostilities, such as being recruited into the armed forces, and they are to be looked after if separated from their families.[5]

Protected Persons

The Fourth Geneva Convention of 1949 is directed specifically at the protected person who is defined in Article 4 as anyone who, at a given moment and in any manner whatsoever, finds himself, in case of a conflict or occupation, in the hands of a party to the conflict or occupying power of whom he is not a national. It should be noted here that, in general, international law is not concerned with the treatment that a State metes out to its own nationals and so Article 4 is concerned with non-nationals. But this statement must be qualified by adding that a State may be under obligation to its own nationals because of treaty commitments. So, for example, the European Convention on Human Rights of 1950 lays down basic human rights, owed by a State to anyone within its jurisdiction (which, of course, will be predominently its own citizens). Some of these continue to apply during time of war. There can be no departure by a State from its obligations under the Convention to refrain from torture, inhuman or degrading treatment or from holding any person in slavery or servitude. A breach of the Convention gives the victim, whether he is a national or not, or indeed, any other State that is a party to it, a right to bring a petition to the European Commission of Human Rights at Strasbourg. A further protection offered to all persons, whether in their own territory or not and whether in war or peace, is the Genocide Convention of 1948. This makes it a crime against international law to kill or injure members of a group with the intent to destroy, in whole or in part, that national, ethnical, racial or religious group.

A rather ambiguous Article 5 allows a State to deny some of the rights of a protected person to a civilian who, in its own territory, is 'definitely suspected of, or engaged in, activities hostile to the security of the State'. In reality there may be little point in spelling out in great detail limitations for its own security upon a State in its national territory. In any event, those who pose such a threat to the State will usually be interned or placed in an assigned residence and the Article is concerned with suspected 'individuals' and not whole groups.[6] The greater problem is posed in occupied territory by those protected persons who are detained as spies or saboteurs or persons under definite suspicion of activity hostile to the security of the occupying power. Should the occupying power have the right to treat them at will since they are, in effect, unprivileged belligerents, or should the detainees merely lose all rights that they would have enjoyed as protected persons? Article 5 goes on to provide that such persons shall forfeit the rights of communication (with the protecting power, or with the International Committee of the Red Cross and with his relatives), but shall in all cases be treated with humanity and if placed on trial, the fundamental guarantee of fairness must be accorded to him.[7] Unlawful confinement, or wilfully depriving a protected person of a fair and regular trial, is a grave breach of the Convention.

Article 27 of the Convention of 1949 spells out the rights of protected persons and provides that they are entitled to respect for their persons, honour, family rights, religion, manners and customs, and without distinction based on race, religion or political opinion, but, perhaps, more importantly, they are entitled to be treated humanely. A breach of the Convention would occur, for instance, if an occupying power separated mothers from their very young children, or banned the practice of religion among a particular sect or indeed treated one group (for example, Jews) differently from others. A specific mode of dealing with protected persons that is prohibited is their being placed in an area or in a place to render it immune from military operations. An example of what it was intended to prohibit here was the practice of placing protected persons in trains alongside ammunition trains to deter attack or, indeed, the act of compelling prominent members of a community to ride at the front of a train to safeguard it from attack.[8] An additional ground for condemning such action is the prohibition on the taking of hostages contained in Article 34. Along with the proscription on reprisals, this article illustrates that a protected person is not to be used by a belligerent State for its own military purposes. Finally, the protected person is not to be subjected to physical suffering or extermination by either the civil (for example, the police or an irregular force created by a political party) or military agents of the State concerned.

The system of protecting powers described in Chapter 10 is designed, it will be recalled, to offer protection to the victims of war and its operation under the Civilians Convention is similar to that in relation to prisoners of war. In practice, supervision of civilians is performed by the International Committee of the Red Cross.

The Treatment of Foreigners

Foreigners in the territory of a party to the conflict, who are nationals of an adversary, have traditionally been treated as enemy aliens. English law, for instance, prevents them from suing in the English courts, except by permission of the Crown, but they can be sued and they have often been interned.[9] However, some of these foreigners may be refugees from their State of origin and no longer entitled to protection from it. Since they have not become nationals of the State in which they reside, they lack the protection of any State. Article 44 of the Civilians Convention directs the State that holds them not to treat them automatically as enemy aliens. A good example of the working of the article can be taken from the experience during the Second World War when many Germans came to England to escape from conditions in their native land. By so leaving, they were denied any further protection from Germany, but since they had not become British citizens they were not entitled to the protection of any State. The First Protocol adds to the category of refugee[10] those who, before the beginning of hostilities, were considered as stateless persons or refugees. They are entitled to be treated as protected persons under the Fourth Geneva Convention of 1949. People who are displaced by the war and who find their way to another State in an attempt to escape from the effect of hostilities would not be able to take the benefit of these provisions directly, since they will not have relinquished their nationality nor will they be stateless persons. If they reach a State that is involved in the conflict, they will be protected persons, but if they enter a neutral State, the laws of war are silent as to their treatment. A useful example might be a conventional war in northern Europe in which civilians, in an attempt to avoid the fighting taking place in Norway, cross the border into neutral Sweden. The Swedish authorities are under no obligation to permit them to enter their territory, but once admitted they must be treated in accordance with general international law standards.

It is often in the interests of all concerned at the outset of, or even during, hostilities that protected persons (who, it will be remembered are not nationals of the State in which they find themselves) should be able to leave the territory if they wish to do so, providing that their departure is not contrary to the national interests of the State concerned. So, British subjects in Argentina had the right to leave that country during the Falklands War and, indeed, there is no evidence that Argentina prevented them from doing so. What though of the Falkland Islander who wished to leave at the outset of the invasion by the Argentinian forces? If the Argentinian argument, that the Falkland Islands were their sovereign territory, was correct, the islanders, as British subjects, would be in no different position from their co-nationals in Argentina. However, it is suggested that once they had landed on the island the true status of the Argentinian forces was that they were an occupying power and so the islanders had no right to leave, although Argentina enabled some to do so.[11]

Enemy civilians who remain in the territory of a State which is engaged in an armed conflict may be subject to internment or to an assigned residence. Their treatment is very similar to that for prisoners of war, but unlike the latter they cannot be compelled to work and there are other differences relating in particular to managing their property or taking part in legal proceedings.

The Occupation of Territory

In time of war the civilian in invaded or occupied territory has always suffered. In characteristic style, Best summed up the position in the following way, 'Civilian sufferings during the revolutionary and Napoleonic wars were enormous, mainly because French armies could not operate without inflicting them. An army marches on its stomach, said or is reported to have said Napoleon. He could better have said, armies march on civilian stomachs for that is what really happened.'[12] In truth, the occupier's needs will always prevail over the pre-existing rights of the inhabitants of the territory. The danger point for the inhabitants has traditionally been where the occupying forces have felt themselves to be insecure from attack or where for economic reasons the inhabitants have been exploited by the occupier. In 1946 the Nuremberg War Crimes Tribunal concentrated, to a large extent, on the activities of the defendants as being responsible for the treatment of civilians in the territories occupied by Germany and styled these as war crimes and crimes against humanity. The standards set by the Nuremberg judgment of an occupying power eventually found their way into the 1949 Geneva Civilians Convention, which at least has had the merit of formulating reasonably clear rules for the treatment of the civilian population.

The Convention applies (by Article 2) to all cases of partial or total occupation of the territory of a High Contracting Party. It may happen, however, that the status of occupied territory is unclear before the occupation and the question then arises as to whether it is the territory of a High Contracting Party to which the Convention applies. This is the argument of Israel with respect to the West Bank and Gaza. The First Protocol of 1977 now makes the position clearer, since it applies the 1949 Convention to all cases of 'alien occupation', a term wide enough to cover the Israeli occupation, but which does not bind Israel since it is not a party to the Protocol.

From a legal point of view the effect of occupation can raise extremely complex issues, not least because the laws of the ousted sovereign and the occupying power may well conflict. It is no answer to say, as will be discussed later, that the laws of the occupier should be ignored once the ousted sovereign regains his territory or, indeed, that the laws of the ousted sovereign are void during the period of occupation. The latter will not wish, for instance, to set free ordinary criminals merely because they were convicted during the period of occupation, nor will he seek to annul marriages or wills. He may, however, treat as a nullity the convictions of those sentenced for crimes against the occupying power and he may seek the return of property taken. Into this milieu the Regulations annexed to the Hague Convention of 1907 (called the Hague Rules) and the Fourth Geneva Convention of 1949 struggle to provide the minimum standards of conduct.

Territory will be occupied when it is actually placed under the authority of the hostile army;[13] in other words, the lawful government (or sovereign) has been replaced over the whole or a part of the territory by the occupier. He cannot do as he wills over the territory, its inhabitants or their property, nor can he refuse to govern it. Article 43 of the Hague Rules 1907 directs the occupier to 'take all the measures in his power to restore, and ensure, as far as possible, public order and safety, while respecting, unless absolutely prevented, the laws in force in the country'. He becomes administrator rather than sovereign and this implies that his law-making powers are more limited. It was certainly the intention of those who framed the Hague Convention that the occupier's law-making powers could be exercised only where it was a matter of military necessity that they should and not merely where the occupier considered it expedient to do so.[14] An occupier could not, for instance, introduce his own laws into the territory that he occupied unless those laws related solely to the needs of his army. In the Second World War Germany unlawfully incorporated into its occupied territories certain provisions of German law, perhaps the most extreme form being 'punishment by analogy', whereby an inhabitant of occupied territory could be punished for any act that was analogous to any other act that was contrary to law. This meant, in effect, that a crime was anything that the occupier said was a crime after the act had been done.[15]

It is often said that hard cases make bad law, and one particular hard case was the occupation of Germany by the Allies in 1945. Were the Allies to enforce German law that was already in existence or would they be justified in supplanting it? The latter option was adopted, and the Supreme Commander was vested with 'supreme legislative, judicial and executive authority within the occupied territories', which led Freeman to conclude that 'Never in the history of military occupation have such extensive powers been wielded by a military government as are now being exercised in Germany.'[16] This was perhaps a unique situation, justified only by the necessity to replace a system of law that was, on any analysis, totally unacceptable to world opinion.[17] It certainly is not authority that would justify a State in replacing all the laws of the country that it occupies.

Article 64 of the 1949 Civilians Convention takes up the theme of the law-making powers of the occupier and permits it to subject the population of the territory to provisions that are essential to enable it to fulfil its obligations under the present Convention, to maintain the orderly government of the territory, and to ensure its safety. It was no doubt on the basis of this Article that General Menendez, the Argentinian commander on the Falkland Islands, ordered curfews and imposed penalties of imprisonment for a failure to obey his rules or for aggravating his soldiers. Further radical changes were introduced which required motorists to drive on the right-hand side of the road, and 'it was made clear that the Britons would be expected to learn Spanish'.[18] It might well be argued that since the Argentinians based their case on the ground of sovereignty and not merely on the right of a belligerent occupier to make laws for the territory, that General Menendez's proclamations were not obviously illegal. It will be appreciated that the laws of war anticipate that the legal system of the occupied territory will continue to function and indeed the legal rights and duties of the inhabitants are not to be abolished or suspended.

One obvious way in which an occupier could manipulate the legal system would be to alter the status of judges, or to coerce them into a particular course of action. An example of the type of activity contemplated here would be the punishment by analogy law described above. Once the occupier takes these steps, there is little protection for those subjected to the military might of occupier; there is no-one to stand between those exercising such power and those against whom such power is exercised.

It has been stressed that the nature of occupation during war is that it gives to the occupier a mere right to administer the territory; he does not become sovereign with all the rights to make any changes that that implies. In his role of administering the territory the occupier can compel the inhabitants to work either on behalf of the civilian population, such as in providing public utility services, or in providing services for his armed forces. They cannot, however, be compelled to serve in his armed forces, nor be employed on work which would involve them in the obligation of taking part in military operations. General Menendez could therefore have required the Falkland Islanders to continue running the electricity supply, to bake bread for his soldiers, but not to act as ammunition bearers during the battle at Port Stanley, but it would probably have been permissible for him to have compelled the islanders to help to place sand bags around a particular building in preparation for an attack.[19]

As part of his duty to administer the territory the occupier may take steps to control the currency, providing this is necessary for economic order. If, on the other hand, he were to fix an unfair rate of exchange between his own country and that which he occupies, his actions would probably be described as an exploitation of that territory.

The occupier cannot transfer the inhabitants out of occupied territory either to work or to detain them in the occupier's territory. More specifically, Article 49 of the Civilians Convention prohibits such transfers whatever their motive and is a clear rejection of the right of an occupying State to deport workers to its homeland, a practice which led to the conviction of Sauckel at Nuremberg for what was described as 'the systematic exploitation, by force, of the labour resources of the occupied territories'.[20] Article 49 does, however, permit an occupier to transfer civilians out of the territory if this is necessary for their security. It might be argued that this is conduct on the part of the occupier that is to be encouraged in modern warfare where a given area is subject to bombardment or to a nuclear attack.

The occupier cannot transfer its own citizens to the territory it occupies. In so far, therefore, that the Argentine government was planning to settle Argentinians in the Falkland Islands in 1982, the policy could only be condemned from the United Kingdom point of view as contrary to Article 49. This is also the standpoint of the British government with regard to the establishment of Israeli settlements in the territories it occupies in the West Bank.

Resistance to the Occupier

Any occupier can normally expect resistance from the inhabitants to his order, since the latter may conceive it as their patriotic duty to make life as difficult for the occupier as possible. An early form of resistance recognised by the international community was the *levée en masse*, discussed in Chapter 10, but the Second World War showed that modern resistance is a good deal more subtle. It involved what would now be described as guerrilla groups operating secretly but to great effect. The 1977 Protocol I, it will be remembered, declares that members of all organised armed forces under a command responsible to a State or a liberation movement, engaged in the armed conflict, are entitled to prisoner of war status upon falling into the hands of an adversary. They need no longer carry their arms openly nor wear a fixed distinctive sign recognisable at a distance. As prisoners of war they cannot be punished for infringing the occupiers' laws, but only in accordance with Article 85 of the Geneva Prisoners of War Convention 1949. The effect of the Protocol, therefore, is that those who, in a systematic way, resist the occupier are entitled, if captured, to be treated as prisoners of war, since they will have been absorbed into the armed forces of their State. Those who cannot shelter under this umbrella, but who nevertheless conduct acts of defiance to the occupier, are unprivileged belligerents. They are non-combatants who have taken up arms against a belligerent and, as such, the occupier might be excused for taking the view that they have, by their acts, become outlaws, to be dealt with at will. The laws of war do not, however, permit him to do so.

The occupier cannot compel the inhabitants to swear allegiance to him, but in return for his protection he can require them, by virtue of his *de facto* position of strength, to obey his orders[21] and he can punish them as unprivileged belligerents if they do not do so. He is, however, limited in doing so by Article 5 (discussed above) and Article 68 of the Geneva Civilians Convention 1949, which places limits on the power of the occupier to pass a sentence of death and insists that for less serious offences internment or imprisonment are the only sentences permitted. Article 68 also goes on to provide that before a sentence of death can be passed the court must have drawn to its attention the fact that the accused, not being a national of the occupying power, owes it no duty of allegiance. There is a further limitation in the article concerned with the death penalty, and that is that it can only be imposed if it was an available sentence in the territory before the occupation began. The position today is that very few States in Europe permit the imposition of the death penalty at all. The United Kingdom entered a reservation to this article and considers itself not bound by it. The effect, therefore, is that should this country be an occupying power it may impose the death penalty if it considers that course necessary.

A particular problem in the past has been the question of whether an occupier is entitled as a reaction to resistance to exact group punishments for attacks on his forces and whether it is permissible to take hostages. On the one hand, an army may only be able to occupy a large area of territory if its units can establish control over it, and to do this the army may have to take steps to deter the population, or individual members of it, from taking action against it. This will generally involve collective punishments or the taking of hostages. On the other, innocent civilians can suffer greatly if such action on the part of the occupying power is permitted. The Hague Rules of 1907 addresses itself to the problem of collective penalties, which it prohibits, but not specifically to the issue of hostage-taking. The *Manual of Military Law* of 1914 was equivocal on the point and merely stated that 'in modern times it is deemed preferable to resort to (other means) instead of taking hostages'. The actions of Germany during the two World Wars led to demands that the practice be declared illegal. The judgment of the International Military Tribunal at Nuremberg found that Keitel had 'ordered that attacks on soldiers in the East should be met by putting to death 50 to 100 Communists for one German soldier'.[22] Article 33 of the Civilians Convention now prohibits collective penalties and reprisals against protected persons and in Article 34 the taking of hostages.[23] It might be thought that the problem is now solved. But suppose an occupying army is subjected to isolated attacks by individuals who manage to kill its soldiers one by one and the perpetrators are unknown. What can the occupier do? It can hardly ignore such acts and treat them as merely part of the cost of occupying territory. The danger, it may be suggested, is that the law leans too much in favour of the resistance to the occupier and that 'No belligerent will keep to the rules (i.e. Articles 33 and 34) if his very existence is threatened. The new rules will contribute to more anger, more accusation, more reprisal, more deviation from valid law.'[24] Unfortunately, whether this prophecy turns out to be true or not will depend on the existence of a war of the Second World War type.

The Taking of Property

The occupier, like a tenant of property, cannot lawfully take that which he physically controls. The Hague Rules 1907 are couched in the language and style of government of the nineteenth century, with its clear distinction between private and state property, with private property generally being exempt from confiscation. Greenspan explains the difficulties experienced in the Second World War when he states that 'This question assumed importance . . . particularly in territories of totalitarian states, whose governments had interests and exercised control in many nominally private enterprises.'[25]

An army of occupation is permitted to seize all moveable property belonging to the State (but not private property) which may be used for military purposes as well as cash and other State funds, but it must pay compensation for seizing any kind of privately held munitions of war (such as arms and ammunition) which it cannot restore on the conclusion of peace. This also includes vehicles which are to be used by the army of occupation, but it would seem not to cover crude oil while still in the ground. In the case of the *Singapore Oil Stocks* in 1956 the Japanese seized an oil field belonging to the plaintiffs when they occupied Sumatra and shipped some to Singapore for their use. The Singapore Court of Appeal decided that the Japanese had not acquired a good title to the oil field, since the Hague Rules of 1907 permitted an occupier to seize only munitions of war. There were at least two reasons why the oil stocks did not come within the term 'munitions of war'. First, they were a raw material which could only be used for purposes of war after a good deal of civilian effort and second, the oil *in situ* was in reality immoveable and the essence of munitions of war was its moveable nature. Since they did not obtain a good title, neither would the British, who claimed the oil as war booty when they drove the Japanese out of the territory.[26]

The requirement under the Hague Rules that the property seized be used for military purposes was clearly flouted by the activities of the German occupation forces in the Second World War when works of art, furniture and so on were taken from the occupied territories and transported to Germany. The Charter of the International Military Tribunal indicted a number of defendants, *inter alia*, for plunder of public or private property and the argument of the defendant Rosemberg at the Nuremberg Trials, that the treasures were seized in order to protect them from the ravages of war, was clearly not the case and was not accepted. The court set out the true position in the following sentence; 'In many of the occupied countries private collections were robbed, libraries were plundered, and private houses were pillaged.'[27]

The experience of those States which had been occupied showed a need for much more specific rules about cultural property and its protection. A conference in 1954 led to the Hague Convention for the Protection of Cultural Property in the Event of Armed Conflict, which in Article 5 seeks to impose an obligation on an occupying State to assist the territory to safeguard and preserve its cultural property and in Article 1 of the Protocol to this Convention there is an obligation to prevent exportation of such property from the territory occupied by it, or if it is removed, to return it.

Article 52 of the Hague Rules 1907 permits an occupier to make requisitions in kind and in services, but only for the needs of the army of occupation and in any event the requisitions must be in proportion to the resources of the country. Requisitions act as a form of compulsory purchase, since the occupier is required to pay, or to issue a receipt, for any property that he takes. A consequence of this is that he acquires a good title to the property lawfully requisitioned. The failure by the Japanese authorities to give a receipt for the seizure of the crude oil in the *Singapore Oil Stocks* case discussed above also prevented them from acquiring title to the oil.

Historically, the requisitioning of food has caused considerable hardship among the civilian population, even though the occupier has paid for it. The Geneva Civilians Convention of 1949 attempts to protect the inhabitants of occupied territory by placing limitations upon the right of the occupier to requisition. So he may not requisition foodstuffs, articles or medical supplies available in the occupied territory, except for use by the occupation forces and then only if the requirements of the civilian population have been taken into account. Again, he must pay a fair price. But his duty goes beyond merely paying for the food he has requisitioned. He must ensure that the food and medical supplies for the civilian population are adequate and if they are not he must bring them into the territory.[28] This requirement stems principally from the experience of the Second World War when starvation of the Russian population occurred on a vast scale. The Nuremberg Tribunal summarised German policy in their Russian campaign in the following way: 'The German armies were to be fed out of Soviet territory, even if many millions of people (were to) starve to death.'[29]

The right of a belligerent to destroy property or parts of the environment in the conduct of military operations has been discussed in Chapter 8 and it has been shown how the laws of war attempt to strike a balance between the rights of the civilian population and the formulation of realistic rules for belligerents. Both the 1907 Hague Rules and the 1949 Geneva Civilians Convention address themselves to this problem by prohibiting the destruction of property unless it is justified by military necessity and, indeed, the latter classes as a grave breach 'extensive destruction and appropriation of property, not justified by military necessary and carried out unlawfully and wantonly'.[30]

The International Military Tribunal at Nuremberg found Jodl guilty of war crimes and crimes against humanity in ordering in October 1944 the evacuation of all persons in northern Norway and the burning of 30,000 houses in order to prevent their owners from helping the Russians. But, it may be asked, could this action not be justified by military necessity? A retreating army may well feel it necessary to take such measures in order to protect itself. It seems that the necessity is to be judged in the light of the facts known to the commander who ordered it and not the view of any tribunal before which the issue has been raised.[31] A further example that might be raised here is the question of whether Argentina was in breach of these provisions in laying mines over parts of the Falkland Islands when it was in occupation during the Falklands War. Since the mines are virtually undetectable and had been laid over a relatively large area, the effect has been to render the land as useless as if it had been permanently poisoned. However, there is no specific rule in the laws of war requiring combatants to make maps of minefields and in the absence of such a rule it would be difficult to argue that a positive duty to do so was imposed by international law.

Termination of the Occupation

The theoretical basis of the law of belligerent occupation is that of the ousted sovereign (or government) and the temporary, but limited, powers of the occupant. At the close of military operations the occupant may have been driven out to be replaced by the rightful sovereign (as in the case of the Falkland Islands on the British government view of sovereignty) or, if he has been victorious, he may remain in occupation. In this case the 1949 Geneva Civilians Convention continues to impose a number of obligations on the occupier for one year after the general close of military operations,[32] but the First Protocol of 1977 alters this rule. This led Roberts to conclude that the 'abrogation of the "one year after" rule may reflect in part the proper desire of the international community to maintain the full application of the law on occupation to areas occupied by Israel since 1967'.[32a]

The returning sovereign government clearly would not wish to treat as null and void all the laws administered by the occupying State, since the latter had a responsibility to administer the territory and to this end courts would have been functioning during the occupation. It would, for instance, be highly inconvenient if marriages, wills and ordinary commercial contracts were to be considered as void. On the other hand, inhabitants of the territory may have had their property unlawfully confiscated or be in prison for an offence committed solely against the occupying forces. In so far as the occupier has acted within the limits of the powers given to him by the Hague Rules, in particular Articles 43 (dealing with the right to enact laws) and 52 (concerned with requisitions), his laws are binding both on the inhabitants and on the returning sovereign.[33] It would be otherwise if the occupier has acted outside the powers given to him, when his laws could then be treated as absolutely void, even though, of course, he had the physical ability to enforce them. Of this type of law the returning sovereign will usually enact retro-actively for its annulment[34] whilst a third State would be bound not to recognise it.[35]

Notes

1. Judgment of the International Military Tribunal (I.M.T.) (1947) 41 A.J.I.L. 172, 229.
2. Article 4, Geneva Convention Relative to the Protection of Civilian Persons in Time of War 1949 (the Fourth Geneva Convention or the Geneva Civilians Convention). Article 4 does not cover nationals of non-signatory, neutral or co-belligerent states.
3. Articles 13-22 of the Geneva Civilians Convention 1949.
4. Articles 70-71 of the 1977 Protocol I Additional to the Geneva Conventions of 1949. See also Article 69 dealing with the obligation on the part of an occupying power to ensure that the civilian population is provided with essential supplies. Article 54 of the Protocol prohibits the starvation of the civilian population as a method of warfare.
5. See Articles 24, 25 and 26 of the Geneva Civilians Convention 1949 and Articles 74 and 77 of Protocol I.
6. Article 42 of the Geneva Civilians Convention 1949. Draper believes that 'States will tend to exclude such suspected persons from all rights, indeed it may be suggested that the article encourages them to do so', *The Red Cross Conventions*. Stevens & Sons Ltd, London, 1958. Pictet, *Commentary on Geneva Convention IV*, International Committee of the Red Cross, Geneva, 1958, p. 58, considers Article 5 to be a 'regrettable concession to state expediency'.
7. See Articles 71-77 of the Geneva Civilians Convention 1949 and Article 75 of the Protocol I.
8. *Manual of Military Law*, Part III, H.M.S.O., London, 1958, paras. 39 and 651.
9. For an account of internment in the United Kingdom during the Second World War, see Cohn (1941), *Legal Aspects of Internment* 14 M.L.R. 200 who makes the point that liability to internment followed under customary international law only if the national of an enemy State enjoyed the protection of that State. Many German refugees were denied protection by Nazi Germany. The U.K. has repudiated the view that to deny enemy aliens unfettered access to the courts is an infringement of Article 23(h) of the Hague Rules of 1907; see Oppenheim, *International Law*, vol. II, Longmans, London, 1952, p. 310.
10. For the definition of 'refugee' see Convention Relating to the Status of Refugees (1951) 189 U.N.T.S. 12, and the 1967 Protocol, 606 U.N.T.S. 267.
11. Other nationals would be able to do so. Article 48 of the Geneva Civilians Convention 1949; but cf. if they were key personnel in public utilities. See, however, *R. v. Ahlers* (1915) 1 K.B. 616, and for the attitude of States on the outbreak of both World Wars, Oppenheim, *International Law*, vol. II, Longmans, London, 1952, p. 307.
12. *Humanity in Warfare*, Methuen, London, 1983, p. 89.
13. Article 42 of the Regulations annexed to the Hague Convention IV Respecting the Laws and Customs of War on Land 1907. Fighting will therefore have come to an end, although resistance may continue. For the different types of occupation see Roberts, *What is Military Occupation?* (1984) 55 B.Y.I.L. 249.
14. The general limitations on the occupier's powers are contained in the Martens Clause of the Hague Rules 1907 and in Articles 23(h), 43, 46 and 50.
15. See, generally, Freeman, *War Crimes by Enemy Nationals Administering Justice in Occupied Territories* (1947) 41 A.J.I.L. 579, 598. Such action would also breach the fundamental guarantees contained in the Geneva Civilians Convention 1949, Articles 65 and 66.
16. Freeman, *op. cit.*, p. 603. For the military occupation of Berlin, see Bathurst, *Legal Aspects of the Berlin Problem* (1962) 28 B.Y.I.L. 255.
17. 'The authors of the Hague Regulations (1907) did not envisage dictatorial regimes—such as that of National Socialist Germany—utterly contemptuous of human rights and of modern conceptions of legality', Oppenheim *International Law*, vol. II, Longmans, London, 1952. The effect was to place a duty of obedience to the law of the Allies on the inhabitants.
18. Dobson, Miller and Payne, *The Falklands Conflict*, Hodder & Stoughton, London, 1982, p. 118.
19. Oppenheim, *op. cit.*, p. 440.
20. Judgment of the I.M.T. (*supra*), p. 312.
21. For his duty to protect see Article 55 of the Geneva Civilians Convention 1949 and Article 14 of the 1977 Protocol. For the duty of obedience, see generally, Baxter, *The Duty of Obedience to the Belligerent Occupant* (1950) 27 B.Y.I.L. 235, and in particular p. 243.

22. Judgment of the I.M.T., p. 282. See also Lord Wright, *The Killing of Hostages as a War Crime* (1948) 25 B.Y.I.L. 296, who deals critically at p. 297 with the case of *List* (or the *Hostages case*) 8 W.C.R. He concludes by stating that, 'the practice (of shooting innocent non-combatants) amounts to a mere terror killing, and may properly be called terroristic murder' (at p. 310).

23. See also Article 46 of the Hague Rules 1907.

24. Roling, *Recueil Des Cours* (1960) vol. 2, pp. 400, 428.

25. *The Modern Law of Land Warfare*, Univ. Calif. Press, 1959, p. 292, and see Robinson, *Transfer of Property in Enemy Occupied Territory* (1945) 39 A.J.I.L. 216, 218, dealing with Soviet conceptions of public and private property.

26. McNair and Watts, *The Legal Effects of War*, Cambridge U.P., 1966 (4th edn), p. 412. Further discussion of this case can be found in 'B', *The Case of the Singapore Oil Stocks* (1956) 5 I.C.L.Q. 84, 95, and Lauterpacht, *The Hague Regulations and the Seizure of Munitions de Guerre*, (1955-56) 32 B.Y.I.L. 218, 230-231.

27. Judgment of the I.M.T., at p. 238.

28. Article 55. Cf. his more limited duty under Article 43 of the Hague Rules 1907. See also Article 14 of the 1977 Protocol which prohibits requisitions of medical supplies or personnel if they are required for the civilian population.

29. Judgment of the I.M.T., at p. 237.

30. Article 147. See also Article 23(g) of the Hague Rules 1907 which is concerned with all property wherever situated; Article 53 of the Geneva Civilians Convention 1949 which deals only with the destruction of property in occupied territory and, generally, Part IV of 1977 Protocol. The 1977 U.N. Convention on the Prohibition of Military or any other Hostile Use of Environmental Modification Techniques deals with widespread long-lasting or severe effects on the environment.

31. See the High Command Trial, 12 W.C.R., at p. 93.

32. Article 6. Suppose, however, the ousted sovereign is unable to return because it ceases to exist (the German government at the end of the Second World War). It has been argued that in this situation the occupant is no longer bound by the laws of occupation, but see Greenspan, *op. cit.*, at p. 216, n. 25.

32a. Roberts, *op. cit.* (n. 13), at p. 272.

33. Morgenstern, *Validity of the Acts of the Belligerent Occupant* (1951) 28 B.Y.I.L. 291, 320.

34. For examples see (1945) 39 A.J.I.L. pp. 222 et seq.

35. Compare *Bank of Ethiopia v. National Bank of Egypt and Liquori* (1937) Ch. 513, a decision strongly criticised by McNair and Watts, *op. cit.*, at p. 397.

12

Protection of the Wounded, the Sick and the Shipwrecked

'Of guns and drums, and wounds ...' *King Henry IV, Part 1*

The second half of the nineteenth century saw the development of humanitarian concern which, in England, led to the abolition of the slave trade and, amongst other issues, control by Parliament of an activity whose capacity to kill could only be matched by warfare, that of merchant and passenger shipping. On the continent, where pitched battles were more of a feature of life than in England, Henry Dunant, a Swiss national, had witnessed the aftermath of the Battle of Solferino in 1859 during the Franco-Austrian War and had been shocked. His book, *Un Souvenir de Solferino*, was published in 1862 and along with Dunant's persuasive efforts it led to the founding of the Red Cross in 1863 and in the following year to the First Geneva International Convention to deal with the wounded and sick of armies in the field.[1] In the previous decade Florence Nightingale had been improving the after-battle survivability rate by applying elementary principles of nursing care to the wounded following the Battle of Inkerman in 1854 during the Crimean War. 'Medical science', wrote A. J. P. Taylor, 'protected the forces in France from Typhoid and other fevers, which in the Boer war had killed five men for every one killed in battle.'[2]

The First Geneva Convention of 1949 deals with the wounded and sick in armed forces in the field, whilst the Second is concerned with the wounded, sick and shipwrecked members of armed forces at sea; both have been supplemented by the First Protocol of 1977. These Conventions now protect not only sick, wounded and shipwrecked members of the armed forces, who, upon capture, would be treated as prisoners of war, but also civilians (other than those entitled to prisoner of war status) who are in need of medical assistance or who are in peril on the sea and who refrain from any act of hostility.

All those who are wounded and sick or who have been shipwrecked[3] are protected persons and are entitled to be treated humanely and to receive the fullest possible medical attention and care without any distinctions based on race, nationality, religion, political opinions or sex. Following any large-scale battle there are likely to be casualties from the enemy as well as from one's own forces, and in such numbers that medical teams have to make a decision as to priority of treatment. Any decision that the enemy wounded will have to wait for treatment, whatever their condition, until the wounded of one's own forces have been dealt with is a breach of Article 12 of the 1949 Conventions.[4] They must not be subjected to torture or to biological experiments or to any other similar conduct, since they are also to be considered as prisoners of war.

The habit of some soldiers of taking items of property from the dead or wounded on the battlefield was known as marauding. The *Manual of Military Law* describes this practice as consisting of 'ranging over battlefields and following advancing or retreating armies in quest of loot, robbing, maltreating and killing stragglers and wounded and plundering the dead'. This type of activity can, of course, have no military purpose and although the *Manual* considers it to be a war crime, it is also the offence of looting within the Army Act 1955.[5]

Article 15 of the First Geneva Convention of 1949 imposes an obligation to search for and to collect the wounded and sick and for this purpose agreement may be made with an adversary to enable this to be done, or, indeed, to exchange wounded and sick and to permit the passage of medical personnel or chaplains. One of the purposes of the Geneva Conventions is not only to offer direct protection to the victims of war but also to relieve the stress of uncertainty to their families and in order to do this accurate records must be kept of those enemy persons who come into the hands of a party to the conflict. This information can then be passed directly to the State which the protected persons serve or indirectly through the Central Tracing Agency run by the International Committee of the Red Cross.[6]

The dead are to be buried, wherever possible, according to the rites of their religion, and after a careful examination with a view to confirming death and identity. Their graves are to be marked so that they may always be found and the necessary records will therefore serve the same purpose as described above.

At the conclusion of a battle the civilian population may feel inhibited from assisting the wounded and sick through fear of the reaction of the adverse party to their action. The earliest multilateral Convention to deal with the wounded and sick, the Geneva Convention of 1864, treated those who assisted on the battlefield at the end of military operations as neutrals who obtained distinct advantages in taking the wounded and sick into their homes. They were spared the obligation to quarter soldiers and some relief from paying contributions to an occupying State. These advantages were deleted from the 1906 Convention and have not subsequently reappeared. The 1949 Convention permits the military authorities to appeal to civilians to help them deal with the wounded and sick and it expressly provides that no one may be molested or convicted for having nursed them. In practice, however, the most useful service to those *hors de combat* will be provided by what are termed aid societies, such as the Red Cross, who are permitted to act on their own initiative in collecting and caring for them. In addition, duties are placed on the civilian population by the First Protocol of 1977 to respect the wounded, sick and shipwrecked even though they may be the enemy. At sea, neutral merchant ships may be called upon to assist with the wounded, sick and shipwrecked and they will enjoy the same protection as civilians acting in a like capacity on land.

One might be forgiven for wondering whether the provisions just described really reflect warfare of a past age. Then, it was not uncommon to find the wounded and sick in fairly large numbers scattered over a relatively small area in which the civilian population would have been largely unaffected, providing they had evacuated the immediate battle zone. Modern warfare, especially if it is fought in Europe, will be totally different. There is unlikely to be a sufficient number of civilians within the immediate area able to render assistance in time to those *hors de combat* and the same may be said of the Red Cross. If it were to be assumed, in addition, that the battle had been fought with tactical nuclear weapons the importance of the civilian population in the rescue process would remain in the realms of pious hope rather than reality. Having said that, however, it should be emphasised that this scenario is not the only conceivable one. The Falklands War was of an entirely different nature. Moreover, the impact of the First Protocol of 1977 is to treat certain civil wars, in which international law provided only a very rudimentary set of principles, in the same way as if they had been an international conflict and in which the laws of war are to apply.[7] When this is borne in mind the rights and duties of the civilian population in relation to those *hors de combat*, including now a civilian, can be understood and it is perhaps in this type of conflict that these principles are most required.

It is not, of course, sufficient merely to provide for the victims of war. Those who attend to them as stretcher bearers, medical personnel or chaplains would not be able to perform their functions if they were considered as legitimate targets. Nor would it serve the victims if the hospitals or medical units to where they had been despatched might also come under attack. So, the First Geneva Convention of 1949 specifically provides that fixed establishments (hospitals) and mobile medical units (temporary field medical units) may in no circumstances be attacked.[8] But there are two sides to this coin. Medical establishments must not be placed so as to render immune from attack a military objective and the privilege against attack may be lost where it is abused. So, if they are used to commit acts harmful to the enemy, such as by sheltering soldiers who have not been wounded or by concealing weapons the protection will cease, but only after any warning given has been ignored. The carrying of arms by medical personnel will not, by itself, cause loss of the privilege, providing such weapons are for self-protection or protection, for example, against marauders or those for whom they are responsible. Medical transport, such as ambulances, may be obtained from military or civilian sources and are equally well protected from attack, providing they are clearly marked with the distinctive emblem of the Red Cross.[9] There is no prohibition on ambulances travelling in convoy with other military vehicles and, like hospital ships, they may be stopped by an adversary and searched. Should they be seized, the adversary will assume the responsibility to care for the sick and wounded, who will then become prisoners of war, but medical personnel or chaplains accompanying them will not.[10] Medical transport will, of course, lose its protection if it is used in a way hostile to the adversary. Thus, if an ambulance is used to carry ammunition or fighting troops to the front line, a war crime is committed by those responsible,[11] but it may act in this way if the distinctive emblems are removed.

In modern armed conflicts the evacuation of the wounded is carried out by helicopter from the battle zone and it was the Vietnam War that showed how effective this could be, particularly when operating against a guerrilla army. This type of conflict usually involves relatively small numbers of combatants engaging a like number in situations where they become detached from the main body of their forces. Good radio communications and speedy evacuation is therefore essential if the dilemma experienced in Burma during the Second World War is to be avoided. At that time there was often no alternative but to leave a wounded man behind in the hope that the enemy would secure medical treatment for him. The 1977 First Protocol makes it plain that the term 'medical aircraft' would include a helicopter and so any medical transport by air will be subject to the same rules. These aircraft, providing that they are properly marked with the distinctive emblem, are entitled to protection as would an ambulance on land. The main difference, of course, is that to troops on the ground an approaching helicopter could either be a gun ship or medical evacuation transport and it is only when the aircraft has landed that its mission can be discovered. This is why the 1977 Protrocol stresses that in a contact zone medical aircraft operate at their own risk, but once they have been recognised as such they are to be protected. It may be necessary for longer-range medical aircraft to fly over either the territory controlled by an adversary or over the territory of a neutral State in order to secure proper medical treatment for the wounded, sick or shipwrecked. In each case they may do so, providing permission is granted by the State concerned, and even if it is they may still be required during their passage to land and to submit to inspection. One reason for this is that under international law each State has exclusive jurisdiction over its own airspace, in which, unlike the territorial sea, there is no right of innocent passage.[12] Should a medical aircraft abuse the immunity from attack that it is given, it loses its special status immediately, unlike medical transports and establishments on land, where a warning must first be given concerning any suspected hostile acts. This is no more than a realistic rule, since the scope for abuse by aircraft and the effect that it may have on an adversary is much greater than in the case of land transport. Hostile acts committed from both forms involve an element of perfidy, but the scope to commit direct physical damage from an aircraft is unlikely to be exceeded by the crew of an ambulance.[13] Moreover, in order to avoid confusion of purpose, medical aircraft are not permitted to engage in a search for the sick, wounded or shipwrecked.[14]

The Conventions also deal with the transport of the wounded, sick and shipwrecked by sea in hospital ships. Until the Second Geneva Convention 1949 there was uncertainty whether any ship could, merely by affixing to it the Red Cross emblem, attain the status and privilege of a hospital ship. Draper writes that in '1940 the United Kingdom refused to recognise small vessels marked with the Red Cross used by Germany for rescuing aircrew shot down in the sea. The date is significant; an invasion of these shores was imminent and it was alleged that their use would interfere with naval activities.'[15] Article 26 of the Second Geneva Convention 1949 now provides that a hospital ship may be of any size, but if a long journey is to be undertaken it should normally be of over 2000 tons to ensure suitable conditions for her passengers. The lifeboats of the R.N.L.I. or of any similar organisation, although not hospital ships, are to be respected and protected from attack in the same way as their larger sisters.

Hospital ships will comprise those ships that are either built or equipped for the specific purpose by one of the parties to the conflict, or they may be chartered by National Red Cross Societies. In addition, they may be made available by a neutral or by the International Committee of the Red Cross.[16] Hospital ships are not, however, immune from interference by belligerent warships. They may be searched, ordered to take a particular course, their wireless transmissions may be controlled and they may even be detained.[17] This liability to search is really no different to that imposed on merchant vessels of neutral States during an armed conflict and it serves the purpose of permitting a belligerent warship to satisfy itself that the vessel is taking no part in military or naval operations.

The *quid pro quo* for the protection of hospital ships is that they should not undertake acts harmful to the enemy, nor should they hamper the movements of the combatants. There were attacks on hospital ships during the First World War, ostensibly on the ground that they had been positively assisting the military operations of the British. The trials of the commanders of the submarines responsible are discussed in Chapter 9. But it was in the Falklands War that the subject became animated once again. The first problem that was faced was that of acquiring a suitable vessel to undertake the operation at such a distance from the United Kingdom. The P. & O. liner *Uganda* was requisitioned by the British government as a hospital ship and, in accordance with Article 22 of the Second Geneva Convention of 1949, the Argentinians were notified of its purpose. Some difficulty was experienced over the proper markings to be placed on the vessel, but the International

Committee of the Red Cross confirmed that the details were those contained in Article 43 of the Convention and that the 1949 Convention had replaced the Tenth Hague Convention of 1907 for parties to both Conventions.[18]

One of the problems faced during the conflict in the South Atlantic was the difficulty in identifying a hospital ship. In good sea conditions the distinctive markings were visible for about 1 nautical mile, but at night or in poor weather they might not be visible at all. The British experimented with a blue flashing light which increased identification of the hospital ships for up to 7 nautical miles. Further, a hospital ship will, in practice, not be in radio contact with its own forces because it is prohibited from using a secret code by Article 34 of the Second Geneva Convention 1949 and by using a normal transmission the main force would reveal to the enemy its whereabouts. Moreover, on a radar screen a hospital ship will look like any other ship of similar size in the same way that the cargo ship *Atlantic Conveyor* may have looked to the Argentinian forces similar to the aircraft carrier H.M.S. *Hermes*. The problem is compounded when a submarine is preparing to attack a surface vessel. How can it be sure that the contact is not a hospital ship when visual identification is not possible? A special transponder attached to a hospital ship enabling it to be identified would seem to be the answer.[19]

Hospital ships may not be used to impede military operations.[20] This principle finds expression throughout the Geneva Conventions in the form of an immunity from attack in return for a promise to stay out of the field of military operations. The intricate balancing act between military necessity on the one hand and humanitarian concern on the other is more easily resolved when attention is drawn to the wounded, sick and shipwrecked. This is because it is in the interests of military commanders, who may wish to press home an attack, to have those *hors de combat* removed as quickly as possible. In this instance, military necessity is, in other words, synonymous with humanitarian concern. Unlike medical aircraft, hospital ships may be used to search for the wounded, sick and shipwrecked and so, it was perfectly permissible for the *Uganda* to come close into shore in the Falklands Sound on 27 May 1982 in order to receive British and Argentinian wounded. *The Times* reported the incident by stating that the 'Foreign Office had received a threat from Argentina that hospital ships not unmistakably removed from the war zone would be treated as hostile'. The Foreign Office had 'rejected Argentine suggestions that the hospital ships were impeding the movement of troops (or) were otherwise engaged in military operations.'[21]

The obligation imposed by the Second Geneva Convention 1949 to search for and collect the shipwrecked, wounded and sick after each engagement is difficult to comply with where submarines are involved in an attack. Apart from the lack of space for receiving the victims, the submarine itself will be at great risk if it surfaces to comply with this obligation. Thus, H.M.S. *Conqueror* was in no position to surface to assist the survivors of the *General*

Belgrano which it sank on 2 May 1982. In addition, a surface warship would often run what would be considered to be an unacceptable risk if it set about picking up survivors when submarines were suspected of still being in the area, a dilemma well described by Nicholas Monsarrat in *The Cruel Sea*.[22]

Those who serve the medical services or are chaplains to their armed forces have a special status under the Conventions. They are non-combatants. Should they fall into the hands of an adversary they are not prisoners of war, although they are entitled to treatment no less favourable than their combatant colleagues.[23] Where the interests of prisoners of war are adequately catered for, additional medical personnel or chaplains need not be retained by the belligerent into whose hands they have fallen and they may be returned to the force from whence they came. It might be thought here that a belligerent would be very unwilling to return such personnel, since they will have been in a position to acquire intelligence information that they could pass on to their own forces upon their return. This risk is one that a belligerent takes on every occasion that he repatriates prisoners of war before the close of military operations. In these cases the conventions direct that prisoners of war so returned may not serve for the duration of the war or take part in active military operations.[24] Since medical personnel and chaplains perform merely a humanitarian role, military requirements do not compel their activities to be so confined.

Within the term medical personnel are included all those members of the armed forces who are exclusively engaged in the search for, collection or treatment of the wounded, sick and shipwrecked or in the administration of medical units and establishments along with the crews of hospital ships.[25] The 1977 Protocol also brings within this protection civilian medical personnel.[26] The staff of the National Red Cross (or Red Crescent) Societies are also entitled to this protection, providing they are subject to military law and perform medical functions,[27] along with medical delegates of the International Committee of the Red Cross if the necessary consent and notification is forthcoming.[28]

The Red Cross (or Red Crescent) emblem must be displayed by all persons protected by these Conventions and on all such equipment and establishments. It has been shown that the protection afforded to medical units and transports may be lost by abuse. In practice, claims and counterclaims concerning the activities of these medical establishments (and hospital ships) are part of the stock-in-trade of the war propagandist, just as the tales of German atrocities were at the beginning of the First World War. It will be recalled that a ruse of war is a permitted activity, but that perfidy is not. The improper use of the Red Cross (or Red Crescent) emblem will not only entitle an adversary to give a warning concerning the activities of the offender, but the act in itself will be a war crime,[29] since it is a breach of the Regulations annexed to the Hague Convention IV of 1907 and of the First Protocol of 1977.

Notes

1. Geneva Convention for the Amelioration of the Condition of the Wounded in Armies of the Field 1864. Further such conventions were adopted in 1906, 1929 and 1949 with two Additional Protocols in 1977.
2. Taylor, *English History, 1914-1945*, Oxford U.P., 1965, p. 121.
3. Which includes forced landings at sea by, or from, aircraft, Article 12 of the Second Geneva Convention of 1949. There is a definition of 'wounded and sick' in Article 8(c) of the First Protocol of 1977. The Falklands War was the first time that the Second Geneva Convention of 1949 had applied fully during an armed conflict.
4. See also Article 10 of the 1977 First Protocol.
5. The creation of this offence was necessary because of the requirement in Article 15 of the First Geneva Convention 1949 that signatory States protect the wounded and sick against pillage and ill-treatment. See s. 30 of the Army Act 1955.
6. Article 33 of the 1977 First Protocol imposes an obligation at the end of active hostilities to search for persons reported by an adversary to be missing in action.
7. See Article 1(4) of the 1977 First Protocol. The Protocol also widened the concept of prisoner of war to include the guerrilla fighter. It should also be remembered that an occupier cannot requisition medical services or equipment from the inhabitants so long as they are needed by the civilian population; Article 14 of the 1977 First Protocol.
8. Article 19. See also 1977 First Protocol, Articles 8, 9 and 12. The protection also applies to Red Cross establishments.
9. Or the Red Crescent. See Article 38 of the First Geneva Convention 1949.
10. See Article 33 of the Third Geneva Convention 1949 and Article 43(2) of the 1977 First Protocol.
11. For the view that such conduct would amount to a war crime if the ambulance bore the emblem of the Red Cross, see *Manual of Military Law* Part III, London, H.M.S.O., 1958, para. 626. It is also an offence under English law; s. 6 Geneva Conventions Act 1957 and s. 70 Army Act 1955.
12. Chicago Convention on International Civil Aviation 1944, U.K.T.S. 8 (1953) Cmnd 8742. See also Chapter 6.
13. See Article 28, 1977 First Protocol.
14. *Ibid.*
15. Draper, *The Red Cross Conventions*, Stevens and Sons, London, 1958, p. 88.
16. See Articles 24 and 25 of the Second Geneva Convention 1949 and for the I.C.R.C. Article 9 and Article 22 of the First Protocol of 1977.
17. Article 31 of the Second Geneva Convention of 1949. They may adopt a specific radio frequency for identification purposes.
18. See, generally, (1982) 53 B.Y.I.L. 520-521. Merchant ships converted to hospital ships must not be reconverted during the period of conflict. For a good account of the law relating to hospital ships, see O'Connell, *The International Law of the Sea*, Vol. 2, Clarendon Press, 1984, pp. 1119-1122. There were four British and two Argentinian hospital ships operating during the Falklands War. Details of them can be found in *Protection of the Victims of Armed Conflict, Falkland-Malvinas Islands 1982*, I.C.R.C., 1984, p. 24.
19. See *ibid.*, p. 25. See also Resolutions 18 and 19 adopted at the fourth session of the Diplomatic Conference on the Reaffirmation and Development of International Humanitarian Law applicable in Armed Conflicts of 1977. For a discussion of attacks on hospital ships see Mossop, *Hospital Ships in the Second World War*, (1947) 24 B.Y.I.L. 402.
20. Article 30 of the Second Geneva Convention 1949.
21. *The Times*, 31 May 1982. Another British hospital ship, the *Hecla*, was also reported as making for Montevideo with between forty-three and forty-five British Servicemen and twenty-two Argentinian wounded on board. Under Article 17 of the Second Geneva Convention 1949 members of the armed forces of a belligerent landed in a neutral port must not become involved subsequently in operations of war. Since the *Hecla* was not a warship, it could enter and leave neutral ports, Article 32, Second Geneva Convention 1949. Delegates of the International Committee of the Red Cross also travelled on the hospital ships, see Article 31 of the Second Geneva Convention 1949. See also (1982) 53 B.Y.I.L. 521. For an account of the Red Cross Box, a neutral zone at sea in which hospital ships

could hold position and exchange the wounded, see *Protection of the Victims of Armed Conflict, Falkland-Malvinas Islands 1982*, I.C.R.C., 1984, p. 26.

22. For the problems concerned in the sinking of enemy merchant ships by submarines, see Chapter 8, and for the difficulties caused when combat helicopters assist those *hors de combat*, see *Protection of the Victims of Armed Conflict, Falkland-Malvinas Islands 1982*, I.C.R.C., 1984, pp. 26-27.

23. Article 33, Third Geneva Convention 1949. See also Article 28, First Geneva Convention 1949; Article 37 Second Geneva Convention 1949; Article 43(2) 1977 First Protocol. Hospital orderlies, nurses and stretcher-bearers will be considered as prisoners of war.

24. See, for example, Article 16, Second Geneva Convention 1949 and Article 117, Third Geneva Convention 1949.

25. See Article 24 of the First Geneva Convention 1949, Articles 36 and 37 of the Second Geneva Convention 1949.

26. See Article 15, 1977 First Protocol. Those exclusively involved in the administration of medical units or establishments would cover, for instance, cooks and drivers. See also Article 8(c), 1977 First Protocol, dealing with civil defence organisations.

27. Which they will be; see s. 209 and Schedule 5, Army Act 1955. If they are authorised to accompany the armed forces, they are entitled to be treated, on capture, as prisoners of war, Article 4(A)(4) Third Geneva Convention 1949. If they are not otherwise protected, they will be entitled to the protection of the Geneva Civilians Convention (Fourth Convention of 1949) and the 1977 First Protocol, see Article 8(c)(i).

28. This is the practical effect of Articles 9 and 44 of the First Geneva Convention 1949 and is given formal recognition by Article 8(c)(iii) of the First Protocol 1977.

29. Article 32(f), Hague Rules 1907; Article 85(3)(f) of the First Protocol 1977. It will also be an offence under s. 6 of the Geneva Conventions Act 1957 and s. 70 of the Army Act 1955.

APPENDIX

*(Reproduced by permission of the
International Committee of the Red Cross)*

I

**Geneva Convention for the
Amelioration of the Condition of
the Wounded and Sick in Armed Forces
in the Field of August 12, 1949**

CHAPTER I

GENERAL PROVISIONS

ARTICLE 1

Respect for
the Convention

The High Contracting Parties undertake to respect and to ensure respect for the present Convention in all circumstances.

ARTICLE 2

Application
of the
Convention

In addition to the provisions which shall be implemented in peacetime, the present Convention shall apply to all cases of declared war or of any other armed conflict which may arise between two or more of the High Contracting Parties, even if the state of war is not recognized by one of them.

The Convention shall also apply to all cases of partial or total occupation of the territory of a High Contracting Party, even if the said occupation meets with no armed resistance.

Although one of the Powers in conflict may not be a party to the present Convention, the Powers who are parties thereto shall remain bound by it in their mutual relations. They shall furthermore be bound by the Convention in relation to the said Power, if the latter accepts and applies the provisions thereof.

ARTICLE 3

In the case of armed conflict not of an international character occurring in the territory of one of the High Contracting Parties, each Party to the conflict shall be bound to apply, as a minimum the following provisions:

Conflicts not of an international character

(1) Persons taking no active part in the hostilities, including members of armed forces who have laid down their arms and those placed *hors de combat* by sickness, wounds, detention, or any other cause, shall in all circumstances be treated humanely, without any adverse distinction founded on race, colour, religion or faith, sex, birth or wealth, or any other similar criteria.

To this end, the following acts are and shall remain prohibited at any time and in any place whatsoever with respect to the above-mentioned persons:

(a) violence to life and person, in particular murder of all kinds, mutilation, cruel treatment and torture;

(b) taking of hostages;

(c) outrages upon personal dignity, in particular humiliating and degrading treatment;

(d) the passing of sentences and the carrying out of executions without previous judgment pronounced by a regularly constituted court, affording all the judicial guarantees which are recognized as indispensable by civilized peoples.

(2) The wounded and sick shall be collected and cared for.

An impartial humanitarian body, such as the International Committee of the Red Cross, may offer its services to the Parties to the conflict.

The Parties to the conflict should further endeavour to bring into force, by means of special agreements, all or part of the other provisions of the present Convention.

The application of the preceding provisions shall not affect the legal status of the Parties to the conflict.

ARTICLE 4

Application by
neutral Powers

Neutral Powers shall apply by analogy the provisions of the present Convention to the wounded and sick, and to members of the medical personnel and to chaplains of the armed forces of the Parties to the conflict, received or interned in their territory, as well as to dead persons found.

ARTICLE 5

Duration of
application

For the protected persons who have fallen into the hands of the enemy, the present Convention shall apply until their final repatriation.

ARTICLE 6

Special
agreements

In addition to the agreements expressly provided for in Articles 10, 15, 23, 28, 31, 36, 37 and 52, the High Contracting Parties may conclude other special agreements for all matters concerning which they may deem it suitable to make separate provision. No special agreement shall adversely affect the situation of the wounded and sick, of members of the medical personnel or of chaplains, as defined by the present Convention, nor restrict the rights which it confers upon them.

Wounded and sick, as well as medical personnel and chaplains, shall continue to have the benefit of such agreements as long as the Convention is applicable to them, except where express provisions to the contrary are contained in the aforesaid or in subsequent agreements, or where more favourable measures have been taken with regard to them by one or other of the Parties to the conflict.

ARTICLE 7

Non-
renunciation
of rights

Wounded and sick, as well as members of the medical personnel and chaplains, may in no circumstances renounce in part or in entirety the rights secured to them by the present Convention, and by the special agreements referred to in the foregoing Article, if such there be.

ARTICLE 8

The present Convention shall be applied with the co-operation and under the scrutiny of the Protecting Powers whose duty it is to safeguard the interests of the Parties to the confict. For this purpose, the Protecting Powers may appoint, apart from their diplomatic or consular staff, delegates from amongst their own nationals or the nationals of other neutral Powers. The said delegates shall be subject to the approval of the Power with which they are to carry out their duties.

The Parties to the conflict shall facilitate, to the greatest extent possible, the task of the representatives or delegates of the Protecting Powers.

The representatives or delegates of the Protecting Powers shall not in any case exceed their mission under the present Convention. They shall, in particular, take account of the imperative necessities of security of the State wherein they carry out their duties. Their activities shall only be restricted as an exceptional and temporary measure when this is rendered necessary by imperative military necessities.

Protecting Powers

ARTICLE 9

The provisions of the present Convention constitute no obstacle to the humanitarian activities which the International Committee of the Red Cross or any other impartial humanitarian organization may, subject to the consent of the Parties to the conflict concerned, undertake for the protection of wounded and sick, medical personnel and chaplains, and for their relief.

Activities of the International Committee of the Red Cross

ARTICLE 10

The High Contracting Parties may at any time agree to entrust to an organization which offers all guarantees of impartiality and efficacy the duties incumbent on the Protecting Powers by virtue of the present Convention.

When wounded and sick, or medical personnel and chaplains do not benefit or cease to benefit, no matter for what reason, by the activities of a Protecting Power or of an organisation provided for in the first paragraph above, the

Substitutes for Protecting Powers

Detaining Power shall request a neutral State, or such an organization, to undertake the functions performed under the present Convention by a Protecting Power designated by the Parties to a conflict.

If protection cannot be arranged accordingly, the Detaining Power shall request or shall accept, subject to the provisions of this Article, the offer of the services of a humanitarian organization, such as the International Committee of the Red Cross, to assume the humanitarian functions performed by Protecting Powers under the present Convention.

Any neutral Power, or any organization invited by the Power concerned or offering itself for these purposes, shall be required to act with a sense of responsibility towards the Party to the conflict on which persons protected by the present Convention depend, and shall be required to furnish sufficient assurances that it is in a position to undertake the appropriate functions and to discharge them impartially.

No derogation from the preceding provisions shall be made by special agreements between Powers one of which is restricted, even temporarily, in its freedom to negotiate with the other Power or its allies by reason of military events, more particularly where the whole, or a substantial part, of the territory of the said Power is occupied.

Whenever in the present Convention mention is made of a Protecting Power, such mention also applies to substitute organizations in the sense of the present Article.

ARTICLE 11

Conciliation procedure

In cases where they deem it advisable in the interest of protected persons, particularly in cases of disagreement between the Parties to the conflict as to the application or interpretation of the provisions of the present Convention, the Protecting Powers shall lend their good offices with a view to settling the disagreement.

For this purpose, each of the Protecting Powers may, either at the invitation of one Party or on its own initiative, propose to the Parties to the conflict a meeting of their representatives, in particular of the authorities responsible for the wounded and sick, members of medical personnel and chaplains, possibly on neutral territory suitably chosen. The Parties to the conflict shall be bound to give effect to the proposals made to them for this purpose. The Protecting Powers may, if necessary, propose for apporoval by the Parties to the conflict a person belonging to a neutral Power or delegated by the International Committee of the Red Cross, who shall be invited to take part in such a meeting.

CHAPTER II

WOUNDED AND SICK

ARTICLE 12

Members of the armed forces and other persons mentioned in the following Article, who are wounded or sick, shall be respected and protected in all circumstances.

Protection and care

They shall be treated humanely and cared for by the Party to the conflict in whose power they may be, without any adverse distinction founded on sex, race, nationality, religion, political opinions, or any other similar criteria. Any attempts upon their lives, or violence to their persons, shall be strictly prohibited; in particular, they shall not be murdered or exterminated, subjected to torture or to biological experiments; they shall not wilfully be left without medical assistance and care, nor shall conditions exposing them to contagion or infection be created.

Only urgent medical reasons will authorize priority in the order of treatment to be administered.

Women shall be treated with all consideration due to their sex.

The Party to the conflict which is compelled to abandon wounded or sick to the enemy shall, as far as military considerations permit, leave with them a part of its medical personnel and material to assist in their care.

ARTICLE 13

The present Convention shall apply to the wounded and sick belonging to the following categories:

Protected persons

(1) Members of the armed forces of a Party to the conflict as well as members of militias or volunteer corps forming part of such armed forces.

(2) Members of other militias and members of other volunteer corps, including those of organized

(2)   resistance movements, belonging to a Party to the conflict and operating in or outside their own territory, even if this territory is occupied, provided that such militias or volunteer corps, including such organized resistance movements, fulfil the following conditions:

    (a)   that of being commanded by a person responsible for his subordinates;

    (b)   that of having a fixed distinctive sign recognizable at a distance;

    (c)   that of carrying arms openly;

    (d)   that of conducting their operations in accordance with the laws and customs of war.

(3)   Members of regular armed forces who profess allegiance to a Government or an authority not recognized by the Detaining Power.

(4)   Persons who accompany the armed forces without actually being members thereof, such as civil members of military aircraft crews, war correspondents, supply contractors, members of labour units or of services responsible for the welfare of the armed forces, provided that they have received authorization from the armed forces which they accompany.

(5)   Members of crews, including masters, pilots and apprentices of the merchant marine and the crews of civil aircraft of the Parties to the confict, who do not benefit by more favourable treatment under any other provisions in international law.

(6)   Inhabitants of a non-occupied territory who on the approach of the enemy spontaneously take up arms to resist the invading forces, without having had time to form themselves into regular armed units, provided they carry arms openly and respect the laws and customs of war.

ARTICLE 14

Status   Subject to the provisions of Article 12, the wounded and sick of a belligerent who fall into enemy hands shall be prisoners of war, and the provisions of international law concerning prisoners of war shall apply to them.

ARTICLE 15

At all times, and particularly after an engagement, Parties to the conflict shall, without delay, take all possible measures to search for and collect the wounded and sick, to protect them against pillage and ill-treatment, to ensure their adequate care, and to search for the dead and prevent their being despoiled.

Whenever circumstances permit, an armistice or a suspension of fire shall be arranged, or local arrangements made, to permit the removal, exchange and transport of the wounded left on the battlefield.

Likewise, local arrangements may be concluded between Parties to the conflict for the removal or exchange of wounded and sick from a besieged or encircled area, and for the passage of medical and religious personnel and equipment on their way to that area.

Search for casualties. Evacuation

ARTICLE 16

Parties to the conflict shall record as soon as possible, in respect of each wounded, sick or dead person of the adverse Party falling into their hands, any particulars which may assist in his identification.

These records should if possible include:

(a) designation of the Power on which he depends;

(b) army, regimental, personal or serial number;

(c) surname;

(d) first name or names;

(e) date of birth;

(f) any other particulars shown on his identity card or disc;

(g) date and place of capture or death;

(h) particulars concerning wounds or illness, or cause of death.

As soon as possible the above mentioned information shall be forwarded to the Information Bureau described in Article 122 of the Geneva Convention relative to the Treatment of Prisoners of War of August 12, 1949, which shall transmit this information to the Power on which these persons depend through the intermediary of the Protecting Power and of the Central Prisoners of War Agency.

Parties to the conflict shall prepare and forward to each other through the same bureau, certificates of death or duly authenticated lists of the dead. They shall likewise collect

Recording and forwarding of information

and forward through the same bureau one half of a double identity disc, last wills or other documents of importance to the next of kin, money and in general all articles of an intrinsic or sentimental value, which are found on the dead. These articles, together with unidentified articles, shall be sent in sealed packets, accompanied by statements giving all particulars necessary for the identification of the deceased owners, as well as by a complete list of the contents of the parcel.

ARTICLE 17

Prescriptions regarding the dead. Graves Registration Service

Parties to the conflict shall ensure that burial or cremation of the dead, carried out individually as far as circumstances permit, is preceded by a careful examination, if possible by a medical examination, of the bodies, with a view to confirming death, establishing identity and enabling a report to be made. One half of the double identity disc, or the identity disc itself if it is a single disc, should remain on the body.

Bodies shall not be cremated except for imperative reasons of hygiene or for motives based on the religion of the deceased. In case of cremation, the circumstances and reasons for cremation shall be stated in detail in the death certificate or on the authenticated list of the dead.

They shall further ensure that the dead are honourably interred, if possible according to the rites of the religion to which they belonged, that their graves are respected, grouped if possible according to the nationality of the deceased, properly maintained and marked so that they may always be found. For this purpose, they shall organize at the commencement of hostilities an Official Graves Registration Service, to allow subsequent exhumations and to ensure the identification of bodies, whatever the site of the graves, and the possible transportation to the home country. These provisions shall likewise apply to the ashes, which shall be kept by the Graves Registration Service until proper disposal thereof in accordance with the wishes of the home country.

As soon as circumstances permit, and at latest at the end of the hostilities, these Services shall exchange, through the Information Bureau mentioned in the second paragraph of Article 16, lists showing the exact location and markings of the graves together with particulars of the dead interred therein.

ARTICLE 18

The military authorities may appeal to the charity of the inhabitants voluntarily to collect and care for, under their direction, the wounded and sick, granting persons who have responded to this appeal the necessary protection and facilities. Should the adverse party take or retake control of the area, he shall likewise grant these persons the same protection and the same facilities.

The military authorities shall permit the inhabitants and relief societies, even in invaded or occupied areas, spontaneously to collect and care for wounded or sick of whatever nationality. The civilian population shall respect these wounded and sick, and in particular abstain from offering them violence.

No one may ever be molested or convicted for having nursed the wounded or sick.

The provisions of the present Article do not relieve the occupying Power of its obligation to give both physical and moral care to the wounded and sick.

Role of the population

CHAPTER III

MEDICAL UNITS AND ESTABLISHMENTS

ARTICLE 19

Fixed establishments and mobile medical units of the Medical Service may in no circumstances be attacked, but shall at all times be respected and protected by the Parties to the conflict. Should they fall into the hands of the adverse Party, their personnel shall be free to pursue their duties, as long as the capturing Power has not itself ensured the necessary care of the wounded and sick found in such establishments and units.

The responsible authorities shall ensure that the said medical establishments and units are, as far as possible, situated in such a manner that attacks against military objectives cannot imperil their safety.

Protection

ARTICLE 20

Protection of
hospital
ships

Hospital ships entitled to the protection of the Geneva
Convention for the Amelioration of the Condition of Woun-
ded, Sick and Shipwrecked Members of Armed Forces at
Sea of August 12, 1949, shall not be attacked from the land.

ARTICLE 21

Discontinuance
of protection of
medical
establishments
and units

The protection to which fixed establishments and mobile
medical units of the Medical Service are entitled shall not
cease unless they are used to commit, outside their humanitarian duties, acts harmful to the enemy. Protection may,
however, cease only after a due warning has been given,
naming, in all appropriate cases, a reasonable time limit and
after such warning has remained unheeded.

ARTICLE 22

Conditions not
depriving
medical units
and
establishments
of protection

The following conditions shall not be considered as depriving
a medical unit or establishment of the protection guaranteed
by Article 19:

(1)   That the personnel of the unit or establishment are
       armed, and that they use the arms in their own
       defence, or in that of the wounded and sick in their
       charge.

(2)   That in the absence of armed orderlies, the unit or
       establishment is protected by a picket or by sentries
       or by an escort.

(3)   That small arms and ammunition, taken from the
       wounded and sick and not yet handed to the proper
       service, are found in the unit or establishment.

(4)   That personnel and material of the veterinary
       service are found in the unit or establishment,
       without forming an integral part thereof.

(5)   That the humanitarian activities of medical units
       and establishments or of their personnel extend to
       the care of civilian wounded or sick.

ARTICLE 23

In time of peace, the High Contracting Parties and, after the outbreak of hostilities, the Parties to the confict, may establish in their own territory, and, if the need arises, in occupied areas, hospital zones and localities so organized as to protect the wounded and sick from the effects of war, as well as the personnel entrusted with the organization and administration of these zones and localities and with the care of the persons therein assembled.

Upon the outbreak and during the course of hostilities, the Parties concerned may conclude agreements on mutual recognition of the hospital zones and localities they have created. They may for this purpose implement the provisions of the Draft Agreement annexed to the present Convention, with such amendments as they may consider necessary.

The Protecting Powers and the International Committee of the Red Cross are invited to lend their good offices in order to facilitate the institution and recognition of these hospital zones and localities.

Hospital zones and localities

CHAPTER IV

PERSONNEL

ARTICLE 24

Medical personnel exclusively engaged in the search for, or the collection, transport or treatment of the wounded or sick, or in the prevention of disease, staff exclusively engaged in the administration of medical units and establishments, as well as chaplains attached to the armed forces, shall be respected and protected in all circumstances.

Protection permanent personnel

ARTICLE 25

Members of the armed forces specially trained for employment, should the need arise, as hospital orderlies, nurses or auxiliary stretcher-bearers, in the search for or the collection, transport or treatment of the wounded and sick shall likewise be respected and protected if they are carrying out these duties at the time when they come into contact with the enemy or fall into his hands.

Protection auxiliary personnel

ARTICLE 26

Personnel of   The staff of National Red Cross Societies and that of other
aid societies   Voluntary Aid Societies, duly recognized and authorized by
their Governments, who may be employed on the same
duties as the personnel named in Article 24, are placed on
the same footing as the personnel named in the said Article,
provided that the staff of such societies are subject to
military laws and regulations.

Each High Contracting Party shall notify to the other,
either in time of peace or at the commencement of or during
hostilities, but in any case before actually employing them,
the names of the societies which it has authorized, under its
responsibility, to render assistance to the regular medical
service of its armed forces.

ARTICLE 27

Societies of   A recognized Society of a neutral country can only lend
neutral   the assistance of its medical personnel and units to a Party
countries   to the conflict with the previous consent of its own Government and the authorization of the Party to the conflict
concerned. That personnel and those units shall be placed
under the control of that Party to the conflict.

The neutral Government shall notify this consent to the
adversary of the State which accepts such assistance. The
Party to the conflict who accepts such assistance is bound
to notify the adverse Party thereof before making any use of
it.

In no circumstances shall this assistance be considered as
interference in the conflict.

The members of the personnel named in the first
paragraph shall be duly furnished with the identity cards
provided for in Article 40 before leaving the neutral country
to which they belong.

ARTICLE 28

Retained   Personnel designated in Articles 24 and 26 who fall into
personnel   the hands of the adverse Party, shall be retained only in so
far as the state of health, the spiritual needs and the number
of prisoners of war require.

Personnel thus retained shall not be deemed prisoners of
war. Nevertheless they shall at least benefit by all the

provisions of the Geneva Convention relative to the Treatment of Prisoners of War of August 12, 1949. Within the
framework of the military laws and regulations of the
Detaining Power, and under the authority of its competent
service, they shall continue to carry out, in accordance with
their professional ethics, their medical and spiritual duties
on behalf of prisoners of war, preferably those of the armed
forces to which they themselves belong. They shall further
enjoy the following facilities for carrying out their medical
or spiritual duties:

    (a)   They shall be authorized to visit periodically the
             prisoners of war in labour units or hospitals outside
             the camp. The Detaining Power shall put at their
             disposal the means of transport required.

    (b)   In each camp the senior medical officer of the
             highest rank shall be responsible to the military
             authorities of the camp for the professional activity
             of the retained medical personnel. For this
             purpose, from the outbreak of hostilities, the
             Parties to the conflict shall agree regarding the
             corresponding seniority of the ranks of their
             medical personnel, including those of the societies
             designated in Article 26. In all questions arising out
             of their duties, this medical officer, and the
             chaplains, shall have direct access to the military
             and medical authorities of the camp who shall grant
             them the facilities they may require for correspon-
             dence relating to these questions.

    (c)   Although retained personnel in a camp shall be
             subject to its internal discipline, they shall not,
             however, be required to perform any work outside
             their medical or religious duties.

During hostilities the Parties to the conflict shall make
arrangements for relieving where possible retained
personnel, and shall settle the procedure of such relief.

None of the preceding provisions shall relieve the
Detaining Power of the obligations imposed upon it with
regard to the medical and spiritual welfare of the prisoners
of war.

ARTICLE 29

Status of
auxiliary
personnel

Members of the personnel designated in Article 25 who have fallen into the hands of the enemy, shall be prisoners of war, but shall be employed on their medical duties in so far as the need arises.

ARTICLE 30

Return of
medical and
religious
personnel

Personnel whose retention is not indispensable by virtue of the provisions of Article 28 shall be returned to the Party to the conflict to whom they belong, as soon as a road is open for their return and military requirements permit.

Pending their return, they shall not be deemed prisoners of war. Nevertheless they shall at least benefit by all the provisions of the Geneva Convention relative to the Treatment of Prisoners of War of August 12, 1949. They shall continue to fulfil their duties under the orders of the adverse Party and shall preferably be engaged in the care of the wounded and sick of the Party to the conflict to which they themselves belong.

On their departure, they shall take with them the effects, personal belongings, valuables and instruments belonging to them.

ARTICLE 31

Selection of
personnel for
return

The selection of personnel for return under Article 30 shall be made irrespective of any consideration of race, religion or political opinion, but preferably according to the chronological order of their capture and their state of health.

As from the outbreak of hosilities, Parties to the conflict may determine by special agreement the percentage of personnel to be retained, in proportion to the number of prisoners and the distribution of the said personnel in the camps.

ARTICLE 32

Return of
personnel
belonging to
neutral
countries

Persons designated in Article 27 who have fallen into the hands of the adverse Party may not be detained.

Unless otherwise agreed, they shall have permission to return to their country, or if this is not possible, to the territory of the Party to the conflict in whose service they were, as soon as a route for their return is open and military considerations permit.

Pending their release, they shall continue their work under the direction of the adverse Party; they shall preferably be engaged in the care of the wounded and sick of the Party to the conflict in whose service they were.

On their departure, they shall take with them their effects, personal articles and valuables and the instruments, arms and if possible the means of transport belonging to them.

The Parties to the conflict shall secure to this personnel, while in their power, the same food, lodging, allowances and pay as are granted to the corresponding personnel of their armed forces. The food shall in any case be sufficient as regards quantity, quality and variety to keep the said personnel in a normal state of health.

CHAPTER V

BUILDINGS AND MATERIAL

ARTICLE 33

The material of mobile medical units of the armed forces which fall into the hands of the enemy, shall be reserved for the care of wounded and sick.

Buildings and stores

The buildings, material and stores of fixed medical establishments of the armed forces shall remain subject to the laws of war, but may not be diverted from that purpose as long as they are required for the care of wounded and sick. Nevertheless, the commanders of forces in the field may make use of them, in case of urgent military necessity, provided that they make previous arrangements for the welfare of the wounded and sick who are nursed in them.

The material and stores defined in the present Article shall not be intentionally destroyed.

ARTICLE 34

The real and personal property of aid societies which are admitted to the privileges of the Convention shall be regarded as private property.

Property of aid societies

The right of requisition recognized for belligerents by the laws and customs of war shall not be exercised except in case

of urgent necessity, and only after the welfare of the
wounded and sick has been ensured.

CHAPTER VI

MEDICAL TRANSPORTS

ARTICLE 35

Protection   Transports of wounded and sick or of medical equipment
shall be respected and protected in the same way as mobile
medical units.

Should such transports or vehicles fall into the hands of
the adverse Party, they shall be subject to the laws of war,
on condition that the Party to the conflict who captures
them shall in all cases ensure the care of the wounded and
sick they contain.

The civilian personnel and all means of transport obtained
by requisition shall be subject to the general rules of international law.

ARTICLE 36

Medical   Medical aircraft, that is to say, aircraft exclusively employed
aircraft   for the removal of wounded and sick and for the transport
of medical personnel and equipment, shall not be attacked,
but shall be respected by the belligerents, while flying at
heights, times and on routes specifically agreed upon
between the belligerents concerned.

They shall bear, clearly marked, the distinctive emblem
prescribed in Article 38, together with their national colours,
on their lower, upper and lateral surfaces. They shall be
provided with any other markings or means of identification
that may be agreed upon between the belligerents upon the
outbreak or during the course of hostilities.

Unless agreed otherwise, flights over enemy or enemy-
occupied territory, are prohibited.

Medical aircraft shall obey every summons to land. In the
event of a landing thus imposed, the aircraft with its
occupants may continue its flight after examination, if any.

In the event of an involuntary landing in enemy or enemy-
occupied territory, the wounded and sick, as well as the
crew of the aircraft shall be prisoners of war. The

medical personnel shall be treated according to Article 24, and the Articles following.

ARTICLE 37

Subject to the provisions of the second paragraph, medical aircraft of Parties to the conflict may fly over the territory of neutral Powers, land on it in case of necessity, or use it as a port of call. They shall give the neutral Powers previous notice of their passage over the said territory and obey all summons to alight, on land or water. They will be immune from attack only when flying on routes, at heights and at times specifically agreed upon between the Parties to the conflict and the neutral Power concerned.

The neutral Powers may, however, place conditions or restrictions on the passage or landing of medical aircraft on their territory. Such possible conditions or restrictions shall be applied equally to all Parties to the conflict.

Unless agreed otherwise between the neutral Power and the Parties to the conflict, the wounded and sick who are disembarked, with the consent of the local authorities, on neutral territory by medical aircraft, shall be detained by the neutral Power, where so required by international law, in such a manner that they cannot again take part in operations of war. The cost of their accommodation and internment shall be borne by the Power on which they depend.

Flight over neutral countries. Landing of wounded

CHAPTER VII
THE DISTINCTIVE EMBLEM

ARTICLE 38

As a compliment to Switzerland, the heraldic emblem of the red cross on a white ground, formed by reversing the Federal colours, is retained as the emblem and distinctive sign of the Medical Service of armed forces.

Nevertheless, in the case of countries which already use as emblem, in place of the red cross, the red crescent or the red lion and sun on a white ground, those emblems are also recognized by the terms of the present Convention.

Emblem of the Convention

ARTICLE 39

Use of the   Under the direction of the competent military authority,
emblem   the emblem shall be displayed on the flags, armlets and on
all equipment employed in the Medical Service.

ARTICLE 40

Identification   The personnel designated in Article 24 and in Articles 26
of medical and   and 27 shall wear, affixed to the left arm, a water-resistant
religious   armlet bearing the distinctive emblem, issued and stamped
personnel   by the military authority.

Such personnel, in addition to wearing the identity disc
mentioned in Article 16, shall also carry a special identity
card bearing the distinctive emblem. This card shall be
water-resistant and of such size that it can be carried in the
pocket. It shall be worded in the national language, shall
mention at least the surname and first names, the date of
birth, the rank and the service number of the bearer, and
shall state in what capacity he is entitled to the protection
of the present Convention. The card shall bear the
photograph of the owner and also either his signature or his
fingerprints or both. It shall be embossed with the stamp of
the military authority.

The identity card shall be uniform throughout the same
armed forces and, as far as possible, of a similar type in the
armed forces of the High Contracting Parties. The Parties
to the conflict may be guided by the model which is
annexed, by way of example, to the present Convention.
They shall inform each other, at the outbreak of hostilities,
of the model they are using. Identity cards should be made
out, if possible, at least in duplicate, one copy being kept
by the home country.

In no circumstances may the said personnel be deprived
of their insignia or identity cards nor of the right to wear the
armlet. In case of loss, they shall be entitled to receive
duplicates of the cards and to have the insignia replaced.

ARTICLE 41

Identification   The personnel designated in Article 25 shall wear, but only
of auxiliary   while carrying out medical duties, a white armlet bearing in
personnel   its centre the distinctive sign in miniature; the armlet shall
be issued and stamped by the military authority.

Military identity documents to be carried by this type of personnel shall specify what special training they have received, the temporary character of the duties they are engaged upon, and their authority for wearing the armlet.

ARTICLE 42

The distinctive flag of the Convention shall be hoisted only over such medical units and establishments as are entitled to be respected under the Convention, and only with the consent of the military authorities.

In mobile units, as in fixed establishments, it may be accompanied by the national flag of the Party to the conflict to which the unit or establishment belongs.

Nevertheless, medical units which have fallen into the hands of the enemy shall not fly any flag other than that of the Convention.

Parties to the conflict shall take the necessary steps, in so far as military considerations permit, to make the distinctive emblems indicating medical units and establishments clearly visible to the enemy land, air or naval forces, in order to obviate the possibility of any hostile action.

Marking of medical units and establishments

ARTICLE 43

The medical units belonging to neutral countries, which may have been authorized to lend their services to a belligerent under the conditions laid down in Article 27, shall fly, along with the flag of the Convention, the national flag of that belligerent, wherever the latter makes use of the faculty conferred on him by Article 42.

Subject to orders to the contrary by the responsible military authorities, they may, on all occasions, fly their national flag, even if they fall into the hands of the adverse Party.

Marking of units of neutral countries

ARTICLE 44

With the exception of the cases mentioned in the following paragraphs of the present Article, the emblem of the Red Cross on a white ground and the words "Red Cross", or "Geneva Cross" may not be employed, either in time of peace or in time of war, except to indicate or to protect the

Restrictions in the use of the emblem. Exceptions

medical units and establishments, the personnel and material protected by the present Convention and other Conventions dealing with similar matters. The same shall apply to the emblems mentioned in Article 38, second paragraph, in respect of the countries which use them. The National Red Cross Societies and other Societies designated in Article 26 shall have the right to use the distinctive emblem conferring the protection of the Convention only within the framework of the present paragraph.

Furthermore, National Red Cross (Red Crescent, Red Lion and Sun) Societies may, in time of peace, in accordance with their national legislation, make use of the name and emblem of the Red Cross for their other activities which are in conformity with the principles laid down by the International Red Cross Conferences. When those activities are carried out in time of war, the conditions for the use of the emblem shall be such that it cannot be considered as conferring the protection of the Convention; the emblem shall be comparatively small in size and may not be placed on armlets or on the roofs of buildings.

The international Red Cross organizations and their duly authorized personnel shall be permitted to make use, at all times, of the emblem of the Red Cross on a white ground.

As an exceptional measure, in conformity with national legislation and with the express permission of one of the National Red Cross (Red Crescent, Red Lion and Sun) Societies, the emblem of the Convention may be employed in time of peace to identify vehicles used as ambulances and to mark the position of aid stations exclusively assigned to the purpose of giving free treatment to the wounded or sick.

CHAPTER VIII

EXECUTION OF THE CONVENTION

ARTICLE 45

Detailed execution. Unforeseen cases

Each Party to the conflict, acting through its commanders-in-chief, shall ensure the detailed execution of the preceding Articles and provide for unforeseen cases, in conformity with the general principles of the present Convention.

ARTICLE 46

Reprisals against the wounded, sick, personnel, buildings or equipment protected by the Convention are prohibited.

Prohibition of reprisals

ARTICLE 47

The High Contracting Parties undertake, in time of peace as in time of war, to disseminate the text of the Present Convention as widely as possible in their respective countries, and, in particular, to include the study thereof in their programmes of military and, if possible, civil instruction, so that the principles thereof may become known to the entire population, in particular to the armed fighting forces, the medical personnel and the chaplains.

Dissemination of the Convention

ARTICLE 48

The High Contracting Parties shall communicate to one another through the Swiss Federal Council and, during hostilities, through the Protecting Powers, the official translations of the present Convention, as well as the laws and regulations which they may adopt to ensure the application thereof.

Translations. Rules of application

CHAPTER IX
REPRESSION OF ABUSES AND INFRACTIONS

ARTICLE 49

The High Contracting Parties undertake to enact any legislation necessary to provide effective penal sanctions for persons committing, or ordering to be committed, any of the grave breaches of the present Convention defined in the following Article.

Penal sanctions
I. General observations

Each High Contracting Party shall be under the obligation to search for persons alleged to have committed, or to have ordered to be committed, such grave breaches, and shall bring such persons, regardless of their nationality, before its own courts. It may also, if it prefers, and in accordance with the provisions of its own legislation, hand such persons over for trial to another High Contracting

Party concerned, provided such High Contracting Party has made out a *prima facie* case.

Each High Contracting Party shall take measures necessary for the suppression of all acts contrary to the provisions of the present Convention other than the grave breaches defined in the following Article.

In all circumstances, the accused persons shall benefit by safeguards of proper trial and defence, which shall not be less favourable than those provided by Article 105 and those following of the Geneva Convention relative to the Treatment of Prisoners of War of August 12, 1949.

ARTICLE 50

II. Grave breaches

Grave breaches to which the preceding Article relates shall be those involving any of the following acts, if committed against persons or property protected by the Convention: wilful killing, torture or inhuman treatment, including biological experiments, wilfully causing great suffering or serious injury to body or health, and extensive destruction and appropriation of property, not justified by military necessity and carried out unlawfully and wantonly.

ARTICLE 51

III. Responsibilities of the Contracting Parties

No High Contracting Party shall be allowed to absolve itself or any other High Contracting Party of any liability incurred by itself or by another High Contracting Party in respect of breaches referred to in the preceding Article.

ARTICLE 52

Enquiry procedure

At the request of a Party to the conflict, an enquiry shall be instituted, in a manner to be decided between the interested Parties, concerning any alleged violation of the Convention.

If agreement has not been reached concerning the procedure for the enquiry, the Parties should agree on the choice of an umpire who will decide upon the procedure to be followed.

Once the violation has been established, the Parties to the conflict shall put an end to it and shall repress it with the least possible delay.

ARTICLE 53

The use by individuals, societies, firms or companies either public or private, other than those entitled thereto under the present Convention, of the emblem or the designation "Red Cross" or "Geneva Cross", or any sign or designation constituting an imitation thereof, whatever the object of such use, and irrespective of the date of its adoption, shall be prohibited at all times.

By reason of the tribute paid to Switzerland by the adoption of the reversed Federal colours, and of the confusion which may arise between the arms of Switzerland and the distinctive emblem of the Convention, the use by private individuals, societies or firms, of the arms of the Swiss Confederation, or of marks constituting an imitation thereof, whether as trademarks or commercial marks, or as parts of such marks, or for a purpose contrary to commercial honesty, or in circumstances capable of wounding Swiss national sentiment, shall be prohibited at all times.

Nevertheless, such High Contracting Parties as were not party to the Geneva Convention of July 27, 1929, may grant to prior users of the emblems, designations, signs or marks designated in the first paragraph, a time limit not to exceed three years from the coming into force of the present Convention to discontinue such use, provided that the said use shall not be such as would appear, in time of war, to confer the protection of the Convention.

The prohibition laid down in the first paragraph of the present Article shall also apply, without effect on any rights acquired through prior use, to the emblems and marks mentioned in the second paragraph of Article 38.

Misuse of the emblem

ARTICLE 54

The High Contracting Parties shall, if their legislation is not already adequate, take measures necessary for the prevention and repression, at all times, of the abuses referred to under Article 53.

Prevention of misuse

FINAL PROVISIONS

ARTICLE 55

Languages   The present Convention is established in English and in French. Both texts are equally authentic.

The Swiss Federal Council shall arrange for official translations of the Convention to be made in the Russian and Spanish languages.

ARTICLE 56

Signature   The present Convention, which bears the date of this day, is open to signature until February 12, 1950, in the name of the Powers represented at the Conference which opened at Geneva on April 21, 1949; furthermore, by Powers not represented at that Conference but which are parties to the Geneva Conventions of 1864, 1906 or 1929 for the Relief of the Wounded and Sick in Armies in the Field.

ARTICLE 57

Ratification   The present Convention shall be ratified as soon as possible and the ratifications shall be deposited at Berne.

A record shall be drawn up of the deposit of each instrument of ratification and certified copies of this record shall be transmitted by the Swiss Federal Council to all the Powers in whose name the Convention has been signed, or whose accession has been notified.

ARTICLE 58

Coming into   The present Convention shall come into force six months
force   after not less than two instruments of ratification have been deposited.

Thereafter, it shall come into force for each High Contracting Party six months after the deposit of the instrument of ratification.

ARTICLE 59

Relation to   The present Convention replaces the Conventions of August
previous   22, 1864, July 6, 1906, and July 27, 1929, in relations
Conventions   between the High Contracting Parties.

ARTICLE 60

From the date of its coming into force, it shall be open to any Power in whose name the present Convention has not been signed, to accede to this Convention.

Accession

ARTICLE 61

Accessions shall be notified in writing to the Swiss Federal Council, and shall take effect six months after the date on which they are received.

The Swiss Federal Council shall communicate the accessions to all the Powers in whose name the Convention has been signed, or whose accession has been notified.

Notification of accessions

ARTICLE 62

The situations provided for in Articles 2 and 3 shall give immediate effect to ratifications deposited and accessions notified by the Parties to the conflict before or after the beginning of hostilities or occupation. The Swiss Federal Council shall communicate by the quickest method any ratifications or accessions received from Parties to the conflict.

Immediate effect

ARTICLE 63

Each of the High Contracting Parties shall be at liberty to denounce the present Convention.

Denunciaton

The denunciation shall be notified in writing to the Swiss Federal Council, which shall transmit it to the Governments of all the High Contracting Parties.

The denunciaton shall take effect one year after the notification thereof has been made to the Swiss Federal Council. However, a denunciation of which notification has been made at a time when the denouncing Power is involved in a conflict shall not take effect until peace has been concluded, and until after operations connected with the release and repatriation of the persons protected by the present Convention have been terminated.

The denunciation shall have effect only in respect of the denouncing Power. It shall in no way impair the obligations which the Parties to the conflict shall remain bound to fulfil by virtue of the principles of the law of nations, as they result from the usages established among civilized peoples, from the laws of humanity and the dictates of the public conscience.

GENEVA CONVENTION FOR THE AMELIORATION OF THE CONDITION OF WOUNDED, SICK AND SHIPWRECKED MEMBERS OF ARMED FORCES AT SEA OF AUGUST 12, 1949.

CHAPTER 1

GENERAL PROVISIONS

ARTICLE 1

Respect for the Convention

The High Contracting Parties undertake to respect and to ensure respect for the present Convention in all circumstances.

ARTICLE 2

Application of the Convention

In addition to the provisions which shall be implemented in peacetime, the present Convention shall apply to all cases of declared war or of any other armed conflict which may arise between two or more of the High Contracting Parties, even if the state of war is not recognized by one of them.

The Convention shall also apply to all cases of partial or total occupation of the territory of a High Contracting Party even if the said occupation meets with no armed resistance.

Although one of the Powers in conflict may not be a party to the present Convention, the Powers who are parties thereto shall remain bound by it in their mutual relations. They shall furthermore be bound by the Convention in relation to the said Power, if the latter accepts and applies the provisions thereof.

ARTICLE 3

Conflicts not of an international character

In the case of armed conflict not of an international character occurring in the territory of one of the High Contracting Parties, each Party to the conflict shall be bound to apply, as a minimum, the following provisions:

ARTICLE 3

(1)   Persons taking no active part in the hostilities,
      including members of armed forces who have laid
      down their arms and those placed *hors de combat* by
      sickness, wounds, detention, or any other cause,
      shall in all circumstances be treated humanely,
      without any adverse distinction founded on race,
      colour, religion or faith, sex, birth or wealth, or any
      other similar criteria.
      To this end, the following acts are and shall remain
      prohibited at any time and in any place whatsoever
      with respect to the above-mentioned persons:

      (*a*)   violence to life and person, in particular
              murder of all kinds, mutilation, cruel
              treatment and torture;

      (*b*)   taking of hostages;

      (*c*)   outrages upon personal dignity, in particular,
              humiliating and degrading treatment;

      (*d*)   the passing of sentences and the carrying out
              of executions without previous judgment
              pronounced by a regularly constituted court,
              affording all the judicial guarantees which are
              recognized as indispensable by civilized
              peoples.

(2)   The wounded, sick and shipwrecked shall be
      collected and cared for.

An impartial humanitarian body, such as the International
Committee of the Red Cross, may offer its services to the
Parties to the conflict.

The Parties to the conflict should further endeavour to
bring into force, by means of special agreements, all or part
of the other provisions of the present Convention.

The application of the preceding provisions shall not
affect the legal status of the Parties to the conflict.

ARTICLE 4

In case of hostilities between land and naval forces of   Field of
Parties to the conflict, the provisions of the present Con-   application
vention shall apply only to forces on board ship.

Forces put ashore shall immediately become subject to the provisions of the Geneva Convention for the Amelioration of the Condition of the Wounded and Sick in Armed Forces in the Field of August 12, 1949.

ARTICLE 5

Application by
neutral Powers

Neutral Powers shall apply by analogy the provisions of the present Convention to the wounded, sick and ship-wrecked, and to members of the medical personnel and to chaplains of the armed forces of the Parties to the conflict received or interned in their territory, as well as to dead persons found.

ARTICLE 6

Special
agreements

In addition to the agreements expressly provided for in Articles 10, 18, 31, 38, 39, 40, 43 and 53, the High Contrac-ting Parties may conclude other special agreements for all matters concerning which they may deem it suitable to make separate provision. No special agreement shall adversely affect the situation of wounded, sick and ship-wrecked persons, of members of the medical personnel or of chaplains, as defined by the present Convention, nor restrict the rights which it confers upon them.

Wounded, sick, and shipwrecked persons, as well as medical personnel and chaplains, shall continue to have the benefit of such agreements as long as the Convention is applicable to them, except where express provisions to the contrary are contained in the aforesaid or in subsequent agreements, or where more favourable measures have been taken with regard to them by one or other of the Parties to the conflict.

ARTICLE 7

Non-renunciation
of rights

Wounded, sick and shipwrecked persons, as well as members of the medical personnel and chaplains, may in no circumstances renounce in part or in entirety the rights secured to them by the present Convention, and by the special agreements referred to in the foregoing Article, if such there be.

ARTICLE 8

The present Convention shall be applied with the cooperation and under the scrutiny of the Protecting Powers whose duty it is to safeguard the interests of the Parties to the conflict. For this purpose, the Protecting Powers may appoint, apart from their diplomatic or consular staff, delegates from amongst their own nationals or the nationals of other neutral Powers. The said delegates shall be subject to the approval of the Power with which they are to carry out their duties.

The Parties to the conflict shall facilitate to the greatest extent possible the task of the representatives or delegates of the Protecting Powers.

The representatives or delegates of the Protecting Powers shall not in any case exceed their mission under the present Convention. They shall, in particular, take account of the imperative necessities of security of the State wherein they carry out their duties. Their activities shall only be restricted as an exceptional and temporary measure when this is rendered necessary by imperative military necessities.

Protecting Powers

ARTICLE 9

The provisions of the Present Convention constitute no obstacle to the humanitarian activities which the International Committee of the Red Cross or any other impartial humanitarian organization may, subject to the consent of the Parties to the conflict concerned, undertake for the protection of wounded, sick and shipwrecked persons, medical personnel and chaplains, and for their relief.

Activities of the International Committee of the Red Cross

ARTICLE 10

The High Contracting Parties may at any time agree to entrust to an organization which offers all guarantees of impartiality and efficacy the duties incumbent on the Protecting Powers by virtue of the present Convention.

When wounded, sick and shipwrecked, or medical personnel and chaplains do not benefit or cease to benefit, no matter for what reason, by the activities of a Protecting Power or of an organization provided for in the first paragraph above, the Detaining Power shall request a neutral State, or such an organization, to undertake the functions performed under

Substitutes for Protecting Powers

the present Convention by a Protecting Power designated by the Parties to a conflict.

If protection cannot be arranged accordingly, the Detaining Power shall request or shall accept, subject to the provisions of this Article, the offer of the services of a humanitarian organization, such as the International Committee of the Red Cross, to assume the humanitarian functions performed by Protecting Powers under the present Convention.

Any neutral Power, or any organization invited by the Power concerned or offering itself for these purposes, shall be required to act with a sense of responsibility towards the Party to the conflict on which persons protected by the present Convention depend, and shall be required to furnish sufficient assurances that it is in a position to undertake the appropriate functions and to discharge them impartially.

No derogation from the preceding provisions shall be made by special agreeements between Powers one of which is restricted, even temporarily, in its freedom to negotiate with the other Power or its allies by reason of military events, more particularly where the whole, or a substantial part, of the territory of the said Power is occupied.

Whenever, in the present Convention, mention is made of a Protecting Power, such mention also applies to substitute organizations in the sense of the present Article.

ARTICLE 11

Conciliation procedure

In cases where they deem it advisable in the interest of protected persons, particularly in cases of disagreement between the Parties to the conflict as to the application or interpretation of the provisions of their present Convention, the Protecting Powers shall lend their good offices with a view to settling the disagreement.

For this purpose, each of the Protecting Powers may, either at the invitation of one Party or on its own initiative, propose to the Parties to the conflict a meeting of their representatives, in particular of the authorities responsible for the wounded, sick and shipwrecked, medical personnel and chaplains, possibly on neutral territory suitably chosen. The Parties to the conflict shall be bound to give effect to the proposals made to them for this purpose. The Protecting Powers may, if necessary, propose for approval by the

Parties to the conflict, a person belonging to a neutral Power or delegated by the International Committee of the Red Cross, who shall be invited to take part in such a meeting.

CHAPTER II

WOUNDED, SICK AND SHIPWRECKED

ARTICLE 12

Members of the armed forces and other persons mentioned in the following Article, who are at sea and who are wounded, sick or shipwrecked, shall be respected and protected in all circumstances, it being understood that the term "shipwreck" means shipwreck from any cause and includes forced landings at sea by or from aircraft.

Protection and care

Such persons shall be treated humanely and cared for by the Parties to the conflict in whose power they may be, without any adverse distinction founded on sex, race, nationality, religion, political opinions, or any other similar criteria. Any attempts upon their lives, or violence to their persons, shall be strictly prohibited; in particular, they shall not be murdered or exterminated, subjected to torture or to biological experiments; they shall not wilfully be left without medical assistance and care, nor shall conditions exposing them to contagion or infection be created.

Only urgent medical reasons will authorize priority in the order of treatment to be administered.

Women shall be treated with all consideration due to their sex.

ARTICLE 13

The present Convention shall apply to the wounded, sick and shipwrecked at sea belonging to the following categories:

Protected persons

(1)   Members of the armed forces of a Party to the conflict, as well as members of militias or volunteer corps forming part of such armed forces.

(2)   Members of other militias and members of other volunteer corps, including those of organized resistance movements, belonging to a Party to the

conflict and operating in or outside their own territory, even if this territory is occupied, provided that such militias or volunteer corps, including such organized resistance movements, fulfil the following conditions:

(*a*)   that of being commanded by a person responsible for his subordinates;

(*b*)   that of having a fixed distinctive sign recognizable at a distance;

(*c*)   that of carrying arms openly;

(*d*)   that of conducting their operations in accordance with the laws and customs of war.

(3)   Members of regular armed forces who profess allegiance to a Government or an authority not recognized by the Detaining Power.

(4)   Persons who accompany the armed forces without actually being members thereof, such as civilian members of military aircraft crews, war correspondents, supply contractors, members of labour units or of services responsible for the welfare of the armed forces, provided that they have received authorization from the armed forces which they accompany.

(5)   Members of crews, including masters, pilots and apprentices of the merchant marine and the crews of civil aircraft of the Parties to the conflict, who do not benefit by more favourable treatment under any other provisions of international law.

(6)   Inhabitants of a non-occupied territory who, on the approach of the enemy, spontaneously take up arms to resist the invading forces, without having had time to form themselves into regular armed units, provided they carry arms openly and respect the laws and customs of war.

ARTICLE 14

Handing over
to a belligerent

All warships of a belligerent Party shall have the right to demand that the wounded, sick, or shipwrecked on board military hospital ships, and hospital ships belonging to relief societies or to private individuals, as well as merchant vessels, yachts and other craft shall be surrendered, whatever their nationality, provided that the wounded and sick are in a fit state to be moved and that the warship can provide adequate facilities for necessary medical treatment.

ARTICLE 15

If wounded, sick or shipwrecked persons are taken on board a neutral warship or a neutral military aircraft, it shall be ensured, where so required by international law, that they can take no further part in operations of war.

Wounded taken
on board a
neutral warship

ARTICLE 16

Subject to the provisions of Article 12, the wounded, sick and shipwrecked of a belligerent who fall into enemy hands shall be prisoners of war, and the provisions of international law concerning prisoners of war shall apply to them. The captor may decide, according to circumstances, whether it is expedient to hold them, or to convey them to a port in the captor's own country, to a neutral port or even to a port in enemy territory. In the last case, prisoners of war thus returned to their home country may not serve for the duration of the war.

Wounded
falling into
enemy hands

ARTICLE 17

Wounded, sick or shipwrecked persons who are landed in neutral ports with the consent of the local authorities, shall, failing arrangements to the contrary between the neutral and the belligerent Powers, be so guarded by the neutral Power, where so required by international law, that the said persons cannot again take part in operations of war.

Wounded
landed in a
neutral port

The costs of hospital accommodation and internment shall be borne by the Power on whom the wounded, sick or shipwrecked persons depend.

ARTICLE 18

After each engagement, Parties to the conflict shall, without delay, take all possible measures to search for and collect the shipwrecked, wounded and sick, to protect them against pillage and ill-treatment, to ensure their adequate care, and to search for the dead and prevent their being despoiled.

Search for
casualties after
an engagement

Whenever circumstances permit, the Parties to the conflict shall conclude local arrangements for the removal of the wounded and sick by sea from a besieged or encircled area and for the passage of medical and religious personnel and equipment on their way to that area.

ARTICLE 19

Recording and forwarding of information

The Parties to the conflict shall record as soon as possible, in respect of each shipwrecked, wounded, sick or dead person of the adverse Party falling into their hands, any particulars which may assist in his identification. These records should if possible include:

(*a*)   designation of the Power on which he depends;

(*b*)   army, regimental, personal or serial number;

(*c*)   surname;

(*d*)   first name or names;

(*e*)   date of birth;

(*f*)   any other particulars shown on his identity card or disc;

(*g*)   date and place of capture or death;

(*h*)   particulars concerning wounds or illness, or cause of death.

As soon as possible the above-mentioned information shall be forwarded to the information bureau described in Article 122 of the Geneva Convention relative to the Treatment of Prisoners of War of August 12, 1949, which shall transmit this information to the Power on which these persons depend through the intermediary of the Protecting Power and of the Central Prisoners of War Agency.

Parties to the conflict shall prepare and forward to each other through the same bureau, certificates of death or duly authenticated lists of the dead. They shall likewise collect and forward through the same bureau one half of the double identity disc, or the identity disc itself if it is a single disc, last wills or other documents of importance to the next of kin, money and in general all articles of an intrinsic or sentimental value, which are found on the dead. These articles, together with unidentified articles, shall be sent in sealed packets, accompanied by statements giving all particulars necessary for the identification of the deceased owners, as well as by a complete list of the contents of the parcel.

ARTICLE 20

Parties to the conflict shall ensure that burial at sea of the dead, carried out individually as far as circumstances permit, is preceded by a careful examination, if possible by a medical examination, of the bodies, with a view to confirming death, establishing identity and enabling a report to be made. Where a double identity disc is used, one half of the disc should remain on the body.

Prescriptions regarding the dead

If dead persons are landed, the provisions of the Geneva Convention for the Amelioration of the Condition of the Wounded and Sick in Armed Forces in the Field of August 12, 1949, shall be applicable.

ARTICLE 21

The Parties to the conflict may appeal to the charity of commanders of neutral merchant vessels, yachts or other craft, to take on board and care for wounded, sick or shipwrecked persons, and to collect the dead.

Appeals to neutral vessels

Vessels of any kind responding to this appeal, and those having of their own accord collected wounded, sick or shipwrecked persons, shall enjoy special protection and facilities to carry out such assistance.

They may, in no case, be captured on account of any such transport; but, in the absence of any promise to the contrary, they shall remain liable to capture for any violations of neutrality they may have committed.

CHAPTER III

HOSPITAL SHIPS

ARTICLE 22

Military hospital ships, that is to say, ships built or equipped by the Powers specially and solely with a view to assisting the wounded, sick and shipwrecked, to treating them and to transporting them, may in no circumstances be attacked or captured, but shall at all times be respected and protected, on condition that their names and descriptions have been notified to the Parties to the conflict ten days before those ships are employed.

Notification and protection of military hospital ships

The characteristics which must appear in the notification

shall include registered gross tonnnage, the length from stem to stern and the number of masts and funnels.

ARTICLE 23

Protection of medical establishments ashore

Establishments ashore entitled to the protection of the Geneva Convention for the Amelioration of the Condition of the Wounded and Sick in Armed Forces in the Field of August 12, 1949, shall be protected from bombardment or attack from the sea.

ARTICLE 24

Hospital ships utilized by relief societies and private individuals of I. Parties to the conflict

Hospital ships utilized by National Red Cross Societies, by officially recognized relief societies or by private persons shall have the same protection as military hospital ships and shall be exempt from capture, if the Party to the conflict on which they depend has given them an official commission and in so far as the provisions of Article 22 concerning notification have been complied with.

These ships must be provided with certificates from the responsible authorities, stating that the vessels have been under their control, while fitting out and on departure.

ARTICLE 25

II. Neutral countries

Hospital ships utilized by National Red Cross Societies, officially recognised relief societies, or private persons of neutral countries shall have the same protection as military hospital ships and shall be exempt from capture, on condition that they have placed themselves under the control of one of the Parties to the conflict, with the previous consent of their own governments and with the authorization of the Party to the conflict concerned, in so far as the provisions of Article 22 concerning notification have been complied with.

ARTICLE 26

Tonnage

The protection mentioned in Articles 22, 24 and 25 shall apply to hospital ships of any tonnage and to their lifeboats, wherever they are operating. Nevertheless, to ensure the maximum comfort and security, the Parties to the conflict shall endeavour to utilize, for the transport of wounded, sick and shipwrecked over long distances and on the high seas, only hospital ships of over 2,000 tons gross.

ARTICLE 27

Under the same conditions as those provided for in Articles 22 and 24, small craft employed by the State or by the officially recognized lifeboat institutions for coastal rescue operations, shall also be respected and protected, so far as operational requirements permit.

Coastal rescue craft

The same shall apply so far as possible to fixed coastal installations used exclusively by these craft for their humanitarian missions.

ARTICLE 28

Should fighting occur on board a warship, the sick-bays shall be respected and spared as far as possible. Sick-bays and their equipment shall remain subject to the laws of warfare, but may not be diverted from their purpose so long as they are required for the wounded and sick. Nevertheless, the commander into whose power they have fallen may, after ensuring the proper care of the wounded and sick who are accommodated therein, apply them to other purposes in case of urgent military necessity.

Protection of sick-bays

ARTICLE 29

Any hospital ship in a port which falls into the hands of the enemy shall be authorized to leave the said port.

Hospital ships in occupied ports

ARTICLE 30

The vessels described in Articles 22, 24, 25 and 27 shall afford relief and assistance to the wounded, sick and shipwrecked without distinction of nationality.

Employment of hospital ships and small craft

The High Contracting Parties undertake not to use these vessels for any military purpose.

Such vessels shall in no way hamper the movements of the combatants.

During and after an engagement, they will act at their own risk.

DLI-I

ARTICLE 31

Right of
control and
search

The Parties to the conflict shall have the right to control
and search the vessels mentioned in Articles 22, 24, 25 and
27. They can refuse assistance from these vessels, order
them off, make them take a certain course, control the use
of their wireless and other means of communication, and
even detain them for a period not exceeding seven days from
the time of interception, if the gravity of the circumstances
so requires.

They may put a commissioner temporarily on board
whose sole task shall be to see that orders given in virtue of
the provisions of the preceding paragraphs are carried out.

As far as possible, the Parties to the conflict shall enter in
the log of the hospital ship, in a language he can understand, the orders they have given the captain of the vessel.

Parties to the conflict may, either unilaterally or by
particular agreements, put on board their ships neutral
observers who shall verify the strict observation of the
provisions contained in the present Convention.

ARTICLE 32

Stay in a
neutral port

Vessels described in Articles 22, 24, 25 and 27 are not
classed as warships as regards their stay in a neutral port.

ARTICLE 33

Converted
merchant
vessels

Merchant vessels which have been transformed into hospital
ships cannot be put to any other use throughout the duration of hostilities.

ARTICLE 34

Discontinuance
of protection

The protection to which hospital ships and sick-bays are
entitled shall not cease unless they are used to commit,
outside their humanitarian duties, acts harmful to the
enemy. Protection may, however, cease only after due
warning has been given, naming in all appropriate cases a
reasonable time limit, and after such warning has remained
unheeded.

In particular, hospital ships may not possess or use a
secret code for their wireless or other means of
communication.

ARTICLE 35

The following conditions shall not be considered as depriving hospital ships or sick-bays of vessels of the protection due to them:

(1)   The fact that the crews of ships or sick-bays are armed for the maintenance of order, for their own defence or that of the sick and wounded.

(2)   The presence on board of apparatus exclusively intended to facilitate navigation or communication.

(3)   The discovery on board hospital ships or in sick-bays of portable arms and ammunition taken from the wounded, sick and shipwrecked and not yet handed to the proper service.

(4)   The fact that the humanitarian activities of hospital ships and sick-bays of vessels or of the crews extend to the care of wounded, sick or shipwrecked civilians.

(5)   The transport of equipment and of personnel intended exclusively for medical duties, over and above the normal requirements.

CHAPTER IV

PERSONNEL

ARTICLE 36

The religious, medical and hospital personnel of hospital ships and their crews shall be respected and protected; they may not be captured during the time they are in the service of the hospital ship, whether or not there are wounded and sick on board.

ARTICLE 37

The religious, medical and hospital personnel assigned to the medical or spiritual care of the persons designated in Articles 12 and 13 shall, if they fall into the hands of the enemy, be respected and protected; they may continue to carry out their duties as long as this is necessary for the care of the wounded and sick. They shall afterwards be sent back as soon as the Commander-in-Chief, under whose authority they are, considers it practicable. They make take with them, on leaving the ship, their personal property.

If, however, it proves necessary to retain some of this personnel owing to the medical or spiritual needs of prisoners of war, everything possible shall be done for their earliest possible landing.

Retained personnel shall be subject, on landing, to the provisions of the Geneva Convention for the Amelioration of the Condition of the Wounded and Sick in Armed Forces in the Field of August 12, 1949.

CHAPTER V

MEDICAL TRANSPORTS

ARTICLE 38

Ships used for the conveyance of medical equipment

Ships chartered for that purpose shall be authorized to transport equipment exclusively intended for the treatment of wounded and sick members of armed forces or for the prevention of disease, provided that the particulars regarding their voyage have been notified to the adverse Power and approved by the latter. The adverse Power shall preserve the right to board the carrier ships, but not to capture them or seize the equipment carried.

By agreement amongst the Parties to the conflict, neutral observers may be placed on board such ships to verify the equipment carried. For this purpose, free access to the equipment shall be given.

ARTICLE 39

Medical aircraft

Medical aircraft, that is to say, aircraft exclusively employed for the removal of wounded, sick and shipwrecked, and for the transport of medical personnel and equipment, may not be the object of attack, but shall be respected by the Parties to the conflict, while flying at heights, at times and on routes specifically agreed upon between the Parties to the conflict concerned.

They shall be clearly marked with the distinctive emblem prescribed in Article 41, together with their national colours, on their lower, upper and lateral surfaces. They shall be provided with any other markings or means of identification which may be agreed upon between the Parties to the conflict upon the outbreak or during the course of hostilities.

Unless agreed otherwise, flights over enemy or enemy-occupied territory are prohibited.

Medical aircraft shall obey every summons to alight on land or water. In the event of having thus to alight, the aircraft with its occupants may continue its flight after examination, if any.

In the event of alighting involuntarily on land or water in enemy or enemy-occupied territory, the wounded, sick and shipwrecked, as well as the crew of the aircraft shall be prisoners of war. The medical personnel shall be treated according to Articles 36 and 37.

ARTICLE 40

Subject to the provisions of the second paragraph, medical aircraft of Parties to the conflict may fly over the territory of neutral Powers, land thereon in case of necessity, or use it as a port of call. They shall give neutral Powers prior notice of their passage over the said territory, and obey every summons to alight, on land or water. They will be immune from attack only when flying on routes, at heights and at times specifically agreed upon between the Parties to the conflict and the neutral Power concerned.

Flight over neutral countries, Landing of wounded

The neutral Powers may, however, place conditions on restrictions of the passage or landing of medical aircraft on their territory. Such possible conditions or restrictions shall be applied equally to all Parties to the conflict.

Unless otherwise agreed between the neutral Powers and the Parties to the conflict, the wounded, sick or ship-wrecked who are disembarked with the consent of the local authorities on neutral territory by medical aircraft shall be detained by the neutral Power, where so required by international law, in such a manner that they cannot again take part in operations of war. The cost of their accommodation and internment shall be borne by the Power on which they depend.

CHAPTER VI

THE DISTINCTIVE EMBLEM

ARTICLE 41

Use of the emblem

Under the direction of the competent military authority, the emblem of the red cross on a white ground shall be displayed on the flags, armlets and on all equipment employed in the Medical Service.

Nevertheles, in the case of countries which already use as emblem, in place of the red cross, the red crescent or the red lion and sun on a white ground, these emblems are also recognized by the terms of the present Convention.

ARTICLE 42

Identification of medical and religious personnel

The personnel designated in Articles 36 and 37 shall wear, affixed to the left arm, a water-resistant armlet bearing the distinctive emblem, issued and stamped by the military authority.

Such personnel, in addition to wearing the identity disc mentioned in Article 19, shall also carry a special identity card bearing the distinctive emblem. This card shall be water-resistant and of such size that it can be carried in the pocket. It shall be worded in the national language, shall mention at least the surname and first names, the date of birth, the rank and the service number of the bearer, and shall state in what capacity he is entitled to the protection of the present Convention. The card shall bear the photograph of the owner and also either his signature or his fingerprints or both. It shall be embossed with the stamp of the military authority.

The identity card shall be uniform throughout the same armed forces and, as far as possible, of a similar type in the armed forces of the High Contracting Parties. The Parties to the conflict may be guided by the model which is annexed, by way of example, to the present Convention. They shall inform each other, at the outbreak of hostilities, of the model they are using. Identity cards should be made out, if possible, at least in duplicate, one copy being kept by the home country.

In no circumstances may the said personnel be deprived of their insignia or identity cards nor of the right to wear the armlet. In cases of loss they shall be entitled to receive duplicates of the cards and to have the insignia replaced.

ARTICLE 43

The ships designated in Articles 22, 24, 25 and 27 shall be distinctively marked as follows:

Marking of
hospital ships
and small craft

(a)   All exterior surfaces shall be white.

(b)   One or more dark red crosses, as large as possible, shall be painted and displayed on each side of the hull and on the horizontal surfaces, so placed as to afford the greatest possible visibility from the sea and from the air.

All hospital ships shall make themselves known by hoisting their national flag and further, if they belong to a neutral state, the flag of the Party to the conflict whose direction they have accepted. A white flag with a red cross shall be flown at the mainmast as high as possible.

Lifeboards of hospital ships, coastal lifeboats and all small craft used by the Medical Service shall be painted white with dark red crosses prominently displayed and shall, in general, comply with the identification system prescribed above for hospital ships.

The above-mentioned ships and craft, which may wish to ensure by night and in times of reduced visibility the protection to which they are entitled, must, subject to the assent of the Party to the conflict under whose power they are, take the necessary measures to render their painting and distinctive emblems sufficiently apparent.

Hospital ships which, in accordance with Article 31, are provisionally detained by the enemy, must haul down the flag of the Party to the conflict in whose service they are or whose direction they have accepted.

Coastal lifeboats, if they continue to operate with the consent of the Occupying Power from a base which is occupied, may be allowed, when away from their base, to continue to fly their own national colours along with a flag carrying a red cross on a white ground, subject to prior notification to all the Parties to the conflict concerned.

All the provisions in this Article relating to the red cross shall apply equally to the other emblems mentioned in Article 41.

Parties to the conflict shall at all times endeavour to conclude mutual agreements, in order to use the most modern methods available to facilitate the identification of hospital ships.

ARTICLE 44

Limitation in the use of markings

The distinguishing signs referred to in Article 43 can only be used, whether in time of peace or war, for indicating or protecting the ships therein mentioned, except as may be provided in any other international Convention or by agreement between all the Parties to the conflict concerned.

ARTICLE 45

Prevention of misuse

The High Contracting Parties shall, if their legislation is not already adequate, take the measures necessary for the prevention and repression, at all times, of any abuse of the distinctive signs provided for under Article 43.

CHAPTER VII

EXECUTION OF THE CONVENTION

ARTICLE 46

Detailed execution. Unforeseen cases

Each Party to the conflict, acting through its Commanders-in-Chief, shall ensure the detailed execution of the preceding Articles and provide for unforeseen cases, in conformity with the general principles of the present Convention.

ARTICLE 47

Prohibition of reprisals

Reprisals against the wounded, sick and shipwrecked persons, the personnel, the vessels or the equipment protected by the Convention are prohibited.

ARTICLE 48

Dissemination of the Convention

The High Contracting Parties undertake, in time of peace as in time of war, to disseminate the text of the present Convention as wide as possible in their respective countries, and,

in particular, to include the study thereof in their programmes of military and, if possible, civil instruction, so
that the principles thereof may become known to the entire
population, in particular to the armed fighting forces, the
medical personnel and the chaplains.

ARTICLE 49

The High Contracting Parties shall communicate to one
another through the Swiss Federal Council and, during
hostilities, through the Protecting Powers, the official translations of the present Convention, as well as the laws and
regulations which they may adopt to ensure the application
thereof.

Translations.
Rules of
application

CHAPTER VIII

REPRESSION OF ABUSES AND INFRACTIONS

ARTICLE 50

The High Contracting Parties undertake to enact any legislation necessary to provide effective penal sanctions for
persons committing, or ordering to be committed, any of
the grave breaches of the present Convention defined in the
following Article.

Penal sanctions
I.
General
observations

Each High Contracting Party shall be under the obligation to search for persons alleged to have committed, or to
have ordered to be committed, such grave breaches, and
shall bring such persons, regardless of their nationality,
before its own courts. It may also, if it prefers, and in
accordance with the provisions of its own legislation, hand
such persons over for trial to another High Contracting
Party concerned, provided such High Contracting Party has
made out a *prima facie* case.

Each High Contracting Party shall take measures necessary for the suppression of all acts contrary to the provisions
of the present Convention other than the grave breaches
defined in the following Article.

In all circumstances, the accused persons shall benefit by
safeguards of proper trial and defence, which shall not be
less favourable than those provided by Article 105 and those
following of the Geneva Convention relative to the Treatment of Prisoners of War of August 12, 1949.

ARTICLE 51

II.   Grave breaches to which the preceding Article relates shall
Grave   be those involving any of the following acts, if committed
breaches against persons or property protected by the Convention:
wilful killing, torture or inhuman treatment, including biological experiments, wilfully causing great suffering or
serious injury to body or health, and extensive destruction
and appropriation of property, not justified by military
necessity and carried out unlawfully and wantonly.

ARTICLE 52

III.   No High Contracting Party shall be allowed to absolve
Responsibilies itself or any other High Contracting Party of any liability
of the   incurred by itself or by another High Contracting Party in
Contracting respect of breaches referred to in the preceding Article.
Parties

ARTICLE 53

Enquiry   At the request of a Party to the conflict, an enquiry shall
procedure be instituted, in a manner to be decided between the
interested Parties, concerning any alleged violation of the
Convention.

If agreement has not been reached concerning the procedure for the enquiry, the Parties should agree on the choice
of an umpire, who will decide upon the procedure to be
followed.

Once the violation has been established, the Parties to the
conflict shall put an end to it and shall repress it with the
least possible delay.

**GENEVA CONVENTION
RELATIVE TO THE TREATMENT
OF PRISONERS OF WAR
OF AUGUST 12, 1949**

PART I

GENERAL PROVISIONS

ARTICLE 1

The High Contracting Parties undertake to respect and to ensure respect for the present Convention in all circumstances.

Respect for the Convention

ARTICLE 2

In addition to the provisions which shall be implemented in peace time, the present Convention shall apply to all cases of declared war or of any other armed conflict which may arise between two or more of the High Contracting Parties, even if the state of war is not recognized by one of them.

Application of the Convention

The Convention shall also apply to all cases of partial or total occupation of the territory of a High Contracting Party, even if the said occupation meets with no armed resistance.

Although one of the Powers in conflict may not be a party to the present Convention, the Powers who are parties thereto shall remain bound by it in their mutual relations. They shall furthermore be bound by the Convention in relation to the said Power, if the latter accepts and applies the provisions thereof.

ARTICLE 3

In the case of armed conflict not of an international character occurring in the territory of one of the High Contracting Parties, each Party to the conflict shall be bound to apply, as a minimum, the following provisions:

Conflicts not of an international character

(1)   Persons taking no active part in the hostilities, including members of armed forces who have laid down their arms and those placed *hors de combat* by sickness, wounds, detention, or any other cause, shall in all circumstances be treated humanely, without any adverse distinction founded on race, colour, religion or faith, sex, birth or wealth, or any other similar criteria.

To this end the following acts are and shall remain prohibited at any time and in any place whatsoever with respect to the above-mentioned persons:

(a)   violence to life and person, in particular murder of all kinds, mutilation, cruel treatment and torture;

(b)   taking of hostages;

(c)   outrages upon personal dignity, in particular, humiliating and degrading treatment;

(d)   the passing of sentences and the carrying out of executions without previous judgment pronounced by a regularly constituted court affording all the judicial guarantees which are recognized as indispensable by civilized peoples.

(2)   The wounded and sick shall be collected and cared for.

An impartial humanitarian body, such as the International Committee of the Red Cross, may offer its services to the Parties to the conflict.

The Parties to the conflict should further endeavour to bring into force, by means of special agreements, all or part of the other provisions of the present Convention.

The application of the preceding provisions shall not affect the legal status of the Parties to the conflict.

ARTICLE 4

Prisoners   A.   Prisoners of war, in the sense of the present Con-
of war   vention, are persons belonging to one of the following categories, who have fallen into the power of the enemy:

(1)   Members of the armed forces of a Party to the conflict as well as members of militias or volunteer

corps forming part of such armed forces.

(2) Members of other militias and members of other volunteer corps, including those of organized resistance movements, belonging to a Party to the conflict and operating in or outside their own territory, even if this territory is occupied, provided that such militias or volunteer corps, including such organized resistance movements, fulfil the following conditions:

   (a) that of being commanded by a person responsible for his subordinates;

   (b) that of having a fixed distinctive sign recognizable at a distance;

   (c) that of carrying arms openly;

   (d) that of conducting their operations in accordance with the laws and customs of war.

(3) Members of regular armed forces who profess allegiance to a government or an authority not recognized by the Detaining Power.

(4) Persons who accompany the armed forces without actually being members thereof, such as civilian members of military aircraft crews, war correspondents, supply contractors, members of labour units or of services responsible for the welfare of the armed forces, provided that they have received authorization from the armed forces which they accompany, who shall provide them for that purpose with an identity card similar to the annexed model.

(5) Members of crews, including masters, pilots and apprentices, of the merchant marine and the crews of civil aircraft of the Parties to the conflict, who do not benefit by more favourable treatment under any other provisions of international law.

(6) Inhabitants of a non-occupied territory, who on the approach of the enemy spontaneously take up arms to resist the invading forces, without having had time to form themselves into regular armed units, provided they carry arms openly and respect the laws and customs of war.

B.   The following shall likewise be treated as prisoners of war under the present Convention:

(1)   Persons belonging, or having belonged, to the armed forces of the occupied country, if the occupying Power considers it necessary by reason of such allegiance to intern them, even though it has originally liberated them while hostilities were going on outside the territory it occupies, in particular where such persons have made an unsuccessful attempt to rejoin the armed forces to which they belong and which are engaged in combat, or where they fail to comply with a summons made to them with a view to internment.

(2)   The persons belonging to one of the categories enumerated in the present Article, who have been received by neutral or non-belligerent Powers on their territory and whom these Powers are required to intern under international law, without prejudice to any more favourable treatment which these Powers may choose to give and with the exception of Articles 8, 10, 15, 30, fifth paragraph, 58-67, 92, 126 and, where diplomatic relations exist between the Parties to the conflict and the neutral or non-belligerent Power concerned, those Articles concerning the Protecting Power. Where such diplomatic relations exist, the Parties to a conflict on whom these persons depend shall be allowed to perform towards them the functions of a Protecting Power as provided in the present Convention, without prejudice to the functions which these Parties normally exercise in conformity with diplomatic and consular usage and treaties.

C.   This Article shall in no way affect the status of medical personnel and chaplains as provided for in Article 33 of the present Convention.

ARTICLE 5

Beginning and end of application

The present Convention shall apply to the persons referred to in Article 4 from the time they fall into the power of the enemy and until their final release and repatriation.

Should any doubt arise as to whether persons, having committed a belligerant act and having fallen into the hands of the enemy, belong to any of the categories enumerated in Article 4, such persons shall enjoy the protection of the present Convention until such time as their status has been determined by a competent tribunal.

ARTICLE 6

In addition to the agreements expressly provided for in Articles 10, 23, 28, 33, 60, 65, 66, 67, 72, 73, 75, 109, 110, 118, 119, 122 and 132, the High Contracting Parties may conclude other special agreements for all matters concerning which they may deem it suitable to make separate provision. No special agreement shall adversely affect the situation of prisoners of war, as defined by the present Convention, nor restrict the rights which it confers upon them.

Special agreements

Prisoners of war shall continue to have the benefit of such agreements as long as the Convention is applicable to them, except where express provisions to the contrary are contained in the aforesaid or in subsequent agreements, or where more favourable measures have been taken with regard to them by one or other of the Parties to the conflict.

ARTICLE 7

Prisoners of war may in no circumstances renounce in part or in entirety the rights secured to them by the present Convention, and by the special agreements referred to in the foregoing Article, if such there be.

Non-renunciation of rights

ARTICLE 8

The present Convention shall be applied with the cooperation and under the scrutiny of the Protecting Powers whose duty it is to safeguard the interests of the Parties to the conflict. For this purpose, the Protecting Powers may appoint, apart from their diplomatic or consular staff, delegates from amongst their own nationals or the nationals of other neutral Powers. The said delegates shall be subject to the approval of the Power with which they are to carry out their duties.

Protecting Powers

The Parties to the confict shall facilitate to the greatest extent possible the task of the representatives or delegates of the Protecting Powers.

The representatives or delegates of the Protecting Powers shall not in any case exceed their mission under the present Convention. They shall, in particular, take account of the imperative necessities of security of the State wherein they carry out their duties.

ARTICLE 9

Activities of the International Committee of the Red Cross

The provisions of the present Convention constitute no obstacle to the humanitarian activities which the International Committee of the Red Cross or any other impartial humanitarian organization may, subject to the consent of the Parties to the conflict concerned, undertake for the protection of prisoners of war and for their relief.

ARTICLE 10

Substitutes for Protecting Powers

The High Contracting Parties may at any time agree to entrust to an organization which offers all guarantees of impartiality and efficacy the duties incumbent on the Protecting Powers by virtue of the present Convention.

When prisoners of war do not benefit or cease to benefit, no matter for what reason, by the activities of a Protecting Power or of an organization provided for in the first paragraph above, the Detaining Power shall request a neutral State, or such an organization, to undertake the functions performed under the present Convention by a Protecting Power designated by the Parties to a conflict.

If protection cannot be arranged accordingly, the Detaining Power shall request or shall accept, subject to the provisions of this Article, the offer of the services of a humanitarian organization, such as the International Committee of the Red Cross, to assume the humanitarian functions performed by Protecting Powers under the present Convention.

Any neutral Power or any organization invited by the Power concerned or offering itself for these purposes, shall be required to act with a sense of responsibility towards the Party to the conflict on which persons protected by the present Convention depend, and shall be required to furnish sufficient assurances that it is in a position to undertake the appropriate functions and to discharge them impartially.

No derogation from the preceding provisions shall be made by special agreements between Powers one of which is restricted, even temporarily, in its freedom to negotiate with the other Power or its allies by reason of military events, more particularly where the whole, or a substantial part, of the territory of the said Power is occupied.

Whenever in the present Convention mention is made of a Protecting Power, such mention applies to substitute organizations in the sense of the present Article.

ARTICLE 11

In cases where they deem it advisable in the interest of protected persons, particularly in cases of disagreement between the Parties to the conflict as to the application or interpretation of the provisions of the present Convention, the Protecting Powers shall lend their good offices with a view to settling the disagreement.   *Conciliation procedure*

For this purpose, each of the Protecting Powers may, either at the invitation of one Party or on its own initiative, propose to the Parties to the conflict a meeting of their representatives, and in particular of the authorities responsible for prisoners of war, possibly on neutral territory suitably chosen. The Parties to the conflict shall be bound to give effect to the proposals made to them for this purpose. The Protecting Powers may, if necessary, propose for approval by the Parties to the conflict a person belonging to a neutral Power, or delegated by the International Committee of the Red Cross, who shall be invited to take part in such a meeting.

PART II

GENERAL PROTECTION OF PRISONERS OF WAR

ARTICLE 12

Prisoners of war are in the hands of the enemy Power, but not of the individuals or military units who have captured them. Irrespective of the individual responsibilities that may exist, the Detaining Power is responsible for the treatment given them.   *Responsibility for the treatment of prisoners*

Prisoners of war may only be transferred by the Detaining Power to a Power which is a party to the Convention and after the Detaining Power has satisfied itself of the willingness and ability of such transferee power to apply the Convention. When prisoners of war are transferred under such circumstances, responsibility for the application of the Convention rests on the Power accepting them while they are in its custody.

Nevertheless if that power fails to carry out the provisions of the Convention in any important respect, the Power by whom the prisoners of war were transferred shall, upon being notified by the Protecting Power, take effective measures to correct the situation or shall request the return of the prisoners of war. Such requests must be complied with.

ARTICLE 13

Humane
treatment
of prisoners

Prisoners of war must at all times be humanely treated. Any unlawful act or omission by the Detaining Power causing death or seriously endangering the health of a prisoner of war in its custody is prohibited, and will be regarded as a serious breach of the present Convention. In particular, no prisoner of war may be subjected to physical mutiliation or to medical or scientific experiments of any kind which are not justified by the medical, dental or hospital treatment of the prisoner concerned and carried out in his interest.

Likewise, prisoners of war must at all times be protected, particularly against acts of violence or intimidation and against insults and public curiosity.

Measures of reprisal against prisoners of war are prohibited.

ARTICLE 14

Respect for
the person
of prisoners

Prisoners of war are entitled in all circumstances to respect for their persons and their honour.

Women shall be treated with all the regard due to their sex and shall in all cases benefit by treatment as favourable as that granted to men.

Prisoners of war shall retain the full civil capacity which they enjoyed at the time of their capture. The Detaining Power may not restrict the exercise, either within or without its own territory, of the rights such capacity confers except in so far as the captivity requires.

ARTICLE 15

The Power detaining prisoners of war shall be bound to provide free of charge for their maintenance and for the medical attention required by their state of health.

Maintenance of prisoners

ARTICLE 16

Taking into consideration the provisions of the present Convention relating to rank and sex, and subject to any privileged treatment which may be accorded to them by reason of their state of health, age or professional qualifications, all prisoners of war shall be treated alike by the Detaining Power, without any adverse distinction based on race, nationality, religious belief or political opinions, or any other distinction founded on similar criteria.

Equality of treatment

PART III

CAPTIVITY

SECTION I

BEGINNING OF CAPTIVITY

ARTICLE 17

Every prisoner of war, when questioned on the subject, is bound to give only his surname, first names and rank, date of birth, and army, regimental, personal or serial number, or failing this, equivalent information.

Questioning of prisoners

If he wilfully infringes this rule, he may render himself liable to a restriction of the privileges accorded to his rank or status.

Each Party to a conflict is required to furnish the persons under its jurisdiction who are liable to become prisoners of war, with an identity card showing the owner's surname, first names, rank, army, regimental, personal or serial number or equivalent information, and date of birth. The identity card may, furthermore, bear the signature or the fingerprints, or both, of the owner, and may bear, as well, any other information the Party to the conflict may wish to add concerning persons belonging to its armed forces. As far as possible the card shall measure 6.5 × 10 cm. and shall be issued in duplicate. The identity card shall be shown by the prisoner of war upon demand, but may in no case be taken away from him.

No physical or mental torture, nor any other form of coercion, may be inflicted on prisoners of war to secure from them information of any kind whatever. Prisoners of war who refuse to answer may not be threatened, insulted, or exposed to any unpleasant or disadvantageous treatment of any kind.

Prisoners of war who, owing to their physical or mental condition, are unable to state their identity, shall be handed over to the medical service. The identity of such prisoners shall be established by all possible means, subject to the provisions of the preceding paragraph.

The questioning of prisoners of war shall be carried out in a language which they understand.

ARTICLE 18

Property
of prisoners

All effects and articles of personal use, except arms, horses, military equipment and military documents, shall remain in the possession of prisoners of war, likewise their metal helmets and gas masks and like articles issued for personal protection. Effects and articles used for their clothing or feeding shall likewise remain in their possession, even if such effects and articles belong to their regulation military equipment.

At no time should prisoners of war be without identity documents. The detaining Power shall supply such documents to prisoners of war who possess none.

Badges of rank and nationality, decorations and articles having above all a personal or sentimental value may not be taken from prisoners of war.

Sums of money carried by prisoners of war may not be taken away from them except by order of an officer, and after the amount and particulars of the owner have been recorded in a special register and an itemized receipt has been given, legibly inscribed with the name, rank and unit of the person issuing the said receipt. Sums in the currency of the Detaining Power, or which are changed into such currency at the prisoner's request, shall be placed to the credit of the prisoner's account as provided in Article 64.

The Detaining Power may withdraw articles of value from prisoners of war only for reasons of security; when such articles are withdrawn, the procedure laid down for sums of money impounded shall apply.

Such objects, likewise the sums taken away in any currency other than that of the Detaining Power and the conversion of which has not been asked for by the owners, shall be kept in the custody of the Detaining Power and shall be returned in their initial shape to prisoners of war at the end of their captivity.

ARTICLE 19

Prisoners of war shall be evacuated, as soon as possible after their capture, to camps situated in an area far enough from the combat zone for them to be out of danger.

Only those prisoners of war who, owing to wounds or sickness, would run greater risks by being evacuated than by remaining where they are, may be temporarily kept back in a danger zone.

Prisoners of war shall not be unnecessarily exposed to danger while awaiting evacuation from a fighting zone.

Evacuation of prisoners

ARTICLE 20

The evacuation of prisoners of war shall always be effected humanely and in conditions similar to those for the forces of the Detaining Power in their changes of station.

The Detaining Power shall supply prisoners of war who are being evacuated with sufficient food and potable water, and with the necessary clothing and medical attention. The Detaining Power shall take all suitable precautions to ensure their safety during evacuation, and shall establish as soon as possible a list of the prisoners of war who are evacuated.

If prisoners of war must, during evacuation, pass through transit camps, their stay in such camps shall be as brief as possible.

Conditions of evacuation

SECTION II

INTERNMENT OF PRISONERS OF WAR

CHAPTER I

GENERAL OBSERVATIONS

ARTICLE 21

Restriction
of liberty
of movement

The Detaining Power may subject prisoners of war to internment. It may impose on them the obligation of not leaving, beyond certain limits, the camp where they are interned, or if the said camp is fenced in, of not going outside its perimeter. Subject to the provisions of the present Convention relative to penal and disciplinary sanctions, prisoners of war may not be held in close confinement except where necessary to safeguard their health and then only during the continuation of the circumstances which make such confinement necessary.

Prisoners of war may be partially or wholly released on parole or promise, in so far as is allowed by the laws of the Power on which they depend. Such measures shall be taken particularly in cases where this may contribute to the improvement of their state of health. No prisoner of war shall be compelled to accept liberty on parole or promise.

Upon the outbreak of hostilities, each Party to the conflict shall notify the adverse Party of the laws and regulations allowing or forbidding its own nationals to accept liberty on parole or promise. Prisoners of war who are paroled or who have given their promise in conformity with the laws and regulations so notified, are bound on their personal honour scrupulously to fulfil, both towards the Power on which they depend and towards the Power which has captured them, the engagements of their paroles or promises. In such cases, the Power on which they depend is bound neither to require nor to accept from them any service incompatible with the parole or promise given.

ARTICLE 22

Places and
conditions of
internment

Prisoners of war may be interned only in premises located on land and affording every guarantee of hygiene and healthfulness. Except in particular cases which are justified by the interest of the prisoners themselves, they shall not be interned in penitentiaries.

Prisoners of war interned in unhealthy areas, or where the climate is injurious for them, shall be removed as soon as possible to a more favourable climate.

The Detaining Power shall assemble prisoners of war in camps or camp compounds according to their nationality, language and customs, provided that such prisoners shall not be separated from prisoners of war belonging to the armed forces with which they were serving at the time of their capture, except with their consent.

ARTICLE 23

No prisoner of war may at any time be sent to, or detained in areas where he may be exposed to the fire of the combat zone, nor may his presence be used to render certain points or areas immune from military operations.

Security of prisoners

Prisoners of war shall have shelters against air bombardment and other hazards of war, to the same extent as the local civilian population. With the exception of those engaged in the protection of their quarters against the aforesaid hazards, they may enter such shelters as soon as possible after the giving of the alarm. Any other protective measure taken in favour of the population shall also apply to them.

Detaining Powers shall give the Powers concerned, through the intermediary of the Protecting Powers, all useful information regarding the geographic location of prisoner of war camps.

Whenever military considerations permit, prisoner of war camps shall be indicated in the day-time by the letters PW or PG, placed so as to be clearly visible from the air. The Powers concerned may, however, agree upon any other system of marking. Only prisoner of war camps shall be marked as such.

ARTICLE 24

Transit or screening camps of a permanent kind shall be fitted out under conditions similar to those described in the present Section, and the prisoners therein shall have the same treatment as in other camps.

Permanent transit camps

CHAPTER II

QUARTERS, FOOD AND CLOTHING
OF PRISONERS OF WAR

ARTICLE 25

Quarters   Prisoners of war shall be quartered under conditions as
favourable as those for the forces of the Detaining Power
who are billeted in the same areas. The said conditions shall
make allowance for the habits and customs of the prisoners
and shall in no case be prejudicial to their health.

The foregoing provisions shall apply in particular to the
dormitories of prisoners of war as regards both total surface
and minimum cubic space, and the general installations,
bedding and blankets.

The premises provided for the use of prisoners of war
individually or collectively, shall be entirely protected from
dampness and adequately heated and lighted, in particular
between dusk and lights out. All precautions must be taken
against the danger of fire.

In any camps in which women prisoners of war, as well
as men, are accommodated, separate dormitories shall be
provided for them.

ARTICLE 26

Food   The basic daily food rations shall be sufficient in quantity,
quality and variety to keep prisoners of war in good health
and to prevent loss of weight or the development of
nutritional deficiences. Account shall also be taken of the
habitual diet of the prisoners.

The Detaining Power shall supply prisoners of war who
work with such additional rations as are necessary for the
labour on which they are employed.

Sufficient drinking water shall be supplied to prisoners of
war. The use of tobacco shall be permitted.

Prisoners of war shall, as far as possible, be associated
with the preparation of their meals; they may be employed
for that purpose in the kitchens. Furthermore, they shall be
given the means of preparing, themselves, the additional
food in their possession.

Adequate premises shall be provided for messing.

Collective disciplinary measures affecting food are
prohibited.

ARTICLE 27

Clothing, underwear and footwear shall be supplied to   Clothing
prisoners of war in sufficient quantities by the Detaining
Power, which shall make allowance for the climate of the
region where the prisoners are detained. Uniforms of enemy
armed forces captured by the Detaining Power should, if
suitable for the climate, be made available to clothe
prisoners of war.

The regular replacement and repair of the above articles
shall be assured by the Detaining Power. In addition,
prisoners of war who work shall receive appropriate
clothing, wherever the nature of the work demands.

ARTICLE 28

Canteens shall be installed in all camps, where prisoners of   Canteens
war may procure foodstuffs, soap and tobacco and ordinary
articles in daily use. The tariff shall never be in excess of
local market prices.

The profits made by camp canteens shall be used for the
benefit of the prisoners; a special fund shall be created for
this purpose. The prisoners' representative shall have the
right to collaborate in the management of the canteen and
of this fund.

When a camp is closed down, the credit balance of the
special fund shall be handed to an international welfare
organization, to be employed for the benefit of prisoners of
war of the same nationality as those who have contributed
to the fund. In case of a general repatriation, such profits
shall be kept by the Detaining Power, subject to any
agreement to the contrary between the Powers concerned.

CHAPTER III

HYGIENE AND MEDICAL ATTENTION

ARTICLE 29

The Detaining Power shall be bound to take all sanitary   Hygiene
measures necessary to ensure the cleanliness and healthfulness of camps and to prevent epidemics.

Prisoners of war shall have for their use, day and night,
conveniences which conform to the rules of hygiene and are

maintained in a constant state of cleanliness. In any camps in which women prisoners of war are accommodated, separate conveniences shall be provided for them.

Also, apart from the baths and showers with which the camps shall be furnished, prisoners of war shall be provided with sufficient water and soap for their personal toilet and for washing their personal laundry; the necessary installations, facilities and time shall be granted them for that purpose.

ARTICLE 30

Medical attention

Every camp shall have an adequate infirmary where prisoners of war may have the attention they require, as well as appropriate diet. Isolation wards shall, if necessary, be set aside for cases of contagious or mental disease.

Prisoners of war suffering from serious disease, or whose condition necessitates special treatment, a surgical operation or hospital care, must be admitted to any military or civilian medical unit where such treatment can be given, even if their repatriation is contemplated in the near future. Special facilities shall be afforded for the care to be given to the disabled, in particular to the blind, and for their rehabilitation, pending repatriation.

Prisoners of war shall have the attention, preferably, of medical personnel of the Power on which they depend and, if possible, of their nationality.

Prisoners of war may not be prevented from presenting themselves to the medical authorities for examination. The detaining authorities shall, upon request, issue to every prisoner who has undergone treatment, an official certificate indicating the nature of his illness or injury, and the duration and kind of treatment received. A duplicate of this certificate shall be forwarded to the Central Prisoners of War Agency.

The costs of treatment, including those of any apparatus necessary for the maintenance of prisoners of war in good health, particularly dentures and other artificial appliances, and spectacles, shall be borne by the Detaining Power.

ARTICLE 31

Medical inspections

Medical inspections of prisoners of war shall be held at least once a month. They shall include the checking and the recording of the weight of each prisoner of war. Their purpose shall be, in particular, to supervise the general state of health, nutrition and cleanliness of prisoners and to detect contagious diseases, especially tuberculosis, malaria and venereal disease. For this purpose the most efficient methods available shall be employed, e.g. periodic mass miniature radiography for the early detection of tuberculosis.

ARTICLE 32

Prisoners of war who, though not attached to the medical service of their armed forces, are physicians, surgeons, dentists, nurses or medical orderlies, may be required by the Detaining Power to exercise their medical functions in the interests of prisoners of war dependent on the same Power. In that case they shall continue to be prisoners of war, but shall receive the same treatment as corresponding medical personnel retained by the Detaining Power. They shall be exempted from any other work under Article 49.

Prisoners engaged on medical duties

CHAPTER IV

MEDICAL PERSONNEL AND CHAPLAINS
RETAINED TO ASSIST PRISONERS OF WAR

ARTICLE 33

Members of the medical personnel and chaplains while retained by the Detaining Power with a view to assisting prisoners of war, shall not be considered as prisoners of war. They shall, however, receive as a minimum the benefits and protection of the present Convention, and shall also be granted all facilities necessary to provide for the medical care of, and religious ministration to prisoners of war.

Rights and privileges of retained personnel

They shall continue to exercise their medical and spiritual functions for the benefit of prisoners of war, preferably those belonging to the armed forces upon which they depend, within the scope of the military laws and regulations of the Detaining Power and under the control of its competent services, in accordance with their professional etiquette. They shall also benefit by the following facilities in the exercise of their medical or spiritual functions:

(a)   They shall be authorized to visit periodically prisoners of war situated in working detachments or in hospitals outside the camp. For this purpose, the Detaining Power shall place at their disposal the necessary means of transport.

(b)   The senior medical officer in each camp shall be responsible to the camp military authorities for everything connected with the activities of retained medical personnel. For this purpose, Parties to the conflict shall agree at the outbreak of hostilities on the subject of the corresponding ranks of the medical personnel, including that of societies mentioned in Article 26 of the Geneva Convention for the Amelioration of the Condition of the Wounded and Sick in Armed Forces in the Field of August 12, 1949. This senior medical officer, as well as chaplains, shall have the right to deal with the competent authorities of the camp on all questions relating to their duties. Such authorities shall afford them all necessary facilities for correspondence relating to these questions.

(c)   Although they shall be subject to the internal discipline of the camp in which they are retained, such personnel may not be compelled to carry out any work other than that concerned with their medical or religious duties.

During hostilities, the Parties to the conflict shall agree concerning the possible relief of retained personnel and shall settle the procedure to be followed.

None of the preceding provisions shall relieve the Detaining Power of its obligations with regard to prisoners of war from the medical or spiritual point of view.

CHAPTER V

RELIGIOUS, INTELLECTUAL AND PHYSICAL ACTIVITIES

ARTICLE 34

Religious duties   Prisoners of war shall enjoy complete latitude in the exercise of their religious duties, including attendance at the service of their faith, on condition that they comply with the disciplinary routine prescribed by the military authorities.

Adequate premises shall be provided where religious services may be held.

ARTICLE 35

Chaplains who fall into the hands of the enemy Power and who remain or are retained with a view to assisting prisoners of war, shall be allowed to minister to them and to exercise freely their ministry amongst prisoners of war of the same religion, in accordance with their religious conscience. They shall be allocated among the various camps and labour detachments containing prisoners of war belonging to the same forces, speaking the same language or practising the same religion. They shall enjoy the necessary facilities, including the means of transport provided for in Article 33, for visiting the prisoners of war outside their camp. They shall be free to correspond, subject to censorship, on matters concerning their religious duties with the ecclesiastical authorities in the country of detention and with international religious organizations. Letters and cards which they may send for this purpose shall be in addition to the quota provided for in Article 71.

Retained
chaplains

ARTICLE 36

Prisoners of war who are ministers of religion, without having officiated as chaplains to their own forces, shall be at liberty, whatever their denomination, to minister freely to the members of their community. For this purpose, they shall receive the same treatment as the chaplains retained by the Detaining Power. They shall not be obliged to do any other work.

Prisoners who
are ministers
of religion

ARTICLE 37

When prisoners of war have not the assistance of a retained chaplain or of a prisoner of war minister of their faith, a minister belonging to the prisoners' or a similar denominination, or in his absence a qualified layman, if such a course is feasible from a confessional point of view, shall be appointed, at the request of the prisoners concerned, to fill this office. This appointment, subject to the approval of the Detaining

Prisoners without
a minister of
their religion

Power, shall take place with the agreement of the community of prisoners concerned and, wherever necessary, with the approval of the local religious authorities of the same faith. The person thus appointed shall comply with all regulations established by the Detaining Power in the interests of discipline and military security.

ARTICLE 38

Recreation, study, sports and games

While respecting the individual preferences of every prisoner, the Detaining Power shall encourage the practice of intellectual, educational, and recreational pursuits, sports and games amongst prisoners, and shall take the measures necessary to ensure the exercise thereof by providing them with adequate premises and necessary equipment.

Prisoners shall have opportunities for taking physical exercise, including sports and games, and for being out of doors. Sufficient open spaces shall be provided for this purpose in all camps.

CHAPTER VI

DISCIPLINE

ARTICLE 39

Administration. Saluting

Every prisoner of war camp shall be put under the immediate authority of a responsible commissioned officer belonging to the regular armed forces of the Detaining Power. Such officer shall have in his possession a copy of the present Convention; he shall ensure that its provisions are known to the camp staff and the guard and shall be responsible, under the direction of his government, for its application.

Prisoners of war, with the exception of officers, must salute and show to all officers of the Detaining Power the external marks of respect provided for by the regulations applying in their own forces.

Officer prisoners of war are bound to salute only officers of a higher rank of the Detaining Power; they must, however, salute the camp commander regardless of his rank.

ARTICLE 40

The wearing of badges of rank and nationality, as well as decorations, shall be permitted.

Badges and decorations

ARTICLE 41

In every camp the text of the present Convention and its Annexes and the contents of any special agreement provided for in Article 6, shall be posted, in the prisoners' own language, at places where all may read them. Copies shall be supplied, on request, to the prisoners who cannot have access to the copy which has been posted.

Regulations, orders, notices and publications of every kind relating to the conduct of prisoners of war shall be issued to them in a language which they understand. Such regulations, orders and publications shall be posted in the manner described above and copies shall be handed to the prisoners' representative. Every order and command addressed to prisoners of war individually must likewise be given in a language which they understand.

Posting of the Convention, and of regulations and orders concerning prisoners

ARTICLE 42

The use of weapons against prisoners of war, especially against those who are escaping or attempting to escape, shall constitute an extreme measure, which shall always be preceded by warnings appropriate to the circumstances.

Use of weapons

CHAPTER VII

RANK OF PRISONERS OF WAR

ARTICLE 43

Upon the outbreak of hostilities, the Parties to the conflict shall communicate to one another the titles and ranks of all the persons mentioned in Article 4 of the present Covention, in order to ensure equality of treatment between prisoners of equivalent rank. Titles and ranks which are subsequently created shall form the subject of similar communications.

The Detaining Power shall recognize promotions in rank which have been accorded to prisoners of war and which

Notification of ranks

have been duly notified by the Power on which these prisoners depend.

ARTICLE 44

Treatment of officers

Officers and prisoners of equivalent status shall be treated with the regard due to their rank and age.

In order to ensure service in officers' camps, other ranks of the same armed forces who, as far as possible, speak the same language, shall be assigned in sufficient numbers, account being taken of the rank of officers and prisoners of equivalent status. Such orderlies shall not be required to perform any other work.

Supervision of the mess by the officers themselves shall be facilitated in every way.

ARTICLE 45

Treatment of other prisoners

Prisoners of war other than officers and prisoners of equivalent status shall be treated with the regard due to their rank and age.

Supervision of the mess by the prisoners themselves shall be facilitated in every way.

CHAPTER VIII

TRANSFER OF PRISONERS OF WAR
AFTER THEIR ARRIVAL IN CAMP

ARTICLE 46

Conditions

The Detaining Power, when deciding upon the transfer of prisoners of war, shall take into acount the interests of the prisoners themselves, more especially so as not to increase the difficulty of their repatriation.

The transfer of prisoners of war shall always be effected humanely and in conditions not less favourable than those under which the forces of the Detaining Powers are transferred. Account shall always be taken of the climatic conditions to which the prisoners of war are accustomed and the conditions of transfer shall in no case be prejudicial to their health.

The Detaining Power shall supply prisoners of war during transfer with sufficient food and drinking water to keep them in good health, likewise with the necessary clothing, shelter and medical attention. The Detaining Power shall take adequate precautions especially in case of transport by sea or by air, to ensure their safety during transfer, and shall draw up a complete list of all transferred prisoners before their departure.

ARTICLE 47

Sick or wounded prisoners of war shall not be transferred as long as their recovery may be endangered by the journey, unless their safety imperatively demands it.

If the combat zone draws closer to a camp, the prisoners of war in the said camp shall not be transferred unless their transfer can be carried out in adequate conditions of safety, or if they are exposed to greater risks by remaining on the spot than by being transferred.

Circumstances precluding transfer

ARTICLE 48

In the event of transfer, prisoners of war shall be officially advised of their departure and of their new postal address. Such notifications shall be given in time for them to pack their luggage and inform their next of kin.

Procedure for transfer

They shall be allowed to take with them their personal effects, and the correspondence and parcels which have arrived for them. The weight of such baggage may be limited, if the conditions of transfer so require, to what each prisoner can reasonably carry, which shall in no case be more than twenty-five kilograms per head.

Mail and parcels addressed to their former camp shall be forwarded to them without delay. The camp commander shall take, in agreement with the prisoners' representative, any measures needed to ensure the transport of the prisoners' community property and of the luggage they are unable to take with them in consequence of restrictions imposed by virtue of the second paragraph of this Article.

The costs of transfers shall be borne by the Detaining Power.

SECTION III

LABOUR OF PRISONERS OF WAR

ARTICLE 49

General
observations

The Detaining Power may utilize the labour of prisoners of war who are physically fit, taking into account their age, sex, rank and physical aptitude, and with a view particularly to maintaining them in a good state of physical and mental health.

Non-commissioned officers who are prisoners of war shall only be required to do supervisory work. Those not so required may ask for other suitable work which shall, so far as possible, be found for them.

If officers or persons of equivalent status ask for suitable work, it shall be found for them, so far as possible, but they may in no circumstances be compelled to work.

ARTICLE 50

Authorized work

Besides work connected with camp administration, installation or maintenance, prisoners of war may be compelled to do only such work as is included in the following classes:

(a)   agriculture;

(b)   industries connected with the production or the extraction of raw materials, and manufacturing industries, with the exception of metallurgical, machinery and chemical industries; public works and building operations which have no military character or purpose;

(c)   transport and handling of stores which are not military in character or purpose;

(d)   commercial business, and arts and crafts;

(e)   domestic service;

(f)   public utility services having no military character or purpose.

Should the above provisions be infringed, prisoners of war shall be allowed to exercise their right of complaint, in conformity with Article 78.

Prisoners of war must be granted suitable working conditions, especially as regards accommodation, food, clothing and equipment; such conditions shall not be inferior to those enjoyed by nationals of the Detaining Power employed in similar work; account shall also be taken of climatic conditions.

Working conditions

The Detaining Power, in utilizing the labour of prisoners of war, shall ensure that in areas in which prisoners are employed, the national legislation concerning the protection of labour, and, more particularly, the regulations for the safety of workers, are duly applied.

Prisoners of war shall receive training and be provided with the means of protection suitable to the work they will have to do and similar to those accorded to the nationals of the Detaining Power. Subject to the provisions of Article 52, prisoners may be submitted to the normal risks run by these civilian workers.

Conditions of labour shall in no case be rendered more arduous by disciplinary measures.

ARTICLE 52

Unless he be a volunteer, no prisoner of war may be employed on labour which is of an unhealthy or dangerous nature.

Dangerous or humiliating labour

No prisoner of war shall be assigned to labour which would be looked upon as humiliating for a member of the Detaining Power's own forces.

The removal of mines or similar devices shall be considered as dangerous labour.

ARTICLE 53

The duration of the daily labour of prisoners of war, including the time of the journey to and fro, shall not be excessive, and must in no case exceed that permitted for civilian workers in the district, who are nationals of the Detaining Power and employed on the same work.

Duration of labour

Prisoners of war must be allowed, in the middle of the day's work, a rest of not less than one hour. This rest will be the same as that to which workers of the Detaining Power are entitled, if the latter is of longer duration. They shall be allowed in addition a rest of twenty-four consecutive hours every week, preferably on Sunday or the day of rest in their country of origin. Furthermore, every prisoner who has worked for one year shall be granted a rest of eight consecutive days, during which his working pay shall be paid him.

If methods of labour such as piece work are employed, the length of the working period shall not be rendered excessive thereby.

ARTICLE 54

Working pay. Occupational accidents and diseases

The working pay due to prisoners of war shall be fixed in accordance with the provisions of Article 62 of the present Convention.

Prisoners of war who sustain accidents in connection with work, or who contract a disease in the course, or in consequence of their work, shall receive all the care their condition may require. The Detaining Power shall furthermore deliver to such prisoners of war a medical certificate enabling them to submit their claims to the Power on which they depend, and shall send a duplicate to the Central Prisoners of War Agency provided for in Article 123.

ARTICLE 55

Medical supervision

The fitness of prisoners of war for work shall be periodically verified by medical examinations at least once a month. The examinations shall have particular regard to the nature of the work which prisoners of war are required to do.

If any prisoner of war considers himself incapable of working, he shall be permitted to appear before the medical authorities of his camp. Physicians or surgeons may recommend that the prisoners who are, in their opinion, unfit for work, be exempted therefrom.

ARTICLE 56

Labour detachments

The organization and administration of labour detachments shall be similar to those of prisoner of war camps.

Every labour detachment shall remain under the control of and administratively part of a prisoner of war camp. The military authorities and the commander of the said camp shall be responsible, under the direction of their government, for the observance of the provisions of the present Convention in labour detachments.

The camp commander shall keep an up-to-date record of the labour detachments dependent on his camp, and shall communicate it to the delegates of the Protecting Power, of the International Committee of the Red Cross, or of other agencies giving relief to prisoners of war, who may visit the camp.

ARTICLE 57

The treatment of prisoners of war who work for private persons, even if the latter are responsible for guarding and protecting them, shall not be inferior to that which is provided for by the present Convention. The Detaining Power, the military authorities and the commander of the camp to which such prisoners belong shall be entirely responsible for the maintenance, care, treatment, and payment of the working pay of such prisoners of war.

Such prisoners of war shall have the right to remain in communication with the prisoners' representatives in the camps on which they depend.

Prisoners
working for
private employers

SECTION IV

FINANCIAL RESOURCES OF PRISONERS OF WAR

ARTICLE 58

Upon the outbreak of hostilities, and pending an arrangement on this matter with the Protecting Power, the Detaining Power may determine the maximum amount of money in cash or in similar form, that prisoners may have in their possession. Any amount in excess, which was properly in their possession and which has been taken or withheld from them, shall be placed to their account, together with any monies deposited by them, and shall not be converted into any other currency without their consent.

If prisoners of war are permitted to purchase services or commodities outside the cap against payments in cash, such payments shall be made by the prisoner himself or by the camp administration who will charge them to the accounts

Ready money

of the prisoners concerned. The Detaining Power will establish the necessary rules in this respect.

ARTICLE 59

Amounts in cash taken from prisoners

Cash which was taken from prisoners of war, in accordance with Article 18, at the time of their capture, and which is in the currency of the Detaining Power, shall be placed to their separate accounts, in accordance with the provisions of Article 64 of the present Section.

The amounts, in the currency of the Detaining Power, due to the conversion of sums in other currencies that are taken from the prisoners of war at the same time, shall also be credited to their separate accounts.

ARTICLE 60

Advances of pay

The Detaining Power shall grant all prisoners of war a monthly advance of pay, the amount of which shall be fixed by conversion, into the currency of the said Power, of the following amounts:

Category I: Prisoners ranking below sergeants: eight Swiss francs.

Category II: Sergeants and other non-commissioned officers, or prisoners of equivalent rank: twelve Swiss Francs.

Category III: Warrant officers and commissioned officers below the rank of major or prisoners of equivalent rank: fifty Swiss francs.

Category IV: Majors, lieutenant-colonels, colonels or prisoners of equivalent rank: sixty Swiss francs.

Category V: General officers or prisoners of war of equivalent rank: seventy-five Swiss Francs.

However, the Parties to the conflict concerned may by special agreement modify the amount of advances of pay due to prisoners of the preceding categories.

Furthermore, if the amounts indicated in the first paragraph above would be unduly high compared with the pay of the Detaining Power's armed forces or would, for any reason, seriously embarrass the Detaining Power, then, pending the conclusion of a special agreement with the Power on which the prisoners depend to vary the amounts indicated above, the Detaining Power:

(*a*)   shall continue to credit the accounts of the prisoners with the amounts indicated in the first paragraph above:

(*b*)   may temporarily limit the amount made available from these advances of pay to prisoners of war for their own use, to sums which are reasonable, but which, for Category I, shall never be inferior to the amount that the Detaining Power gives to the members of its own armed forces.

The reasons for any limitations will be given without delay to the Protecting Power.

ARTICLE 61

The Detaining Power shall accept for distribution as supplementary pay to prisoners of war sums which the Power on which the prisoners depend may forward to them, on condition that the sums to be paid shall be the same for each prisoner of the same category, shall be payable to all prisoners of that category depending on that Power, and shall be placed in their separate accounts, at the earliest opportunity, in accordance with the provisions of Article 64. Such supplementary pay shall not relieve the Detaining Power of any obligation under this Convention.

Supplementary pay

ARTICLE 62

Prisoners of war shall be paid a fair working rate of pay by the detaining authorities direct. The rate shall be fixed by the said authorities, but shall at no time be less than one-fourth of one Swiss franc for a full working day. The Detaining Power shall inform prisoners of war, as well as

Working pay

the Power on which they depend, through the intermediary
of the Protecting Power, of the rate of daily working pay
that it has fixed.

Working pay shall likewise be paid by the detaining
authority to prisoners of war permanently detailed to duties
or to a skilled or semi-skilled occupation in connection with
the administration, installation or maintenance of camps,
and to the prisoners who are required to carry out spiritual
or medical duties on behalf of their comrades.

The working pay of the prisoners' representative, of his
advisers, if any, and of his assistants, shall be paid out of the
fund maintained by canteen profits. The scale of this
working pay shall be fixed by the prisoners' representative
and approved by the camp commander. If there is no such
fund, the detaining authorities shall pay these prisoners a
fair working rate of pay.

ARTICLE 63

Transfer
of funds

Prisoners of war shall be permitted to receive remittances
of money addressed to them individually or collectively.

Every prisoner of war shall have at his disposal the credit
balance of his account as provided for in the following
Article, within the limits fixed by the Detaining Power,
which shall make such payments as are requested. Subject
to financial or monetary restrictions which the Detaining
Power regards as essential, prisoners of war may also have
payments made abroad. In this case payments addressed by
prisoners of war to dependents shall be given priority.

In any event, and subject to the consent of the Power on
which they depend, prisoners may have payments made in
their own country, as follows: the Detaining Power shall
send to the aforesaid Power through the Protecting Power,
a notification giving all the necessary particulars concerning
the prisoners of war, the beneficiaries of the payments, and
the amount of the sums to be paid, expressed in the
Detaining Power's currency. The said notification shall be
signed by the prisoners and countersigned by the camp
commander. The Detaining Power shall debit the prisoners'
account by a corresponding amount; the sums thus debited
shall be placed by it to the credit of the Power on which the
prisoners depend.

To apply the foregoing provisions, the Detaining Power

may usefully consult the Model Regulations in Annex V of the present Convention.

ARTICLE 64

The Detaining Power shall hold an account for each prisoner of war, showing at least the following:

Prisoners accounts

(1) The amounts due to the prisoner or received by him as advances of pay, as working pay or derived from any other source; the sums in the currency of the Detaining Power which were taken from him; the sums taken from him and converted at his request into the currency of the said Power.

(2) The payments made to the prisoner in cash, or in any other similar form; the payments made on his behalf and at his request; the sums tranferred under Article 63, third paragraph.

ARTICLE 65

Every item entered in the account of a prisoner of war shall be countersigned or initialled by him, or by the prisoners' representative acting on his behalf.

Management of prisoners' accounts

Prisoners of war shall at all times be afforded reasonable facilities for consulting and obtaining copies of their accounts, which may likewise be inspected by the representatives of the Protecting Powers at the time of visits to the camp.

When prisoners of war are transferred from one camp to another, their personal accounts will follow them. In case of transfer from one Detaining Power to another, the monies which are their property and are not in the currency of the Detaining Power will follow them. They shall be given certificates for any other monies standing to the credit of their accounts.

The Parties to the conflict concerned may agree to notify to each other at specific intervals through the Protecting Power, the amount of the accounts of the prisoners of war.

ARTICLE 66

On the termination of captivity, through the release of a prisoner of war or his repatriation, the Detaining Power shall give him a statement, signed by an authorized officer of that Power, showing the credit balance then due to him.

Winding up of accounts

The Detaining Power shall also send through the Protecting Power to the government upon which the prisoner of war depends, lists giving all appropriate particulars of all prisoners of war whose captivity has been terminated by repatriation, release, escape, death or any other means, and showing the amount of their credit balances. Such lists shall be certified on each sheet by an authorized representative of the Detaining Power.

Any of the above provisions of this Article may be varied by mutual agreement between any two Parties to the confict.

The Power on which the prisoner of war depends shall be responsible for settling with him any credit balance due to him from the Detaining Power on the termination of his captivity.

ARTICLE 67

Adjustments between Parties to the Conflict

Advances of pay, issued to prisoners of war in conformity with Article 60, shall be considered as made on behalf of the Power on which they depend. Such advances of pay, as well as all payments made by the said Power under Article 63, third paragraph, and Article 68, shall form the subject of arrangements between the Powers concerned, at the close of hostilities.

ARTICLE 68

Claims for compensation

Any claim by a prisoner of war for compensation in respect of any injury or other disability arising out of work shall be referred to the Power on which he depends, through the Protecting Power. In accordance with Article 54, the Detaining Power will, in all cases, provide the prisoner of war concerned with a statement showing the nature of the injury or disability, the circumstances in which it arose and particulars of medical or hospital treatment given for it. This statement will be signed by a responsible officer of the Detaining Power and the medical particulars certified by a medical officer.

Any claim by a prisoner of war for compensation in respect of personal effects, monies or valuables impounded by the Detaining Power under Article 18 and not forthcoming on his repatriation, or in respect of loss alleged to be due to the fault of the Detaining Power or any of its servants, shall likewise be referred to the Power on which he depends. Nevertheless, any such personal effects required for use by the prisoners of war whilst in captivity shall be replaced at the expense of the Detaining Power. The Detaining Power will, in all cases, provide the prisoner of war with a statement, signed by a responsible officer, showing all available information regarding the reasons why such effects, monies or valuables have not been restored to him. A copy of this statement will be forwarded to the Power on which he depends through the Central Prisoners of War Agency provided for in Article 123.

SECTION V

RELATIONS OF PRISONERS OF WAR
WITH THE EXTERIOR

ARTICLE 69

Immediately upon prisoners of war falling into its power, the Detaining Power shall inform them and the Powers on which they depend, through the Protecting Power, of the measures taken to carry out the provisions of the present Section. They shall likewise inform the parties concerned of any subsequent modifications of such measures.

Notification of
measures taken

ARTICLE 70

Immediately upon capture, or not more than one week after arrival at a camp, even if it is a transit camp, likewise in case of sickness or transfer to hospital or another camp, every prisoner of war shall be enabled to write direct to his family, on the one hand, and to the Central Prisoners of War Agency provided for in Article 123, on the other hand, a card similar, if possible, to the model annexed to the present Convention, informing his relatives of his capture, address and state of health. The said cards shall be forwarded as rapidly as possible and may not be delayed in any manner.

Capture card

ARTICLE 71

Prisoners of war shall be allowed to send and receive letters and cards. If the Detaining Power deems it necessary to

Correspondence

limit the numbers of letters and cards sent by each prisoner of war, the said number shall not be less than two letters and four cards monthly, exclusive of the capture cards provided for in Article 70, and conforming as closely as possible to the models annexed to the present Convention. Further limitations may be imposed only if the Protecting Power is satisfied that it would be in the interests of the prisoners of war concerned to do so owing to difficulties of translation caused by the Detaining Power's inability to find sufficient qualified linguists to carry out the necessary censorship. If limitations must be placed on the correspondence addressed to prisoners of war, they may be ordered only by the Power on which the prisoners depend, possibly at the request of the Detaining Power. Such letters and cards must be conveyed by the most rapid method at the disposal of the Detaining Power; they may not be delayed or retained for disciplinary reasons.

Prisoners of war who have been without news for a long period, or who are unable to receive news from their next of kin or to give them news by the ordinary postal route, as well as those who are at a great distance from their homes, shall be permitted to send telegrams, the fees being charged against the prisoners of war's accounts with the Detaining Power or paid in the currency at their disposal. They shall likewise benefit by this measure in cases of urgency.

As a general rule, the correspondence of prisoners of war shall be written in their native language. The Parties to the conflict may allow correspondence in other languages.

Sacks containing prisoner of war mail must be securely sealed and labelled so as clearly to indicate their contents, and must be addressed to offices of destination.

ARTICLE 72

Relief shipments
I.
General
principles

Prisoners of war shall be allowed to receive by post or by any other means individual parcels or collective shipments containing, in particular, foodstuffs, clothing, medical supplies and articles of a religious, educational or recreational character which may meet their needs, including books, devotional articles, scientific equipment, examination papers, musical instruments, sports outfits and materials allowing prisoners of war to pursue their studies or their cultural activities.

Such shipments shall in no way free the Detaining Power

from the obligations imposed upon it by virtue of the present Convention.

The only limits which may be placed on these shipments shall be those proposed by the Protecting Power in the interest of the prisoners themselves, or by the International Committee of the Red Cross or any other organization giving assistance to the prisoners, in respect of their own shipments only, on account of exceptional strain on transport or communications.

The conditions for the sending of individual parcels and collective relief shall, if necessary, be the subject of special agreements between the Powers concerned, which may in no case delay the receipt by the prisoners of relief supplies. Books may not be included in parcels of clothing and foodstuffs. Medical supplies shall, as a rule, be sent in collective parcels.

ARTICLE 73

In the absence of special agreements between the Powers concerned on the conditions for the receipt and distribution of collective relief shipments, the rules and regulations concerning collective shipments, which are annexed to the present Convention shall be applied.

II.
Collective relief

The special agreements referred to above shall in no case restrict the right of prisoners' representatives to take possesion of collective relief shipments intended for prisoners of war, to proceed to their distribution or to dispose of them in the interest of the prisoners.

Nor shall such agreements restrict the right of representatives of the Protecting Power, the International Committee of the Red Cross or any other organization giving assistance to prisoners of war and responsible for the forwarding of collective shipments, to supervise their distribution to the recipients.

ARTICLE 74

All relief shipments for prisoners of war shall be exempt from import, customs and other dues.

Exemption from
postal and
transport charges

Correspondence, relief shipments and authorized remittances of money addressed to prisoners of war or despatched by them through the post office, either direct or through the Information Bureaux provided for in Article 122 and the

Central Prisoners of War Agency provided for in Article 123, shall be exempt from any postal dues, both in the countries of origin and destination, and in intermediate countries.

If relief shipments intended for prisoners of war cannot be sent through the post office by reason of weight or for any other cause, the cost of transportation shall be borne by the Detaining Power in all the territories under its control. The other Powers party to the Convention shall bear the cost of transport in their respective territories.

In the absence of special agreements between the Parties concerned, the costs connected with transport of such shipments, other than costs covered by the above exemption, shall be charged to the senders.

The High Contracting Parties shall endeavour to reduce, so far as possible, the rates charge for telegrams sent by prisoners of war, or addressed to them.

ARTICLE 75

Special means
of transport

Should military operations prevent the Powers concerned from fulfilling their obligation to assure the transport of the shipments referred to in Articles 70, 71, 72 and 77, the Protecting Powers concerned, the International Committee of the Red Cross or any other organization duly approved by the Parties to the conflict may undertake to ensure the conveyance of such shipments by suitable means (railway wagons, motor vehicles, vessels or aircraft, etc.). For this purpose, the High Contracting Parties shall endeavour to supply them with such transport and to allow its circulation, especially by granting the necessary safe-conducts.

Such transport may also be used to convey:

(a)   correspondence, lists and reports exchanged between the Central Information Agency referred to in Article 123 and the National Bureau referred to in Article 122;

(b)   correspondence and reports relating to prisoners of war which the Protecting Powers, the International Committee of the Red Cross or any other body assisting the prisoners, exchange either with their own delegates or with the Parties to the conflict.

These provisions in no way detract from the right of any Party to the conflict to arrange other means of transport, if it should so prefer, not preclude the granting of safe-conducts, under mutually agreed conditions, to such means of transport.

In the absence of special agreements, the costs occasioned by the use of such means of transport shall be borne proportionally by the Parties to the conflict whose nationals are benefitted thereby.

ARTICLE 76

The censoring of correspondence addressed to prisoners of war or despatched by them shall be done as quickly as possible. Mail shall be censored only by the despatching State and the receiving State, and once only by each.

Censorship and examination

The examination of consignments intended for prisoners of war shall not be carried out under conditions that will expose the goods contained in them to deterioration; except in the case of written or printed matter, it shall be done in the presence of the addressee, or of a fellow-prisoner duly delegated by him. The delivery to prisoners of individual or collective consignments shall not be delayed under the pretext of difficulties of censorship.

Any prohibition or correspondence ordered by Parties to the conflict, either for military or political reasons, shall be only temporary and its duration shall be as short as possible.

ARTICLE 77

The Detaining Powers shall provide all facilities for the transmission, through the Protecting Power or the Central Prisoners of War Agency provided for in Article 123, of instruments, papers or documents intended for prisoners of war or despatched by them, especially powers of attorney and wills.

Preparation execution and and transmission of legal documents

In all cases, they shall facilitate the preparation and execution of such documents on behalf of prisoners of war; in particular, they shall allow them to consult a lawyer and shall take what measures are necessary for the authentication of their signatures.

SECTION VI

RELATIONS BETWEEN PRISONERS OF WAR
AND THE AUTHORITIES

CHAPTER 1

COMPLAINTS OF PRISONERS OF WAR
RESPECTING THE CONDITIONS OF CAPTIVITY

ARTICLE 78

Complaints
and requests

Prisoners of war shall have the right to make known to the military authorities in whose power they are, their requests regarding the conditions of captivity to which they are subjected.

They shall also have the unrestricted right to apply to the representatives of the Protecting Powers either through their prisoners' representative or, if they consider it necessary, direct, in order to draw their attention to any points on which they may have complaints to make regarding their conditions of captivity.

These requests and complaints shall not be limited nor considered to be a part of the correspondence quota referred to in Article 71. They must be transmitted immediately. Even if they are recognized to be unfounded, they may not give rise to any punishment.

Prisoners' representatives may send periodic reports on the situation in the camps and the need of the prisoners of war to the representatives of the Protecting Powers.

CHAPTER II

PRISONER OF WAR REPRESENTATIVES

ARTICLE 79

Election

In all places where there are prisoners of war, except in those where there are officers, the prisoners shall freely elect by secret ballot, every six months, and also in case of vacancies, prisoners' representatives entrusted with representing them before the military authorities, the Protecting Powers, the International Committee of the Red Cross and any other organization which may assist them.

These prisoners' representatives shall be eligible for re-election.

In camps for officers and persons of equivalent status or in mixed camps, the senior officer among the prisoners of war shall be recognized as the camp prisoners' representative. In camps for officers, he shall be assisted by one or more advisers chosen by the officers; in mixed camps, his assistants shall be chosen from among the prisoners of war who are not officers and shall be elected by them.

Officer prisoners of war of the same nationality shall be stationed in labour camps for prisoners of war, for the purpose of carrying out the camp administration duties for which the prisoners of war are responsible. These officers may be elected as prisoners' representatives under the first paragraph of this Article. In such a case the assistants to the prisoners' representatives shall be chosen from among those prisoners of war who are not officers.

Every representative elected must be approved by the Detaining Power before he has the right to commence his duties. Where the Detaining Power refuses to approve a prisoner of war elected by his fellow prisoners of war, it must inform the Protecting Power of the reason for such refusal.

In all cases the prisoners' representative must have the same nationality, language and customs as the prisoners of war whom he represents. Thus, prisoners of war distributed in different sections of a camp, according to their nationality, language or customs, shall have for each section their own prisoners' representative, in accordance with the foregoing paragraphs.

ARTICLE 80

Prisoners' representatives shall further the physical, spiritual and intellectual well-being of prisoners of war.   Duties

In particular, where the prisoners decide to organize amongst themselves a system of mutual assistance, this organization will be within the province of the prisoners' representative, in addition to the special duties entrusted to him by other provisions of the present Convention.

Prisoners' representatives shall not be held responsible, simply by reason of their duties, for any offences committed by prisoners of war.

ARTICLE 81

Prerogatives   Prisoners' representatives shall not be required to perform any other work, if the accomplishment of their duties is thereby made more difficult.

Prisoners' representatives may appoint from amongst the prisoners such assistants as they may require. All material facilities shall be granted them, particularly a certain freedom of movement necessary for the accomplishment of their duties (inspection of labour detachments, receipt of supplies, etc.).

Prisoners' representatives shall be permitted to visit premises where prisoners of war are detained, and every prisoner of war shall have the right to consult freely his prisoners' representative.

All facilities shall likewise be accorded to the prisoners' representatives for communication by post and telegraph with the detaining authorities, the Protecting Powers, the International Committee of the Red Cross and their delegates, the Mixed Medical Commissions and with the bodies which give assistance to prisoners of war. Prisoners' representatives of labour detachments shall enjoy the same facilities for communication with the prisoners' representatives of the principal camp. Such communications shall not be restricted, nor considered as forming a part of the quota mentioned in Article 71.

Prisoners' representatives who are transferred shall be allowed a reasonable time to acquaint their successors with current affairs.

In case of dismissal, the reasons therefore shall be communicated to the Protecting Power.

CHAPTER III

PENAL AND DISCIPLINARY SANCTIONS

I. General Provisions

ARTICLE 82

Applicable   A prisoner of war shall be subject to the laws, regulations
legislation   and orders in force in the armed forces of the Detaining Power; the Detaining Power shall be justified in taking judicial or disciplinary measures in respect of any offence committed by a prisoner of war against such laws, regulations

or orders. However, no proceedings or punishments contrary to the provisions of this Chapter shall be allowed.

If any law, regulation or order of the Detaining Power shall declare acts committed by a prisoner of war to be punishable, whereas the same acts would not be punishable if committed by a member of the forces of the Detaining Power, such acts shall entail disciplinary punishments only.

ARTICLE 83

In deciding whether proceedings in respect of an offence alleged to have been committed by a prisoner of war shall be judicial or disciplinary, the Detaining Power shall ensure that the competent authorities exercise the greatest leniency and adopt, wherever possible, disciplinary rather than judicial measures.

Choice of disciplinary or judicial proceedings

ARTICLE 84

A prisoner of war shall be tried only by a military court, unless the existing laws of the Detaining Power expressly permit the civil courts to try a member of the armed forces of the Detaining Power in respect of the particular offence alleged to have been committed by the prisoner of war.

Courts

In no circumstances whatever shall a prisoner of war be tried by a court of any kind which does not offer the essential guarantees of independence and impartiality as generally recognized, and, in particular, the procedure of which does not afford the accused the rights and means of defence provided for in Article 105.

ARTICLE 85

Prisoners of war prosecuted under the laws of the Detaining Power for acts committed prior to capture shall retain, even if convicted, the benefits of the present Convention.

Offences committed before capture

ARTICLE 86

No prisoner of war may be punished more than once for the same act, or on the same charge.

"Non bis in idem"

Penalties   Prisoners of war may not be sentenced by the military authorities and courts of the Detaining Power to any penalties except those provided for in respect of members of the armed forces of the said Power who have committed the same acts.

When fixing the penalty, the courts or authorities of the Detaining Power shall take into consideration, to the widest extent possible, the fact that the accused, not being a national of the Detaining Power, is not bound to it by any duty of allegiance, and that he is in its power as the result of circumstances independent of his own will. The said courts or authorities shall be at liberty to reduce the penalty provided for the violation of which the prisoner of war is accused, and shall therefore not be bound to apply the minimum penalty prescribed.

Collective punishment for individual acts, corporation punishments, imprisonment in premises without daylight and, in general, any form of torture or cruelty, are forbidden.

No prisoner of war may be deprived of his rank by the Detaining Power, or prevented from wearing his badges.

Execution   Officers, non-commissioned officers and men who are
of penalties   prisoners of war undergoing a disciplinary or judicial punishment, shall not be subjected to more severe treatment than that applied in respect of the same punishment to members of the armed forces of the Detaining Power of equivalent rank.

A woman prisoner of war shall not be awarded or sentenced to a punishment more severe, or treated whilst undergoing punishment more severely, than a woman member of the armed forces of the Detaining Power dealt with for a similar offence.

In no case may a woman prisoner of war be awarded or sentenced to a punishment more severe, or treated whilst undergoing punishment more severely, than a male member of the armed forces of the Detaining Power dealt with for a similar offence.

Prisoners of war who have served disciplinary or judicial sentences may not be treated differently from other prisoners of war.

II. Disciplinary Sanctions

ARTICLE 89

The disciplinary punishments applicable to prisoners of war are the following:

(1)   A fine which shall not exceed 50 per cent of the advances of pay and working pay which the prisoner of war would otherwise receive under the provisions of Articles 60 and 62 during a period of not more than thirty days.

(2)   Discontinuance of privileges granted over and above the treatment provided for by the present Convention.

(3)   Fatigue duties not exceeding two hours daily.

(4)   Confinement.

The punishment referred to under (3) shall not be applied to officers.

In no case shall disciplinary punishments be inhuman, brutal or dangerous to the health of prisoners of war.

General observations I. Forms of punishment

ARTICLE 90

The duration of any single punishment shall in no case exceed thirty days. Any period of confinement awaiting the hearing of a disciplinary offence or the award of disciplinary punishment shall be deducted from an award pronounced against a prisoner of war.

The maximum of thirty days provided above may not be exceeded, even if the prisoner of war is answerable for several acts at the same time when he is awarded punishment, whether such acts are related or not.

The period between the pronouncing of an award of disciplinary punishment and its execution shall not exceed one month.

When a prisoner of war is awarded a further disciplinary punishment, a period of at least three days shall elapse between the execution of any two of the punishments, if the duration of one of these is ten days or more.

II. Duration of punishments

ARTICLE 91

Escapes
I.

The escape of a prisoner of war shall be deemed to have succeeded when:

Successful
escape

(1)   he has joined the armed forces of the Power on which he depends, or those of an allied Power;

(2)   he has left the territory under the control of the Detaining Power, or of an ally of the said Power;

(3)   he has joined a ship flying the flag of the Power on which he depends, or of an allied Power, in the territorial waters of the Detaining Power, the said ship not being under the control of the last named Power.

Prisoners of war who have made good their escape in the sense of this Article and who are recaptured, shall not be liable to any punishment in respect of their previous escape.

ARTICLE 92

II.
Unsuccessful
escape

A prisoner of war who attempts to escape and is recaptured before having made good his escape in the sense of Article 91 shall be liable only to a disciplinary punishment in respect of this act, even if it is a repeated offence.

A prisoner of war who is recaptured shall be handed over without delay to the competent military authority.

Article 88, fourth paragraph, notwithstanding, prisoners of war punished as a result of an unsuccessful escape may be subjected to special surveillance. Such surveillance must not affect the state of their health, must be undergone in a prisoner of war camp, and must not entail the suppression of any of the safeguards granted them by the present Convention.

ARTICLE 93

III.
Connected
offences

Escape or attempt to escape, even if it is a repeated offence, shall not be deemed an aggravating circumstance if the prisoner of war is subjected to trial by judicial proceedings in respect of an offence committed during his escape or attempt to escape.

In conformity with the principle stated in Article 83, offences committed by prisoners of war with the sole intention of facilitating their escape and which do not entail any violence against life or limb, such as offences against public property, theft without intention of self-enrichment, the drawing up or use of false papers, the wearing of civilian clothing shall occasion disciplinary punishment only.

Prisoners of war who aid or abet an escape or an attempt to escape shall be liable on this count to disciplinary punishment only.

ARTICLE 94

If an escaped prisoner of war is recaptured, the Power on which he depends shall be notified thereof in the manner defined in Article 122, provided notification of his escape has been made.

IV.
Notification
of recapture

ARTICLE 95

A prisoner of war accused of an offence against discipline shall not be kept in confinement pending the hearing unless a member of the armed forces of the Detaining Power would be so kept if he were accused of a similar offence, or if it is essential in the interests of camp order and discipline.

Procedure
I.
Confinement
awaiting hearing

Any period spent by a prisoner of war in confinement awaiting the disposal of an offence against discipline shall be reduced to an absolute minimum and shall not exceed fourteen days.

The provisions of Articles 97 and 98 of this Chapter shall apply to prisoners of war who are in confinement awaiting the disposal of offences against discipline.

ARTICLE 96

Acts which constitute offences against discipline shall be investigated immediately.

II.
Competent
authorities and
right of defence

Without prejudice to the competence of courts and superior military authorities, disciplinary punishment may be ordered only by an officer having disciplinary powers in his capacity as camp commander, or by a responsible officer who replaces him or to whom he has delegated his disciplinary powers.

In no case may such powers be delegated to a prisoner of war or be exercised by a prisoner of war.

Before any disciplinary award is pronounced, the accused shall be given precise information regarding the offences of which he is accused, and given an opportunity of explaining his conduct and of defending himself. He shall be permitted, in particular, to call witnesses and to have recourse, if necessary, to the services of a qualified interpreter. The decision shall be announced to the accused prisoner of war and to the prisoners' representative.

A record of disciplinary punishments shall be maintained by the camp commander and shall be open to inspection by representatives of the Protecting Power.

ARTICLE 97

Execution of
punishment
I.
Premises

Prisoners of war shall not in any case be transferred to penitentiary establishments (prisons, penitentiaries, convict prisons, etc.) to undergo disciplinary punishment therein.

All premises in which disciplinary punishments are undergone shall conform to the sanitary requirements set forth in Article 25. A prisoner of war undergoing punishment shall be enabled to keep himself in a state of cleanliness, in conformity with Article 29.

Officers and persons of equivalent status shall not be lodged in the same quarters as non-commissioned officers or men.

Women prisoners of war undergoing disciplinary punishment shall be confined in separate quarters from male prisoners of war and shall be under the immediate supervision of women.

ARTICLE 98

II.
Essential
safeguards

A prisoner of war undergoing confinement as a disciplinary punishment, shall continue to enjoy the benefits of the provisions of this Convention except in so far as these are necessarily rendered inapplicable by the mere fact that he is confined. In no case may he be deprived of the benefits of the provisions of Articles 78 and 126.

A prisoner of war awarded disciplinary punishment may not be deprived of the prerogatives attached to his rank.

Prisoners of war awarded disciplinary punishment shall be allowed to exercise and to stay in the open air at least two hours daily.

They shall be allowed, on their request, to be present at the daily medical inspections. They shall receive the attention which their state of health requires and, if necessary, shall be removed to the camp infirmary or to a hospital.

They shall have permission to read and write, likewise to
send and receive letters. Parcels and remittances of money
however, may be withheld from them until the completion
of the punishment; they shall meanwhile be entrusted to the
prisoners' representative, who will hand over to the
infirmary the perishable goods contained in such parcels.

III. Judicial Proceedings

ARTICLE 99

No prisoner of war may be tried or sentenced for an act
which is not forbidden by the law of the Detaining Power or
by international law, in force at the time the said act was
committed.

No moral or physical coercion may be exerted on a
prisoner of war in order to induce him to admit himself
guilty of the act of which he is accused.

No prisoner of war may be convicted without having had
an opportunity to present his defence and the assistance of
a qualified advocate or counsel.

Essential rules
I.
General
principles

ARTICLE 100

Prisoners of war and the Protecting Powers shall be informed as soon as possible of the offences which are punishable
by the death sentence under the laws of the Detaining
Power.

Other offences shall not thereafter be made punishable by
the death penalty without the concurrence of the Power
upon which the prisoners of war depend.

The death sentence cannot be pronounced on a prisoner
of war unless the attention of the court has, in accordance
with Article 87, second paragraph, been particularly called
to the fact that since the accused is not a national of the
Detaining Power, he is not bound to it by a duty of
allegiance, and that he is in its power as the result of
circumstances independent of his own will.

II.
Death penalty

ARTICLE 101

If the death penalty is pronounced on a prisoner of war,
the sentence shall not be executed before the expiration of a

III.
Delay in

execution of the
death penalty

period of at least six months from the date when the Protecting Power receives, at an indicated address, the detailed communication provided for in Article 107.

ARTICLE 102

Procedure
I.
Conditions for
validity of
sentence

A prisoner of war can be validly sentenced only if the sentence has been pronounced by the same courts according to the same procedure as in the case of members of the armed forces of the Detaining Power, and if, furthermore, the provisions of the present Chapter have been observed.

ARTICLE 103

II.
Confinement
awaiting trial
(Deduction from
sentence,
treatment)

Judicial investigations relating to a prisoner of war shall be conducted as rapidly as circumstances permit and so that his trial shall take place as soon as possible. A prisoner of war shall not be confined while awaiting trial unless a member of the armed forces of the Detaining Power would be so confined if he were accused of a similar offence, or if it is essential to do so in the interests of national security. In no circumstances shall this confinement exceed three months.

Any period spent by a prisoner of war in confinement awaiting trial shall be deducted from any sentence of imprisonment passed upon him and taken into account in fixing any penalty.

The provisions of Articles 97 and 98 of this Chapter shall apply to a prisoner of war whilst in confinement awaiting trial.

ARTICLE 104

III.
Notification
of proceedings

In any case in which the Detaining Power has decided to institute judicial proceedings against a prisoner of war, it shall notify the Protecting Power as soon as possible and at least three weeks before the opening of the trial. This period of three weeks shall run as from the day on which such notification reaches the Protecting Power at the address previously indicated by the latter to the Detaining Power.

The said notification shall contain the following information:

    (1)   surname and first names of the prisoner of war, his rank, his army, regimental, personal or serial number, his date of birth, and his profession or trade, if any;

    (2)   place of internment or confinement;

    (3)   specification of the charge or charges on which the prisoner of war is to be arraigned, giving the legal provisions applicable;

    (4)   designation of the court which will try the case, likewise the date and place fixed for the opening of the trial.

The same communication shall be made by the Detaining Power to the prisoners' representative.

If no evidence is submitted, at the opening of a trial, that the notification referred to above was received by the Protecting Power, by the prisoner of war and by the prisoners' representative concerned, at least three weeks before the opening of the trial, then the latter cannot take place and must be adjourned.

ARTICLE 105

The prisoner of war shall be entitled to assistance by one of his prisoner comrades, to defence by a qualified advocate or counsel of his own choice, to the calling of witnesses and, if he deems necessary, to the services of a competent interpreter. He shall be advised of these rights by the Detaining Power in due time before the trial.

IV.
Rights and means
of defence

Failing a choice by the prisoner of war, the Protecting Power shall find him an advocate or counsel, and shall have at least one week at its disposal for the purpose. The Detaining Power shall deliver to the said Power, on request, a list of persons qualified to present the defence. Failing a choice of an advocate or counsel by the prisoner of war or the Protecting Power, the Detaining Power shall appoint a competent advocate or counsel to conduct the defence.

The advocate or counsel conducting the defence on behalf of the prisoner of war shall have at his disposal a period of two weeks at least before the opening of the trial, as well as the necessary facilities to prepare the defence of the accused. He may, in particular, freely visit the accused and interview him in private. He may also confer with any witnesses for the defence, including prisoners of war. He shall have the benefit of these facilities until the term of appeal or petition has expired.

Particulars of the charge or charges on which the prisoner of war is to be arraigned, as well as the documents which are generally communicated to the accused by virtue of the laws in force in the armed forces of the Detaining Power, shall be communicated to the accused prisoner of war in a language which he understands, and in good time before the opening of the trial. The same communication in the same circumstances shall be made to the advocate or counsel conducting the defence on behalf of the prisoner of war.

The representatives of the Protecting Power shall be entitled to attend the trial of the case, unless, exceptionally, this is held *in camera* in the interest of State security. In such a case the Detaining Power shall advise the Protecting Power accordingly.

ARTICLE 106

V.
Appeals

Every prisoner of war shall have, in the same manner as the members of the armed forces of the Detaining Power, the right of appeal or petition from any sentence pronounced upon him, with a view to the quashing or revising of the sentence or the reopening of the trial. He shall be fully informed of his right to appeal or petition and of the time limit within which he may do so.

ARTICLE 107

VI.
Notification of
findings and
sentence

Any judgment and sentence pronounced upon a prisoner of war shall be immediately reported to the Protecting Power in the form of a summary communication, which shall also indicate whether he has the right of appeal with a view to the quashing of the sentence or the reopening of the trial. This communication shall likewise be sent to the prisoners' representative concerned. It shall also be sent to the accused prisoner of war in a language he understands, if the sentence was not pronounced in his presence. The Detaining Power shall also immediately communicate to the Protecting Power the decision of the prisoner of war to use or to waive his right of appeal.

Furthermore, if a prisoner of war is finally convicted or if a sentence pronounced on a prisoner of war in the first instance is a death sentence, the Detaining Power shall as soon as possible address to the Protecting Power a detailed communication containing:

(1)   the precise wording of the finding and sentence;

(2)   a summarized report of any preliminary investigation and of the trial, emphasizing in particular the elements of the prosecution and the defence;

(3)   notification, where applicable, of the establishment where the sentence will be served.

The communications provided for in the foregoing subparagraphs shall be sent to the Protecting Power at the address previously made known to the Detaining Power.

ARTICLE 108

Sentences pronounced on prisoners of war after a conviction has become duly enforceable, shall be served in the same estabishments and under the same conditons as in the case of members of the armed forces of the Detaining Power. These conditions shall in all cases conform to the requirements of health and humanity.

Execution of penalties. Penal regulations

A woman prisoner of war on whom such a sentence has been pronounced shall be confined in separate quarters and shall be under the supervision of women.

In any case, prisoners of war sentenced to a penalty depriving them of their liberty shall retain the benefit of the provisions of Articles 78 and 126 of the present Convention. Furthermore, they shall be entitled to receive and despatch correspondence, to receive at least one relief parcel monthly, to take regular exercise in the open air, to have the medical care required by their state of health, and the spiritual assistance they may desire. Penalties to which they may be subjected shall be in accordance with the provisions of Article 87, third paragraph.

PART IV

TERMINATION OF CAPTIVITY

SECTION 1

DIRECT REPATRIATION AND ACCOMMODATION IN NEUTRAL COUNTRIES

ARTICLE 109

General
observations

Subject to the provisions of the third paragraph of this Article, Parties to the conflict are bound to send back to their own country, regardless of number or rank, seriously wounded and seriously sick prisoners of war, after having cared for them until they are fit to travel, in accordance with the first paragraph of the following Article.

Throughout the duration of hostilities, Parties to the conflict shall endeavour, with the cooperation of the neutral Powers concerned, to make arrangements for the accommodation in neutral countries of the sick and wounded prisoners of war referred to in the second paragraph of the following Article. They may, in addition, conclude agreements with a view to the direct repatriation or internment in a neutral country of able-bodied prisoners of war who have undergone a long period of captivity.

No sick or injured prisoner of war who is eligible for repatriation under the first paragraph of this Article, may be repatriated against his will during hostilities.

ARTICLE 110

Cases of
repatriation and
accommodation

The following shall be repatriated direct:

(1) Incurably wounded and sick whose mental or physical fitness seems to have been gravely diminished.

(2) Wounded and sick who, according to medical opinion, are not likely to recover within one year, whose condition requires treatment and whose mental or physical fitness seems to have been gravely diminished.

(3) Wounded and sick who have recovered, but whose mental or physical fitness seems to have been gravely and permanently diminished.

The following may be accommodated in a neutral country:

(1)   Wounded and sick whose recovery may be expected within one year of the date of the wound or the beginning of the illness, if treatment in a neutral country might increase the prospects of a more certain and speedy recovery.

(2)   Prisoners of war whose mental or physical health, according to medical opinion, is seriously threatened by continued captivity, but whose accommodation in a neutral country might remove such a threat.

The conditions which prisoners of war accommodated in a neutral country must fulfil in order to permit their repatriation shall be fixed, as shall likewise their status, by agreement between the Powers concerned. In general, prisoners of war who have been accommodated in a neutral country, and who belong to the following categories, should be repatriated:

(1)   those whose state of health has deteriorated so as to fulfil the conditions laid down for direct repatriation;

(2)   those whose mental or physical powers remain, even after treatment, considerably impaired.

If no special agreements are concluded between the Parties to the conflict concerned, to determine the cases of disablement or sickness entailing direct repatriation or accommodation in a neutral country, such cases shall be settled in accordance with the principles laid down in the Model Agreement concerning direct repatriation and accommodation in neutral countries of wounded and sick prisoners of war and in the Regulations concerning Mixed Medical Commissions annexed to the present Convention.

ARTICLE 111

The Detaining Power, the Power on which the prisoners of war depend, and a neutral Power agreed upon by these two Powers, shall endeavour to conclude agreements which will enable prisoners of war to be interned in the territory of the said neutral Power until the close of hostilities.

Internment in a neutral country

ARTICLE 112

Mixed Medical Commissions

Upon the outbreak of hostilities, Mixed Medical Commissions shall be appointed to examine sick and wounded prisoners of war, and to make all appropriate decisions regarding them. The appointment, duties and functioning of these Commissions shall be in conformity with the provisions of the Regulations annexed to the present Convention.

However, prisoners of war who, in the opinion of the medical authorities of the Detaining Power, are manifestly seriously injured or seriously sick, may be repatriated without having to be examined by a Mixed Medical Commission.

ARTICLE 113

Prisoners entitled to examination by Mixed Medical Commissions

Besides those who are designated by the medical authorities of the Detaining Power, wounded or sick prisoners of war belonging to the categories listed below shall be entitled to present themselves for examination by the Mixed Medical Commissions provided for in the foregoing Article:

(1) Wounded and sick proposed by a physician or surgeon who is of the same nationality, or a national of a Party to the conflict allied with the Power on which the said prisoners depend, and who exercises his functions in the camp.

(2) Wounded and sick proposed by their prisoners' representative.

(3) Wounded and sick proposed by the Power on which they depend, or by an organization duly recognized by the said Power and giving assistance to the prisoners.

Prisoners of war who do not belong to one of the three foregoing categories may nevertheless present themselves for examination by Mixed Medical Commission, but shall be examined only after those belonging to the said categories.

The physician or surgeon of the same nationality as the prisoners who present themselves for examination by the Mixed Medical Commission, likewise the prisoners' representative of the said prisoners, shall have permission to be present at the examination.

ARTICLE 114

Prisoners of war who meet with accidents shall, unless the injury is self-inflicted, have the benefit of the provisions of this Convention as regards repatriation or accommodation in a neutral country.

Prisoners meeting with accidents

ARTICLE 115

No prisoner of war on whom a disciplinary punishment has been imposed and who is eligible for repatriation or for accommodation in a neutral country, may be kept back on the plea that he has not undergone his punishment.

Prisoners serving a sentence

Prisoners of war detained in connection with a judicial prosecution or conviction and who are designated for repatriation or accommodation in a neutral country, may benefit by such measures before the end of the proceedings or the completion of the punishment, if the Detaining Power consents.

Parties to the conflict shall communicate to each other the names of those who will be detained untl the end of the proceedings or the completion of the punishment.

ARTICLE 116

The costs of repatriating prisoners of war or of transporting them to a neutral country shall be borne, from the frontiers of the Detaining Power, by the Power on which the said prisoners depend.

Costs of repatriation

ARTICLE 117

No repatriated person may be employed on active military service.

Activity after repatriation

SECTION II

RELEASE AND REPATRIATION
OF PRISONERS OF WAR
AT THE CLOSE OF HOSTILITIES

ARTICLE 118

Release and
repatriation
Prisoners of war shall be released and repatriated without delay after the cessation of active hostilities.

In the absence of stipulations to the above effect in any agreement concluded between the Parties to the conflict with a view to the cessation of hostilities, or failing any such agreement, each of the Detaining Powers shall itself establish and execute without delay a plan of repatriation in conformity with the principle laid down in the foregoing paragraph.

In either case, the measures adopted shall be brought to the knowledge of the prisoners of war.

The cost of repatriation of prisoners of war shall in all cases be equitably apportioned between the Detaining Power and the Power on which the prisoners depend. This apportionment shall be carried out on the following basis:

(a)   If the two Powers are contiguous, the Power on which the prisoners of war depend shall bear the costs of repatriation from the frontiers of the Detaining Power.

(b)   If the two Powers are not contiguous, the Detaining Power shall bear the costs of transport of prisoners of war over its own territory as far as its frontier or its port of embarkation nearest to the territory of the Power on which the prisoners of war depend. The Parties concerned shall agree between themselves as to the equitable apportionment of the remaining costs of the repatriation. The conclusion of this agreement shall in no circumstances justify any delay in the repatriation of the prisoners of war.

ARTICLE 119

Details of
procedure
Repatriation shall be effected in conditions similar to those laid down in Articles 46 to 48 inclusive of the present

Convention for the transfer of prisoners of war, having regard to the provisions of Article 118 and to those of the following paragraphs.

On repatriation, any articles of value impounded from prisoners of war under Article 18, and any foreign currency which has not been converted into the currency of the Detaining Power, shall be restored to them. Articles of value and foreign currency which, for any reason whatever, are not restored to prisoners of war on repatriation, shall be despatched to the Information Bureau set up under Article 122.

Prisoners of war shall be allowed to take with them their personal effects, and any correspondence and parcels which have arrived for them. The weight of such baggage may be limited, if the conditions of repatriation so require, to what each prisoner can reasonably carry. Each prisoner shall in all cases be authorized to carry at least twenty-five kilograms.

The other personal effects of the repatriated prisoner shall be left in the charge of the Detaining Power which shall have them forwarded to him as soon as it has concluded an agreement to this effect, regulating the conditions of transport and the payment of the costs involved, with the Power on which the prisoner depends.

Prisoners of war against whom criminal proceedings for an indictable offence are pending may be detained until the end of such proceedings, and, if necessary, until the completion of the punishment. The same shall apply to prisoners of war already convicted for an indictable offence.

Parties to the conflict shall communicate to each other the names of any prisoners of war who are detained until the end of the proceedings or until punishment has been completed.

By agreement between the Parties to the conflict, commissions shall be established for the purpose of searching for dispersed prisoners of war and of assuring their repatriation with the least possible delay.

SECTION III

DEATH OF PRISONERS OF WAR

ARTICLE 120

Wills, death
certificates,
burial, cremation

Wills of prisoners of war shall be drawn up so as to satisfy the conditions of validity required by the legislation of their country of origin, which will take steps to inform the Detaining Power of its requirements in this respect. At the request of the prisoner of war and, in all cases, after death, the will shall be transmitted without delay to the Protecting Power; a certified copy shall be sent to the Central Agency.

Death certificates in the form annexed to the present Convention, or lists certified by a responsible officer, of all persons who die as prisoners of war shall be forwarded as rapidly as possible to the Prisoner of War Information Bureau established in accordance with Article 122. The death certificates or certified lists shall show particulars of identity as set out in the third paragraph of Article 17, and also the date and place of death, the cause of death, the date and place of burial and all particulars necessary to identify the graves.

The burial or cremation of a prisoner of war shall be preceded by a medical examination of the body with a view to confirming death and enabling a report to be made and, where necessary, establishing identity.

The detaining authorities shall ensure that prisoners of war who have died in captivity are honourably buried, if possible according to the rites of the religion to which they belonged, and that their graves are respected, suitably maintained and marked so as to be found at any time. Wherever possible, deceased prisoners of war who depended on the same Power shall be interred in the same place.

Deceased prisoners of war shall be buried in individual graves unless unavoidable circumstances require the use of collective graves. Bodies may be cremated only for imperative reasons of hygiene, on account of the religion of the deceased or in accordance with his express wish to this effect. In case of cremation, the fact shall be stated and the reasons given in the death certificate of the deceased.

In order that graves may always be found, all particulars of burials and graves shall be recorded with a Graves Registration Service established by the Detaining Power. Lists of graves and particulars of the prisoners of war interred in cemeteries and elsewhere shall be transmitted to the Power on which such prisoners of war depended. Responsibility for the care of these graves and for records of any subsequent moves of the bodies shall rest on the Power controlling the territory, if a Party to the present Convention. These provisions shall also apply to the ashes, which shall be kept by the Graves Registration Service until proper disposal thereof in accordance with the wishes of the home country.

ARTICLE 121

Every death or serious injury of a prisoner of war caused or suspected to have been caused by a sentry, another prisoner of war, or any other person, as well as any death the cause of which is unknown, shall be immediately followed by an official enquiry by the Detaining Power.

Prisoners killed or injured in special circumstances

A communication on this subject shall be sent immediately to the Protecting Power. Statements shall be taken from witnesses, especially from those who are prisoners of war, and a report including such statements shall be forwarded to the Protecting Power.

If the enquiry indicates the guilt of one or more persons, the Detaining Power shall take all measures for the prosecution of the person or persons responsible.

PART V

INFORMATION BUREAU AND
RELIEF SOCIETIES
FOR PRISONERS OF WAR

ARTICLE 122

Upon the outbreak of a conflict and in all cases of occupation, each of the Parties to the conflict shall institute an official Information Bureau for prisoners of war who are in its power. Neutral or non-belligerent Powers who may have received within their territory persons belonging to one of the categories referred to in Article 4, shall take the same action with respect to such persons. The Power concerned shall ensure that the Prisoners of War Information Bureau is provided with the necessary accommodation, equipment

National Bureaux

and staff to ensure its efficient working. It shall be at liberty to employ prisoners of war in such a Bureau under the conditions laid down in the Section of the present Convention dealing with work by prisoners of war.

Within the shortest possible period, each of the Parties to the conflict shall give its Bureau the information referred to in the fourth, fifth and sixth paragraphs of this Article regarding any enemy person belonging to one of the categories referred to in Article 4, who has fallen into its power. Neutral or non-belligerent Powers shall take the same action with regard to persons belonging to such categories whom they have received within their territory.

The Bureau shall immediately forward such information by the most rapid means to the Power concerned, through the intermediary of the Protecting Powers and likewise of the Central Agency provided for in Article 123.

This information shall make it possible quickly to advise the next of kin concerned. Subject to the provisions of Article 17, the information shall include, in so far as available to the Information Bureau, in respect of each prisoner of war, his surname, first names, rank, army, regimental, personal or serial number, place and full date of birth, indication of the Power on which he depends, first name of the father and maiden name of the mother, name and address of the person to be informed and the address to which correspondence for the prisoner may be sent.

The Information Bureau shall receive from the various departments concerned information regarding transfers, releases, repatriations, escapes, admissions to hospital, and deaths, and shall transmit such information in the manner described in the third paragraph above.

Likewise, information regarding the state of health of prisoners of war who are seriously ill or seriously wounded shall be supplied regularly, every week if possible.

The Information Bureau shall also be responsible for replying to all enquiries sent to it concerning prisoners of war, including those who have died in captivity; it will make any enquiries necessary to obtain the information which is asked for if this is not in its possession.

All written communications made by the Bureau shall be authenticated by a signature or a seal.

The Information Bureau shall furthermore be charged with collecting all personal valuables, including sums in currencies other than that of the Detaining Power and documents of importance to the next of kin, left by prisoners of war who have been repatriated or released, or who have escaped or died, and shall forward the said valuables to the Powers concerned. Such articles shall be sent by the Bureau in sealed packets which shall be accompanied by statements giving clear and full particulars of the identity of the person to whom the articles belonged, and by a complete list of the contents of the parcel. Other personal effects of such prisoners of war shall be transmitted under arrangements agreed upon between the Parties to the conflict concerned.

ARTICLE 123

A Central Prisoners of War Information Agency shall be created in a neutral country. The International Committee of the Red Cross shall, if it deems necessary, propose to the Powers concerned the organization of such an Agency.

Central Agency

The function of the Agency shall be to collect all the information it may obtain through official or private channels respecting prisoners of war, and to transmit it as rapidly as possible to the country of origin of the prisoners of war or to the Power on which they depend. It shall receive from the Parties to the conflict all facilities for effecting such transmissions.

The High Contracting Parties, and in particular those whose nationals benefit by the services of the Central Agency, are requested to give the said Agency the financial aid it may require.

The foregoing provisions shall in no way be interpreted as restricting the humanitarian activities of the International Committee of the Red Cross, or of the relief Societies provided for in Article 125.

ARTICLE 124

The national Information Bureaux and the Central Information Agency shall enjoy free postage for mail, likewise all the exemptions provided for in Article 74, and further, so far as possible, exemption from telegraphic charges or, at least, greatly reduced rates.

Exemption from charges

ARTICLE 125

Relief societies
and other
organizations

Subject to the measures which the Detaining Powers may consider essential to ensure their security or to meet any other reasonable need, the representatives of religious organizations, relief societies, or any other organization assisting prisoners of war, shall receive from the said Powers, for themselves and their duly accredited agents, all necessary facilities for visiting the prisoners, distributing relief supplies and material, from any source, intended for religious, educational or recreative purposes, and for assisting them in organizing their leisure time within the camps. Such societies or organizations may be constituted in the territory of the Detaining Power or in any other country, or they may have an international character.

The Detaining Power may limit the number of societies and organizations whose delegates are allowed to carry out their activities in its territory and under its supervision, on condition, however, that such limitation shall not hinder the effective operation of adequate relief to all prisoners of war.

The special position of the International Committee of the Red Cross in this field shall be recognized and respected at all times.

As soon as relief supplies or material intended for the above-mentioned purposes are handed over to prisoners of war, or very shortly afterwards, receipts for each consignment, signed by the prisoners' representative, shall be forwarded to the relief society or organization making the shipment. At the same time, receipts for these consignments shall be supplied by the administrative authorities responsible for guarding the prisoners.

PART VI
EXECUTION OF THE CONVENTION

SECTION 1
GENERAL PROVISIONS

ARTICLE 126

Supervision

Representatives or delegates of the Protecting Powers shall have permission to go to all places where prisoners of war may be, particularly to places of internment, imprisonment and labour, and shall have access to all premises occupied by prisoners of war; they shall also be allowed to go to the places of departure, passage and arrival of prisoners who are being transferred. They shall be able to interview the prisoners, and in particular the prisoners' representatives, without witnesses, either personally or through an interpreter.

Representatives and delegates of the Protecting Powers shall have full liberty to select the places they wish to visit. The duration and frequency of these visits shall not be restricted. Visits may not be prohibited except for reasons of imperative military necessity, and then only as an exceptional and temporary measure.

The Detaining Power and the Power on which the said prisoners of war depend may agree, if necessary, that compatriots of these prisoners of war be permitted to participate in the visits.

The delegates of the International Committee of the Red Cross shall enjoy the same prerogatives. The appointment of such delegates shall be submitted to the approval of the Power detaining the prisoners of war to be visited.

ARTICLE 127

The High Contracting Parties undertake, in time of peace as in time of war, to disseminate the text of the present Convention as widely as possible in their respective countries, and, in particular, to include the study thereof in their programmes of military and, if possible, civil instruction, so that the principles thereof may become known to all their armed forces and to the entire population.

Dissemination of the Convention

Any military or other authorities, who in time of war assume responsibilities in respect of prisoners of war, must possess the text of the Convention and be specially instructed as to its provisions.

ARTICLE 128

The High Contracting Parties shall communicate to one another through the Swiss Federal Council and, during hostilities, through the Protecting Powers, the official translations of the present Convention, as well as the laws and regulations which they may adopt to ensure the application thereof.

Translation Rules of application

DLI-K*

ARTICLE 129

Penal sanctions   The High Contracting Parties undertake to enact any legis-
I. General   lation necessary to provide effective penal sanctions for
observations   persons committing, or ordering to be committed, any of
the grave breaches of the present Convention defined in the
following Article.

Each High Contracting Party shall be under the
obligation to search for persons alleged to have committed,
or to have ordered to be committed, such grave breaches,
and shall bring such persons, regardless of their nationality,
before its own courts. It may also, if it prefers, and in
accordance with the provisions of its own legislation, hand
such persons over for trial to another High Contracting
Party concerned, provided such High Contracting Party has
made out a *prima facie* case.

Each High Contracting Party shall take measures
necessary for the suppression of all acts contrary to the
provisions of the present Convention other than the grave
breaches defined in the following Article.

In all circumstances, the accused persons shall benefit by
safeguards of proper trial and defence, which shall not be
less favourable than those provided by Article 105 and those
following of the present Convention.

ARTICLE 130

II.   Grave breaches to which the preceding Article relates shall
Grave breaches   be those involving any of the following acts, if committed
against persons or property protected by the Convention:
wilful killing, torture or inhuman treatment, including
biological experiments, wilfully causing great suffering or
serious injury to body or health, compelling a prisoner of
war to serve in the forces of the hostile Power, or wilfully
depriving a prisoner of war of the rights of fair and regular
trial prescribed in this Convention.

ARTICLE 131

III. Responsibil-   No High Contracting Party shall be allowed to absolve itself
ities of the   or any other High Contracting Party of any liability incurred
Contracting   by itself or by another High Contracting Party in respect
Parties   of breaches referred to in the preceding Article.

ARTICLE 132

At the request of a Party to the conflict, an enquiry shall be instituted, in a manner to be decided between the interested Parties, concerning any alleged violation of the Convention.

If agreement has not been reached concerning the procedure for an enquiry, the Parties should agree on the choice of an umpire who will decide upon the procedure to be followed.

Once the violation has been established, the Parties to the conflict shall put an end to it and shall repress it with the least possible delay.

Enquiry
procedure

**Geneva Convention
Relative to the
Protection of Civilian
Persons in Time of War
of August 12, 1949.**

VI

PART I

GENERAL PROVISIONS

ARTICLE 1

Respect for the
Convention

The High Contracting Parties undertake to respect and to ensure respect for the present Convention in all circumstances.

ARTICLE 2

Application of
the Convention

In addition to the provisions which shall be implemented in peacetime, the present Convention shall apply to all cases of declared war or of any other armed conflict which may arise between two or more of the High Contracting Parties, even if the state of war is not recognized by one of them.

The Convention shall also apply to all cases of partial or total occupation of the territory of a High Contracting Party, even if the said occupation meets with no armed resistance.

Although one of the powers in conflict may not be a party to the present Convention, the Powers who are parties thereto shall remain bound by it in their mutual relations. They shall furthermore be bound by the Convention in relation to the said Power, if the latter accepts and applies the provisions thereof.

ARTICLE 3

Conflicts not of
an, international
character

In the case of armed conflict not of an international character occurring in the territory of one of the High Contracting Parties, each Party to the conflict shall be bound to apply, as a minimum, the following provisions:

(1)   Persons taking no active part in the hostilities, including members of armed forces who have laid down their arms and those placed *hors de combat* by sickness, wounds, detention, or any other cause, shall in all circumstances be treated humanely, without any adverse distinction founded on race, colour, religion or faith, sex, birth or wealth, or any other similar criteria.

   To this end, the following acts are and shall remain prohibited at any time and in any place whatsoever with respect to the above-mentioned persons:

   (*a*)   violence to life and person, in particular murder of all kinds, mutilation, cruel treatment and torture;

   (*b*)   taking of hostages;

   (*c*)   outrages upon personal dignity, in particular humiliating and degrading treatment;

   (*d*)   the passing of sentences and the carrying out of executions without previous judgment pronounced by a regularly constituted court, affording all the judicial guarantees which are recognized as indispensable by civilized peoples.

(2)   The wounded and sick shall be collected and cared for.

An impartial humanitarian body, such as the International Committee of the Red Cross, may offer its services to the Parties to the conflict.

The Parties to the conflict should further endeavour to bring into force, by means of special agreements, all or part of the other provisions of the present Convention.

The application of the preceding provisions shall not affect the legal status of the Parties to the conflict.

ARTICLE 4

Persons protected by the Convention are those who, at a given moment and in any manner whatsoever, find themselves, in case of a conflict of occupation, in the hands of a Party to the conflict or Occupying Power of which they are not nationals.

Definition of protected persons

Nationals of a State which is not bound by the Convention are not protected by it. Nationals of a neutral State who find themselves in the territory of a belligerent State, and nationals of a co-belligerent State, shall not be regarded as protected persons while the State of which they are nationals has normal diplomatic representation in the State in whose hands they are.

The provisions of Part II are, however, wider in application, as defined in Article 13.

Persons protected by the Geneva Convention for the Amelioration of the Condition of the Wonded and Sick in Armed Forces in the Field of August 12, 1949, or by the Geneva Convention for the Amelioration of the Condition of Wounded, Sick and Shipwrecked Members of Armed Forces at Sea of August 12, 1949, or by the Geneva Convention relative to the Treatment of Prisoners of War of August 12, 1949, shall not be considered as protected persons within the meaning of the present Convention.

ARTICLE 5

Derogations   Where, in the territory of a Party to the conflict, the latter is satisfied that an individual protected person is definitely suspected of or engaged in activities hostile to the security of the State, such individual person shall not be entitled to claim such rights and privileges under the present Convention as would, if exercised in the favour of such individual person, be prejudicial to the security of such State.

Where in occupied territory an individual protected person is detained as a spy or saboteur, or as a person under definite suspicion of activity hostile to the security of the Occupying Power, such person shall, in those cases where absolute military security so requires, be regarded as having forfeited rights of communication under the present Convention.

In each case, such persons shall nevertheless be treated with humanity, and in case of trial, shall not be deprived of the rights of fair and regular trial prescribed by the present Convention. They shall also be granted the full rights and privileges of a protected person under the present Convention at the earliest date consistent with the security of the State or occupying Power, as the case may be.

ARTICLE 6

The present Convention shall apply from the outset of any conflict or occupation mentioned in Article 2.

In the territory of Parties to the conflict, the application of the present Convention shall cease on the general close of military operations.

In the case of occupied territory, the application of the present Convention shall cease one year after the general close of military operations; however, the Occupying Power shall be bound, for the duration of the occupation, to the extent that such Power exercises the functions of government in such territory, by the provisions of the following Articles of the present Convention: 1 to 12, 27, 29 to 34, 47, 49, 51, 52, 53, 59, 61 to 77, 143.

Protected persons whose release, repatriation or re-establishment may take place after such dates shall meanwhile continue to benefit by the present Convention.

Beginning
and end of
application

ARTICLE 7

In additon to the agreements expressly provided for in Articles 11, 14, 15, 17, 36, 108, 109, 132, 133 and 149, the High Contracting Parties may conclude other special agreements for all matters concerning which they may deem it suitable to make separate provision. No special agreement shall adversely affect the situation of protected persons, as defined by the present Convention, nor restrict the rights which it confers upon them.

Protected persons shall continue to have the benefit of such agreements as long as the Convention is applicable to them, except where express provisions to the contrary are contained in the aforesaid or in subsequent agreements, or where more favourable measures have been taken with regard to them by one or other of the Parties to the conflict.

Special
agreements

ARTICLE 8

Protected persons may in no circumstances renounce in part or in entirety the rights secured to them by the present Convention, and by the special agreements referred to in the foregoing Article, if such there be.

Non-renunciation
of rights

ARTICLE 9

Protecting
Powers

The present Convention shall be applied with the cooperation and under the scrutiny of the Protecting Powers whose
duty it is to safeguard the interests of the Parties to the
conflict. For this purpose, the Protecting Powers may
appoint, apart from their diplomatic or consular staff, delegates from amongst their own nationals or the nationals of
other neutral Powers. The said delegates shall be subject to
the approval of the Power with which they are to carry out
their duties.

The Parties to the conflict shall facilitate to the greatest
extent possible the task of the representatives or delegates
of the Protecting Powers.

The representatives or delegates of the Protecting Powers
shall not in any case exceed their mission under the present
Convention. They shall, in particular, take account of the
imperative necessities of security of the State wherein they
carry out their duties.

ARTICLE 10

Activities of the
International
Committee of
the Red Cross

The provisions of the present Convention constitute no
obstacle to the humanitarian activities which the International Committee of the Red Cross or any other impartial
humanitarian organization may, subject to the consent of
the Parties to the conflict concerned, undertake for the
protection of civilian persons and for their relief.

ARTICLE 11

Substitutes for
Protecting
Powers

The High Contracting Parties may at any time agree to
entrust to an organization which offers all guarantees of
impartiality and efficacy the duties incumbent on the
Protecting Powers by virtue of the present Convention.

When persons protected by the present Convention do
not benefit or cease to benefit, no matter for what reason,
by the activities of a Protecting Power or of an organization
provided for in the first paragraph above, the Detaining
Power shall request a neutral State, or such an organization,
to undertake the functions performed under the present
Convention by a Protecting Power designated by the Parties
to a conflict.

If protection cannot be arranged accordingly, the Detaining

Power shall request or shall accept, subject to the provisions of this Article, the offer of the services of a humanitarian organization, such as the International Committee of the Red Cross, to assume the humanitarian functions performed by Protecting Powers under the present Convention.

Any neutral Power, or any organization invited by the Power concerned or offering itself for these purposes, shall be required to act with a sense of responsibility towards the Party to the conflict on which persons protected by the present Convention depend, and shall be required to furnish sufficient assurances that it is in a position to undertake the appropriate functions and to discharge them impartially.

No derogation from the preceding provisions shall be made by special agreements between Powers one of which is restricted, even temporarily, in its freedom to negotiate with the other Power or its allies by reason of military events, more particularly where the whole, or a substantial part, of the territory of the said Power is occupied.

Whenever in the present Convention mention is made of a Protecting Power, such mention applies to substitute organizations in the sense of the present Article.

The provisions of this Article shall extend and be adapted to cases of nationals of a neutral State who are in occupied territory or who find themselves in the territory of a belligerent State in which the State of which they are nationals has not normal diplomatic representation.

ARTICLE 12

In cases where they deem it advisable in the interest of protected persons, particularly in cases of disagreement between the Parties to the conflict as to the application or interpretation of the provisions of the present Convention, the Protecting Powers shall lend their good offices with a view to settling the disagreement. *(Conciliation procedure)*

For this purpose, each of the Protecting Powers may, either at the invitation of one Party or on its own initiative, propose to the Parties to the conflict a meeting of their representatives, and in particular of the authorities responsible for protected persons, possibly on neutral territory suitably chosen. The Parties to the conflict shall be bound to give effect to the proposals made to them for this purpose.

The Protecting Powers may, if necessary, propose for approval by the Parties to the conflict, a person belonging to a neutral Power or delegated by the International Committee of the Red Cross, who shall be invited to take part in such a meeting.

PART II

GENERAL PROTECTION OF POPULATIONS AGAINST CERTAIN CONSEQUENCES OF WAR

ARTICLE 13

Field of
application of
Part II

The provisions of Part II cover the whole of the populations of the countries in conflict, without any adverse distinction based, in particular, on race, nationality, religion or political opinion, and are intended to alleviate the sufferings caused by war.

ARTICLE 14

Hospital and
safety zones
and localities

In time of peace, the High Contracting Parties and, after the outbreak of hostilities, the Parties thereto, may establish in their own territory and, if the need arises, in occupied areas, hospital and safety zones and localities so organized as to protect from the effects of war, wounded, sick and aged persons, children under fifteen, expectant mothers and mothers of children under seven.

Upon the outbreak and during the course of hostilities, the Parties concerned may conclude agreements on mutual recognition of the zones and localities they have created. They may for this purpose implement the provisions of the Draft Agreement annexed to the present Convention, with such amendments as they may consider necessary.

The Protecting Powers and the International Committee of the Red Cross are invited to lend their good offices in order to facilitate the institution and recognition of these hospital and safety zones and localities.

ARTICLE 15

Neutralized
zones

Any Party to the conflict may, either direct or through a neutral State or some humanitarian organization, propose to the adverse Party to establish, in the regions where fighting is taking place, neutralized zones intended to shelter from the effects of war the following persons, without distinction:

(*a*) wounded and sick combatants or non-combatants;

(*b*) civilian persons who take no part in hostilities, and who, while they reside in the zones, perform no work of a military character.

When the Parties concerned have agreed upon the geographical position, adminstration, food supply and supervision of the proposed neutralized zone, a written agreement shall be concluded and signed by the representatives of the Parties to the conflict. The agreement shall fix the beginning and the duration of the neutralization of the zone.

ARTICLE 16

The wounded and sick, as well as the infirm, and expectant mothers, shall be the object of particular protection and respect.

As far as military considerations allow, each Party to the conflict shall facilitate the steps taken to search for the killed and wounded, to assist the shipwrecked and other persons exposed to grave danger, and to protect them against pillage and ill-treatment.

Wounded and sick
I.
General protection

ARTICLE 17

The Parties to the conflict shall endeavour to conclude local agreements for the removal from besieged or encircled areas, of wounded, sick, infirm, and aged persons, children and maternity cases, and for the passage of ministers of all religions, medical personnel and medical equipment on their way to such areas.

II.
Evacuation

ARTICLE 18

Civilian hospitals organized to give care to the wounded and sick, the infirm and maternity cases, may in no circumstances be the object of attack, but shall at all times be respected and protected by the Parties to the conflict.

States which are Parties to a conflict shall provide all civilian hospitals with certificates showing that they are civilian hospitals and that the buildings which they occupy

III.
Protection of hospitals

are not used for any purpose which would deprive these hospitals of protection in accordance with Article 19.

Civilian hospitals shall be marked by means of the emblem provided for in Article 38 of the Geneva Convention for the Amelioration of the Condition of the Wounded and Sick in Armed Forces in the Field of August 12, 1949, but only if so authorized by the State.

The Parties to the conflict shall, in so far as military considerations permit, take the necessary steps to make the distinctive emblems indicating civilian hospitals clearly visible to the enemy land, air and naval forces in order to obviate the possibility of any hostile action.

In view of the dangers to which hospitals may be exposed by being close to military objectives, it is recommended that such hospitals be situated as far as possible from such objectives.

ARTICLE 19

IV.
Discontinuance
of protection
of hospitals

The protection to which civilian hospitals are entitled shall not cease unless they are used to commit, outside their humanitarian duties, acts harmful to the enemy. Protection may, however, cease only after due warning has been given, naming, in all appropriate cases, a reasonable time limit, and after such warning has remained unheeded.

The fact that sick or wounded members of the armed forces are nursed in these hospitals, or the presence of small arms and ammunition taken from such combatants which have not yet been handed to the proper service, shall not be considered to be acts harmful to the enemy.

ARTICLE 20

V.
Hospital staff

Persons regularly and solely engaged in the operation and administration of civilian hospitals, including the personnel engaged in the search for, removal and transporting of and caring for wounded and sick civilians, the infirm and maternity cases, shall be respected and protected.

In occupied territory and in zones of military operations, the above personnel shall be recognizable by means of an identity card certifying their status, bearing the photograph of the holder and embossed with the stamp of the responsible authority, and also by means of a stamped, water-resistant armlet which they shall wear on the left arm while carrying out their duties. This armlet shall be issued by the State and shall bear the emblem provided for in Article 38 of the Geneva Convention for the Amelioration of the Condition of the Wounded and Sick in Armed Forces in the Field of August 12, 1949.

Other personnel who are engaged in the operation and administration of civilian hospitals shall be entitled to respect and protection and to wear the armlet, as provided in and under the conditions prescribed in this Article, while they are employed on such duties. The identity card shall state the duties on which they are employed.

The management of each hospital shall at all times hold at the disposal of the competent national or occupying authorities an up-to-date list of such personnel.

ARTICLE 21

Convoys of vehicles or hospital trains on land or specially provided vessels on sea, conveying wounded and sick civilians, the infirm and maternity cases, shall be respected and protected in the same manner as the hospitals provided for in Article 18, and shall be marked, with the consent of the State, by the display of the distinctive emblem provided for in Article 38 of the Geneva Convention for the Amelioration of the Conditon of the Wounded and Sick in Armed Forces in the Field of August 12, 1949.

VI.
Land and sea transport

ARTICLE 22

Aircraft exclusively employed for the removal of wounded and sick civilians, the infirm and maternity cases, or for the transport of medical personnel and equipment, shall not be attacked, but shall be respected while flying at heights, times and on routes specifically agreed upon between all the Parties to the conflict concerned.

VII.
Air transport

They may be marked with the distinctive emblem provided for in Article 38 of the Geneva Convention for the Amelioration of the Condition of the Wounded and Sick in Armed Forces in the Field of August 12, 1949.

Unless agreed otherwise, flights over enemy or enemy-occupied territory are prohibited.

Such aircraft shall obey every summons to land. In the event of a landing thus imposed, the aircraft with its occupants may continue its flight after examination, if any.

ARTICLE 23

Consignment of
medical supplies,
food and clothing

Each High Contracting Party shall allow the free passage of all consignments of medical and hospital stores and objects necessary for religious worship intended only for civilians of another High Contracting Party, even if the latter is its adversary. It shall likewise permit the free passage of all consignments of essential foodstuffs, clothing and tonics intended for children under fifteen, expectant mothers and maternity cases.

The obligation of a High Contracting Party to allow the free passage of the consignments indicated in the preceding paragraph is subject to the condition that this Party is satisfied that there are no serious reasons for fearing:

(*a*)   that the consignments may be diverted from their destination,

(*b*)   that the control may not be effective, or

(*c*)   that a definite advantage may accrue to the military efforts or economy of the enemy through the substitution of the above-mentioned consignments for goods which would otherwise be provided or produced by the enemy or through the release of such material, services or facilities as would otherwise be required for the production of such goods.

The Power which allows the passage of the consignments indicated in the first paragraph of this Article may make such permission conditional on the distribution to the persons benefited thereby being made under the local supervision of the Protecting Powers.

Such consignments shall be forwarded as rapidly as possible, and the Power which permits their free passage shall have the right to prescribe the technical arrangements under which such passage is allowed.

ARTICLE 24

Measures
relating to
child welfare

The Parties to the conflict shall take the necessary measures to ensure that children under fifteen, who are orphaned or are separated from their families as a result of the war, are not left to their own resources, and that their maintenance, the exercise of their religion and their education are facilitated in all circumstances. Their education shall, as far as possible, be entrusted to persons of a similar cultural tradition.

The Parties to the conflict shall facilitate the reception of such children in a neutral country for the duration of the conflict with the consent of the Protecting Power, if any, and under due safeguards for the observance of the principles stated in the first paragraph.

They shall, furthermore, endeavour to arrange for all children under twelve to be identified by the wearing of identity discs, or by some other means.

ARTICLE 25

All persons in the territory of a Party to the conflict, or in a territory occupied by it, shall be enabled to give news of a strictly personal nature to members of their families, wherever they may be, and to receive news from them. This correspondence shall be forwarded speedily and without undue delay.

Family news

If, as a result of circumstances, it becomes difficult or impossible to exchange family correspondence by the ordinary post, the Parties to the conflict concerned shall apply to a neutral intermediary, such as the Central Agency provided for in Article 140, and shall decide in consultation with it how to ensure the fulfilment of their obligations under the best possible conditions, in particular with the cooperation of the National Red Cross (Red Crescent, Red Lion and Sun) Societies.

If the Parties to the conflict deem it necessary to restrict family correspondence, such restrictions shall be confined to the compulsory use of standard forms containing twenty-five freely chosen words, and to the limitation of the number of these forms despatched to one each month.

ARTICLE 26

Each Party to the conflict shall facilitate enquiries made by members of families dispersed owing to the war, with the object of renewing contact with one another and of meeting, if possible. It shall encourage, in particular, the work of organizations engaged on this task provided they are acceptable to it and conform to its security regulations.

Dispersed families

PART III

STATUS AND TREATMENT OF PROTECTED PERSONS

SECTION I

PROVISIONS COMMON TO THE TERRITORIES OF THE PARTIES TO THE CONFLICT AND TO OCCUPIED TERRITORIES

ARTICLE 27

Treatment

I.

General observations

Protected persons are entitled, in all circumstances, to respect for their persons, their honour, their family rights, their religious convictions and practices, and their manners and customs. They shall at all times be humanely treated, and shall be protected especially against all acts of violence or threats thereof and against insults and public curiosity.

Women shall be especially protected against any attack on their honour, in particular against rape, enforced prostitution, or any form of indecent assault.

Without prejudice to the provisions relating to their state of health, age and sex, all protected persons shall be treated with the same consideration by the Party to the conflict in whose power they are, without any adverse distinction based, in particular, on race, religion or political opinion.

However, the Parties to the conflict may take such measures of control and security in regard to protected persons as may be necessary as a result of the war.

ARTICLE 28

II.

Danger zones

The presence of a protected person may not be used to render certain points or areas immune from military operations.

ARTICLE 29

III.

Responsibilities

The Party to the conflict in whose hands protected persons may be, is responsible for the treatment accorded to them by its agents, irrespective of any individual responsibility which may be incurred.

ARTICLE 30

Protected persons shall have every facility for making application to the Protecting Powers, the International Committee of the Red Cross, the National Red Cross (Red Crescent, Red Lion and Sun) Society of the country where they may be, as well as to any organization that might assist them.

These several organizations shall be granted all facilities for that purpose by the authorities, within the bounds set by military or security considerations.

Apart from the visits of the delegates of the Protecting Powers and of the International Committee of the Red Cross, provided for by Article 143, the Detaining or Occupying Powers shall facilitate as much as possible visits to protected persons by the representatives of other organizations whose object is to give spiritual aid or material relief to such persons.

Application to Protecting Powers and relief organizations

ARTICLE 31

No physical or moral coercion shall be exercised against protected persons, in particular to obtain information from them or from third parties.

Prohibition of coercion

ARTICLE 32

The High Contracting Parties specifically agree that each of them is prohibited from taking any measure of such a character as to cause the physical suffering or extermination of protected persons in their hands. This prohibition applies not only to murder, torture, corporal punishment, mutilation and medical or scientific experiments not necessitated by the medical treatment of a protected person, but also to any other measures of brutality whether applied by civilian or military agents.

Prohibition of corporal punishment, torture, etc.

ARTICLE 33

No protected person may be punished for an offence he or she has not personally committed. Collective penalties and likewise all measures of intimidation or of terrorism are prohibited.

Pillage is prohibited.

Reprisals against protected persons and their property are prohibited.

Individual responsibility, collective penalties, pillage, reprisals

ARTICLE 34

Hostages   The taking of hostages is prohibited.

SECTION II

ALIENS IN THE TERRITORY
OF A PARTY TO THE CONFLICT

ARTICLE 35

Right to leave   All protected persons who may desire to leave the territory
the territory   at the outset of, or during a conflict, shall be entitled to do
so, unless their departure is contrary to the national
interests of the State. The applications of such persons to
leave shall be decided in accordance with regularly established procedures and the decision shall be taken as rapidly
as possible. Those persons permitted to leave may provide
themselves with the necessary funds for their journey and
take with them a reasonable amount of their effects and
articles of personal use.

If any such person is refused permission to leave the territory, he shall be entitled to have such refusal reconsidered
as soon as possible by an appropriate court or administrative
board designated by the Detaining Power for that purpose.

Upon request, representatives of the Protecting Power
shall, unless reasons of security prevent it, or the persons
concerned object, be furnished with the reasons for refusal
of any requests for permission to leave the territory and be
given, as expeditiously as possible, the names of all persons
who have been denied permission to leave.

ARTICLE 36

Method of   Departures permitted under the foregoing Article shall
repatriation   be carried out in satisfactory conditions as regards safety,
hygiene, sanitation and food. All costs in connection therewith, from the point of exit in the territory of the Detaining
Power, shall be borne by the country of destination, or, in
the case of accommodation in a neutral country, by the
Power whose nationals are benefited. The practical details
of such movements may, if necessary, be settled by special
agreements between the Powers concerned.

The foregoing shall not prejudice such special agreements as may be concluded between Parties to the conflict concerning the exchange and repatriation of their nationals in enemy hands.

ARTICLE 37

Protected persons who are confined pending proceedings or serving a sentence involving loss of liberty, shall during their confinement be humanely treated.

As soon as they are released, they may ask to leave the territory in conformity with the foregoing Articles.

Persons in confinement

ARTICLE 38

With the exception of special measures authorized by the present Convention, in particular by Articles 27 and 41 thereof, the situation of protected persons shall continue to be regulated, in principle, by the provisions concerning aliens in time of peace. In any case, the following rights shall be granted to them:

Non-repatriated persons
I.
General observations

(1) They shall be enabled to receive the individual or collective relief that may be sent to them.

(2) They shall, if their state of health so requires, receive medical attention and hospital treatment to the same extent as the nationals of the State concerned.

(3) They shall be allowed to practise their religion and to receive spiritual assistance from ministers of their faith.

(4) If they reside in an area particularly exposed to the dangers of war, they shall be authorized to move from that area to the same extent as the nationals of the State concerned.

(5) Children under fifteen years, pregnant women and mothers of children under seven years shall benefit by any preferential treatment to the same extent as the nationals of the State concerned.

ARTICLE 39

II.

Means of

existence

Protected persons who, as a result of the war, have lost their gainful employment, shall be granted the opportunity to find paid employment. That opportunity shall, subject to security considerations and to the provisions of Article 40, be equal to that enjoyed by the nationals of the Power in whose territory they are.

Where a Party to the conflict applies to a protected person methods of control which result in his being unable to support himself, and especially if such a person is prevented for reasons of security from finding paid employment on reasonable conditions, the said Party shall ensure his support and that of his dependents.

Protected persons may in any case receive allowances from their home country, the Protecting Power, or the relief societies referred to in Article 30.

ARTICLE 40

III.

Employment

Protected persons may be compelled to work only to the same extent as nationals of the Party to the conflict in whose territory they are.

If protected persons are of enemy nationality, they may only be compelled to do work which is normally necessary to ensure the feeding, sheltering, clothing, transport and health of human beings and which is not directly related to the conduct of military operations.

In the cases mentioned in the two preceding paragraphs, protected persons compelled to work shall have the benefit of the same working conditions and of the same safeguards as national workers, in particular as regards wages, hours of labour, clothing and equipment, previous training and compensation for occupational accidents and diseases.

If the above provisions are infringed, protected persons shall be allowed to exercise their right of complaint in accordance with Article 30.

ARTICLE 41

IV.

Assigned

residence.

Internment

Should the Power in whose hands protected persons may be consider the measures of control mentioned in the present Convention to be inadequate, it may not have recourse to any other measure of control more severe than that of assigned residence or internment, in accordance with the provisions of Articles 42 and 43.

In applying the provisions of Article 39, second paragraph, to the cases of persons required to leave their usual places of residence by virtue of a decision placing them in assigned residence elsewhere, the Detaining Power shall be guided as closely as possible by the standards of welfare set forth in Part III, Section IV of this Convention.

ARTICLE 42

The internment or placing in assigned residence of protected persons may be ordered only if the security of the Detaining Power makes it absolutely necessary.

If any person, acting through the representatives of the Protecting Power, voluntarily demands internment, and if his situation renders this step necessary, he shall be interned by the Power in whose hands he may be.

V.
Grounds for internment or assigned residence. Voluntary internment.

ARTICLE 43

Any protected person who has been interned or placed in assigned residence shall be entitled to have such action reconsidered as soon as possible by an appropriate court or administrative board designated by the Detaining Power for that purpose. If the internment or placing in assigned residence is maintained, the court or administrative board shall periodically, and at least twice yearly, give consideration to his or her case, with a view to the favourable amendment of the initial decision, if circumstances permit.

Unless the protected persons concerned object, the Detaining Power shall, as rapidly as possible, give the Protecting Power the names of any protected persons who have been interned or subjected to assigned residence, or who have been released from internment or assigned residence. The decisions of the courts or boards mentioned in the first paragraph of the present Article shall also, subject to the same conditions, be notified as rapidly as possible to the Protecting Power.

VI.
Procedure

ARTICLE 44

In applying the measures of control mentioned in the present Convention, the Detaining Power shall not treat as

VII.
Refugees

enemy aliens exclusively on the basis of their nationality *de jure* of an enemy State, refugees who do not, in fact, enjoy the protection of any government.

ARTICLE 45

VIII.
Transfer to
another Power

Protected persons shall not be transferred to a Power which is not a party to the Convention.

This provision shall in no way constitute an obstacle to the repatriation of protected persons, or to their return to their country of residence after the cessation of hostilities.

Protected persons may be transferred by the Detaining Power only to a Power which is a party to the present Convention and after the Detaining Power has satisfied itself of the willingness and ability of such transferee Power to apply the present Convention. If protected persons are transferred under such circumstances, responsibility for the application of the present Convention rests on the Power accepting them, while they are in its custody. Nevertheless, if that Power fails to carry out the provisions of the present Convention in any important respect, the Power by which the protected persons were transferred shall, upon being so notified by the Protecting Power, take effective measures to correct the situation or shall request the return of the protected persons. Such request must be complied with.

In no circumstances shall a protected person be transferred to a country where he or she may have reason to fear persecution for his or her political opinions or religous beliefs.

The provisions of this Article do not constitute an obstacle to the extradition, in pursuance of extradition treaties concluded before the outbreak of hostilities, of protected persons accused of offences against ordinary criminal law.

ARTICLE 46

Cancellation
restrictive
measures

In so far as they have not been previously withdrawn, restrictive measures taken regarding protected persons shall be cancelled as soon as possible after the close of hostilities.

Restrictive measures affecting their property shall be cancelled, in accordance with the law of the Detaining Power, as soon as possible after the close of hostilities.

SECTION III

OCCUPIED TERRITORIES

ARTICLE 47

Protected persons who are in occupied territory shall not be deprived, in any case or in any manner whatsoever, of the benefits of the present Convention by any change introduced, as the result of the occupation of a territory, into the institutions or government of the said territory, nor by any agreement concluded between the authorities of the occupied territories and the Occupying Power, nor by any annexation by the latter of the whole or part of the occupied territory.

Inviolability of rights

ARTICLE 48

Protected persons who are not nationals of the Power whose territory is occupied, may avail themselves of the right to leave the territory subject to the provisions of Article 35, and decisions thereon shall be taken according to the procedure which the Occupying Power shall establish in accordance with the said Article.

Special cases of repatriation

ARTICLE 49

Individual or mass forcible transfers, as well as deportations of protected persons from occupied territory to the territory of the Occupying Power or to that of any other country, occupied or not, are prohibited, regardless of their motive.

Deportations, transfers, evacuations

Nevertheless, the Occupying Power may undertake total or partial evacuation of a given area if the security of the population or imperative military reasons so demand. Such evacuations may not involve the displacement of protected persons outside the bounds of the occupied territory except when for material reasons it is impossible to avoid such displacement. Persons thus evacuated shall be transferred back to their homes as soon as hostilities in the area in question have ceased.

The Occupying Power undertaking such transfers or evacuations shall ensure, to the greatest practicable extent, that proper accommodation is provided to receive the protected persons, that the removals are effected in satisfactory conditions of hygiene, health, safety and nutrition, and that members of the same family are not separated.

The Protecting Power shall be informed of any transfers and evacuations as soon as they have taken place.

The Occupying Power shall not detain protected persons in an area particularly exposed to the dangers of war unless the security of the population or imperative military reasons so demand.

The Occupying Power shall not deport or transfer parts of its own civilian population into the territory it occupies.

ARTICLE 50

Children

The Occupying Power shall, with the cooperation of the national and local authorities, facilitate the proper working of all institutions devoted to the care and education of children.

The Occupying Power shall take all necessary steps to facilitate the identification of children and the registration of their parentage. It may not, in any case, change their personal status, nor enlist them in formations or organizations subordinate to it.

Should the local institutions be inadequate for the purpose, the Occupying Power shall make arrangements for the maintenance and education, if possible by persons of their own nationality, language and religion, of children who are orphaned or separated from their parents as a result of the war and who cannot be adequately cared for by a near relative or friend.

A special section of the Bureau set up in accordance with Article 136 shall be responsible for taking all necessary steps to identify children whose identity is in doubt. Particulars of their parents or other near relatives should always be recorded if available.

The Occupying Power shall not hinder the application of any preferential measures in regard to food, medical care and protection against the effects of war, which may have been adopted prior to the occupation in favour of children under fifteen years, expectant mothers, and mothers of children under seven years.

ARTICLE 51

The Occupying Power may not compel protected persons to serve in its armed or auxiliary forces. No pressure or propaganda which aims at securing voluntary enlistment is permitted.

Enlistment.
Labour

The Occupying Power may not compel protected persons to work unless they are over eighteen years of age, and then only on work which is necessary either for the needs of the army of occupation, or for the public utility services, or for the feeding, sheltering, clothing, transportation or health of the population of the occupied country. Protected persons may not be compelled to undertake any work which would involve them in the obligation of taking part in military operations. The Occupying Power may not compel protected persons to employ forcible means to ensure the security of the installations where they are performing compulsory labour.

The work shall be carried out only in the occupied territory where the persons whose services have been requisitioned are. Every such person shall, so far as possible, be kept in his usual place of employment. Workers shall be paid a fair wage and the work shall be proportionate to their physical and intellectual capacities. The legislation in force in the occupied country concerning working conditions, and safeguards as regards, in particular, such matters as wages, hours of work, equipment, preliminary training and compensation for occupational accidents and diseases, shall be applicable to the protected persons assigned to the work referred to in this Article.

In no case shall requisition of labour lead to a mobilization of workers in an organization of a military or semi-military character.

ARTICLE 52

No contract, agreement or regulation shall impair the right of any worker, whether voluntary or not and wherever he may be, to apply to the representatives of the Protecting Power in order to request the said Power's intervention.

Protection of
workers

All measures aiming at creating unemployment or at restricting the opportunities offered to workers in an occupied territory, in order to induce them to work for the Occupying Power, are prohibited.

ARTICLE 53

Prohibited
destruction

Any destruction by the Occupying Power of real or personal property belonging individually or collectively to private persons, or to the State, or to other public authorities, or to social or cooperative organizations, is prohibited, except where such destruction is rendered absolutely necessary by military operations.

ARTICLE 54

Judges and
public officials

The Occupying Power may not alter the status of public officials or judges in the occupied territories, or in any way apply sanctions to or take any measures of coercion or discrimination against them, should they abstain from fulfilling their functions for reasons of conscience.

This prohibition does not prejudice the application of the second paragraph of Article 51. It does not affect the right of the Occupying Power to remove public officials from their posts.

ARTICLE 55

Food and medical
supplies for
the population

To the fullest extent of the means available to it, the Occupying Power has the duty of ensuring the food and medical supplies of the population; it should, in particular, bring in the necessary foodstuffs, medical stores and other articles if the resources of the occupied territory are inadequate.

The Occupying Power may not requisition foodstuffs, articles or medical supplies available in the occupied territory, except for use by the occupation forces and administration pesonnel, and then only if the requirements of the civilian population have been taken into account. Subject to the provisions of other international Conventions, the Occupying Power shall make arrangements to ensure that fair value is paid for any requisitioned goods.

The Protecting Power shall, at any time, be at liberty to verify the state of the food and medical supplies in occupied territories, except where temporary restrictions are made necessary by imperative military requirements.

ARTICLE 56

To the fullest extent of the means available to it, the Occupying Power has the duty of ensuring and maintaining, with the cooperation of national and local authorities, the medical and hospital establishments and services, public health and hygiene in the occupied territory, with particular reference to the adoption and application of the prophylactic and preventive measures necessary to combat the spread of contagious diseases and epidemics. Medical personnel of all categories shall be allowed to carry out their duties.

Hygiene and public health

If new hospitals are set up in occupied territory and if the competent organs of the occupied State are not operating there, the occupying authorities shall, if necessary, grant them the recognition provided for in Article 18. In similar circumstances, the occupying authorities shall also grant recognition to hospital personnel and transport vehicles under the provisions of Articles 20 and 21.

In adopting measures of health and hygiene and in their implementation, the Occupying Power shall take into consideration the moral and ethical susceptibilities of the population of the occupied territory.

ARTICLE 57

The Occupying Power may requisition civilian hospitals only temporarily and only in cases of urgent necessity for the care of military wounded and sick, and then on condition that suitable arrangements are made in due time for the care and treatment of the patients and for the needs of the civilian population for hospital accommodation.

Requisition of hospitals

The material and stores of civilian hospitals cannot be requisitioned so long as they are necessary for the needs of the civilian population.

ARTICLE 58

The Occupying Power shall permit ministers of religion to give spiritual assistance to the members of their religious communities.

Spiritual assistance

The Occupying Power shall also accept consignments of books and articles required for religious needs and shall facilitate their distribution in occupied territory.

ARTICLE 59

Relief
I.
Collective relief

If the whole or part of the population of an occupied territory is inadequately supplied, the Occupying Power shall
agree to relief schemes on behalf of the said poulation, and
shall facilitate them by all the means at its disposal.

Such schemes, which may be undertaken either by States
or by impartial humanitarian organizations such as the
International Committee of the Red Cross, shall consist, in
particular, of the provision of consignments of foodstuffs,
medical supplies and clothing.

All Contracting Parties shall permit the free passage of
these consignments and shall guarantee their protection.

A Power granting free passage to consignments on their
way to territory occupied by an adverse Party to the conflict
shall, however, have the right to search the consignments,
to regulate their passage according to prescribed times and
routes, and to be reasonably satisfied through the Protecting
Power that these consignments are to be used for the relief
of the needy population and are not to be used for the
benefit of the Occupying Power.

ARTICLE 60

II.
Responsibilities
of the Occupying
Power

Relief consignments shall in no way relieve the Occupying
Power of any of its responsibilities under Articles 55, 56 and
59. The Occupying Power shall in no way whatsoever divert
relief consignments from the purpose for which they are
intended, except in cases of urgent necessity, in the interests
of the population of the occupied territory and with the
consent of the Protecting Power.

ARTICLE 61

III.
Distribution

The Distribution of the relief consignments referred to in
the foregoing Articles shall be carried out with the
cooperation and under the supervision of the Protecting
Power. This duty may also be delegated, by agreement
between the Occupying Power and the Protecting Power, to
a neutral Power, to the International Committee of the Red
Cross or to any other impartial humanitarian body.

Such consignments shall be exempt in occupied territory
from all charges, taxes or customs duties unless these are
necessary in the interests of the economy of the territory.

The Occupying Power shall facilitate the rapid distribution of these consignments.

All Contracting Parties shall endeavour to permit the transit and transport, free of charge, of such relief consignments on their way to occupied territories.

ARTICLE 62

Subject to imperative reasons of security, protected persons in occupied territories shall be permitted to receive the individual relief consignments sent to them.

IV.
Individual relief

ARTICLE 63

Subject to temporary and exceptional measures imposed for urgent reasons of security by the Occupying Power:

National Red Cross and other relief societies

(*a*)   recognized National Red Cross (Red Crescent, Red Lion and Sun) Societies shall be able to pursue their activities in accordance with Red Cross principles, as defined by the International Red Cross Conferences. Other relief societies shall be permitted to continue their humanitarian activities under similar conditions;

(*b*)   the Occupying Power may not require any changes in the personnel or structure of these societies, which would prejudice the aforesaid activities.

The same principles shall apply to the activities and personnel of special organizations of a non-military character, which already exist or which may be established, for the purpose of ensuring the living conditions of the civilian population by the maintenance of the essential public utility services, by the distribution of relief and by the organization of rescues.

ARTICLE 64

The penal laws of the occupied territory shall remain in force, with the exception that they may be repealed or suspended by the Occupying Power in cases where they constitute a threat to its security or an obstacle to the application of the present Convention. Subject to the latter consideration and to the necessity for ensuring the effective administration of justice, the tribunals of the occupied

Penal legislation.
I.
General observations

territory shall continue to function in respect of all offences covered by the said laws.

The Occupying Power may, however, subject the population of the occupied territory to provisions which are essential to enable the Occupying Power to fulfil its obligations under the present Convention, to maintain the orderly government of the territory, and to ensure the security of the Occupying Power, of the members and property of the occupying forces or administration, and likewise of the establishments and lines of communication used by them.

ARTICLE 65

II.
Publication

The penal provisions enacted by the Occupying Power shall not come into force before they have been published and brought to the knowledge of the inhabitants in their own language. The effect of these penal provisions shall not be retroactive.

ARTICLE 66

III.
Competent courts

In case of a breach of the penal provisions promulgated by it by virtue of the second paragraph of Article 64, the Occupying Power may hand over the accused to its properly constituted, non-political military courts, on condition that the said courts sit in the occupied country. Courts of appeal shall preferably sit in the occupied country.

ARTICLE 67

IV.
Applicable
provisions

The Courts shall apply only those provisions of law which were applicable prior to the offence, and which are in accordance with general principles of law, in particular the principle that the penalty shall be proportioned to the offence. They shall take into consideration the fact that the accused is not a national of the Occupying Power.

ARTICLE 68

V.
Penalties.
Death penalty

Protected persons who commit an offence which is solely intended to harm the Occupying Power, but which does not constitute an attempt on the life or limb of members of the occupying forces or administration, nor a grave collective danger, nor seriously damage the property of the occupying forces or administration or the installations used by them, shall be liable to internment or simple imprisonment, provided the duration of such internment or imprisonment, is proportionate to the offence committed. Furthermore, internment or imprisonment shall, for such offences, be the only measure adopted for depriving protected persons of liberty. The courts provided for under Article 66 of the present Convention may at their discretion convert a sentence of imprisonment to one of internment for the same period.

The penal provisions promulgated by the Occupying Power in accordance with Articles 64 and 65 may impose the death penalty on a protected person only in cases where the person is guilty of espionage, of serious acts of sabotage against the military installations of the Occupying Power or of intentional offences which have caused the death of one or more persons, provided that such offences were punishable by death under the law of the occupied territory in force before the occupation began.

The death penalty may not be pronounced against a protected person unless the attention of the court has been particularly called to the fact that since the accused is not a national of the Occupying Power, he is not bound to it by any duty of allegiance.

In any case, the death penalty may not be pronounced against a protected person who was under eighteen years of age at the time of the offence.

ARTICLE 69

In all cases, the duration of the period during which a protected person accused of an offence is under arrest awaiting trial or punishment shall be deducted from any period of imprisonment awarded.

VI.
Deduction from sentence of period spent under arrest

ARTICLE 70

Protected persons shall not be arrested, prosecuted or convicted by the Occupying Power for acts committed or for opinions expressed before the occupation, or during a temporary interruption thereof, with the exception of breaches of the laws and customs of war.

VII.
Offences committed before occupation

Nationals of the occupying Power who, before the outbreak of hostilities, have sought refuge in the territory of the occupied State, shall not be arrested, prosecuted, convicted or deported from the occupied territory, except for offences committed after the outbreak of hostilities, or for offences under common law committed before the outbreak of hostilities which, according to the law of the occupied State, would have justified extradition in time of peace.

ARTICLE 71

Penal procedure
I.
General
observation

No sentence shall be pronounced by the competent courts of the Occupying Power except after a regular trial.

Accused persons who are prosecuted by the Occupying Power shall be promptly informed, in writing, in a language which they understand, of the particulars of the charges preferred against them, and shall be brought to trial as rapidly as possible. The Protecting Power shall be informed of all proceedings instituted by the Occupying Power against protected persons in respect of charges involving the death penalty or imprisonment for two years or more; it shall be enabled, at any time, to obtain information regarding the state of such proceedings. Furthermore, the Protecting Power shall be entitled, on request, to be furnished with all particulars of these and of any other proceedings instituted by the Occupying Power against protected persons.

The notification of the Protecting Power, as provided for in the second paragraph above, shall be sent immediately, and shall in any case reach the Protecting Power three weeks before the date of the first hearing. Unless, at the opening of the trial, evidence is submitted that the provisions of this Article are fully complied with, the trial shall not proceed. The notification shall include the following particulars:

(a) description of the accused;

(b) place of residence or detention;

(c) specification of the charge or charges (with mention of the penal provisions under which it is brought);

(d) designation of the court which will hear the case;

(e) place and date of the first hearing.

ARTICLE 72

Accused persons shall have the right to present evidence necessary to their defence and may, in particular, call witnesses. They shall have the right to be assisted by a qualified advocate or counsel of their own choice, who shall be able to visit them freely and shall enjoy the necessary facilities for preparing the defence.

Failing a choice by the accused, the Protecting Power may provide him with an advocate or counsel. When an accused person has to meet a serious charge and the Protecting Power is not functioning, the Occupying Power, subject to the consent of the accused, shall provide an advocate or counsel.

Accused persons shall, unless they freely waive such assistance, be aided by an interpreter, both during preliminary investigation and during the hearing in court. They shall have the right at any time to object to the interpreter and to ask for his replacement.

II.
Right of defence

ARTICLE 73

A convicted person shall have the right of appeal provided for by the laws applied by the court. He shall be fully informed of his right to appeal or petition and of the time limit within which he may do so.

The penal procedure provided in the present Section shall apply, as far as it is applicable, to appeals. Where the laws applied by the Court make no provision for appeals, the convicted person shall have the right to petition against the finding and sentence to the competent authority of the Occupying Power.

III.
Right of appeal

ARTICLE 74

Representatives of the Protecting Power shall have the right to attend the trial of any protected person, unless the hearing has, as an exceptional measure, to be held *in camera* in the interests of the security of the Occupying Power, which shall then notify the Protecting Power. A notification in respect of the date and place of trial shall be sent to the Protecting Power.

Any judgment involving a sentence of death, or imprisonment for two years or more, shall be communicated, with

IV.
Assistance by the Protecting Power

the relevant grounds, as rapidly as possible to the Protecting
Power. The notification shall contain a reference to the
notification made under Article 71, and, in the case of
sentences of imprisonment, the name of the place where the
sentence is to be served. A record of judgments other than
those referred to above shall be kept by the court and shall
be open to inspection by representatives of the Protecting
Power. Any period allowed for appeal in the case of sentences involving the death penalty, or imprisonment of two
years or more, shall not run until notification of judgment
has been received by the Protecting Power.

ARTICLE 75

V.
Death sentence

In no case shall persons condemned to death be deprived
of the right of petition for pardon or reprieve.

No death sentence shall be carried out before the expiration of a period of at least six months from the date of
receipt by the Protecting Power of the notification of the
final judgment confirming such death sentence, or of an
order denying pardon or reprieve.

The six months period of suspension of the death sentence herein prescribed may be reduced in individual cases
in circumstances of grave emergency involving an organized
threat to the security of the Occupying Power or its forces,
provided always that the Protecting Power is notified of
such reduction and is given reasonable time and
opportunity to make representations to the competent
occupying authorities in respect of such death sentences.

ARTICLE 76

Treatment of
detainees

Protected persons accused of offences shall be detained in
the occupied country, and if convicted they shall serve their
sentences therein. They shall, if possible, be separated from
other detainees and shall enjoy conditions of food and
hygiene which will be sufficient to keep them in good
health, and which will be at least equal to those obtaining
in prisons in the occupied country.

They shall receive the medical attention required by their
state of health.

They shall also have the right to receive any spiritual
assistance which they may require.

Women shall be confined in separate quarters and shall be under the direct supervision of women.

Proper regard shall be paid to the special treatment due to minors.

Protected persons who are detained shall have the right to be visited by delegates of the Protecting Power and of the International Committee of the Red Cross, in accordance with the provisions of Article 143.

Such persons shall have the right to receive at least one relief parcel monthly.

ARTICLE 77

Protected persons who have been accused of offences or convicted by the courts in occupied territory, shall be handed over at the close of occupation, with the relevant records, to the authorities of the liberated territory.

Handing over of detainees at the close of occupation

ARTICLE 78

If the Occupying Power considers it necessary, for imperative reasons of security, to take safety measures concerning protected persons, it may, at the most, subject them to assigned residence or to internment.

Decisions regarding such assigned residence or internment shall be made according to a regular procedure to be prescribed by the Occupying Power in accordance with the provisions of the present Convention. This procedure shall include the right of appeal for the parties concerned. Appeals shall be decided with the least possible delay. In the event of the decision being upheld, it shall be subject to periodical review, if possible every six months, by a competent body set up by the said Power.

Protected persons made subject to assigned residence and thus required to leave their homes shall enjoy the full benefit of Article 39 of the present Convention.

Security measures. Internment and assigned residence. Right of appeal

SECTION IV

REGULATIONS FOR THE TREATMENT
OF INTERNEES

CHAPTER I

GENERAL PROVISIONS

ARTICLE 79

Cases of intern-
ment and
applicable
provisions

The Parties to the conflict shall not intern protected persons, except in accordance with the provisions of Articles 41, 42, 43, 68 and 78.

ARTICLE 80

Civil capacity

Internees shall retain their full civil capacity and shall exercise such attendant rights as may be compatible with their status.

ARTICLE 81

Maintenance

Parties to the conflict who intern protected persons shall be bound to provide free of charge for their maintenance, and to grant them also the medical attention required by their state of health.

No deduction from the allowances, salaries or credits due to the internees shall be made for the repayment of these costs.

The Detaining Power shall provide for the support of those dependent on the internees, if such dependents are without adequate means of support or are unable to earn a living.

ARTICLE 82

Grouping of
internees

The Detaining Power shall, as far as possible, accommodate the internees according to their nationality, language and customs. Internees who are nationals of the same country shall not be separated merely because they have different languages.

Throughout the duration of their internment, members of

the same family, and in particular parents and children, shall be lodged together in the same place of internment, except when separation of a temporary nature is necessitated for reasons of employment or health or for the purposes of enforcement of the provisions of Chapter IX of the present Section. Internees may request that their children who are left at liberty without parental care shall be interned with them.

Wherever possible, interned members of the same family shall be housed in the same premises and given separate accommodation from other internees, together with facilities for leading a proper family life.

CHAPTER II

PLACES OF INTERNMENT

ARTICLE 83

The Detaining Power shall not set up places of internment in areas particularly exposed to the dangers of war.

The Detaining Power shall give the enemy Powers, through the intermediary of the Protecting Powers, all useful information regarding the geographical location of places of internment.

Whenever military considerations permit, internment camps shall be indicated by the letters IC, placed so as to be clearly visible in the daytime from the air. The Powers concerned may, however, agree upon any other system of marking. No place other than an internment camp shall be marked as such.

Location of places of internment. Marking of camps

ARTICLE 84

Internees shall be accommodated and administered separately from prisoners of war and from persons deprived of liberty for any other reason.

Separate internment

ARTICLE 85

The Detaining Power is bound to take all necessary and and possible measures to ensure that protected persons shall from the outset of their internment, be accommodated in

Accommodation, hygiene

buildings or quarters which afford every possible safeguard as regards hygiene and health, and provide efficient protection against the rigours of the climate and the effects of the war. In no case shall permanent places of internment be situated in unhealthy areas or in districts the climate of which is injurious to the internees. In all cases where the district, in which a protected person is temporarily interned, is in an unhealthy area or has a climate which is harmful to his health, he shall be removed to a more suitable place of internment as rapidly as circumstances permit.

The premises shall be fully protected from dampness, adequately heated and lighted, in particular between dusk and lights out. The sleeping quarters shall be sufficiently spacious and well ventilated, and the internees shall have suitable bedding and sufficient blankets, account being taken of the climate, and the age, sex, and state of health of the internees.

Internees shall have for their use, day and night, sanitary conveniences which conform to the rules of hygiene and are constantly maintained in a state of cleanliness. They shall be provided with sufficient water and soap for their daily personal toilet and for washing their personal laundry; installations and facilities necessary for this purpose shall be granted to them. Showers or baths shall also be available. The necessary time shall be set aside for washing and for cleaning.

Whenever it is necessary, as an exceptional and temporary measure, to accommodate women internees who are not members of a family unit in the same place of internment as men, the provision of separate sleeping quarters and sanitary conveniences for the use of such women internees shall be obligatory.

ARTICLE 86

Premises for
religious services

The Detaining Power shall place at the disposal of interned persons of whatever denomination, premises suitable for the holding of their religious services.

ARTICLE 87

Canteens

Canteens shall be installed in every place of internment, except where other suitable facilities are available. Their purpose shall be to enable internees to make purchases, at prices not higher than local market prices, of foodstuffs and articles of everyday use, including soap and tobacco, such as would increase their personal well-being and comfort.

Profits made by canteens shall be credited to a welfare fund to be set up for each place of internment, and administered for the benefit of the internees attached to such place of internment. The Internee Committee provided for in Article 102 shall have the right to check the management of the canteen and of the said fund.

When a place of internment is closed down, the balance of the welfare fund shall be transferred to the welfare fund of a place of internment for internees of the same nationality, or, if such a place does not exist, to a central welfare fund which shall be administered for the benefit of all internees remaining in the custody of the Detaining Power. In case of a general release, the said profits shall be kept by the Detaining Power, subject to any agreement to the contrary between the Powers concerned.

ARTICLE 88

In all places of internment exposed to air raids and other hazards of war, shelters adequate in number and structure to ensure the necessary protection shall be installed. In case of alarms, the internees shall be free to enter such shelters as quickly as possible, excepting those who remain for the protection of their quarters against the aforesaid hazards. Any protective measures taken in favour of the population shall also apply to them.

Air raid shelters.
Protective measures

All due precautions must be taken in places of internment against the danger of fire.

CHAPTER III

FOOD AND CLOTHING

ARTICLE 89

Daily food rations for internees shall be sufficient in quantity, quality and variety to keep internees in a good state of health and prevent the development of nutritional deficiencies. Account shall also be taken of the customary diet of the internees.

Food

Internees shall also be given the means by which they can prepare for themselves any additional food in their possession.

Sufficient drinking water shall be supplied to internees. The use of tobacco shall be permitted.

Internees who work shall receive additional rations in proportion to the kind of labour which they perform.

Expectant and nursing mothers and children under fifteen years of age, shall be given additional food, in proportion to their physiological needs.

ARTICLE 90

Clothing   When taken into custody, internees shall be given all facilities to provide themselves with the necessary clothing, footwear and change of underwear, and later on, to procure further supplies if required. Should any internees not have sufficient clothing, account being taken of the climate, and be unable to procure any, it shall be provided free of charge to them by the Detaining Power.

The clothing supplied by the Detaining Power to internees and the outward markings placed on their own clothes shall not be ignominious nor expose them to ridicule.

Workers shall receive suitable working outfits, including protective clothing whenever the nature of their work so requires.

CHAPTER IV

HYGIENE AND MEDICAL ATTENTION

ARTICLE 91

Medical attention   Every place of internment shall have an adequate infirmary, under the direction of a qualified doctor, where internees may have the attention they require, as well as an appropriate diet. Isolation wards shall be set aside for cases of contagious or mental diseases.

Maternity cases and internees suffering from serious diseases, or whose condition requires special treatment, a surgical operation or hospital care, must be admitted to any institution where adequate treatment can be given and shall receive care not inferior to that provided for the general population.

Internees shall, for preference, have the attention of medical personnel of their own nationality.

Internees may not be prevented from presenting themselves to the medical authorities for examination. The medical authorities of the Detaining Power shall, upon request, issue to every internee who has undergone treatment an official certificate showing the nature of his illness or injury, and the duration and nature of the treatment given. A duplicate of this certificate shall be forwarded to the Central Agency provided for in Article 140.

Treatment, including the provision of any apparatus necessary for the maintenance of internees in good health, particularly dentures and other artificial appliances and spectacles, shall be free of charge to the internee.

ARTICLE 92

Medical inspections of internees shall be made at least once a month. Their purpose shall be, in particular, to supervise the general state of health, nutrition and cleanliness of internees, and to detect contagious diseases, especially tuberculosis, malaria, and venereal diseases. Such inspections shall include, in particular, the checking of weight of each internee and, at least once a year, radioscopic examination.

Medical inspections

CHAPTER V

RELIGIOUS, INTELLECTUAL AND PHYSICAL ACTIVITIES

ARTICLE 93

Internees shall enjoy complete latitude in the exercise of their religious duties, including attendance at the services of their faith, on condition that they comply with the disciplinary routine prescribed by the detaining authorities.

Religious duties

Ministers of religion who are interned shall be allowed to minister freely to the members of their community. For this purpose, the Detaining Power shall ensure their equitable allocation amongst the various places of internment in which there are internees speaking the same language and belonging to the same religion. Should such ministers be too few in number, the Detaining Power shall provide them with the necessary facilities, including means of transport, for moving from one place to another, and they shall be authorized to visit any internees who are in hospital. Ministers of religion shall be at liberty to correspond on matters concerning their ministry with the religious authorities in the country of detention and, as far as possible, with the international religious organizations of their faith. Such correspondence shall not be considered as forming a part of the quota mentioned in Article 107. It shall, however, be subject to the provisions of Article 112.

When internees do not have at their disposal the assistance of ministers of their faith, or should these latter be too few in number, the local religious authorities of the same faith may appoint, in agreement with the Detaining Power, a minister of the internees' faith or, if such a course is feasible from a denominational point of view, a minister of similar religion or a qualified layman. The latter shall enjoy the facilities granted to the ministry he has assumed. Persons so appointed shall comply with all regulations laid down by the Detaining Power in the interests of discipline and security.

ARTICLE 94

Recreation, study, sports and games

The Detaining Power shall encourage intellectual, educational and recreational pursuits, sports and games amongst internees, whilst leaving them free to take part in them or not. It shall take all practicable measures to ensure the exercise thereof, in particular by providing suitable premises.

All possible facilities shall be granted to internees to continue their studies or to take up new subjects. The education of children and young people shall be ensured; they shall be allowed to attend schools either within the place of internment or outside.

Internees shall be given opportunities for physical exercise, sports and outdoor games. For this purpose, sufficient open spaces shall be set aside in all places of internment. Special playgrounds shall be reserved for children and young people.

ARTICLE 95

The Detaining Power shall not employ internees as workers, unless they so desire. Employment which, if undertaken under compulsion by a protected person not in internment, would involve a breach of Articles 40 or 51 of the present Convention, and employment on work which is of a degrading or humiliating character are in any case prohibited.

Working conditions

After a working period of six weeks, internees shall be free to give up work at any moment, subject to eight days' notice.

These provisions constitute no obstacle to the right of the Detaining Power to employ interned doctors, dentists and other medical personel in their professional capacity on behalf of their fellow internees, or to employ internees for administration and maintenance work in places of internment and to detail such persons for work in the kitchens or for other domestic tasks, or to require such persons to undertake duties connected with the protection of internees against aerial bombardment or other war risks. No internee may, however, be required to perform tasks for which he is, in the opinion of a medical officer, physically unsuited.

The Detaining Power shall take entire responsibility for all working conditions, for medical attention, for the payment of wages, and for ensuring that all employed internees receive compensation for occupational accidents and diseases. The standards prescribed for the said working conditions and for compensation shall be in accordance with the national laws and regulations, and with the existing practice; they shall in no case be inferior to those obtaining for work of the same nature in the same district. Wages for work done shall be determined on an equitable basis by special agreements between the internees, the Detaining Power, and, if the case arises, employers other than the Detaining Power, due regard being paid to the obligation of the Detaining Power to provide for free maintenance of internees and for the medical attention which their state of health may require. Internees permanently detailed for categories of work mentioned in the third paragraph of this Article, shall be paid fair wages by the Detaining Power. The working conditions and the scale of compensation for occupational accidents and diseases to internees thus detailed,

shall not be inferior to those applicable to work of the same
nature in the same district.

Labour   All labour detachments shall remain part of and dependent
detachments   upon a place of internment. The competent authorities of
the Detaining Power and the commandant of a place of
internment shall be responsible for the observance in a
labour detachment of the provisions of the present Convention. The commandant shall keep an up-to-date list of the
labour detachments subordinate to him and shall communicate it to the delegates of the Protecting Power, of the
International Committee of the Red Cross and of other
humanitarian organisations who may visit the places of
internment.

CHAPTER VI

PERSONAL PROPERTY AND FINANCIAL RESOURCES

Valuables and   Internees shall be permitted to retain articles of personal
personal effects   use. Monies, cheques, bonds, etc., and valuables in their
possesion may not be taken from them except in accordance
with established procedure. Detailed receipts shall be given
therefore.

The amounts shall be paid into the account of every internee as provided for in Article 98. Such amounts may not be
converted into any other currency unless legislation in force
in the territory in which the owner is interned so requires
or the internee gives his consent.

Articles which have above all a personal or sentimental
value may not be taken away.

A woman internee shall not be searched except by a
woman.

On release or repatriation, internees shall be given all
articles, monies or other valuables taken from them during
internment and shall receive in currency the balance of any
credit to their accounts kept in accordance with Article 98,

with the exception of any articles or amounts withheld by the Detaining Power by virtue of its legislation in force. If the property of an internee is so withheld, the owner shall receive a detailed receipt.

Family or identity documents in the possession of internees may not be taken away without a receipt being given. At no time shall internees be left without identity documents. If they have none, they shall be issued with special documents drawn up by the detaining authorities, which will serve as their identity papers until the end of their internment.

Internees may keep on their persons a certain amount of money, in cash or in the shape of purchase coupons, to enable them to make purchases.

ARTICLE 98

All internees shall receive regular allowances, sufficient to enable them to purchase goods and articles, such as tobacco, toilet requisites, etc. Such allowances may take the form of credits or purchase coupons.

Financial resources and individual accounts

Furthermore, internees may receive allowances from the Power to which they owe allegiance, the Protecting Powers, the organizations which may assist them, or their families, as well as the income on their property in accordance with the law of the Detaining Power. The amount of allowances granted by the Power to which they owe allegiance shall be the same for each category of internees (infirm, sick, pregnant women, etc.), but may not be allocated by that Power or distributed by the Detaining Power on the basis of discriminations between internees which are prohibited by Article 27 of the present Convention.

The Detaining Power shall open a regular account for every internee, to which shall be credited the allowances named in the present Article, the wages earned and the remittances received, together with such sums taken from him as may be available under the legislation in force in the territory in which he is interned. Internees shall be granted all facilities consistent with the legislation in force in such territory to make remittances to their families and to other dependants. They may draw from their accounts the amounts necessary for their personal expenses, within the limits fixed by the Detaining Power. They shall at all times be afforded reasonable facilities for consulting and obtaining copies of their accounts. A statement of accounts shall be furnished to the Protecting Power on request, and shall accompany the internee in case of transfer.

CHAPTER VII

ADMINISTRATION AND DISCIPLINE

ARTICLE 99

Camp administration. Posting of the Convention and of orders

Every place of internment shall be put under the authority of a responsible officer, chosen from the regular military forces or the regular civil administration of the Detaining Power. The officer in charge of the place of internment must have in his possession a copy of the present Convention in the official language, or one of the official languages, of his country and shall be responsible for its application. The staff in control of internees shall be instructed in the provisions of the present Convention and of the administrative measures adopted to ensure its application.

The text of the present Convention and the texts of special agreements concluded under the said Convention shall be posted inside the place of internment, in a language which the internees understand, or shall be in the possession of the Internee Comittee.

Regulations, orders, notices and publications of every kind shall be communicated to the internees and posted inside the places of internment, in a language which they understand.

Every order and command addressed to internees individually, must likewise be given in a language which they understand.

ARTICLE 100

General discipline

The disciplinary regime in places of internment shall be consistent with humanitarian principles, and shall in no circumstances include regulations imposing on internees any physical exertion dangerous to their health or involving physical or moral victimization. Identification by tattooing or imprinting signs or markings on the body, is prohibited.

In particular, prolonged standing and roll-calls, punishment drill, military drill and manœuvres, or the reduction of food rations, are prohibited.

ARTICLE 101

Internees shall have the right to present to the authorities in whose power they are, any petition with regard to the conditions of internment to which they are subjected.

They shall also have the right to apply without restriction through the Internee Committee or, if they consider it necessary, direct to the representatives of the Protecting Power, in order to indicate to them any points on which they may have complaints to make with regard to the conditions of internment.

Such petitions and complaints shall be transmitted forthwith and without alteration, and even if the latter are recognized to be unfounded, they may not occasion any punishment.

Periodic reports on the situation in places of internment and as to the needs of the internees, may be sent by the Internee Committees to the representatives of the Protecting Powers.

Complaints and petitions

ARTICLE 102

In every place of internment, the internees shall freely elect by secret ballot every six months, the members of a Committee empowered to represent them before the Detaining and the Protecting Powers, the International Committee of the Red Cross and any other organization which may assist them. The members of the Committee shall be eligible for re-election.

Internees so elected shall enter upon their duties after their election has been approved by the detaining authorities. The reasons for any refusals or dismissals shall be communicated to the Protecting Powers concerned.

*Internee committees
I.
Election of members*

ARTICLE 103

The Internee Committee shall further the physical, spiritual and intellectual well-being of the internees.

In case the internees decide, in particular, to organize a system of mutual assistance amongst themselves, this organization would be within the competence of the Committees in addition to the special duties entrusted to them under other provisions of the present Convention.

*II.
Duties*

ARTICLE 104

III.
Prerogatives

Members of Internee Committees shall not be required to perform any other work, if the accomplishment of their duties is rendered more difficult thereby.

Members of Internee Committees may appoint from amongst the internees such assistants as they may require. All material facilities shall be granted to them, particularly a certain freedom of movement necessary for the accomplishment of their duties (visits to labour detachments, receipt of supplies, etc.).

All facilities shall likewise be accorded to members of Internee Committees for communication by post and telegraph with the detaining authorities, the Protecting Powers, the International Committee of the Red Cross and their delegates, and with the organizations which give assistance to internees. Committee members in labour detachments shall enjoy similar facilities for communication with their Internee Committee in the principal place of internment. Such communications shall not be limited, nor considered as forming a part of the quota mentioned in Article 107.

Members of Internee Committees who are transferred shall be allowed a reasonable time to acquaint their successors with current affairs.

CHAPTER VIII

RELATIONS WITH THE EXTERIOR

ARTICLE 105

Notification of measures taken

Immediately upon interning protected persons, the Detaining Powers shall inform them, the Power to which they owe allegiance and their Protecting Power of the measures taken for executing the provisions of the present Chapter. The Detaining Powers shall likewise inform the Parties concerned of any subsequent modifications of such measures.

ARTICLE 106

Internment card

As soon as he is interned, or at the latest not more than one week after his arrival in a place of internment, and likewise in cases of sickness or transfer to another place of internment or to a hospital, every internee shall be enabled to send direct to his family, on the one hand, and to the Central Agency provided for by Article 140, on the other, an internment card similar, if possible, to the model annexed to the Present Convention, informing his relatives of his detention, address and state of health. The said cards shall be forwarded as rapidly as possible and may not be delayed in any way.

ARTICLE 107

Internees shall be allowed to send and receive letters and cards. If the Detaining Power deems it necessary to limit the numbers of letters and cards sent by each internee, the said number shall not be less than two letters and four cards monthly; these shall be drawn up so as to conform as closely as possible to the models annexed to the present Convention. If limitations must be placed on the correspondence addressed to internees, they may be ordered only by the Power to which such internees owe allegiance, possibly at the request of the Detaining Power. Such letters and cards must be conveyed with reasonable despatch; they may not be delayed or retained for disciplinary reasons.

Internees who have been a long time without news, or who find it impossible to receive news from their relatives, or to give them news by the ordinary postal route, as well as those who are at a considerable distance from their homes, shall be allowed to send telegrams, the charges being paid by them in the currency at their disposal. They shall likewise benefit by this provision in cases which are recognized to be urgent.

As a rule, internees' mail shall be written in their own language. The Parties to the conflict may authorize correspondence in other languages.

Correspondence

ARTICLE 108

Internees shall be allowed to receive, by post or by any other means, individual parcels or collective shipments containing in particular foodstuffs, clothing, medical supplies, as well as books and objects of a devotional, educational or recreational character which may meet their needs. Such shipments shall in no way free the Detaining Power from

Relief shipments
I.
General
principles

the obligations imposed upon it by virtue of the present Convention.

Should military necessity require the quantity of such shipments to be limited, due notice thereof shall be given to the Protecting Power and to the International Committee of the Red Cross, or to any other organization giving assistance to the internees and responsible for the forwarding of such shipments.

The conditions for the sending of individual parcels and collective shipments shall, if necessary, be the subject of special agreements between the Powers concerned, which may in no case delay the receipt by the internees of relief supplies. Parcels of clothing and foodstuffs may not include books. Medical relief supplies shall, as a rule, be sent in collective parcels.

ARTICLE 109

II.
Collective relief

In the absence of special agreements between Parties to the conflict regarding the conditions for the receipt and distribution of collective relief shipments, the regulations concerning collective relief which are annexed to the present Convention shall be applied.

The special agreements provided for above shall in no case restrict the right of Internee Committees to take possession of collective relief shipments intended for internees, to undertake their distribution and to dispose of them in the interests of the recipients.

Nor shall such agreements restrict the right of representatives of the Protecting Powers, the International Committee of the Red Cross, or any other organization giving assistance to internees and responsible for the forwarding of collective shipments, to supervise their distribution to the recipients.

ARTICLE 110

III.
Exemption from
postal and
transport charges

All relief shipments for internees shall be exempt from import, customs and other dues.

All matter sent by mail, including relief parcels sent by parcel post and remittances of money, addressed from other countries to internees or despatched by them through the post office, either direct or through the Information Bureaux provided for in Article 136 and the Central Information

Agency provided for in Article 140, shall be exempt from all postal dues both in the countries of origin and destination and in intermediate countries. To this end, in particular, the exemption provided by the Universal Postal Convention of 1947 and by the agreements of the Universal Postal Union in favour of civilians of enemy nationality detained in camps or civilian prisons, shall be extended to the other interned persons protected by the present Convention. The countries not signatory to the above-mentioned agreements shall be bound to grant freedom from charges in the same circumstances.

The cost of transporting relief shipments which are intended for internees and which, by reason of their weight or any other cause, cannot be sent through the post office, shall be borne by the Detaining Power in all the territories under its control. Other Powers which are Parties to the present Convention shall bear the cost of transport in their respective territories.

Costs connected with the transport of such shipments, which are not covered by the above paragraphs, shall be charged to the senders.

The High Contracting Parties shall endeavour to reduce, so far as possible, the charges for telegrams sent by internees, or addressed to them.

ARTICLE 111

Should military operations prevent the Powers concerned from fulfilling their obligation to ensure the conveyance of the mail and relief shipments provided for in Articles 106, 107, 108 and 113, the Protecting Powers concerned, the International Committee of the Red Cross or any other organization duly approved by the Parties to the conflict may undertake the conveyance of such shipments by suitable means (rail, motor vehicles, vessels or aircraft, etc.). For this purpose, the High Contracting Parties shall endeavour to supply them with such transport, and to allow its circulation, especially by granting the necessary safe-conducts.

Special means of transport

Such transport may also be used to convey:

(a) correspondence, lists and reports exchanged between the Central Information Agency referred to in Article 140 and the National Bureaux referred to in Article 136;

362	Defence: The Legal Implications

(*b*)	correspondence and reports relating to internees which the Protecting Powers, the International Committee of the Red Cross or any other organization assisting the internees exchange either with their own delegates or with the Parties to the confict.

These provisions in no way detract from the right of any Party to the conflict to arrange other means of transport if it should so prefer, nor preclude the granting of safe-conducts, under mutually agreed conditions, to such means of transport.

The costs occasioned by the use of such means of transport shall be borne, in proportion to the importance of the shipments, by the Parties to the conflict whose nationals are benefited thereby.

ARTICLE 112

Censorship and examination

The censoring of correspondence addressed to internees or despatched by them shall be done as quickly as possible.

The examination of consignments intended for internees shall not be carried out under conditions that will expose the goods contained in them to deterioration. It shall be done in the presence of the addressee, or of a fellow-internee duly delegated by him. The delivery to internees of individual or collective consignments shall not be delayed under the pretext of difficulties of censorship.

Any prohibition of correspondence ordered by the Parties to the conflict either for military or political reasons, shall be only temporary and its duration shall be as short as possible.

ARTICLE 113

Execution and transmission of legal documents

The Detaining Powers shall provide all reasonable facilities for the transmission, through the Protecting Power or the Central Agency provided for in Article 140, or as otherwise required, or wills, powers of attorney, letters of authority, or any other documents intended for internees or despatched by them.

In all cases the Detaining Powers shall facilitate the execution and authentication in due legal form of such documents on behalf of internees, in particular by allowing them to consult a lawyer.

ARTICLE 114

The Detaining Power shall afford internees all facilities to enable them to manage their property, provided this is not incompatible with the conditions of internment and the law which is applicable. For this purpose, the said Power may give them permission to leave the place of internment in urgent cases and if circumstances allow.

Management of property

ARTICLE 115

In all cases where an internee is a party to proceedings in any court, the Detaining Power shall, if he so requests, cause the court to be informed of his detention and shall, within legal limits, ensure that all necessary steps are taken to prevent him from being in any way prejudiced, by reason of his internment, as regards the preparation and conduct of his case or as regards the execution of any judgment of the court.

Facilities for preparation and conduct of cases

ARTICLE 116

Every internee shall be allowed to receive visitors, especially near relatives, at regular intervals and as frequently as possible.

As far as is possible, internees shall be permitted to visit their homes in urgent cases, particularly in cases of death or serious illness of relatives.

Visits

CHAPTER IX

PENAL AND DISCIPLINARY SANCTIONS

ARTICLE 117

Subject to the provisions of the present Chapter, the laws in force in the territory in which they are detained will continue to apply to internees who commit offences during internment.

If general laws, regulations or orders declare acts committed by internees to be punishable, whereas the same acts are not punishable when committed by persons who are not internees, such acts shall entail disciplinary punishments only.

General provisions. Applicable legislation

No internee may be punished more than once for the same act, or on the same count.

Penalties

The courts or authorities shall in passing sentence take as far as possible into account the fact that the defendant is not a national of the Detaining Power. They shall be free to reduce the penalty prescribed for the offence with which the internee is charged and shall not be obligated, to this end, to apply the minimum sentence prescribed.

Imprisonment in premises without daylight, and, in general, all forms of cruelty without exception are forbidden.

Internees who have served disciplinary or judicial sentences shall not be treated differently from other internees.

The duration of preventive detention undergone by an internee shall be deducted from any disciplinary or judicial penalty involving confinement to which he may be sentenced.

Internee Committees shall be informed of all judicial proceedings instituted against internees whom they represent, and of their result.

Disciplinary punishments

The disciplinary punishments applicable to internees shall be the following:

(1) A fine which shall not exceed 50 per cent of the wages which the internee would otherwise receive under the provisions of Article 95 during a period of not more than thirty days.

(2) Discontinuance of privileges granted over and above the treatment provided for by the present Convention.

(3) Fatigue duties, not exceeding two hours daily, in connection with the maintenance of the place of internment.

(4) Confinement.

In no case shall disciplinary penalties be inhuman, brutal

or dangerous for the health of internees. Account shall be taken of the internee's age, sex and state of health.

The duration of any single punishment shall in no case exceed a maximum of thirty consecutive days, even if the internee is answerable for several breaches of discipline when his case is dealt with, whether such breaches are connected or not.

ARTICLE 120

Internees who are recaptured after having escaped or when attempting to escape, shall be liable only to disciplinary punishment in respect of this act, even if it is a repeated offence.

Article 118, paragraph 3, notwithstanding, internees punished as a result of escape or attempt to escape, may be subjected to special surveillance, on condition that such surveillance does not affect the state of their health, that it is exercised in a place of internment and that it does not entail the abolition of any of the safeguards granted by the present Convention.

Internees who aid and abet an escape, or attempt to escape, shall be liable on this count to disciplinary punishment only.

Escapes

ARTICLE 121

Escape, or attempt to escape, even if it is a repeated offence, shall not be deemed an aggravating circumstance in cases where an internee is prosecuted for offences committed during his escape.

The Parties to the conflict shall ensure that the competent authorities exercise leniency in deciding whether punishment inflicted for an offence shall be of a disciplinary or judicial nature, especially in respect of acts committed in connection with an escape, whether successful or not.

Connected offences

ARTICLE 122

Acts which constitute offences against discipline shall be investigated immediately. This rule shall be applied, in particular, in cases of escape or attempt to escape. Recaptured internees shall be handed over to the competent authorities as soon as possible.

In case of offences against discipline, confinement awaiting

Investigations. Confinement awaiting hearing

trial shall be reduced to an absolute minimum for all internees, and shall not exceed fourteen days. Its duration shall
in any case be deducted from any sentence of confinement.

The provisions of Articles 124 and 125 shall apply to
internees who are in confinement awaiting trial for offences
against discipline.

ARTICLE 123

Competent
authorities.
Procedure

Without prejudice to the competence of courts and higher
authorities, disciplinary punishment may be ordered only by
the commandant of the place of internment, or by a responsible officer or official who replaces him, or to whom he has
delegated his disciplinary powers.

Before any disciplinary punishment is awarded, the
accused internee shall be given precise information regarding the offences of which he is accused, and given an
opportunity of explaining his conduct and of defending
himself. He shall be permitted, in particular, to call
witnesses and to have recourse, if necessary, to the services
of a qualified interpreter. The decision shall be announced
in the presence of the accused and of a member of the
Internee Committee.

The period elapsing between the time of award of a disciplinary punishment and its execution shall not exceed one
month.

When an internee is awarded a further disciplinary
punishment, a period of at least three days shall elapse
between the execution of any two of the punishments, if the
duration of one of these is ten days or more.

A record of disciplinary punishments shall be maintained by
the commandant of the place of internment and shall be open
to inspection by representatives of the Protecting Power.

ARTICLE 124

Premises for
disciplinary
punishments

Internees shall not in any case be transferred to penitentiary establishments (prisons, penitentiaries, convict prisons,
etc.) to undergo disciplinary punishment therein.

The premises in which disciplinary punishments are
undergone shall conform to sanitary requirements; they
shall in particular be provided with adequate bedding.
Internees undergoing punishment shall be enabled to keep
themselves in a state of cleanliness.

Women internees undergoing disciplinary punishment shall be confined in separate quarters from male internees and shall be under the immediate supervision of women.

ARTICLE 125

Internees awarded disciplinary punishment shall be allowed to exercise and to stay in the open air at least two hours daily.

They shall be allowed, if they so request, to be present at the daily medical inspections. They shall receive the attention which their state of health requires and, if necessary, shall be removed to the infirmary of the place of internment or to a hospital.

They shall have permission to read and write, likewise to send and receive letters. Parcels and remittances of money, however, may be withheld from them until the completion of their punishment; such consignments shall meanwhile be entrusted to the Internee Committee, who will hand over to the infirmary the perishable goods contained in the parcels.

No internee given a disciplinary punishment may be deprived of the benefit of the provisions of Articles 107 and 143 of the present Convention.

Essential safeguards

ARTICLE 126

The provisions of Articles 71 to 76 inclusive shall apply, by analogy, to proceedings against internees who are in the national territory of the Detaining Power.

Provisions applicable to judicial . proceedings

CHAPTER X

TRANSFER OF INTERNEES

ARTICLE 127

The transfer of internees shall always be effected humanely. As a general rule, it shall be carried out by rail or other means of transport, and under conditions at least equal to those obtaining for the forces of the Detaining Power in their changes of station. If, as an exceptional measure, such removals have to be effected on foot, they may not take place unless the internees are in a fit state of health, and may not in any case expose them to excessive fatigue.

Conditions

The Detaining Power shall supply internees during transfer with drinking water and food sufficient in quantity, quality and variety to maintain them in good health, and also with the necessary clothing, adequate shelter and the necessary medical attention. The Detaining Power shall take all suitable precautions to ensure their safety during transfer, and shall establish before their departure a complete list of all internees transferred.

Sick, wounded or infirm internees and maternity cases shall not be transferred if the journey would be seriously detrimental to them, unless their safety imperatively so demands.

If the combat zone draws close to a place of internment, the internees in the said place shall not be transferred unless their removal can be carried out in adequate conditions of safety, or unless they are exposed to greater risks by remaining on the spot than by being transferred.

When making decisions regarding the transfer of internees, the Detaining Power shall take their interests into account and, in particular, shall not do anything to increase the difficulties of repatriating them or returning them to their own homes.

ARTICLE 128

Method   In the event of transfer, internees shall be officially advised of their departure and of their new postal address. Such notification shall be given in time for them to pack their luggage and inform their next of kin.

They shall be allowed to take with them their personal effects, and the correspondence and parcels which have arrived for them. The weight of such baggage may be limited if the conditions of transfer so require, but in no case to less than twenty-five kilograms per internee.

Mail and parcels addressed to their former place of internment shall be forwarded to them without delay.

The commandant of the place of internment shall take, in agreement with the Internee Committee, any measures needed to ensure the transport of the internees' community property and of the luggage the internees are unable to take with them in consequence of restrictions imposed by virtue of the second paragraph.

CHAPTER XI

DEATHS

ARTICLE 129

The wills of internees shall be received for safe-keeping by the responsible authorities; and in the event of the death of an internee his will shall be transmitted without delay to a person whom he has previously designated.

Wills, Death certificates

Deaths of internees shall be certified in every case by a doctor, and a death certificate shall be made out, showing the causes of death and the conditions under which it occurred.

An official record of the death, duly registered, shall be drawn up in accordance with the procedure relating thereto in force in the territory where the place of internment is situated, and a duly certified copy of such record shall be transmitted without delay to the Protecting Power as well as to the Central Agency referred to in Article 140.

ARTICLE 130

The detaining authorities shall ensure that internees who die while interned are honourably buried, if possible according to the rites of the religion to which they belonged, and that their graves are respected, properly maintained, and marked in such a way that they can always be recognized.

Burial. Cremation

Deceased internees shall be buried in individual graves unless unavoidable circumstances require the use of collective graves. Bodies may be cremated only for imperative reasons of hygiene, on account of the religion of the deceased or in accordance with his expressed wish to this effect. In case of cremation, the fact shall be stated and the reasons given in the death certificate of the deceased. The ashes shall be retained for safe-keeping by the detaining authorities and shall be transferred as soon as possible to the next of kin on their request.

As soon as circumstances permit, and not later than the close of hostilities, the Detaining Power shall forward lists of graves of deceased internees to the Powers on whom the deceased internees depended, through the Information Bureaux provided for in Article 136. Such lists shall include all particulars necessary for the identification of the deceased internees, as well as the exact location of their graves.

ARTICLE 131

Internees killed
or injured in
special
circumstances

Every death or serious injury of an internee, caused or suspected to have been caused by a sentry, another internee or any other person, as well as any death the cause of which is unknown, shall be immediately followed by an official enquiry by the Detaining Power.

A communication on this subject shall be sent immediately to the Protecting Power. The evidence of any witnesses shall be taken, and a report including such evidence shall be prepared and forwarded to the said Protecting Power.

If the enquiry indicates the guilt of one or more persons, the Detaining Power shall take all necessary steps to ensure the prosecution of the person or persons responsible.

CHAPTER XII

RELEASE, REPATRIATION AND ACCOMMODATION IN NEUTRAL COUNTRIES

ARTICLE 132

During hostilities
or occupation

Each interned person shall be released by the Detaining Power as soon as the reasons which necessitated his internment no longer exist.

The Parties to the conflict shall, moreover, endeavour during the course of hostilities, to conclude agreements for the release, the repatriation, the return to places of residence or the accommodation in a neutral country of certain classes of internees, in particular children, pregnant women and mothers with infants and young children, wounded and sick, and internees who have been detained for a long time.

ARTICLE 133

After the close
of hostilities

Internment shall cease as soon as possible after the close of hostilities.

Internees in the territory of a Party to the conflict, against whom penal proceedings are pending for offences not exclusively subject to disciplinary penalties, may be detained until the close of such proceedings and, if circumstances require, until the completion of the penalty. The same shall apply to internees who have been previously sentenced to a punishment depriving them of liberty.

By agreement between the Detaining Power and the Powers concerned, committees may be set up after the close of hostilities, or of the occupation of territories, to search for dispersed internees.

ARTICLE 134

The High Contracting Parties shall endeavour, upon the close of hostilities or occupation, to ensure the return of all internees to their last place of residence, or to facilitate their repatriation.

Repatriation and return to last place of residence

ARTICLE 135

The Detaining Power shall bear the expense of returning released internees to the places where they were residing when interned, or, if it took them into custody while they were in transit or on the high seas, the cost of completing their journey or of their return to their point of departure.

Costs

Where a Detaining Power refuses permission to reside in its territory to a released internee who previously had his permanent domicile therein, such Detaining Power shall pay the cost of the said internee's repatriation. If, however, the internee elects to return to his country on his own responsibility or in obedience to the Government of the Power to which he owes allegiance, the Detaining Power need not pay the expenses of his journey beyond the point of his departure from its territory. The Detaining Power need not pay the costs of repatriation of an internee who was interned at his own request.

If internees are transferred in accordance with Article 45, the transferring and receiving Powers shall agree on the portion of the above costs to be borne by each.

The foregoing shall not prejudice such special agreements as may be concluded between Parties to the conflict concerning the exchange and repatriation of their nationals in enemy hands.

SECTION V

INFORMATION BUREAUX AND CENTRAL AGENCY

ARTICLE 136

National Bureaux   Upon the outbreak of a conflict and in all cases of occupation, each of the Parties to the conflict shall establish an
official Information Bureau responsible for receiving and
transmitting information in respect of the protected persons
who are in its power.

Each of the Parties to the conflict shall, within the
shortest possible period, give its Bureau information of any
measure taken by it concerning any protected persons who
are kept in custody for more than two weeks, who are
subjected to assigned residence or who are interned. It shall,
furthermore, require its various departments concerned
with such matters to provide the aforesaid Bureau promptly
with information concerning all changes pertaining to these
protected persons, as, for example, transfers, releases,
repatriations, escapes, admittances to hospitals, births and
deaths.

ARTICLE 137

Transmission of   Each national Bureau shall immediately forward informa-
information   tion concerning protected persons by the most rapid means
to the Powers of whom the aforesaid persons are nationals,
or to Powers in whose territory they resided, through the
intermediary of the Protecting Powers and likewise through
the Central Agency provided for in Article 140. The
Bureaux shall also reply to all enquiries which may be
received regarding protected persons.

Information Bureaux shall transmit information concerning a protected person unless its transmission might be
detrimental to the person concerned or to his or her
relatives. Even in such a case, the information may not be
withheld from the Central Agency which, upon being
notified of the circumstances, will take the necessary
precautions indicated in Article 140.

All communications in writing made by any Bureau shall
be authenticated by a signature or a seal.

ARTICLE 138

The information received by the national Bureau and trans-   Particulars
mitted by it shall be of such a character as to make it   required
possible to identify the protected person exactly and to
advise his next of kin quickly. The information in respect
of each person shall include at least his surname, first
names, place and date of birth, nationality, last residence
and distinguishing characteristics, the first name of the
father and the maiden name of the mother, the date, place
and nature of the action taken with regard to the individual,
the address at which correspondence may be sent to him
and the name and address of the person to be informed.

Likewise, information regarding the state of health of
internees who are seriously ill or seriously wounded shall be
supplied regularly and if possible every week.

ARTICLE 139

Each national Information Bureau shall, furthermore, be   Forwarding of
responsible for collecting all personal valuables left by   personal
protected persons mentioned in Article 136, in particular   valuables
those who have been repatriated or released, or who have
escaped or died; it shall forward the said valuables to those
concerned, either direct, or, if necessary, through the
Central Agency. Such articles shall be sent by the Bureau in
sealed packets which shall be accompanied by statements
giving clear and full identity particulars of the person to
whom the articles belonged, and by a complete list of the
contents of the parcel. Detailed records shall be maintained
of the receipt and despatch of all such valuables.

ARTICLE 140

A Central Information Agency for protected persons, in   Central Agency
particular for internees, shall be created in a neutral
country. The International Committee of the Red Cross
shall, if it deems necessary, propose to the Powers concerned the organization of such an Agency, which may be the
same as that provided for in Article 123 of the Geneva
Convention relative to the Treatment of Prisoners of War of
August 12, 1949.

The function of the Agency shall be to collect all information of the type set forth in Article 136 which it may obtain

through official or private channels and to transmit it as
rapidly as possible to the countries of origin or of residence
of the persons concerned, except in cases where such transmissions might be detrimental to the persons whom the said
information concerns, or to their relatives. It shall receive
from the Parties to the conflict all reasonable facilities for
effecting such transmission.

The High Contracting Parties, and in particular those
whose nationals benefit by the services of the Central
Agency, are requested to give the said Agency the financial
aid it may require.

The foregoing provisions shall in no way be interpreted as
restricting the humanitarian activities of the International
Committee of the Red Cross and of the relief Societies
described in Article 142.

ARTICLE 141

Exemption from   The national Information Bureaux and the Central Infor-
charges   mation Agency shall enjoy free postage for all mail, likewise
the exemptions provided for in Article 110, and further, so
far as possible, exemption from telegraphic charges or, at
least, greatly reduced rates.

PART IV

EXECUTION OF THE CONVENTION
SECTION I
GENERAL PROVISIONS

ARTICLE 142

Relief societies   Subject to the measures which the Detaining Powers may
and other   consider essential to ensure their security or to meet any
organizations   other reasonable need, the representatives of religious organizations, relief societies, or any other organizations assisting
the protected persons, shall receive from these Powers, for
themselves or their duly accredited agents, all facilities for
visiting the protected persons, for distributing relief
supplies and material from any source, intended for educational, recreational or religious purposes, or for assisting
them in organizing their leisure time within the places of

internment. Such societies or organizations may be constituted in the territory of the Detaining Power, or in any other country, or they may have an international character.

The Detaining Power may limit the number of societies and organizations whose delegates are allowed to carry out their activities in its territory and under its supervision, on condition, however, that such limitation shall not hinder the supply of effective and adequate relief to all protected persons.

The special position of the International Committee of the Red Cross in this field shall be recognized and respected at all times.

ARTICLE 143

Representatives or delegates of the Protecting Powers shall have permission to go to all places where protected persons are, particularly to places of internment, detention and work.

Supervision

They shall have access to all premises occupied by protected persons and shall be able to interview the latter without witnesses, personally or through an interpreter.

Such visits may not be prohibited except for reasons of imperative military necessity, and then only as an exceptional and temporary measure. Their duration and frequency shall not be restricted.

Such representatives and delegates shall have full liberty to select the places they wish to visit. The Detaining or Occupying Power, the Protecting Power and when occasion arises the Power of origin of the persons to be visited, may agree that compatriots of the internees shall be permitted to participate in the visits.

The delegates of the International Committee of the Red Cross shall also enjoy the above prerogatives. The appointment of such delegates shall be submitted to the approval of the Power governing the territories where they will carry out their duties.

ARTICLE 144

The High Contracting Parties undertake, in time of peace as in time of war, to disseminate the text of the present Convention as widely as possible in their respective countries, and, in particular, to include the study thereof in their

Dissemination of the Convention

programmes of military and, if possible, civil instruction, so that the principles thereof may become known to the entire population.

Any civilian, military, police or other authorities, who in time of war assume responsibilities in respect of protected persons, must possess the text of the Convention and be specially instructed as to its provisions.

ARTICLE 145

Translations.
Rules of
application

The High Contracting Parties shall communicate to one another through the Swiss Federal Council and, during hostilities, through the Protecting Powers, the official translations of the present Convention, as well as the laws and regulations which they may adopt to ensure the application thereof.

ARTICLE 146

Penal sanctions
I.
General
observations

The High Contracting Parties undertake to enact any legislation necessary to provide effective penal sanctions for persons committing, or ordering to be committed, any of the grave breaches of the present Convention defined in the following Article.

Each High Contracting Party shall be under the obligation to search for persons alleged to have committed, or to have ordered to be committed, such grave breaches, and shall bring such persons, regardless of their nationality, before its own courts. It may also, if it prefers, and in accordance with the provisions of its own legislation, hand such persons over for trial to another High Contracting party concerned, provided such High Contracting Party has made out a *prima facie* case.

Each High Contracting Party shall take measures necessary for the suppression of all acts contrary to the provisions of the present Convention other than the grave breaches defined in the following Article.

In all circumstances, the accused persons shall benefit by safeguards of proper trial and defence, which shall not be less favourable than those provided by Article 105 and those following of the Geneva Convention relative to the Treatment of Prisoners of War of August 12, 1949.

ARTICLE 147

Grave breaches to which the preceding Article relates shall be those involving any of the following acts, if committed against persons or property protected by the present Convention: wilful killing, torture or inhuman treatment, including biological experiments, wilfully causing great suffering or serious injury to body or health, unlawful deportation or transfer or unlawful confinement of a protected person, compelling a protected person to serve in the forces of a hostile Power, or wilfully depriving a protected person of the rights of fair and regular trial prescribed in the present Convention, taking of hostages and extensive destruction and appropriation of property, not justified by military necessity and carried out unlawfully and wantonly.

II.
Grave breaches

ARTICLE 148

No High Contracting Party shall be allowed to absolve itself or any other High Contracting Party of any liability incurred by itself or by another High Contracting Party in respect of breaches referred to in the preceding Article.

III.
Responsibilities of the Contracting Parties

ARTICLE 149

At the request of a Party to the conflict, an enquiry shall be instituted, in a manner to be decided between the interested Parties, concerning any alleged violation of the Convention.

If agreement has not been reached concerning the procedure for the enquiry, the Parties should agree on the choice of an umpire who will decide upon the procedure to be followed.

Once the violation has been established, the Parties to the conflict shall put an end to it and shall repress it with the least possible delay.

Enquiry procedure

First Protocol 1977 to the Geneva Conventions of 1949

PART I

GENERAL PROVISIONS

Article 1—General principles and scope of application

1. The High Contracting Parties undertake to respect and to ensure respect for this Protocol in all circumstances.
2. In cases not covered by this Protocol or by other international agreements, civilians and combatants remain under the protection and authority of the principles of international law derived from established custom, from the principles of humanity and from the dictates of public conscience.
3. This Protocol, which supplements the Geneva Conventions of 12 August 1949 for the protection of war victims, shall apply in the situations referred to in Article 2 common to those Conventions.
4. The situations referred to in the preceding paragraph include armed conflicts in which peoples are fighting against colonial domination and alien occupation and against racist régimes in the exercise of their right of self-determination, as enshrined in the Charter of the United Nations and the Declaration on Principles of International Law concerning Friendly Relations and Co-operation among States in accordance with the Charter of the United Nations.

Article 2—Definitions

For the purposes of this Protocol:

(a) "First Convention", "Second Convention", "Third Convention" and "Fourth Convention" mean, respectively, the Geneva Convention for the Amelioration of the Condition of the Wounded and Sick in Armed Forces in the Field of 12 August 1949; the Geneva Convention for the Amelioration of the Condition of Wounded, Sick and Shipwrecked Members of Armed Forces at Sea of 12 August 1949; the Geneva Convention relative to the Treatment of Prisoners of War of 12 August 1949; the Geneva Convention relative to the Protection of Civilian Persons in Time of War of 12 August 1949; "the Conventions" means the four Geneva Conventions of 12 August 1949 for the protection of war victims;

(b) "rules of international law applicable in armed conflict" means the rules applicable in armed conflict set forth in international agreements to which the Parties to the conflict are Parties and the generally recognized principles and rules of international law which are applicable to armed conflict;

(c) "Protecting Power" means a neutral or other State not a party to the conflict which has been designated by a Party to the conflict and accepted by the adverse Party and has agreed to carry out the functions assigned to a Protecting Power under the Conventions and this Protocol;

(d) "substitute" means an organization acting in place of a Protecting Power in accordance with Article 5.

Article 3—Beginning and end of application

Without prejudice to the provisions which are applicable at all times:

(a) the Conventions and this Protocol shall apply from the beginning of any situation referred to in Article 1 of this Protocol;

(b) the application of the Conventions and of this Protocol shall cease, in the territory of Parties to the conflict, on the general close of military operations and, in the case of occupied territories, on the termination of the occupation, except, in either circumstance, for those persons whose final release, repatriation or re-establishment takes place thereafter. These persons shall continue to benefit from the relevant provisions of the Conventions and of this Protocol until their final release, repatriation or re-establishment.

Article 4—Legal status of the Parties to the conflict

The application of the Conventions and of this Protocol, as well as the conclusion of the agreements provided for therein, shall not affect the legal status of the Parties to the conflict. Neither the occupation of a territory nor the application of the Conventions and this Protocol shall affect the legal status of the territory in question.

Article 5—Appointment of Protecting Powers and of their substitute

1. It is the duty of the Parties to a conflict from the beginning of that conflict to secure the supervision and implementation of the Conventions and of this Protocol by the application of the system of Protecting Powers, including *inter alia* the designation and acceptance of those Powers, in accordance with the following paragraphs. Protecting

Powers shall have the duty of safeguarding the interests of the Parties to the conflict.

2. From the beginnning of a situation referred to in Article 1, each Party to the conflict shall without delay designate a Protecting Power for the purpose of applying the Conventions and this Protocol and shall, likewise without delay and for the same purpose, permit the activities of a Protecting Power which has been accepted by it as such after designation by the adverse Party.

3. If a Protecting Power has not been designated or accepted from the beginning of a situation referred to in Article 1, the International Committee of the Red Cross, without prejudice to the right of any other impartial humanitarian organization to do likewise, shall offer its good offices to the Parties to the conflict with a view to the designation without delay of a Protecting Power to which the Parties to the conflict consent. For that purpose it may, *inter alia*, ask each Party to provide it with a list of at least five States which that Party considers acceptable to act as Protecting Power on its behalf in relation to an adverse Party, and ask each adverse Party to provide a list of at least five States which it would accept as the Protecting Power of the first Party; these lists shall be communicated to the Committee within two weeks after the receipt of the request; it shall compare them and seek the agreement of any proposed State named on both lists.

4. If, despite the foregoing, there is no Protecting Power, the Parties to the conflict shall accept without delay an offer which may be made by the International Committee of the Red Cross or by any other organization which offers all guarantees of impartiality and efficacy, after due consultations with the said Parties and taking into account the result of these consultations, to act as a substitute. The functioning of such a substitute is subject to the consent of the Parties to the conflict; every effort shall be made by the Parties to the conflict to facilitate the operations of the substitute in the performance of its tasks under the Conventions and this Protocol.

5. In accordance with Article 4, the designation and acceptance of Protecting Powers for the purpose of applying the Conventions and this Protocol shall not affect the legal status of the Parties to the conflict or of any territory, including occupied territory.

6. The maintenance of diplomatic relations between Parties to the conflict or the entrusting of the protection of a Party's interests and those of its nationals to a third State in accordance with the rules of international law relating to diplomatic relations is no obstacle to the designation of Protecting Powers for the purpose of applying the Conventions and this Protocol.

7. Any subsequent mention in this Protocol of a Protecting Power includes also a substitute.

Article 6—Qualified persons

1. The High Contracting Parties shall, also in peacetime, endeavour, with the assistance of the national Red Cross (Red Crescent, Red Lion and Sun) Societies, to train qualified personnel to facilitate the application of the Conventions and of this Protocol, and in particular the activities of the Protecting Powers.

2. The recruitment and training of such personnel are within domestic jurisdiction.

3. The International Committeee of the Red Cross shall hold at the disposal of the High Contracting Parties the lists of persons so trained which the High Contracting Parties may have established and may have transmitted to it for that purpose.

4. The conditions governing the employment of such personnel outside the national territory shall, in each case, be the subject of special agreements between the Parties concerned.

Article 7—Meetings

The depositary of this Protocol shall convene a meeting of the High Contracting Parties, at the request of one or more of the said Parties and upon the approval of the majority of the said Parties, to consider general problems concerning the application of the Conventions and of the Protocol.

PART II

WOUNDED, SICK AND SHIPWRECKED

SECTION 1—GENERAL PROTECTION

Article 8—Terminology

For the purposes of this Protocol:

(*a*) "wounded" and "sick" means persons, whether military or civilian, who, because of trauma, disease or other physical or mental disorder or disability, are in need of medical assistance or care and who refrain from any act of hostility. These terms also cover maternity cases, new-born babies and other persons who may be in need of immediate medical assistance or care, such as the infirm or expectant mothers, and who refrain from any act of hostility;

(b) "shipwrecked" means persons, whether military or civilian, who are in peril at sea or in other waters as a result of misfortune affecting them or the vessel or aircraft carrying them and who refrain from any act of hostility. These persons, provided that they continue to refrain from any act of hostility, shall continue to be considered shipwrecked during their rescue until they acquire another status under the Conventions or this Protocol;

(c) "medical personnel" means those persons assigned, by a Party to the conflict, exclusively to the medical purposes enumerated under sub-paragraph (e) or to the administration of medical units or to the operation or administration of medical transports. Such assignments may be either permanent or temporary. The term includes:

    (i) medical personnel of a Party to the conflict, whether military or civilian, including those described in the First and Second Coventions, and those assigned to civil defence organizations;

    (ii) medical personnel of national Red Cross (Red Crescent, Red Lion and Sun) Societies and other national voluntary aid societies duly recognized and authorized by a Party to the conflict;

    (iii) medical personnel of medical units or medical transports described in Article 9, paragraph 2;

(d) "religious personnel" means military or civilian persons, such as chaplains, who are exclusively engaged in the work of their ministry and attached:

    (i) to the armed forces of a Party to the conflict;

    (ii) to medical units or medical transports of a Party to the conflict;

    (iii) to medical units or medical transports described in Article 9, paragraph 2; or

    (iv) to civil defence organizations of a Party to the conflict.

The attachment of religious personnel may be either permanent or temporary, and the relevant provisions mentioned under sub-paragraph (k) apply to them;

(e) "medical units" means establishments and other units, whether military or civilian, organized for medical purposes, namely the search for, collection, transportation, diagnosis or treatment—including first-aid treatment—of the wounded, sick and shipwrecked, or for the prevention of disease. The term includes, for example, hospital and other similar units, blood transfusion centres, preventive medicine centres and institutes, medical depots and the medical and pharmaceutical stores of such units. Medical units may be fixed or mobile, permanent or temporary;

(f) "medical transportation" means the conveyance by land, water or air of the wounded, sick, shipwrecked, medical personnel, religious personnel, medical equipment or medical supplies protected by the Conventions and by this Protocol;

(g) "medical transports" means any means of transportation, whether military or civilian, permanent or temporary, assigned exclusively to medical transportation and under the control of a competent authority of a Party to the conflict;

(h) "medical vehicles" means any medical transports by land;

(i) "medical ships and craft" means any medical transports by water;

(j) "medical aircraft" means any medical transports by air;

(k) "permanent medical personnel", "permanent medical units" and "permanent medical transports" mean those assigned exclusively to medical purposes for an indeterminate period. "Temporary medical personnel", "temporary medical units" and "temporary medical transports" mean those devoted exclusively to medical purposes for limited periods during the whole of such periods. Unless otherwise specified, the terms "medical personnel", "medical units" and "medical transports" cover both permanent and temporary categories;

(l) "distinctive emblem" means the distinctive emblem of the red cross, red crescent or red lion and sun on a white ground when used for the protection of medical units and transports, or medical and religious personnel, equipment or supplies;

(m) "distinctive signal" means any signal or message specified for the identification exclusively of medical units or transports in Chapter III of Annex I to this Protocol.

Article 9—Field of application

1. This Part, the provisions of which are intended to ameliorate the condition of the wounded, sick and shipwrecked, shall apply to all those affected by a situation referred to in Article 1, without any

adverse distinction founded on race, colour, sex, language, religion or belief, political or other opinion, national or social origin, wealth, birth or other status, or on any other similar criteria.

2. The relevant provisions of Articles 27 and 32 of the First Convention shall apply to permanent medical units and transports (other than hospital ships, to which Article 25 of the Second Convention applies) and their personnel made available to a Party to the conflict for humanitarian purposes:

(a) by a neutral or other State which is not a Party to that conflict;

(b) by a recognized and authorized aid society of such a State;

(c) by an impartial international humanitarian organization.

Article 10—Protection and care

1. All the wounded, sick and shipwrecked, to whichever Party they belong, shall be respected and protected.

2. In all circumstances they shall be treated humanely and shall receive, to the fullest extent practicable and with the least possible delay, the medical care and attention required by their condition. There shall be no distinction among them founded on any grounds other than medical ones.

Article 11—Protection of persons

1. The physical or mental health and integrity of persons who are in the power of the adverse Party or who are interned, detained or otherwise deprived of liberty as a result of a situation referred to in Article 1 shall not be endangered by any unjustified act or omission. Accordingly, it is prohibited to subject the persons described in this Article to any medical procedure which is not indicated by the state of health of the person concerned and which is not consistent with generally accepted medical standards which would be applied under similar medical circumstances to persons who are nationals of the Party conducting the procedure and who are in no way deprived of liberty.

2. It is, in particular, prohibited to carry out on such persons, even with their consent:

(a) physical mutilations;

(b) medical or scientific experiments;

(c) removal of tissue or organs for transplantation,

except where these acts are justified in conformity with the conditions provided for in paragraph 1.

3. Exceptions to the prohibition in paragraph 2 (*c*) may be made only in the case of donations of blood for transfusion or of skin for grafting, provided that they are given voluntarily and without any coercion or inducement, and then only for therapeutic purposes, under conditions consistent with generally accepted medical standards and controls designed for the benefit of both the donor and the recipient.

4. Any wilful act or omission which seriously endangers the physical or mental health or integrity of any person who is in the power of a Party other than the one on which he depends and which either violates any of the prohibitions in paragraphs 1 and 2 or fails to comply with the requirements of paragraph 3 shall be a grave breach of this Protocol.

5. The persons described in paragraph 1 have the right to refuse any surgical operation. In case of refusal, medical personnel shall endeavour to obtain a written statement to that effect, signed or acknowledged by the patient.

6. Each Party to the conflict shall keep a medical record for every donation of blood for transfusion or skin for grafting by persons referred to in paragraph 1, if that donation is made under the responsibility of that Party. In addition, each Party to the conflict shall endeavour to keep a record of all medical procedures undertaken with respect to any person who is interned, detained or otherwise deprived of liberty as a result of a situation referred to in Article 1. These records shall be available at all times for inspection by the Protecting Power.

Article 12—Protection of medical units

1. Medical units shall be respected and protected at all times and shall not be the object of attack.

2. Paragraph 1 shall apply to civilian medical units, provided that they:

    (*a*) belong to one of the Parties to the conflict;

    (*b*) are recognized and authorized by the competent authority of one of the Parties to the conflict; or

    (*c*) are authorized in conformity with Article 9, paragraph 2, of this Protocol or Article 27 of the First Convention.

3. The Parties to the conflict are invited to notify each other of the location of their fixed medical units. The absence of such notification shall not exempt any of the Parties from the obligation to comply with the provisions of paragraph 1.

4. Under no circumstances shall medical units be used in an attempt to shield military objectives from attack. Whenever possible, the Parties to the conflict shall ensure that medical units are so sited that attacks against military objectives do not imperil their safety.

Article 13—Discontinuance of protection of civilian medical units

1. The protection to which civilian medical units are entitled shall not cease unless they are used to commit, outside their humanitarian function, acts harmful to the enemy. Protection may, however, cease only after a warning has been given setting, whenever appropriate, a reasonable time-limit, and after such warning has remained unheeded.

2. The following shall not be considered as acts harmful to the enemy:

    (*a*) That the personnel of the unit are equipped with light individual weapons for their own defence or for that of the wounded and sick in their charge;

    (*b*) that the unit is guarded by a picket or by sentries or by an escort;

    (*c*) that small arms and ammunition taken from the wounded and sick, and not yet handed to the proper service, are found in the units;

    (*d*) that members of the armed forces or other combatants are in the unit for medical reasons.

Article 14—Limitations on requisition of civilian medical units

1. The Occupying Power has the duty to ensure that the medical needs of the civilian population in occupied territory continue to be satisfied.

2. The Occupying Power shall not, therefore, requisition civilian medical units, their equipment, their *matériel* or the services of their personnel, so long as these resources are necessary for the provision of adequate medical services for the civilian population and for the continuing medical care of any wounded and sick already under treatment.

3. Provided that the general rule in paragraph 2 continues to be observed, the Occupying Power may requisition the said resources, subject to the following particular conditions:

    (*a*) that the resources are necessary for the adequate and immediate medical treatment of the wounded and sick members of the armed forces of the Occupying Power or of prisoners of war;

    (*b*) that the requisition continues only while such necessity exists; and

    (*c*) that immediate arrangements are made to ensure that the medical needs of the civilian population, as well as those of any wounded and sick under treatment who are affected by the requisition, continue to be satisfied.

Article 15—Protection of civilian medical and religious personnel

1. Civilian medical personnel shall be respected and protected.

2. If needed, all available help shall be afforded to civilian medical personnel in an area where civilian medical services are disrupted by reason of combat activity.

3. The Occupying Power shall afford civilian medical personnel in occupied territories every assistance to enable them to perform, to the best of their ability, their humanitarian functions. The Occupying Power may not require that, in the performance of those functions, such personnel shall give priority to the treatment of any person except on medical grounds. They shall not be compelled to carry out tasks which are not compatible with their humanitarian mission.

4. Civilian medical personnel shall have access to any place where their services are essential, subject to such supervisory and safety measures as the relevant Party to the conflict may deem necessary.

5. Civilian religious personnel shall be respected and protected. The provision of the Conventions and of this Protocol concerning the protection and identification of medical personnel shall apply equally to such persons.

Article 16—General protection of medical duties

1. Under no circumstances shall any person be punished for carrying out medical activities compatible with medical ethics, regardless of the person benefiting therefrom.

2. Persons engaged in medical activities shall not be compelled to perform acts or to carry out work contrary to the rules of medical ethics or to other medical rules designed for the benefit of the wounded and sick or to the provisions of the Conventions or of this Protocol, or to refrain from performing acts or from carrying out work required by those rules and provisions.

3. No person engaged in medical activities shall be compelled to give to anyone belonging either to an adverse Party, or to his own Party except as required by the law of the latter Party, any information concerning the wounded and sick who are, or who have been, under his care, if such information would, in his opinion, prove harmful to the patients concerned or to their families. Regulations for the compulsory notification of communicable diseases shall, however, be respected.

Article 17—Role of the civilian population and of aid societies

1. The civilian population shall respect the wounded, sick and ship-wrecked, even if they belong to the adverse Party, and shall commit no act of violence against them. The civilian population and aid societies, such as national Red Cross (Red Crescent, Red Lion and Sun) Societies, shall be permitted, even on their own initiative, to collect and care for the wounded, sick and shipwrecked, even in invaded or occupied areas. No one shall be harmed, prosecuted, convicted or punished for such humanitarian acts.

2. The Parties to the conflict may appeal to the civilian population and the aid societies referred to in paragraph 1 to collect and care for the wounded, sick and shipwrecked, and to search for the dead and report their location; they shall grant both protection and the necessary facilities to those who respond to this appeal. If the adverse Party gains or regains control of the area, that Party also shall afford the same protection and facilities for so long as they are needed.

Article 18—Identification

1. Each Party to the conflict shall endeavour to ensure that medical and religious personnel and medical units and transport are identifiable.

2. Each Party to the conflict shall also endeavour to adopt and to implement methods and procedures which will make it possible to recognize medical units and transports which use the distinctive emblem and distinctive signals.

3. In occupied territory and in areas where fighting is taking place or is likely to take place, civilian medical personnel and civilian regilious personnel should be recognizable by the distinctive emblem and an identity card certifying their status.

4. With the consent of the competent authority, medical units and transports shall be marketed by the distinctive emblem. The ships and craft referred to in Article 22 of this Protocol shall be marked in accordance with the provisions of the Second Convention.

5. In addition to the distinctive emblem, a Party to the conflict may, as provided in Chapter III of Annex I to this Protocol, authorize the use of distinctive signals to identify medical units and transports. Exceptionally, in the special cases covered in that Chapter, medical transports may use distinctive signals without displaying the distinctive emblem.

6. The application of the provisions of paragraphs 1 to 5 of this Article is governed by Chapters I to III of Annex I to this Protocol. Signals

designated in Chapter III of the Annex for the exclusive use of medical units and transport shall not, except as provided therein, be used for any purpose other than to identify the medical units and transports specified in that Chapter.

7. This Article does not authorize any wider use of the distinctive emblem in peacetime than is prescribed in Article 44 of the First Convention.

8. The provisions of the Conventions and of this Protocol relating to supervision of the use of the distinctive emblem and to the prevention and repression of any misuse thereof shall be applicable to distinctive signals.

Article 19—Neutral and other States not Parties to the conflict

Neutral and other States not Parties to the conflict shall apply the relevant provisions of this Protocol to persons protected by this Part who may be received or interned within their territory, and to any dead of the Parties to that conflict whom they may find.

Article 29—Prohibition of reprisals

Reprisals against the persons and objects protected by this Part are prohibited.

SECTION II—MEDICAL TRANSPORTATION

Article 21—Medical vehicles

Medical vehicles shall be respected and protected in the same way as mobile medical units under the Conventions and this Protocol.

Article 22—Hospital ships and coastal rescue craft

1. The provisions of the Conventions relating to:

   (*a*) vessels described in Articles 22, 24, 25 and 27 of the Second Convention,

   (*b*) their lifeboats and small craft,

   (*c*) their personnel and crews, and

   (*d*) the wounded, sick and shipwrecked on board,

   shall also apply where these vessels carry civilian wounded, sick and shipwrecked who do not belong to any of the categories mentioned in Article 13 of the Second Convention. Such civilians shall not, however, be subject to surrender to any Party which is not their own, or to capture at sea. If they find themselves in the power of a Party to the conflict other than their own they shall be covered by the Fourth Convention and by this Protocol.

2. The protection provided by the Conventions to vessels described in Article 25 of the Second Convention shall extend to hospital ships made available for humanitarian purposes to a Party to the conflict:

    (a) by a neutral or other State which is not a Party to that conflict; or

    (b) by an impartial international humanitarian organization,

    provided that, in either case, the requirements set out in that Article are complied with.

3. Small craft described in Article 27 of the Second Convention shall be protected even if the notification envisaged by that Article has not been made. The Parties to the conflict are, nevertheless, invited to inform each other of any details of such craft which will facilitate their identification and recognition.

Article 23—Other medical ships and craft

1. Medical ships and craft other than those referred to in Article 22 of this Protocol and Article 38 of the Second Convention shall, whether at sea or in other waters, be respected and protected in the same way as mobile medical units under the Conventions and this Protocol. Since this protection can only be effective if they can be identified and recognized as medical ships or craft, such vessels should be marked with the distinctive emblem and as far as possible comply with the second paragraph of Article 43 of the Second Convention.

2. The ships and craft referred to in paragraph 1 shall remain subject to the laws of war. Any warship on the surface able immediately to enforce its command may order them to stop, order them off, or make them take a certain course, and they shall obey every such command. Such ships and craft may not in any other way be diverted from their medical mission so long as they are needed for the wounded, sick and shipwrecked on board.

3. The protection provided in paragraph 1 shall cease only under the conditions set out in Articles 34 and 35 of the Second Convention. A clear refusal to obey a command given in accordance with paragraph 2 shall be an act harmful to the enemy under Article 34 of the Second Convention.

4. A Party to the conflict may notify any adverse Party as far in advance of sailing as possible of the name, description, expected time of sailing, course and estimated speed of the medical ship or craft, particularly in the case of ships of over 2,000 gross tons, and may provide any other information which would facilitate identification and recognition. The adverse Party shall acknowledge receipt of such information.

5. The provisions of Article 37 of the Second Convention shall apply to medical and religious personnel in such ships and craft.

6. The provisions of the Second Convention shall apply to the wounded, sick and shipwrecked belonging to the categories referred to in Article 13 of the Second Convention and in Article 44 of this Protocol who may be on board such medical ships and craft. Wounded, sick and shipwrecked civilians who do not belong to any of the categories mentioned in Article 13 of the Second Convention shall not be subject, at sea, either to surrender to any Party which is not their own, or to removal from such ships or craft; if they find themselves in the power of a Party to the conflict other than their own, they shall be covered by the Fourth Convention and by this Protocol.

Article 24—Protection of medical aircraft

Medical aircraft shall be respected and protected, subject to the provisions of this Part.

Article 25—Medical aircraft in areas not controlled by an adverse Party

In and over land areas physically controlled by friendly forces, or in and over sea areas not physically controlled by an adverse Party, the respect and protection of medical aircraft of a Party to the conflict is not dependent on any agreement with an adverse Party. For greater safety, however, a Party to the conflict operating its medical aircraft in these areas may notify the adverse Party, as provided in Article 29, in particular when such aircraft are making flights bringing them within range of surface-to-air weapons systems of the adverse Party.

Article 26—Medical aircraft in contact or similar zones

1. In and over those parts of the contact zone which are physically controlled by friendly forces and in and over those areas the physical control of which is not clearly established, protection for medical aircraft can be fully effective only by prior agreement between the competent military authorities of the Parties to the conflict, as provided

for in Article 29. Although, in the absence of such an agreement, medical aircraft operate at their own risk, they shall nevertheless be respected after they have been recognized as such.

2. "Contact zone" means any area on land where the forward elements of opposing forces are in contact with each other, especially where they are exposed to direct fire from the ground.

Article 27—Medical aircraft in areas controlled by an adverse Party

1. The medical aircraft of a Party to the conflict shall continue to be protected while flying over land or sea areas physically controlled by an adverse Party, provided that prior agreement to such flights has been obtained from the competent authority of that adverse Party.

2. A medical aircraft which flies over an area physically controlled by an adverse Party without, or in deviation from the terms of, an agreement provided for in paragraph 1, either through navigational error or because of an emergency affecting the safety of the flight, shall make every effort to identify itself and to inform the adverse Party of the circumstances. As soon as such medical aircraft has been recognized by the adverse Party, that Party shall make all reasonable efforts to give the order to land or to alight on water, referred to in Article 30, paragraph 1, or to take other measures to safeguard its own interests, and, in either case, to allow the aircraft time for compliance, before resorting to an attack against the aircraft.

Article 28—Restrictions on operations of medical aircraft

1. The Parties to the conflict are prohibited from using their medical aircraft to attempt to acquire any military advantage over an adverse Party. The presence of medical aircraft shall not be used in an attempt to render military objectives immune from attack.

2. Medical aircraft shall not be used to collect or transmit intelligence data and shall not carry any equipment intended for such purposes. They are prohibited from carrying any persons or cargo not included within the definition in Article 8, sub-paragraph (f). The carrying on board of the personal effects of the occupants or of equipment intended solely to facilitate navigation, communication or identification shall not be considered as prohibited.

3. Medical aircraft shall not carry any armament except small arms and ammunition taken from the wounded, sick and shipwrecked on board and not yet handed to the proper service, and such light individual weapons as may be necessary to enable the medical personnel on

board to defend themselves and the wounded, sick and shipwrecked in their charge.

4. While carrying out the flights referred to in Articles 26 and 27, medical aircraft shall not, except by prior agreement with the adverse Party, be used to search for the wounded, sick and shipwrecked.

Article 29—Notifications and agreements concerning medical aircraft

1. Notifications under Article 25, or requests for prior agreement under Articles 26, 27, 28 (paragraph 4), or 31 shall state the proposed number of medical aircraft, their flight plans and means of identification, and shall be understood to mean that every flight will be carried out in compliance with Article 28.

2. A Party which receives a notification given under Article 25 shall at once acknowledge receipt of such notification.

3. A Party which receives a request for prior agreement under Articles 26, 27, 28 (paragraph 4), or 31 shall, as rapidly as possible, notify the requesting Party:

(*a*) that the request is agreed to;

(*b*) that the request is denied; or

(*c*) of reasonable alternative proposals to the request. It may also propose a prohibition or restriction of other flights in the area during the time involved. If the Party which submitted the request accepts the alternative proposals, it shall notify the other Party of such acceptance.

4. The Parties shall take the necessary measures to ensure that notifications and agreements can be made rapidly.

5. The Parties shall also take the necessary measures to disseminate rapidly the substance of any such notifications and agreements to the military units concerned and shall instruct those units regarding the means of identification that will be used by the medical aircraft in question.

Article 30—Landing and inspection of medical aircraft

1. Medical aircraft flying over areas which are physically controlled by an adverse Party, or over areas the physical control of which is not clearly established, may be ordered to land or to alight on water, as

appropriate, to permit inspection in accordance with the following paragraphs. Medical aircraft shall obey any such order.

2. If such an aircraft lands or alights on water, whether ordered to do so or for other reasons, it may be subjected to inspection solely to determine the matters referred to in paragraphs 3 and 4. Any such inspection shall be commenced without delay and shall be conducted expeditiously. The inspecting Party shall not require the wounded and sick to be removed from the aircraft unless their removal is essential for the inspection. That Party shall in any event ensure that the condition of the wounded and sick is not adversely affected by the inspection or by the removal.

3. If the inspection discloses that the aircraft:

    (*a*) is a medical aircraft within the meaning of Article 8, sub-paragraph (*j*),

    (*b*) is not in violation of the conditions prescribed in Article 28, and

    (*c*) has not flown without or in breach of a prior agreement where such agreement is required,

    the aircraft and those of its occupants who belong to the adverse Party or to a neutral or other State not a Party to the conflict shall be authorized to continue the flight without delay.

4. If the inspection discloses that the aircraft:

    (*a*) is not a medical aircraft within the meaning of Article 8, sub-paragraph (*j*),

    (*b*) is in violation of the conditions prescribed in Article 28, or

    (*c*) has flown without or in breach of a prior agreement where such agreement is required,

    the aircraft may be seized. Its occupants shall be treated in conformity with the relevant provisions of the Conventions and of this Protocol. Any aircraft seized which had been assigned as a permanent medical aircraft may be used thereafter only as a medical aircraft.

Article 31—Neutral or other States not Parties to the conflict

1. Except by prior agreement, medical aircraft shall not fly over or land in the territory of a neutral or other State not a Party to the conflict. However, with such an agreement, they shall be respected throughout their flight and also for the duration of any calls in the territory. Nevertheless they shall obey any summons to land or to alight on water, as appropriate.

2. Should a medical aircraft, in the absence of an agreement or in deviation

from the terms of an agreement, fly over the territory of a neutral or other State not a Party to the conflict, either through navigational error or because of an emergency affecting the safety of the flight, it shall make every effort to give notice of the flight and to identify itself. As soon as such medical aircraft is recognized, that State shall make all reasonable efforts to give the order to land or to alight on water referred to in Article 30, paragraph 1, or to take other measures to safeguard its own interests, and, in either case, to allow the aircraft time for compliance, before resorting to an attack against the aircraft.

3. If a medical aircraft, either by agreement or in the circumstances mentioned in paragraph 2, lands or alights on water in the territory of a neutral or other State not Party to the conflict, whether ordered to do so or for other reasons, the aircraft shall be subject to inspection for the purposes of determining whether it is in fact a medical aircraft. The inspection shall be commenced without delay and shall be conducted expeditiously. The inspecting Party shall not require the wounded and sick of the Party operating the aircraft to be removed from it unless their removal is essential for the inspection. The inspecting Party shall in any event ensure that the condition of the wounded and sick is not adversely affected by the inspection or the removal. If the inspection discloses that the aircraft is in fact a medical aircraft, the aircraft with its occupants, other than those who must be detained in accordance with the rules of international law applicable in armed conflict, shall be allowed to resume its flight, and reasonable facilities shall be given for the continuation of the flight. If the inspection discloses that the aircraft is not a medical aircraft, it shall be seized and the occupants treated in accordance with paragraph 4.

4. The wounded, sick and shipwrecked disembarked, otherwise than temporarily, from a medical aircraft with the consent of the local authorities in the territory of a neutral or other State not a Party to the conflict shall, unless agreed otherwise between that State and the Parties to the conflict, be detained by that State where so required by the rules of international law applicable in armed conflict, in such a manner that they cannot again take part in the hostilities. The cost of hospital treatment and internment shall be borne by the State to which those persons belong.

5. Neutral or other States not Parties to the conflict shall apply any conditions and restrictions on the passage of medical aircraft over, or on the landing of medical aircraft in, their territory equally to all Parties to the conflict.

SECTION III—MISSING AND DEAD PERSONS

Article 32—General principle

In the implementation of this Section, the activities of the High Contracting Parties, of the Parties to the conflict and of the international humanitarian organizations mentioned in the Conventions and in this Protocol shall be prompted mainly by the right of families to know the fate of their relatives.

Article 33—Missing persons

1. As soon as circumstances permit, and at the latest from the end of active hostilities, each Party to the conflict shall search for the persons who have been reported missing by an adverse Party. Such adverse Party shall transmit all relevant information concerning such persons in order to facilitate such searches.

2. In order to facilitate the gathering of information pursuant to the preceding paragraph, each Party to the conflict shall, with respect to persons who would not receive more favourable consideration under the Conventions and this Protocol:

    (*a*) record the information specified in Article 138 of the Fourth Convention in respect of such persons who have been detained, imprisoned or otherwise held in captivity for more than two weeks as a result of hostilities or occupation, or who have died during any period of detention;

    (*b*) to the fullest extent possible, facilitate and, if need be, carry out the search for and the recording of information concerning such persons if they have died in other circumstances as a result of hostilities or occupation.

3. Information concerning persons reported missing pursuant to paragraph 1 and requests for such information shall be transmitted either directly or through the Protecting Power or the Central Tracing Agency of the International Committee of the Red Cross or national Red Cross (Red Crescent, Red Lion and Sun) Societies. Where the information is not transmitted through the International Committee of the Red Cross and its Central Tracing Agency, each Party to the conflict shall ensure that such information is also supplied to the Central Tracing Agency.

4. The Parties to the conflict shall endeavour to agree on arrangements for teams to search for, identify and recover the dead from battlefield

areas, including arrangements, if appropriate, for such teams to be accompanied by personnel of the adverse Party while carrying out these missions in areas controlled by the adverse Party. Personnel of such teams shall be respected and protected while exclusively carrying out these duties.

Article 34—Remains of deceased

1. The remains of persons who have died for reasons related to occupation or in detention resulting from occupation or hostilities and those of persons not nationals of the country in which they have died as a result of hostilities shall be respected, and the gravesites of all such persons shall be respected, maintained and marked as provided for in Article 130 of the Fourth Convention, where the remains or gravesites would not receive more favourable consideration under the Conventions and this Protocol.

2. As soon as circumstances and the relations between the adverse Parties permit, the High Contracting Parties in whose territories graves and, as the case may be, other locations of the remains of persons who have died as a result of hostilities or during occupation or in detention are situated, shall conclude agreements in order:

   (*a*) to facilitate access to the gravesites by relatives of the deceased and by representatives of official graves registration services and to regulate the practical arrangements for such access;

   (*b*) to protect and maintain such gravesites permanently;

   (*c*) to facilitate the return of the remains of the deceased and of personal effects to the home country upon its request or, unless that country objects, upon the request of the next of kin.

3. In the absence of the agreements provided for in paragraph 2(*b*) or (*c*) and if the home country of such deceased is not willing to arrange at its expense for the maintenance of such gravesites, the High Contracting Party in whose territory the gravesites are situated may offer to facilitate the return of the remains of the deceased to the home country. Where such an offer has not been accepted the High Contracting Party may, after the expiry of five years from the date of the offer and upon due notice to the home country, adopt the arrangements laid down in its own laws relating to cemeteries and graves.

4. A High Contracting Party in whose territory the gravesites referred to in this Article are situated shall be permited to exhume the remains only:

   (*a*) in accordance with paragraphs 2 (*c*) and 3, or

   (*b*) where exhumation is a matter of overriding public necessity, including cases of medical and investigative necessity, in which case the High Contracting Party shall at all times respect the remains, and shall give notice to the home country of its intention to exhume the remains together with details of the intended place of reinternment.

PART III

METHODS AND MEANS OF WARFARE
COMBATANT AND PRISONER-OF-WAR STATUS

SECTION 1—METHODS AND MEANS OF WARFARE

Article 35—Basic rules

1. In any armed conflict, the right of the Parties to the conflict to choose methods or means of warfare is not unlimited.

2. It is prohibited to employ weapons, projectiles and material and methods of warfare of a nature to cause superfluous injury or unnecessary suffering.

3. It is prohibited to employ methods or means of warfare which are intended, or may be expected, to cause widespread, long-term and severe damage to the natural environment.

Article 36—New weapons

In the study, development, acquisition or adoption of a new weapon, means or method of warfare, a High Contracting Party is under an obligation to determine whether its employment would, in some or all circumstances, be prohibited by this Protocol or by any other rule of international law applicable to the High Contracting Party.

Article 37—Prohibition of perfidy

1. It is prohibited to kill, injure or capture an adversary by resort to perfidy. Acts inviting the confidence of an adversary to lead him to believe that he is entitled to, or is obliged to accord, protection under the rules of international law applicable in armed conflict, with intent to betray that confidence, shall constitute perfidy. The following acts are examples of perfidy:

    (*a*) the feigning of an intent to negotiate under a flag of truce or of a surrender;

    (*b*) the feigning of an incapacitation by wounds or sickness;

    (*c*) the feigning of civilian, non-combatant status; and

    (*d*) the feigning of protected status by the use of signs, emblems or uniforms of the United Nations or of neutral or other States not Parties to the conflict.

2. Ruses of war are not prohibited. Such ruses are acts which are intended to mislead an adversary or to induce him to act recklessly but which infringe no rule of international law applicable in armed conflict and which are not perfidious because they do not invite the confidence of an adversary with respect to protection under that law. The following are examples of such ruses: the use of camouflage, decoys, mock operations and misinformation.

Article 38—Recognized emblems

1. It is prohibited to make improper use of the distinctive emblem of the red cross, red crescent or red lion and sun or of other emblems, signs or signals provided for by the Conventions or by this Protocol. It is also prohibited to misuse deliberately in an armed conflict other internationally recognized protective emblems, signs or signals, including the flag of truce, and the protective emblem of cultural property.

2. It is prohibited to make use of the distinctive emblem of the United Nations, except as authorized by that Organization.

Article 39—Emblems of nationality

1. It is prohibited to make use in an armed conflict of the flags or military emblems, insignia or uniforms of neutral or other States not parties to the conflict.

2. It is prohibited to make use of the flags or military emblems, insignia or uniforms of adverse Parties while engaging in attacks or in order to shield, favour, protect or impede military operations.

3. Nothing in this Article or in Article 37, paragraph 1 (*d*), shall affect the existing generally recognized rules of international law applicable to espionage or to the use of flags in the conduct of armed conflict at sea.

Article 40—Quarter

It is prohibited to order that there shall be no survivors, to threaten an adversary therewith or to conduct hostilities on this basis.

Article 41—Safeguard of an enemy hors de combat

1. A person who is recognized or who, in the circumstances, should be recognized to be *hors de combat* shall not be made the object of attack.

2. A person is *hors de combat* if:

    (*a*) he is in the power of an adverse Party;

    (*b*) he clearly expresses an intention to surrender; or

    (*c*) he has been rendered unconscious or is otherwise incapacitated by
           wounds or sickness, and therefore is incapable of defending
           himself;

    provided that in any of these cases he abstains from any hostile act and
    does not attempt to escape.

3. When persons entitled to protection as prisoners of war have fallen
    into the power of an adverse Party under unusual conditions of
    combat which prevent their evacuation as provided for in Part III,
    Section I, of the Third Convention, they shall be released and all
    feasible precautions shall be taken to ensure their safety.

Article 42—Occupants of aircraft

1. No person parachuting from an aircraft in distress shall be made the
    object of attack during his descent.

2. Upon reaching the ground in territory controlled by an adverse Party,
    a person who has parachuted from an aircraft in distress shall be given
    an opportunity to surrender before being made the object of attack,
    unless it is apparent that he is engaging in a hostile act.

3. Airborne troops are not protected by this Article.

SECTION II—COMBATANT AND PRISONER-OF-WAR STATUS

Article 43—Armed forces

1. The armed forces of a Party to a conflict consist of all organized armed
    forces, groups and units which are under a command responsible to
    that Party for the conduct of its subordinates, even if that Party is
    represented by a government or an authority not recognized by an
    adverse Party. Such armed forces shall be subject to an internal
    disciplinary system which, *inter alia*, shall enforce compliance with
    the rules of international law applicable in armed conflict.

2. Members of the armed forces of a party to a conflict (other than
    medical personnel and chaplains covered by Article 33 of the Third
    Convention) are combatants, that is to say, they have the right to
    participate directly in hostilities.

3. Whenever a Party to a conflict incorporates a paramilitary or armed

law enforcement agency into its armed forces it shall so notify the other Parties to the conflict.

Article 44—Combatants and prisoners of war

1. Any combatant, as defined in Article 43, who falls into the power of an adverse Party shall be a prisoner of war.

2. While all combatants are obliged to comply with the rules of international law applicable in armed conflict, violations of these rules shall not deprive a combatant of his right to be a combatant or, if he falls into the power of an adverse Party, of his right to be a prisoner of war, except as provided in paragraphs 3 and 4.

3. In order to promote the protection of the civilian population from the effects of hostilities, combatants are obliged to distinguish themselves from the civilian population while they are engaged in an attack or in a military operation preparatory to an attack. Recognizing, however, that there are situations in armed conflicts where, owing to the nature of the hostilities an armed combatant cannot so distinguish himself, he shall retain his status as a combatant, provided that, in such situations, he carries his arms openly:

    (*a*) during each military engagement, and

    (*b*) during such time as he is visible to the adversary while he is engaged in a military deployment preceding the launching of an attack in which he is to participate.

    Acts which comply with the requirements of this paragraph shall not be considered as perfidious within the meaning of Article 37, paragraph 1 (*c*).

4. A combatant who falls into the power of an adverse Party while failing to meet the requirements set forth in the second sentence of paragraph 3 shall forfeit his right to be a prisoner of war, but he shall, nevertheless, be given protections equivalent in all respects to those accorded to prisoners of war by the Third Convention and by this Protocol. This protection includes protections equivalent to those accorded to prisoners of war by the Third Convention in the case where such a person is tried and punished for any offences he has committed.

5. Any combatant who falls into the power of an adverse Party while not engaged in an attack or in a military operation preparatory to an attack shall not forfeit his rights to be a combatant and a prisoner of war by virtue of his prior activities.

6. This Article is without prejudice to the right of any person to be a prisoner of war pursuant to Article 4 of the Third Convention.

7. This Article is not intended to change the generally accepted practice of States with respect to the wearing of the uniform by combatants assigned to the regular, uniformed armed units of a Party to the conflict.

8. In addition to the categories of persons mentioned in Article 13 of the First and Second Conventions, all members of the armed forces of a Party to the conflict, as defined in Article 43 of this Protocol, shall be entitled to protection under those Conventions if they are wounded or sick or, in the case of the Second Convention, shipwrecked at sea or in other waters.

Article 45—Protection of persons who have taken part in hostilities

1. A person who takes part in hostilities and falls into the power of an adverse Party shall be presumed to be a prisoner of war, and therefore shall be protected by the Third Convention, if he claims the status of prisoner of war, or if he appears to be entitled to such status, or if the Party on which he depends claims such status on his behalf by notificaiton to the detaining Power or to the Protecting Power. Should any doubt arise as to whether any such persons is entitled to the status of prisoner of war, he shall continue to have such status and, therefore, to be protected by the Third Convention and this Protocol until such time as his status has been determined by a competent tribunal.

2. If a person who has fallen into the power of an adverse Party is not held as a prisoner of war and is to be tried by that Party for an offence arising out of the hostilities, he shall have the right to assert his entitlement to prisoner-of-war status before a judicial tribunal and to have that question adjudicated. Whenever possible under the applicable procedure, this adjudication shall occur before the trial for the offence. The representatives of the Protecting Power shall be entitled to attend the proceedings in which that question is adjudicated, unless, exceptionally, the proceedings are held *in camera* in the interest of State security. In such a case the detaining Power shall advise the Protecting Power accordingly.

3. Any person who has taken part in hostilities, who is not entitled to prisoner-of-war status and who does not benefit from more favourable treatment in accordance with the Fourth Convention shall have the right at all times to the protection of Article 75 of this Protocol. In occupied territory, any such person, unless he is held as a spy, shall also be entitled, notwithstanding Article 5 of the Fourth Convention, to his rights of communication under that Convention.

Article 46—Spies

1. Notwithstanding any other provision of the Conventions or of this Protocol, any member of the armed forces of a Party to the conflict who falls into the power of an adverse Party while engaging in espionage shall not have the right to the status of prisoner of war and may be treated as a spy.

2. A member of the armed forces of a party to the conflict who, on behalf of that Party and in territory controlled by an adverse Party, gathers or attempts to gather information shall not be considered as engaging in espionage if, while so acting, he is in the uniform of his armed forces.

3. A member of the armed forces of a Party to the conflict who is a resident of territory occupied by an adverse Party and who, on behalf of the Party on which he depends, gathers or attempts to gather information of military value within that territory shall not be considered as engaging in espionage unless he does so through an act of false pretences or deliberately in a clandestine manner. Moreover, such a resident shall not lose his right to the status of prisoner of war and may not be treated as a spy unless he is captured while engaging in espionage.

4. A member of the armed forces of a Party to the conflict who is not a resident of territory occupied by an adverse Party and who has engaged in espionage in that territory shall not lose his right to the status of prisoner of war and may not be treated as a spy unless he is captured before he has rejoined the armed forces to which he belongs.

Article 47—Mercenaries

1. A mercenary shall not have the right to be a combatant or a prisoner of war.

2. A mercenary is any person who:

    (*a*) is specially recruited locally or abroad in order to fight in an armed conflict;

    (*b*) does, in fact, take a direct part in the hostilities;

    (*c*) is motivated to take part in the hostilities essentially by the desire for private gain and, in fact, is promised, by or on behalf of a Party to the conflict, material compensation substantially in excess of that promised or paid to combatants or similar ranks and functions in the armed forces of that Party;

    (*d*) is neither a national of a Party to the conflict nor a resident of territory controlled by a Party to the conflict;

(*e*) is not a member of the armed forces of a Party to the conflict; and

(*f*) has not been sent by a State which is not a Party to the conflict on official duty as a member of its armed forces.

PART IV

CIVILIAN POPULATION

SECTION 1—GENERAL PROTECTION AGAINST EFFECTS OF HOSTILITIES

CHAPTER 1—BASIC RULE AND FIELD OF APPLICATION

Article 48—Basic rule

In order to ensure respect for and protection of the civilian population and civilian objects, the Parties to the conflict shall at all times distinguish between the civilian population and combatants and between civilian objects and military objectives and accordingly shall direct their operations only against military objectives.

Article 49—Definition of attacks and scope of application

1. "Attacks" mean acts of violence against the adversary, whether in offence or in defence.

2. The provisions of this Protocol with respect to attacks apply to all attacks in whatever territory conducted, including the national territory belonging to a Party to the conflict but under the control of an adverse Party.

3. The provisions of this Section apply to any land, air or sea warfare which may affect the civilian population, individual civilians or civilian objects on land. They further apply to all attacks from the sea or from the air against objectives on land but do not otherwise affect the rules of international law applicable in armed conflict at sea or in the air.

4. The provisions of this Section are additional to the rules concerning humanitarian protection contained in the Fourth Convention, particularly in Part II thereof, and in other international agreements binding upon the High Contracting Parties, as well as to other rules of international law relating to the protection of civilians and civilian objects on land, at sea or in the air against the effects of hostilities.

CHAPTER II—CIVILIANS AND CIVILIAN POPULATION

Article 50—Definition of civilians and civilian population

1. A civilian is any person who does not belong to one of the categories of persons referred to in Article 4 A (1), (2), (3) and (6) of the Third Convention and in Article 43 of this Protocol. In case of doubt whether a person is a civilian, that person shall be considered to be a civilian.

2. The civilian poulation comprises all persons who are civilians.

3. The presence within the civilian population of individuals who do not come within the definition of civilians does not deprive the population of its civilian character.

Article 51—Protection of the civilian population

1. The civilian population and individual civilians shall enjoy general protection against dangers arising from military operations. To give effect to this protection, the following rules, which are additional to other applicable rules of international law, shall be observed in all circumstances.

2. The civilian population as such, as well as individual civilians, shall not be the object of attack. Acts or threats of violence the primary purpose of which is to spread terror among the civilian population are prohibited.

3. Civilians shall enjoy the protection afforded by this Section, unless and for such time as they take a direct part in hostilities.

4. Indiscriminate attacks are prohibited. Indiscriminate attacks are:

   (*a*) those which are not directed at a specific military objective;

   (*b*) those which employ a method or means of combat which cannot be directed at a specific military objective; or

   (*c*) those which employ a method or means of combat the effects of which cannot be limited as required by this Protocol;

   and consequently, in each such case, are of a nature to strike military objectives and civilians or civilian objects without distinction.

5. Among others, the following types of attack are to be considered as indiscriminate:

   (*a*) an attack by bombardment by any methods or means which treats as a single military objective a number of clearly separated and distinct military objectives located in a city, town, village or other area containing a similar concentration of civilians or civilian objects; and (*b*) an attack which may be expected to cause incidental loss of civilian life, injury to civilians, damage to civilian objects, or a combination thereof, which would be excessive in relation to the concrete and direct military advantage anticipated.

6. Attacks against the civilian population or civilians by way of reprisals are prohibited.

7. The presence or movements of the civilian population or individual civilians shall not be used to render certain points or areas immune from military operations, in particular in attempts to shield military objectives from attacks or to shield, favour or impede military operations. The Parties to the conflict shall not direct the movement of the civilian population or individual civilians in order to attempt to shield military objectives from attacks or to shield military operations.

8. Any violation of these prohibitions shall not release the Parties to the conflict from their legal obligations with respect to the civilian population and civilians, including the obligation to take the precautionary measures provided for in Article 57.

CHAPTER III—CIVILIAN OBJECTS

Article 52—General protection of civilian objects

1. Civilian objects shall not be the object of attack or of reprisals. Civilian objects are all objects which are not military objectives as defined in paragraph 2.

2. Attacks shall be limited strictly to military objectives. In so far as objects are concerned, military objectives are limited to those objects which by their nature, location, purpose or use make an effective contribution to military action and whose total or partial destruction, capture or neutralization, in the circumstances ruling at the time, offers a definite military advantage.

3. In case of doubt whether an object which is normally dedicated to civilian purposes, such as a place of worship, a house or other dwelling or a school, is being used to make an effective contribution to military action, it shall be presumed not to be so used.

Article 53—Protection of cultural objects and of places of worship

Without prejudice to the provisions of the Hague Convention for the Protection of Cultural Property in the Event of Armed Conflict of 14 May 1954, and of other relevant international instruments, it is prohibited:

(*a*) to commit any acts of hostility directed against the historic monuments, works of art or places of worship which constitute the cultural or spiritual heritage of peoples;

(*b*) to use such objects in support of the military effort;

(*c*) to make such objects the object of reprisals.

Article 54—Protection of objects indispensable to the survival of the civilian population

1. Starvation of civilians as a method of warfare is prohibited.

2. It is prohibited to attack, destroy, remove or render useless objects indispensable to the survival of the civilian population, such as foodstuffs, agricultural areas for the production of foodstuffs, crops, livestock, drinking water installations and supplies and irrigation works, for the specific purpose of denying them for their sustenance value to the civilian population or to the adverse Party, whatever the motive, whether in order to starve out civilians, to cause them to move away, or for any other motive.

3. The prohibitions in paragraph 2 shall not apply to such of the objects covered by it as are used by an adverse Party:

(*a*) as sustenance solely for the members of its armed forces; or

(*b*) if not as sustenance, then in direct support of military action, provided, however, that in no event shall actions against these objects be taken which may be expected to leave the civilian population with such inadequate food or water as to cause its starvation or force its movement.

4. These objects shall not be made the object of reprisals.

5. In recognition of the vital requirements of any Party to the conflict in the defence of its national territory against invasion, derogation from the prohibitions contained in paragraph 2 may be made by a Party to the conflict within such territory under its own control where required by imperative military necessity.

Article 55—Protection of the natural environment

1. Care shall be taken in warfare to protect the natural environment against widespread, long-term and severe damage. This protection includes a prohibition of the use of methods or means of warfare which are intended or may be expected to cause such damage to the natural environment and thereby to prejudice the health or survival of the population.

2. Attacks against the natural environment by way of reprisals are prohibited.

Article 56—Protection of works and installations containing
dangerous forces

1. Works or installations containing dangerous forces, namely dams, dykes and nuclear electrical generating stations, shall not be made the object of attack, even where these objects are military objectives, if such attack may cause the release of dangerous forces and consequent severe losses among the civilian population. Other military objectives located at or in the vicinity of these works or installations shall not be made the object of attack if such attack may cause the release of dangerous forces from the works or installations and consequent severe losses among the civilian population.

2. The special protection against attack provided by paragraph 1 shall cease:

    (*a*) for a dam or a dyke only if it is used for other than its normal function and in regular, significant and direct support of military operations and if such attack is the only feasible way to terminate such support;

    (*b*) for a nuclear electrical generating station only if it provides electric power in regular, significant and direct support of military operations and if such attack is the only feasible way to terminate such support;

    (*c*) for other military objectives located at or in the vicinity of these works or installations only if they are used in regular, significant and direct support of military operations and if such attack is the only feasible way to terminate such support.

3. In all cases, the civilian population and individual civilians shall remain entitled to all the protection accorded them by international law, including the protection of the precautionary measures provided for in Article 57. If the protection ceases and any of the works, installations or military objectives mentioned in paragaph 1 is attacked, all practical precautions shall be taken to avoid the release of the dangerous forces.

4. It is prohibited to make any of the works, installations or military objectives mentioned in paragraph 1 the object of reprisals.

5. The Parties to the conflict shall endeavour to avoid locating any military objectives in the vicinity of the works or installations mentioned in paragrpah 1. Nevertheless, installations erected for the sole purpose of defending the protected works or installations from attack are permissible and shall not themselves be made the object of attack, provided that they are not used in hostilities except for defensive actions necessary to respond to attacks against the protected

works or installations and that their armament is limited to weapons capable only of repelling hostile action against the protected works or installations.

6. The High Contracting Parties and the Parties to the conflict are urged to conclude further agreements among themselves to provide additional protection for objects containing dangerous forces.

7. In order to facilitate the identification of the objects protected by this article, the Parties to the conflict may mark them with a special sign consisting of a group of three bright orange circles placed on the same axis, as specified in Article 16 of Annex I to this Protocol. The absence of such marking in no way relieves any Party to the conflict of its obligations under this Article.

CHAPTER IV—PRECAUTIONARY MEASURES

Article 57—Precautions in attack

1. In the conduct of military operations, constant care shall be taken to spare the civilian population, civilians and civilian objects.

2. With respect to attacks, the following precautions shall be taken:

   a) those who plan or decide upon an attack shall:

      (i) do everything feasible to verify that the objectives to be attacked are neither civilians nor civilian objects and are not subject to special protection but are military objectives within the meaning of paragraph 2 of Article 52 and that it is not prohibited by the provisions of this Protocol to attack them;

      (ii) take all feasible precautions in the choice of means and methods of attack with a view to avoiding, and in any event to minimizing, incidental loss of civilian life, injury to civilians and damage to civilian objects;

      (iii) refrain from deciding to launch any attack which may be expected to cause incidental loss of civilian life, injury to civilians, damage to civilian objects, or a combination thereof, which would be excessive in relation to the concrete and direct military advantage anticipated;

   (b) an attack shall be cancelled or suspended if it becomes apparent that the objective is not a military one or is subject to special protection or that the attack may be expected to cause incidental loss of civilian life, injury to civilians, damage to civilian objects,

or a combination thereof, which would be excessive in relation to the concrete and direct military advantage anticipated;

(*c*) effective advance warning shall be given of attacks which may affect the civilian population, unless circumstances do not permit.

3. When a choice is possible between several military objectives for obtaining a similar military advantage, the objective to be selected shall be the attack which may be expected to cause the least danger to civilian lives and to civilian objects.

4. In the conduct of military operations at sea or in the air, each Party to the conflict shall, in conformity with its rights and duties under the rules of international law applicable in armed conflict, take all reasonable precautions to avoid losses of civilian lives and damage to civilian objects.

5. No provision of this Article may be construed as authorizing any attacks against the civilian population, civilians or civilian objects.

Article 58—Precautions against the effects of attacks

The Parties to the conflict shall, to the maximum extent feasible:

(*a*) without prejudice to Article 49 of the Fourth Convention, endeavour to remove the civilian population, individual civilians and civilian objects under their control from the vicinity of military objectives;

(*b*) avoid locating military objectives within or near densely populated areas;

(*c*) take the other necessary precautions to protect the civilian population, individual civilians and civilian objects under their control against the dangers resulting from military operations.

CHAPTER V—LOCALITIES AND ZONES UNDER SPECIAL PROTECTION

Article 59—Non-defended localities

1. It is prohibited for the Parties to the conflict to attack, by any means whatsoever, non-defended localities.

2. The appropriate authorities of a Party to the conflict may declare as a non-defended locality any inhabited place near or in a zone where armed forces are in contact which is open for occupation by an adverse Party. Such a locality shall fulfil the following conditions:

(a) all combatants, as well as mobile weapons and mobile military equipment must have been evacuated;

(b) no hostile use shall be made of fixed military installations or establishments;

(c) no acts of hostility shall be committed by the authorities or by the population; and

(d) no activities in support of military operations shall be undertaken.

3. The presence, in this locality, of persons specially protected under the Conventions and this Protocol, and of police forces retained for the sole purpose of maintaining law and order, is not contrary to the conditions laid down in paragraph 2.

4. The declaration made under paragraph 2 shall be addressed to the adverse Party and shall define and describe, as precisely as possible, the limits of the non-defended locality. The Party to the conflict to which the declaration is addressed shall acknowledge its receipt and shall treat the locality as a non-defended locality unless the conditions laid down in paragraph 2 are not in fact fulfilled, in which event it shall immediately so inform the Party making the declaration. Even if the conditions laid down in paragraph 2 are not fulfilled, the locality shall continue to enjoy the protection provided by the other provisons of this Protocol and the other rules of international law applicable in armed conflict.

5. The Parties to the conflict may agree on the establishment of non-defended localities even if such localities do not fulfil the conditions laid down in paragraph 2. The agreement should define and describe, as precisely as possible, the limits of the non-defended locality; if necessary, it may lay down the methods of supervision.

6. The Party which is in control of a locality governed by such an agreement shall mark it, so far as possible, by such signs as may be agreed upon with the other Party, which shall be displayed where they are clearly visible, especially on its perimeter and limits and on highways.

7. A locality loses its status as a non-defended locality when it ceases to fulfil the conditions laid down in paragraph 2 or in the agreement referred to in paragraph 5. In such an eventuality, the locality shall continue to enjoy the protection provided by the other provisions of this Protocol and the other rules of international law applicable in armed conflict.

Article 60—Demilitarized zones

1. It is prohibited for the Parties to the conflict to extend their military operations to zones on which they have conferred by agreement the

status of demilitarized zone, if such extension is contrary to the terms of this agreement.

2. The agreement shall be an express agreement, may be concluded verbally or in writing, either directly or through a Protecting Power or any impartial humanitarian organization, and may consist of reciprocal and concordant declarations. The agreement may be concluded in peacetime, as well as after the outbreak of hostilities, and should define and describe, as precisely as possible, the limits of the demilitarized zone and, if necessary, lay down the methods of supervision.

3. The subject of such an agreement shall normally be any zone which fulfils the following conditions:

   (a) all combatants, as well as mobile weapons and mobile military equipment, must have been evacuated;

   (b) no hostile use shall be made of fixed military installations or establishments;

   (c) no acts of hostility shall be committed by the authorities or by the population; and

   (d) any activity linked to the military effort must have ceased.

   The Parties to the conflict shall agree upon the interpretation to be given to the condition laid down in sub-paragraph (d) and upon persons to be admitted to the demilitarized zone other than those mentioned in paragraph 4.

4. The presence, in this zone, of persons specially protected under the Conventions and this Protocol, and of police forces retained for the sole purpose of maintaining law and order, is not contrary to the conditions laid down in paragraph 3.

5. The Party which is in control of such a zone shall mark it, so far as possible, by such signs as may be agreed upon with the other Party, which shall be displayed where they are clearly visible, especially on its perimeter and limits and on highways.

6. If the fighting draws near to a demilitarized zone, and if the Parties to the conflict have so agreed, none of them may use the zone for purposes related to the conduct of military operations or unilaterally revoke its status.

7. If one of the Parties to the conflict commits a material breach of the provisions of paragraphs 3 or 6, the other Party shall be released from its obligations under the agreement conferring upon the zone the status of demilitarized zone. In such an eventuality, the zone loses its status but shall continue to enjoy the protection provided by the other provisions of this Protocol and the other rules of international law applicable in armed conflict.

CHAPTER VI—CIVIL DEFENCE

Article 61—Definitions and scope

For the purposes of this Protocol:

(*a*) "civil defence" means the performance of some or all of the undermentioned humanitarian tasks intended to protect the civilian population against the dangers, and to help it to recover from the immediate effects, of hostilities or disasters and also to provide the conditions necessary for its survival. These tasks are:

   (i)   warning;
   (ii) evacuation;
   (iii) management of shelters;
   (iv) management of blackout measures;
   (v)   rescue;
   (vi) medical services, including first aid, and religious assistance;
   (vii) fire-fighting;
   (viii) detection and marking of danger areas;
   (ix) decontamination and similar protective measures;
   (x)   provision of emergency accommodation and supplies;
   (xi) emergency assistance in the restoration and maintenance of order in distressed areas;
   (xii) emergency repair of indispensable public utilities;
   (xiii) emergency disposal of the dead;
   (xiv) assistance in the preservation of objects essential for survival;
   (xv) complementary activities necessary to carry out any of the tasks mentioned above, including, but not limited to, planning and organization;

(*b*) "civil defence organizations" means those establishments and other units which are organized or authorized by the competent authorities of a Party to the conflict to perform any of the tasks mentioned under sub-paragraph (*a*), and which are assigned and devoted exclusively to such tasks;

(*c*) "personnel" of civil defence organizations means those persons assigned by a Party to the conflict exclusively to the performance of the tasks mentioned under sub-paragraph (*a*), including personnel assigned by the competent authority of that Party exclusively to the administration of these organizations;

(d) *"matériel"* of civil defence organizations means equipment, supplies and transports used by these organizations for the performance of the tasks mentioned under sub-paragraph (a).

Article 62—General protection

1. Civilian civil defence organizations and their personnel shall be respected and protected, subject to the provisions of this Protocol, particularly the provisions of this Section. They shall be entitled to perform their civil defence tasks except in case of imperative military necessity.

2. The provisions of paragraph 1 shall also apply to civilians who, although not members of civilian civil defence organizations, respond to an appeal from the competent authorities and perform civil defence tasks under their control.

3. Buildings and *matériel* used for civil defence purposes and shelters provided for the civilian population are covered by Article 52. Objects used for civil defence purposes may not be destroyed or diverted from their proper use except by the Party to which they belong.

Article 63—Civil defence in occupied territories

1. In occupied territories, civilian civil defence organizations shall receive from the authorities the facilities necessary for the performance of their tasks. In no circumstances shall their personnel be compelled to perform activities which would interfere with the proper performance of these tasks. The Occupying Power shall not change the structure or personnel of such organizations in any way which might jeopardize the efficient performance of their mission. These organizations shall not be required to give priority to the nationals or interests of that Power.

2. The Occupying Power shall not compel, coerce or induce civilian civil defence organizations to perform their tasks in any manner prejudicial to the interests of the civilian population.

3. The Occupying Power may disarm civil defence personnel for reasons of security.

4. The Occupying Power shall neither divert from their proper use nor requisition buildings or *matériel* belonging to or used by civil defence organizations if such diversions or requisition would be harmful to the civilian population.

5. Provided that the general rule in paragraph 4 continues to be observed, the Occupying Power may requisition or divert these resources, subject to the following particular conditions:

    (a) that the buildings or *matériel* are necessary for other needs of the civilian population; and

    (b) that the requisition or diversion continues only while such necessity exists.

6. The Occupying Power shall neither divert nor requisition shelters provided for the use of the civilian population or needed by such population.

Article 64—Civilian civil defence organizations of neutral or other States not parties to the conflict and international co-ordinating organizations

1. Articles 62, 63, 65 and 66 shall also apply to the personnel and *matériel* of civilian civil defence organizations of neutral or other States not Parties to the conflict which perform civil defence tasks mentioned in Article 61 in the territory of a party to the conflict, with the consent and under the control of that Party. Notification of such assistance shall be given as soon as possible to any adverse Party concerned. In no circumstances shall this activity be deemed to be an interference in the conflict. This activity should, however, be performed with due regard to the security interests of the Parties to the conflict concerned.

2. The Parties to the conflict receiving the assistance referred to in paragraph 1 and the High Contracting Parties granting it should facilitate international co-ordination of such civil defence actions when appropriate. In such cases the relevant international organizations are covered by the provisions of this Chapter.

3. In occupied territories, the Occupying Power may only exclude or restrict the activities of civilian civil defence organizations of neutral or other States not Parties to the conflict and of international co-ordinating organizations if it can ensure the adequate performance of civil defence tasks from its own resources or those of the occupied territory.

Article 65—Cessation of protection

1. The protection to which civilian civil defence organizations, their personnel, buildings, shelters and *matériel* are entitled shall not cease unless they commit or are used to commit, outside their proper tasks, acts harmful to the enemy. Protection may, however, cease only after

a warning has been given setting, whenever appropriate, a reasonable time-limit, and after such warning has remained unheeded.

2. The following shall not be considered as acts harmful to the enemy:

   (a) that civil defence tasks are carried out under the direction or control of military authorities;

   (b) that civilian civil defence personnel co-operate with military personnel in the performance of civil defence tasks, or that some military personnel are attached to civilian civil defence organizations;

   (c) that the performance of civil defence tasks may incidentally benefit military victims, particulary those who are *hors de combat*.

3. It shall also not be considered as an act harmful to the enemy that civilian civil defence personnel bear light individual weapons for the purpose of maintaining order or for self-defence. However, in areas where land fighting is taking place or is likely to take place, the Parties to the conflict shall undertake the appropriate measures to limit these weapons to handguns, such as pistols or revolvers, in order to assist in distinguishing between civil defence personnel and combatants. Although civil defence personnel bear other light individual weapons in such areas, they shall nevertheless be respected and protected as soon as they have been recognized as such.

4. The formation of civilian civil defence organizations along military lines, and compulsory service in them, shall also not deprive them of the protection conferred by this Chapter.

Article 66—Identification

1. Each Party to the conflict shall endeavour to ensure that its civil defence organizations, their personnel, buildings and *matériel*, are identifiable while they are exclusively devoted to the performance of civil defence tasks. Shelters provided for the civilian population should be similarly identifiable.

2. Each Party to the conflict shall also endeavour to adopt and implement methods and procedures which will make it possible to recognize civilian shelters as well as civil defence personnel, buildings and *matériel* on which the international distinctive sign of civil defence is displayed.

3. In occupied territories and in areas where fighting is taking place or is likely to take place, civilian civil defence personnel should be recognizable by the international distinctive sign of civil defence and by an identity card certifying their status.

4. The international distinctive sign of civil defence is an equilateral blue triangle on an orange ground when used for the protection of civil defence organizations, their personnel, buildings and *matériel* and for civilian shelters.

5. In addition to the distinctive sign, Parties to the conflict may agree upon the use of distinctive signals for civil defence identification purposes.

6. The application of the provisions of paragraphs 1 to 4 is governed by Chapter V of Annex I to this Protocol.

7. In time of peace, the sign described in paragraph 4 may, with the consent of the competent national authorities, be used for civil defence identification purposes.

8. The High Contracting Parties and the Parties to the conflict shall take the measures necessary to supervise the display of the international distinctive sign of civil defence and to prevent and repress any misuse thereof.

9. The identification of civil defence medical and religious personnel, medical units and medical transports is also governed by Article 18.

Article 67—Members of the armed forces and military units assigned to civil defence organizations

1. Members of the armed forces and military units assigned to civil defence organizations shall be respected and protected, provided that:

    (*a*) such personnel and such units are permanently assigned and exclusively devoted to the performance of any of the tasks mentioned in Article 61;

    (*b*) if so assigned, such personnel do not perform any other military duties during the conflict;

    (*c*) such personnel are clearly distinguishable from the other members of the armed forces by prominently displaying the international distinctive sign of civil defence, which shall be as large as appropriate, and such personnel are provided with the identity card referred to in Chapter V of Annex I to this Protocol certifying their status;

    (*d*) such personnel and such units are equipped only with light individual weapons for the purpose of maintaining order or for self-defence. The provisions of Article 65, paragraph 3 shall also apply in this case;

    (*e*) such personnel do not participate directly in hostilities, and do not commit, or are not used to commit, outside their civil defence tasks, acts harmful to the adverse Party;

(*f*) such personnel and such units perform their civil defence tasks only within the national territory of their Party.

The non-observance of the conditions stated in (*e*) above by any member of the armed forces who is bound by the conditions prescribed in (*a*) and (*b*) above is prohibited.

2. Military personnel serving within civil defence organizations shall, if they fall into the power of an Adverse Party, be prisoners of war. In occupied territory they may, but only in the interest of the civilian population of that territory, be employed on civil defence tasks in so far as the need arises, provided however that, if such work is dangerous, they volunteer for such tasks.

3. The buildings and major items of equipment and transports of military units assigned to civil defence organizations shall be clearly marked with the international distinctive sign of civil defence. This distinctive sign shall be as large as appropriate.

4. The *matériel* and buildings of military units permanently assigned to civil defence organizations and exclusively devoted to the performance of civil defence tasks shall, if they fall into the hands of an adverse Party, remain subject to the laws of war. They may not be diverted from their civil defence purpose so long as they are required for the performance of civil defence tasks, except in case of imperative military necessity, unless previous arrangements have been made for adequate provison for the needs of the civilian population.

SECTION II—RELIEF IN FAVOUR OF THE CIVILIAN POPULATION

Article 68—Field of application

The provisions of this Section apply to the civilian population as defined in this Protocol and are supplementary to Articles 23, 55, 59, 60, 61 and 62 and other relevant provisions of the Fourth Convention.

Article 69—Basic needs in occupied territories

1. In addition to the duties specified in Article 55 of the Fourth Convention concerning food and medical supplies, the Occupying Power shall, to the fullest extent of the means available to it and without any adverse distinction, also ensure the provision of clothing, bedding, means of shelter, other supplies essential to the survival of the civilian population of the occupied territory and objects necessary for religious worship.

2. Relief actions for the benefit of the civilian population of occupied territories are governed by Articles 59, 60, 61, 62, 108, 109, 110 and 111 of the Fourth Convention, and by Article 71 of this Protocol, and shall be implemented without delay.

Article 70—Relief actions

1. If the civilian population of any territory under the control of a Party to the conflict, other than occupied territory, is not adequately provided with the supplies mentioned in Article 69, relief actions which are humanitarian and impartial in character and conducted without any adverse distinction shall be undertaken, subject to the agreement of the Parties concerned in such relief actions. Offers of such relief shall not be regarded as interference in the armed conflict or as unfriendly acts. In the distribution of relief consignments, priority shall be given to those persons, such as children, expectant mothers, maternity cases and nursing mothers, who, under the Fourth Convention or under this Protocol, are to be accorded privileged treatment or special protection.

2. The Parties to the conflict and each High Contracting Party shall allow and facilitate rapid and unimpeded passage of all relief consignments, equipment and personnel provided in accordance with this Section, even if such assistance is destined for the civilian population of the adverse Party.

3. The Parties to the conflict and each High Contracting Party which allow the passage of relief consignments, equipment and personnel in accordance with paragraph 2;

   (*a*) shall have the right to prescribe the technical arrangements, including search, under which such passage is permitted;

   (*b*) may make such permission conditional on the distribution of this assistance being made under the local supervision of a Protecting Power;

   (*c*) shall, in no way whatsoever, divert relief consignments from the purpose for which they are intended nor delay their forwarding, except in cases of urgent necessity in the interest of the civilian population concerned.

4. The Parties to the conflict shall protect relief consignments and facilitate their rapid distribution.

5. The Parties to the conflict and each High Contracting Party concerned shall encourage and facilitate effective international co-ordination of the relief actions referred to in paragraph 1.

Article 71—Personnel participating in relief actions

1. Where necessary, relief personnel may form part of the assistance provided in any relief action, in particular for the transportation and distribution of relief consignments; the participation of such personnel shall be subject to the approval of the Party in whose territory they will carry out their duties.

2. Such personnel shall be respected and protected.

3. Each Party in receipt of relief consignments shall, to the fullest extent practicable, assist the relief personnel referred to in paragraph 1 in carrying out their relief mission. Only in case of imperative military necessity may the activities of the relief personnel be limited or their movements temporarily restricted.

4. Under no circumstances may relief personnel exceed the terms of their mission under this Protocol. In particular they shall take account of the security requirements of the Party in whose territory they are carrying out their duties. The mission of any of the personnel who do not respect these conditions may be terminated.

SECTION III—TREATMENT OF PERSONS IN THE POWER OF A PARTY TO THE CONFLICT

CHAPTER 1—FIELD OF APPLICATION AND PROTECTION OF PERSONS AND OBJECTS

Article 72—Field of application

The provisions of this Section are additional to the rules concerning humanitarian protection of civilians and civilian objects in the power of a Party to the conflict contained in the Fourth Convention, particularly Parts I and III thereof, as well as to other applicable rules of international law relating to the protection of fundamental human rights during international armed conflict.

Article 73—Refugees and stateless persons

Persons who, before the beginning of hostilities, were considered as stateless persons or refugees under the relevant international instruments accepted by the Parties concerned or under the national legislation of the State of refuge or State of residence shall be protected

persons within the meaning of Parts I and III of the Fourth
Convention, in all circumstances and without any adverse distinction.

Article 74—*Reunion of dispersed families*

The High Contracting Parties and the Parties to the conflict shall
facilitate in every possible way the reunion of families dispersed as a
result of armed conflicts and shall encourage in particular the work of
the humanitarian organizations engaged in this task in accordance
with the provisions of the Conventions and of this Protocol and in
conformity with their respective security regulations.

Article 75—*Fundamental guarantees*

1. In so far as they are affected by a situation referred to in Article 1 of
   this Protocol, persons who are in the power of a Party to the conflict
   and who do not benefit from more favourable treatment under the
   Conventions or under this Protocol shall be treated humanely in all
   circumstances and shall enjoy, as a minimum the protection provided
   by this Article without an adverse distinction based upon race, colour,
   sex, language, religion or belief, political or other opinion, national or
   social origin, wealth, birth or other status, or on any other similar
   criteria. Each Party shall respect the person, honour, convictions and
   religious practices of all such persons.

2. The following acts are and shall remain prohibited at any time and in
   any place whatsoever, whether committed by civilian or by military
   agents:

   (*a*) violence to the life, health, or physical or mental well-being of
   persons, in particular:

       (i) murder;

       (ii) torture of all kinds, whether physical or mental;

       (iii) corporal punishment; and

       (iv) mutilation;

   (*b*) outrages upon personal dignity, in particular humiliating and
   degrading treatment, enforced prostitution and any form of
   indecent assault;

   (*c*) the taking of hostages;

   (*d*) collective punishments; and

   (*e*) threats to commit any of the foregoing acts.

3. Any person arrested, detained or interned for actions related to the

armed conflict shall be informed promptly, in a language he understands, of the reasons why these measures have been taken. Except in
cases of arrest or detention for penal offences, such persons shall be
released with the minimum delay possible and in any event as soon
as the circumstances justifying the arrest, detention or internment
have ceased to exist.

4. No sentence may be passed and no penalty may be executed on a
    person found guilty of a penal offence related to the armed conflict
    except pursuant to a conviction pronounced by an impartial and
    regularly constituted court respecting the generally recognized
    principles of regular judicial procedure, which include the following:

    (*a*) the procedure shall provide for an accused to be informed without
         delay of the particulars of the offence alleged against him and
         shall afford the accused before and during his trial all necessary
         rights and means of defence;

    (*b*) no one shall be convicted of an offence except on the basis of
         individual penal responsibility;

    (*c*) no one shall be accused or convicted of a criminal offence on
         account of any act or omission which did not constitute a criminal
         offence under the national or international law to which he was
         subject at the time when it was committed; nor shall a heavier
         penalty be imposed than that which was applicable at the time
         when the criminal offence was committed. If, after the
         commission of the offence, provision is made by law for the
         imposition of a lighter penalty, the offender shall benefit thereby;

    (*d*) anyone charged with an offence is presumed innocent until
         proved guilty according to law;

    (*e*) anyone charged with an offence shall have the right to be tried in
         his presence;

    (*f*) no one shall be compelled to testify against himself or to confess
         guilt;

    (*g*) anyone charged with an offence shall have the right to examine,
         or have examined, the witnesses against him and to obtain the
         attendance and examination of witnesses on his behalf under the
         same conditions as witnesses against him;

    (*h*) no one shall be prosecuted or punished by the same Party for an
         offence in respect of which a final judgement acquitting or
         convicting that person has been previously pronounced under the
         same law and judicial procedure;

    (*i*) anyone prosecuted for an offence shall have the right to have the
         judgement pronounced publicly; and

(*j*) a convicted person shall be advised on conviction of his judicial and other remedies and of the time-limits within which they may be exercised.

5. Women whose liberty has been restricted for reasons related to the armed conflict shall be held in quarters separated from men's quarters. They shall be under the immediate supervision of women. Nevertheless, in cases where facilities are detained or interned, they shall, whenever possible, be held in the same place and accommodated as family units.

6. Persons who are arrested, detained or interned for reasons related to the armed conflict shall enjoy the protection provided by this Article until their final release, repatriation or re-establishment, even after the end of the armed conflict.

7. In order to avoid any doubt concerning the prosecution and trial of persons accused of war crimes or crimes against humanity, the following principles shall apply:

(*a*) persons who are accused of such crimes should be submitted for the purpose of prosecution and trial in accordance with the applicable rules of international law; and

(*b*) any such persons who do not benefit from more favourable treatment under the Conventions or this Protocol shall be accorded the treatment provided by this Article, whether or not the crimes of which they are accused constitute grave breaches of the Conventions or of this Protocol.

8. No provision of this Article may be construed as limiting or infringing any other more favourable provision granting greater protection, under any applicable rules of international law, to persons covered by paragraph 1.

CHAPTER II—MEASURES IN FAVOUR OF WOMEN AND CHILDREN

Article 76—Protection of women

1. Women shall be the object of special respect and shall be protected in particular against rape, forced prostitution and any other form of indecent assault.

2. Pregnant women and mothers having dependent infants who are arrested, detained or interned for reasons related to the armed conflict, shall have their cases considered with the utmost priority.

3. To the maximum extent feasible, the Parties to the conflict shall endeavour to avoid the pronouncement of the death penalty on pregnant women or mothers having dependent infants, for an offence related to the armed conflict. The death penalty for such offences shall not be executed on such women.

Article 77—Protection of children

1. Children shall be the object of special respect and shall be protected against any form of indecent assault. The Parties to the conflict shall provide them with the care and aid they require, whether because of their age or for any other reason.

2. The Parties to the conflict shall take all feasible measures in order that children who have not attained the age of fifteen years do not take a direct part in hostilities and, in particular, they shall refrain from recruiting them into their armed forces. In recruiting among those persons who have attained the age of fifteen years but who have not attained the age of eighteen years, the Parties to the conflict shall endeavour to give priority to those who are oldest.

3. If, in exceptional cases, despite the provisions of paragraph 2, children who have not attained the age of fifteen years take a direct part in hostilities and fall into the power of an adverse Party, they shall continue to benefit from the special protection accorded by this Article, whether or not they are prisoners of war.

4. If arrested, detained or interned for reasons related to the armed conflict, children shall be held in quarters separate from the quarters of adults, except where families are accommodated as family units as provided in Article 75, paragraph 5.

5. The death penalty for an offence related to the armed conflict shall not be executed on persons who had not attained the age of eighteen years at the time the offence was committed.

Article 78—Evacuation of children

1. No Party to the conflict shall arrange for the evacuation of children, other than its own nationals, to a foreign country except for a temporary evacuation where compelling reasons of the health or medical treatment of the children or, except in occupied territory, their safety, so require. Where the parents or legal guardian can be found, their written consent to such evacuation is required. If these persons cannot be found the written consent to such evacuation of the persons who by law or custom are primarily responsible for the care of the children is required. Any such evacuation shall be supervised

by the Protecting Power in agreement with the Parties concerned, namely, the Party arranging for the evacuation, the Party receiving the children and any Parties whose nationals are being evacuated. In each case, all Parties to the conflict shall take all feasible precautions to avoid endangering the evacuation.

2. Whenever an evacuation occurs pursuant to paragaph 1, each child's education, including his religious and moral education as his parents desire, shall be provided while he is away with the greatest possible continuity.

3. With a view to facilitating the return to their families and country of children evacuated pursuant to this Article, the authorities of the Party arranging for the evacuation and, as appropriate, the authorities of the receiving country shall establish for each child a card with photographs, which they shall send to the Central Tracing Agency of the International Committeee of the Red Cross. Each card shall bear, whenever possible, and whenever it involves no risk of harm to the child, the following information:

(a) surname(s) of the child;

(b) the child's first name(s);

(c) the child's sex;

(d) the place and date of birth (or, if that date is not known, the approximate age);

(e) the father's full name;

(f) the mother's full name and her maiden name;

(g) the child's next-of-kin;

(h) the child's nationality;

(i) the child's native language, and any other languages he speaks;

(j) the address of the child's family;

(k) any identification number for the child;

(l) the child's state of health;

(m) the child's blood group;

(n) any distinguishing features;

(o) the date on which and the place where the child was found;

(p) the date on which and the place from which the child left the country;

(q) the child's religion, if any;

(r) the child's present address in the receiving country;

(s) should the child die before his return, the date, place and circumstances of death and place of interment.

CHAPTER III—JOURNALISTS

Article 79—Measures of protection for journalists

1. Journalists engaged in dangerous professional missions in areas of armed conflict shall be considered as civilians within the meaning of Article 50, paragraph 1.
2. They shall be protected as such under the Conventions and this Protocol, provided that they take no action adversely affecting their status as civilians, and without prejudice to the right of war correspondents accredited to the armed forces to the status provided for in Article 4 A (4) of the Third Convention.
3. They may obtain an identity card similar to the model in Annex II of this Protocol. This card, which shall be issued by the government of the State of which the journalist is a national or in whose territory he resides or in which the news medium employing him is located, shall attest to his status as a journalist.

PART V

EXECUTION OF THE CONVENTIONS
AND OF THIS PROTOCOL

SECTION 1—GENERAL PROVISIONS

Article 80—Measures for execution

1. The High Contracting Parties and the Parties to the conflict shall without delay take all necessary measures for the execution of their obligations under the Conventions and this Protocol.
2. The High Contracting Parties and the Parties to the conflict shall give orders and instructions to ensure observance of the Conventions and this Protocol, and shall supervise their execution.

Article 81—Activities of the Red Cross and other humanitarian organizations

1. The Parties to the conflict shall grant to the International Committee of the Red Cross all facilities within their power so as to enable it to carry out the humanitarian functions assigned to it by the Conventions and this Protocol in order to ensure protection and assistance to the

victims of conflicts; the International Committee of the Red Cross may also carry out any other humanitarian activities in favour of these victims, subject to the consent of the Parties to the conflict concerned.

2. The Parties to the conflict shall grant to their respective Red Cross (Red Crescent, Red Lion and Sun) organizations the facilities necessary for carrying out their humanitarian activities in favour of the victims of the conflict, in accordance with the provisions of the Conventions and this Protocol and the fundamental principles of the Red Cross as formulated by the International Conference of the Red Cross.

3. The High Contracting Parties and the Parties to the conflict shall facilitate in every possible way the assistance which Red Cross (Red Crescent, Red Lion and Sun) organizations and the League of Red Cross Societies extend to the victims of conflicts in accordance with the provisions of the Conventions and this Protocol and with the fundamental principles of the Red Cross as formulated by the International Conferences of the Red Cross.

4. The High Contracting Parties and the Parties to the conflict shall, as far as possible, make facilities similar to those mentioned in paragraphs 2 and 3 available to the other humanitarian organizations referred to in the Conventions and this Protocol which are duly authorized by the respective Parties to the conflict and which perform their humanitarian activities in accordance with the provisions of the Conventions and this Protocol.

Article 82—Legal advisers in armed forces

The High Contracting Parties at all times, and the Parties to the conflict in time of armed conflict, shall ensure that legal advisers are available, when necessary, to advise military commanders at the appropriate level on the application of the Conventions and this Protocol and on the appropriate instruction to be given to the armed forces on this subject.

Article 83—Dissemination

1. The High Contracting Parties undertake, in time of peace as in time of armed conflict, to disseminate the Coventions and this Protocol as widely as possible in their respective countries and, in particular, to include the study thereof in their programmes of military instruction and to encourage the study thereof by the civilian population, so that those instruments may become known to the armed forces and to the civilian population.

2. Any military or civilian authorities who, in time of armed conflict, assume responsibilities in respect of the application of the Conventions and this Protocol shall be fully acquainted with the text thereof.

Article 84—Rules of application

The High Contracting Parties shall communicate to one another, as soon as possible, through the depositary and, as appropriate, through the Protecting Powers, their official translations of this Protocol, as well as the laws and regulations which they may adopt to ensure its application.

SECTION II—REPRESSION OF BREACHES OF THE CONVENTIONS AND OF THIS PROTOCOL

Article 85—Repression of breaches of this Protocol

1. The provisions of the Conventions relating to the repression of breaches and grave breaches, supplemented by this Section, shall apply to the repression of breaches and grave breaches of this Protocol.

2. Acts described as grave breaches in the Conventions are grave breaches of this Protocol if committed against persons in the power of an adverse Party protected by Articles 44, 45 and 73 of this Protocol, or against the wounded, sick and shipwrecked of the adverse Party who are protected by this Protocol, or against those medical or religious personnel, medical units or medical transports which are under the control of the adverse Party and are protected by this Protocol.

3. In addition to the grave breaches defined in Article 11, the following acts shall be regarded as grave breaches of this Protocol, when committed wilfully, in violation of the relevant provisions of this Protocol, and causing death or serious injury to body or health:

    (*a*) making the civilian population or individual civilians the object of attack;

    (*b*) launching an indiscriminate attack affecting the civilian population or civilian objects in the knowledge that such attack will cause excessive loss of life, injury to civilians or damage to civilian objects, as defined in Article 57, paragraph 2 (*a*) (iii);

(c) launching an attack against works or installations containing dangerous forces in the knowledge that such attack will cause excessive loss of life, injury to civilians or damage to civilian objects, as defined in Article 57, paragraph 2 (a) (iii);

(d) making non-defended localities and demilitarized zones the object of attack;

(e) making a person the object of attack in the knowledge that he is *hors de combat*;

(f) the perfidious use, in violation of Article 37, of the distinctive emblem of the red cross, red crescent or red lion and sun or of other protective signs recognized by the Conventions or this Protocol.

4. In addition to the grave breaches defined in the preceding paragraphs and in the Conventions, the following shall be regarded as grave breaches of this Protocol, when committed wilfully and in violation of the Conventions or the Protocol:

(a) the transfer of the Occupying Power of parts of its own civilian population into the territory it occupies, or the deportation or transfer of all or parts of the population of the occupied territory within or outside this territory, in violation of Article 49 of the Fourth Convention;

(b) unjustifiable delay in the repatriation of prisoners of war or civilians;

(c) practices of *apartheid* and other inhuman and degrading practices involving outrages upon personal dignity, based on racial discrimination;

(d) making the clearly-recognized historic monuments, works of art or places of worship which constitute the cultural or spiritual heritage of peoples and to which special protection has been given by special arrangement, for example, within the framework of a competent international organization, the object of attack, causing as a result extensive destruction thereof, where there is no evidence of the violation by the adverse Party of Article 53, sub-paragraph (b), and when such historic monuments, works of art and places of worship are not located in the immediate proximity of military objectives;

(e) depriving a person protected by the Conventions or referred to in paragraph 2 of this Article of the rights of fair and regular trial.

5. Without prejudice to the application of the Conventions and of this Protocol, grave breaches of these instruments shall be regarded as war crimes.

Article 86—Failure to act

1. The High Contracting Parties and the Parties to the conflict shall repress grave breaches, and take measures necessary to suppress all other breaches, of the Conventions or of this Protocol which result from a failure to act when under a duty to do so.

2. The fact that a breach of the Conventions or of this Protocol was committed by a subordinate does not absolve his superiors from penal or disciplinary responsibility, as the case may be, if they knew, or had information which should have enabled them to conclude in the circumstances at the time, that he was committing or was going to commit such a breach and if they did not take all feasible measures within their power to prevent or repress the breach.

Article 87—Duty of commanders

1. The High Contracting Parties and the Parties to the conflict shall require military commanders, with respect to members of the armed forces under their command and other persons under their control, to prevent and, where necessary, to suppress and to report to competent authorities breaches of the Conventions and of this Protocol.

2. In order to prevent and suppress breaches, High Contracting Parties and Parties to the conflict shall require that, commensurate with their level of responsibility, commanders ensure that members of the armed forces under their command are aware of their obligations under the Conventions and this Protocol.

3. The High Contracting Parties and Parties to the conflict shall require any commander who is aware that subordinates or other persons under his control are going to commit or have committed a breach of the Conventions or of this Protocol, to initiate such steps as are necessary to prevent such violations of the Conventions or this Protocol, and, where appropriate, to initiate disciplinary or penal actions against violators thereof.

Article 88—Mutual assistance in criminal matters

1. The High Contracting Parties shall afford one another the greatest measure of assistance in connexion with criminal proceedings brought in respect of grave breaches of the Conventions or of this Protocol.

2. Subject to the rights and obligations established in the Conventions and in Article 85, paragraph 1, of this Protocol, and when circumstances permit, the High Contracting Parties shall co-operate in the matter of extradition. They shall give due consideration to the

request of the State in whose territory the alleged offence has occurred.

3. The law of the High Contracting Party requested shall apply in all cases. The provisions of the preceding paragraphs shall not, however, affect the obligations arising from the provisions of any other treaty of a bilateral or multilateral nature which governs or will govern the whole or part of the subject of mutual assistance in criminal matters.

Article 89—Co-operation

In situations of serious violations of the Conventions or of this Protocol, the High Contracting Parties undertake to act, jointly or individually, in co-operation with the United Nations and in conformity with the United Nations Charter.

Article 90—International Fact-Finding Commission

1. (*a*) An International Fact-Finding Commission (hereinafter referred to as "the Commission") consisting of fifteen members of high moral standing and acknowledged impartiality shall be established.

   (*b*) When not less than twenty High Contracting Parties have agreed to accept the competence of the Commission pursuant to paragraph 2, the depositary shall then, and at intervals of five years thereafter, convene a meeting of representatives of those High Contracting Parties for the purpose of electing the members of the Commission. At the meeting, the representatives shall elect the members of the Commission by secret ballot from a list of persons to which each of those High Contracting Parties may nominate one person.

   (*c*) The members of the Commission shall serve in their personal capacity and shall hold office until the election of new members at the ensuing meeting.

   (*d*) At the election, the High Contracting Parties shall ensure that the persons to be elected to the Commission individually possess the qualifications required and that, in the Commission as a whole, equitable geographical representation is assured.

   (*e*) In the case of a casual vacancy, the Commission itself shall fill the vacancy, having due regard to the provisions of the preceding sub-paragraphs.

   (*f*) The depository shall make available to the Commission the necessary administrative facilities for the performance of its functions.

2. (*a*) The High Contracting Parties may at the time of signing, ratifying or acceding to the Protocol, or at any other subsequent time, declare that they recognize *ipso facto* and without special agreement, in relation to any other High Contracting Party accepting the same obligation, the competence of the Commission to enquire into allegations by such other Party, as authorized by this Article.

(*b*) The declarations referred to above shall be deposited with the depositary, which shall transmit copies thereof to the High Contracting Parties.

(*c*) The Commission shall be competent to:

  (i) enquire into any facts alleged to be a grave breach as defined in the Conventions and this Protocol or other serious violation of the Conventions or of this Protocol;

  (ii) facilitate, through its good offices, the restoration of an attitude of respect for the Conventions and this Protocol.

(*d*) In other situations, the Commission shall institute an enquiry at the request of a party to the conflict only with the consent of the other Party or Parties concerned.

(*e*) Subject to the foregoing provisions of this paragraph, the provisions of Article 52 of the First Convention, Article 53 of the Second Convention, Article 132 of the Third Convention and Article 149 of the Fouth Convention shall continue to apply to any alleged violation of the Coventions and shall extend to any alleged violation of this Protocol.

3. (*a*) Unless otherwise agreed by the Parties concerned, all enquiries shall be undertaken by a Chamber consisting of seven members appointed as follows:

  (i) five members of the Commission, not nationals of any Party to the conflict, appointed by the President of the Commission on the basis of equitable representation of the geographical areas, after consultation with the Parties to the conflict;

  (ii) two *ad hoc* members, not nationals of any Party to the conflict, one to be appointed by each side.

(*b*) Upon receipt of the request for an enquiry, the President of the Commission shall specify an appropriate time limit for setting up a Chamber. If any *ad hoc* member has not been appointed within the time limit, the President shall immediately appoint such additional member or members of the Commission as may be necessary to complete the membership of the Chamber.

4. (*a*) The Chamber set up under paragraph 3 to undertake an enquiry shall invite the Parties to the conflict to assist it and to present evidence. The Chamber may also seek such other evidence as it deems appropriate and may carry out an investigation of the situation *in loco*.

    (*b*) All evidence shall be fully disclosed to the Parties, which shall have the right to comment on it to the Commission.

    (*c*) Each Party shall have the right to challenge such evidence.

5. (*a*) The Commission shall submit to the Parties a report on the findings of fact of the Chamber, with such recommendations as it may deem appropriate.

    (*b*) If the Chamber is unable to secure sufficient evidence for factual and impartial findings, the Commission shall state the reasons for that inability.

    (*c*) The Commission shall not report its findings publicly, unless all the Parties to the conflict have requested the Commission to do so.

6. The Commission shall establish its own rules, including rules for the presidency of the Commission and the presidency of the Chamber. Those rules shall ensure that the functions of the President of the Commission are exercised at all times and that, in the case of an enquiry, they are exercised by a person who is not a national of a Party to the conflict.

7. The administrative expenses of the Commission shall be met by contributions from the High Contracting Parties which made declarations under paragraph 2, and by voluntary contributions. The Party or Parties to the conflict requesting an enquiry shall advance the necessary funds for expenses incurred by a Chamber and shall be reimbursed by the Party or Parties against which the allegations are made to the extent of fifty per cent of the costs of the Chamber. Where there are counter-allegations before the Chamber each side shall advance fifty per cent of the necessary funds.

Article 91—Responsibility

A Party to the conflict which violates the provisions of the Conventions or of this Protocol shall, if the case demands, be liable to pay compensation. It shall be responsible for all acts committed by persons forming part of its armed forces.

PART I

SCOPE OF THIS PROTOCOL

Article 1—Material field of application

1. This Protocol, which develops and supplements Article 3 common to the Geneva Conventions of 12 August 1949 without modifying its existing conditions of application, shall apply to all armed conflicts which are not covered by Article 1 of the Protocol Additional to the Geneva Conventions of 12 August 1949, and relating to the Protection of Victims of International Armed Conflicts (Protocol I) and which take place in the territory of a High Contracting Party between its armed forces and dissident armed forces or other organized armed groups which, under responsible command, exercise such control over a part of its territory as to enable them to carry out sustained and concerted military operations and to implement this Protocol.

2. This Protocol shall not apply to situations of internal disturbances and tensions, such as riots, isolated and sporadic acts of violence and other acts of a similar nature, as not being armed conflicts.

Article 2—Personal field of application

1. This Protocol shall be applied without any adverse distinction founded on race, colour, sex, language, religion or belief, political or other opinion, national or social origin, wealth, birth or other status, or on any other similar criteria (hereinafter referred to as "adverse distinction") to all persons affected by an armed conflict as defined in Article 1.

2. At the end of the armed conflict, all the persons who have been deprived of their liberty or whose liberty has been restricted for reasons related to such conflict, as well as those deprived of their liberty or whose liberty is restricted after the conflict for the same reasons, shall enjoy the protection of Articles 5 and 6 until the end of such deprivation or restriction of liberty.

Article 3—Non-intervention

1. Nothing in this Protocol shall be invoked for the purpose of affecting the sovereignty of a State or the responsibility of the government, by all legitimate means, to maintain or re-establish law and order in the State or to defend the national unity and territorial integrity of the State.

2. Nothing in this Protocol shall be invoked as a justification for intervening, directly or indirectly, for any reason whatever, in the armed
   conflict or in the internal or external affairs of the High Contracting
   Party in the territory of which that conflict occurs.

PART II

HUMANE TREATMENT

Article 4—Fundamental guarantees

1. All persons who do not take a direct part or who have ceased to take
   part in hostilities, whether or not their liberty has been restricted, are
   entitled to respect for their person, honour and convictions and
   religious practices. They shall in all circumstances be treated
   humanely, without any adverse distinction. It is prohibited to order
   that there shall be no survivors.

2. Without prejudice to the generality of the foregoing, the following
   acts against the persons referred to in paragraph 1 are and shall remain
   prohibited at any time and in any place whatsoever:

   (*a*) violence to the life, health and physical or mental well-being of
        persons, in particular murder as well as cruel treatment such as
        torture, mutilation or any form of corporal punishment;

   (*b*) collective punishments;

   (*c*) taking of hostages;

   (*d*) acts of terrorism;

   (*e*) outrages upon personal dignity, in particular humiliating and
        degrading treatment, rape, enforced prostitution and any form of
        indecent assault;

   (*f*) slavery and the slave trade in all their forms;

   (*g*) pillage;

   (*h*) threats to commit any of the foregoing acts.

3. Children shall be provided with the care and aid they require, and in
   particular:

   (*a*) they shall receive an education, including religious and moral
        education, in keeping with the wishes of their parents, or in the
        absence of parents, of those responsible for their care;

   (*b*) all appropriate steps shall be taken to facilitate the reunion of
        families temporarily separated;

(c) children who have not attained the age of fifteen years shall neither be recruited in the armed forces or groups nor allowed to take part in hostilities;

(d) the special protection provided by this Article to children who have not attained the age of fifteen years shall remain applicable to them if they take a direct part in hostilities despite the provisions of sub-paragraph (c) and are captured;

(e) measures shall be taken, if necessary, and whenever possible with the consent of their parents or persons who by law or customs are primarily responsible for their care, to remove children temporarily from the area in which hostilities are taking place to a safer area within the country and ensure that they are accompanied by persons responsible for their safety and well-being.

Article 5—Persons whose liberty has been restricted

1. In addition to the provisions of Article 4, the following provisions shall be respected as a minimum with regard to persons deprived of their liberty for reasons related to the armed conflict, whether they are interned or detained:

    (a) the wounded and the sick shall be treated in accordance with Article 7;

    (b) the persons referred to in this paragraph shall, to the same extent as the local civilian population, be provided with food and drinking water and be afforded safeguards as regards health and hygiene and protection against the rigours of the climate and the dangers of the armed conflict;

    (c) they shall be allowed to receive individual or collective relief;

    (d) they shall be allowed to practise their religion and, if requested and appropriate, to receive spiritual assistance from persons, such as chaplains, performing religious functions;

    (e) they shall, if made to work, have the benefit of working conditions and safeguards similar to those enjoyed by the local civilian population.

2. Those who are responsible for the internment or detention of the persons referred to in paragraph 1 shall also, within the limits of their capabilities, respect the following provisions relating to such persons:

    (a) except when men and women of a family are accommodated together, women shall be held in quarters separated from those of men and shall be under the immediate supervision of women;

(*b*) they shall be allowed to send and receive letters and cards, the number of which may be limited by competent authority if it deems necessary;

(*c*) places of internment and detention shall not be located close to the combat zone. The persons referred to in paragraph 1 shall be evacuated when the places where they are interned or detained become particularly exposed to danger arising out of the armed conflict, if their evacuation can be carried out under adequate conditions of safety;

(*d*) they shall have the benefit of medical examinations;

(*e*) their physical or mental health and integrity shall not be endangered by any unjustified act or ommission. Accordingly, it is prohibited to subject the persons described in this Article to any medical procedure which is not indicated by the state of health of the person concerned, and which is not consistent with the generally accepted medical standards applied to free persons under similar medical circumstances.

3. Persons who are not covered by paragraph 1 but whose liberty has been restricted in any way whatsoever for reasons related to the armed conflict shall be treated humanely in accordance with Article 4 and with paragraphs 1 (*a*), (*c*) and (*d*), and 2 (*b*) of this Article.

4. If it is decided to release persons deprived of their liberty, necessary measures to ensure their safety shall be taken by those so deciding.

Article 6—Penal prosecutions

1. This Article applies to the prosecution and punishment of criminal offences related to the armed conflict.

2. No sentence shall be passed and no penalty shall be executed on a person found guilty of an offence except pursuant to a convention pronounced by a court offering the essential guarantees of independence and impartiality. In particular:

(*a*) the procedure shall provide for an accused to be informed without delay of the particulars of the offence alleged against him and shall afford the accused before and during his trial all necessary rights and means of defence;

(*b*) no one shall be convicted of an offence except on the basis of individual penal responsibility;

(*c*) no one shall be held guilty of any criminal offence on account of any act or omission which did not constitute a criminal offence, under the law, at the time when it was committed; nor shall a heavier penalty be imposed than that which was applicable at the time when the criminal offence was committed; if, after the commission of the offence, provision is made by law for the imposition of a lighter penalty, the offender shall benefit thereby;

(d) anyone charged with an offence is presumed innocent until proved guilty according to law;

(e) anyone charged with an offence shall have the right to be tried in his presence;

(f) no one shall be compelled to testify against himself or to confess guilt.

3. A convicted person shall be advised on conviction of his judicial and other remedies and of the time-limits within which they may be exercised.

4. The death penalty shall not be pronounced on persons who were under the age of eighteen years at the time of the offence and shall not be carried out on pregnant women or mothers of young children.

5. At the end of hostilities, the authorities in power shall endeavour to grant the broadest possible amnesty to persons who have participated in the armed conflict, or those deprived of their liberty for reasons related to the armed conflict, whether they are interned or detained.

PART III

WOUNDED, SICK AND SHIPWRECKED

Article 7—Protection and care

1. All the wounded, sick and shipwrecked, whether or not they have taken part in the armed conflict, shall be respected and protected.

2. In all circumstances they shall be treated humanely and shall receive, to the fullest extent practicable and with the least possible delay, the medical care and attention required by their condition. There shall be no distinction among them founded on any grounds other than medical ones.

Article 8—Search

Whenever circumstances permit, and particularly after an engagement, all possible measure shall be taken, without delay, to search for and collect the wounded, sick and shipwrecked, to protect them against pillage and ill-treatment, to ensure their adequate care, and to search for the dead, prevent their being despoiled, and decently dispose of them.

Article 9—Protection of medical and religious personnel

1. Medical and religious personnel shall be respected and protected and shall be granted all available help for the performance of their duties. They shall not be compelled to carry out tasks which are not compatible with their humanitarian mission.

2. In the performance of their duties medical personnel may not be required to give priority to any person except on medical grounds.

Article 10—General protection of medical duties

1. Under no circumstances shall any person be punished for having carried out medical activities compatible with medical ethics, regardless of the person benefiting therefrom.

2. Persons engaged in medical activities shall neither be compelled to perform acts or to carry out work contrary to, nor be compelled to refrain from acts required by, the rules of medical ethics or other rules designed for the benefit of the wounded and sick, or this Protocol.

3. The professional obligations of persons engaged in medical activities regarding information which they may acquire concerning the wounded and sick under their care shall, subject to national law, be respected.

4. Subject to national law, no person engaged in medical activities may be penalized in any way for refusing or failing to give information concering the wounded and sick who are, or who have been, under his care.

Article 11—Protection of medical units and transports

1. Medical units and transports shall be respected and protected at all times and shall not be the object of attack.

2. The protection to which medical units and transports are entitled shall not cease unless they are used to commit hostile acts, outside their humanitarian function. Protection may, however, cease only after a warning has been given setting, whenever appropriate, a reasonable time-limit, and after such warning has remained unheeded.

Article 12—The distinctive emblem

Under the direction of the competent authority concerned, the distinctive emblem of the red cross, red crescent or red lion and sun on a white ground shall be displayed by medical and religious personnel and medical units, and on medical transports. It shall be respected in all circumstances. It shall not be used improperly.

PART IV

CIVILIAN POPULATION

Article 13—Protection of the civilian population

1. The civilian population and individual civilians shall enjoy general protection against the dangers arising from military operations. To give effect to this protection, the following rule shall be observed in all circumstances.

2. The civilian population as such, as well as individual civilians, shall not be the object of attack. Acts or threats of violence the primary purpose of which is to spread terror among the civilian population are prohibited.

3. Civilians shall enjoy the protection afforded by this Part, unless and for such time as they take a direct part in hostilities.

Article 14—Protection of objects indispensable to the survival of the
civilian population

Starvation of civilians as a method of combat is prohibited. It is therefore prohibited to attack, destroy, remove or render useless, for that purpose, objects indispensable to the survival of the civilian population, such as foodstuffs, agricultural areas for the production of foodstuffs, crops, livestock, drinking water installations and supplies and irrigation works.

Article 15—Protection of works and installations containing dangerous forces

Works or installations containing dangerous forces, namely dams, dykes and nuclear electrical generating stations, shall not be made the object of attack, even where these objects are military objectives, if such attack may cause the release of dangerous forces and consequent severe losses among the civilian population.

Article 16—Protection of cultural objects and of places of worship

Without prejudice to the provisions of the Hague Convention for the Protection of Cultural Property in the Event of Armed Conflict of

14 May 1954, it is prohibited to commit any acts of hostility directed against historic monuments, works of art or places of worship which constitute the cultural or spiritual heritage of peoples, and to use them in support of the military effort.

Article 17—Prohibition of forced movement of civilians

1. The displacement of the civilian population shall not be ordered for reasons related to the conflict unless the security of the civilians involved or imperative military reasons so demand. Should such displacements have to be carried out, all possible measures shall be taken in order that the civilian population may be received under satisfactory condition of shelter, hygiene, health, safety and nutrition.

2. Civilians shall not be compelled to leave their own territory for reasons connnected with the conflict.

Article 18—Relief societies and relief actions

1. Relief societies located in the territory of the High Contracting Party, such as Red Cross (Red Crescent, Red Lion and Sun) organizations, may offer their services for the performance of their traditional functions in relation to the victims of the armed conflict. The civilian population may, even on its own initiative, offer to collect and care for the wounded, sick and shipwrecked.

2. If the civilian population is suffering undue hardship owing to a lack of the supplies essential for its survival, such as foodstuffs and medical supplies, relief actions for the civilian population which are of an exclusively humanitarian and impartial nature and which are conducted without any adverse distinction shall be undertaken subject to the consent of the High Contracting Party concerned.

INDEX